"一带一路"共建国家航运从业人员培训系列教材

本书由辽宁省大连海事大学教育发展基金会和大连泛和集团支持出版

航海科学

Nautical Science

（汉英对照）

主　编 / 刘军坡

副主编 / 肖仲明　王文新

主　审 / 刘德新

大连海事大学出版社

DALIAN MARITIME UNIVERSITY PRESS

图书在版编目(CIP)数据

航海科学 = Nautical Science：汉英对照 / 刘军坡主编. — 大连：大连海事大学出版社，2024.12
"一带一路"共建国家航运从业人员培训系列教材
ISBN 978-7-5632-4482-9

Ⅰ. ①航…　Ⅱ. ①刘…　Ⅲ. ①航海—技术培训—教材—汉、英 Ⅳ. ①U675

中国国家版本馆 CIP 数据核字(2023)第 236543 号

大连海事大学出版社出版
地址:大连市黄浦路523号　邮编:116026　电话:0411-84729665(营销部)　84729480(总编室)
http://press.dlmu.edu.cn　E-mail:dmupress@dlmu.edu.cn

大连金华光彩色印刷有限公司印装　　大连海事大学出版社发行

2024 年 12 月第 1 版　　2024 年 12 月第 1 次印刷
幅面尺寸:184 mm×260 mm　　印张:23
字数:486 千　　印数:1～1700 册

出版人:刘明凯

责任编辑:张　华　　责任校对:刘若实
封面设计:解瑶瑶　　版式设计:解瑶瑶

ISBN 978-7-5632-4482-9　　定价:64.00 元

“一带一路”共建国家
航运从业人员培训系列教材

编委会

总序

习近平总书记指出，航运业是国际贸易发展的重要保障，也是世界各国人民友好往来的重要纽带。2013 年秋，习近平总书记提出了共建丝绸之路经济带和 21 世纪海上丝绸之路重大倡议。在“一带一路”建设中，海运发挥着先导性、战略性作用，它不仅是 21 世纪海上丝绸之路的主要运输方式，而且对丝绸之路经济带的形成和发展起着重要的支持和推动作用。

中华人民共和国成立后，我国海运业经过了 70 多年的发展建设，逐步发展壮大。我国已经成为名副其实的海运大国，正向着海运强国的建设目标迈进。目前，我国海运连接度世界领先，航线网络遍布全球，海运服务能力位居世界前列，海运船队运力规模居世界第二，沿海港口规模和吞吐量稳居世界第一。作为海运业最活跃、最关键、最重要的因素，涉海类专门人才发挥着不可替代的作用，是重要的战略资源。职业素养过硬、业务能力扎实、管理水平高超、心理素质良好的高素质从业人员，在推动海运业发展建设中发挥着关键作用。近年来，世界各国特别是“一带一路”共建国家对涉海类专门人才的需求越来越大，加强相关人才培训培养的需要也越来越迫切。交通运输部党组书记、部长李小鹏在出席 2023 年中国航海日主论坛的致辞中强调：习近平总书记高度重视交通运输事业发展，多次到港口、航运等交通运输一线视察并做出一系列重要指示，为推进交通运输和航运发展指明了前进方向、提供了根本遵循。我们要坚持交通天下，打造开放航运。要推进与“一带一路”共建国家和地区基础设施“硬联通”和规则标准“软联通”，提升国际运输便利化水平。

在此背景下，校友江四元先生建议，由大连海事大学组织力量，专门编写一套面向“一带一路”共建国家航运从业人员培训系列教材，学校慨然应允。一方面，国际合作与人文交流是海事教育的重要职能之一，是实现海事行业科技发展和人才培养以及不同文化交汇融合的有效途径。另一方面，作为我国高等航海教育的引领者和国际海事教育发展的推动者，大连海事大学是我国最早开展境外实质性办学的高校，早在 2007 年就在斯里兰卡建立了海外校区，实现了海事教育的首次输出；目前学校的留学生群体中，“一带一路”共建国家生源占比超 90%。综上，大连海事大学具备开展此项工作的基础和条件。

为提高教材编纂质量，学校专门成立了教材编委会，组织校内外权威专家学者和行业企事业单位精英，围绕航运管理、金融、保险、法律、经纪、船舶经营管理、海事行政管理等领域开展研究，力求保证教材的时代性、创新性、系统性、权威性和指导性。为提高教材的适用性和可读性，本系列教材采用中英文对照的方式进行编写，同时辅之以大量实际案例和生动故事，便于国内外读者的理解和思考。我相信，这套教材一定会成为国家对外开放合作的优秀作品。

大连海事大学原党委书记、校长

2023 年 9 月 28 日

前言

本书为针对甲板部操作级船员工作及生活需求编写的中英文对照教材。本书章节及内容设置参照了《1978 年海员培训、发证和值班标准国际公约马尼拉修正案》对甲板部操作级船员的培训要求。本书力求知识点全面简洁,针对性和实用性强,图文并茂,易于学员学习、理解。本书旨在帮助母语非中文的甲板部船员能够快速在中国籍船舶工作,同时强化甲板部业务学习。

本书共分七章。第一章为航海基础知识,第二章为货物基础知识,第三章为船舶基础知识,第四章为个人安全,第五章为船舶保安,第六章为工作用语,第七章为日常生活用语。每一章都紧密围绕船员的实际需求展开,力求全方位提升船员的专业素养与跨文化交流能力。

本书适用于具备一定英文基础的甲板部船员进行中文学习,也适用于具备一定中文基础的甲板部船员进行英文学习。本书也可作为航海院校师生的教学参考书及航运管理相关人员的学习参考书。

本书由刘军坡担任主编,肖仲明、王文新担任副主编,刘德新担任主审。吕红光、刘新卓、姜朝妍、黄岗、惠小锁参与了本书的编写。全书由刘军坡统稿。本书在编写过程中得到了广大同行的大力支持和热情指导,在此表示衷心感谢。

航海科技日新月异,新理论、新技术、新设备不断涌现并投入航海实践,相关国际公约、各国法律法规、行业标准和规定也在不断进步完善。因此,本书虽已倾注了作者们最大的努力与心血,但难免存在不足之处,敬请广大同人和读者批评指正,不吝赐教。

编　者

2024 年 9 月

目录

第 1 章　航海基础知识

Chapter 1 | Basic Knowledge of Navigation

航海是一门古老的技艺和科学，其发展离不开定位、辨向、海图、助航等技术。

Navigation is an ancient art and science, its development can not be separated from positioning, direction identification, chart, aids to navigation and other technologies.

1.1　坐标

1.1　Geographical Coordinate

要理解航海、海图作业和与船舶航行有关的其他任务，就必须了解地球的形状。陆上和海上航行的主要区别是陆地上有固定的参考标记，而海上没有。如果要定位，就必须把方向、距离与地球的形状联系起来。

To understand navigation, chart work and the other tasks associated with the navigation of a ship, it is essential to understand the shape of the earth. The main difference between travelling on land and at sea is that there are fixed reference marks on land, but not at sea. To find a position it is necessary to relate direction and distance to the shape of the earth.

1.1.1　地球形状

1.1.1　Shape of the Earth

一般而言，对于小比例尺制图，认为地球是球形的，虽然把地球看作一个球而不是它的实际形状会引起一些问题。地球是一个具有不规则形状的岩石块，看起来像一个扁球体，其赤道直径大于极直径。由于地球表面的不规则性,它没有一个精确的数学表达式,因此我们不能在其上进行导航。我们采用的是与地球表面最接近的数学近似称为椭圆体(较早的术语为“扁球体”)。

Generally, for small-scale mapping purposes, the earth is considered to be spherical, although there are some problems caused by viewing the earth as a sphere instead of its actual shape. The earth is an irregular shaped lump of rock that looks like an oblate spheroid with more equatorial diameter than polar diameter. Due to the earth's surface irregularity, it does not have a complete mathematical expression and so we cannot use it for navigation. The closest mathematical approximation to the earth's surface is called an ellipsoid (older term "oblate spheroid").

如图 1.1.1 所示,当地球从西向东绕其最短直径 PP' 旋转时,地球椭圆体的形状是由椭圆($PWP'E$)的形状参数决定的。该椭圆在围绕其短轴(PP')旋转时产生椭圆体。椭圆的长半轴 a 是地球的赤道半径,短半轴 b 是极半径(从中心 O 出发)。在实践中,另两个参数,即扁率(f)和偏心率(e),可用来确定椭圆的形状,它们之间的关系如下:

$$f = \frac{a - b}{a}; e = \frac{\sqrt{a^2 - b^2}}{a}$$

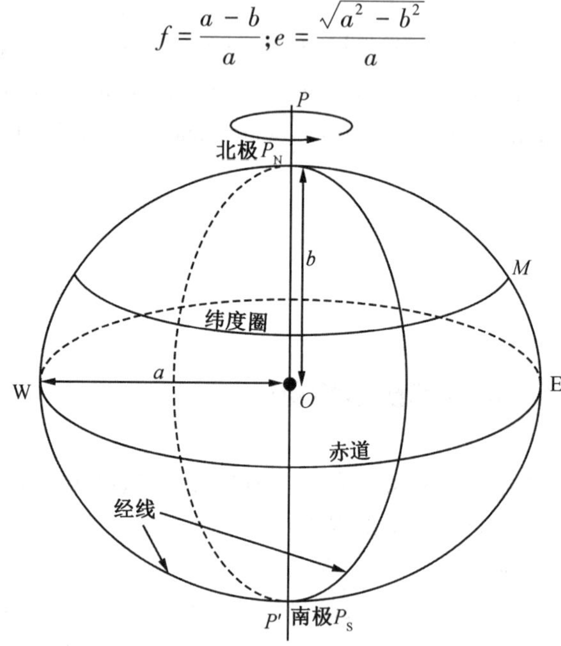

图 1.1.1 地球形状——椭圆体

See Figure 1.1.1, as the earth turns about its shortest diameter PP' from west to east, the shape of an ellipsoid is determined by the shape parameters of that ellipse ($PWP'E$) which generates the ellipsoid when it is rotated about its minor axis (PP'). The semi-major axis of the ellipse, a, is identified as the equatorial radius of the ellipsoid; the semi-minor axis of the ellipse, b, is identified with the polar distances (from the center O). In practice another two parameters, flattening (f) and eccentricity (e), may be used to specify the shape of the ellipsoid, the relationship between them is listed as follows:

$$f = \frac{a - b}{a};e = \frac{\sqrt{a^2 - b^2}}{a}$$

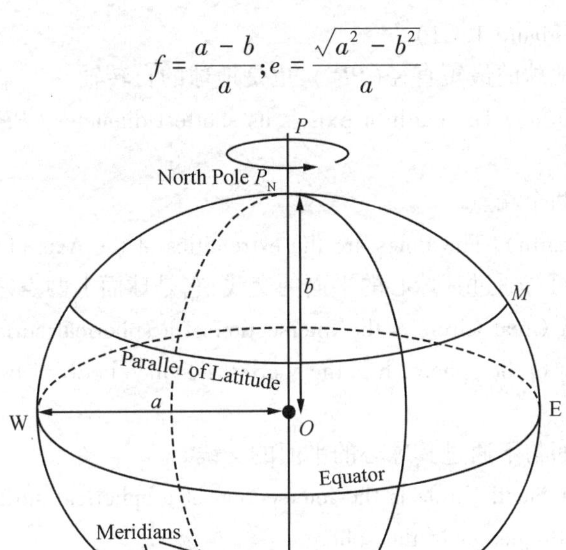

Figure 1.1.1　The shape of the earth—an ellipsoid

为了得到与地球表面尽量吻合的椭圆,针对不同地方就需要很多椭圆表示。因此,许多具有不同中心和大小的参考椭球(地球的精确形状和大小)被采用,作为海图或定位系统的基础。但是,在同一位置使用不同的椭球会导致显示不同的坐标,引起混乱。因此,现代的椭球,如 1980 年大地测量参考系(GRS-80)和 1984 年世界大地测量系统(WGS-84),以地心为坐标原点,在总体平均的基础上更准确地代表整个地球,但它们通常不能为特定区域提供“最佳适合”。对我国而言,目前海图系统采用的是中国大地坐标系 2000(CGCS2000)。该坐标系自 2008 年 7 月起正式作为新的国家大地坐标系,这是一种与地球椭球相关的地心坐标系,其定义与 WGS-84 略有不同。

In order to obtain an ellipse that closely matches the earth's shape, there must be a number of ellipses for different places on the surface of earth. Therefore, a great many reference ellipsoids (the precise shape and size of the earth) have been used with various sizes and centers to form the basis of navigational charts or position fixing systems, but using different spheroids in a particular location will result in different displayed positions, this is awful. Modern ellipsoids such as Geodetic Reference System 1980 (GRS-80) and World Geodetic System 1984 (WGS-84) are centered at the actual center of mass of the earth and represent the entire earth more accurately on an overall, average basis but they do not generally give the "best fit" for a particular region. For our country, China Geodetic Coordinate System 2000 (CGCS2000) has been officially adopted as the new national geodetic coordinate system since July 2008, which is a geocentric coordinate system associated with an earth ellipsoid defined slightly different from WGS-84.

以下定义用于描述地球形状的要素和相关度量(如图 1.1.1 所示)。

The following definitions have been established to describe key aspects and measurements of the earth's shape (see Figure 1.1.1).

(1)地轴:地轴是地球的最短直径(PP'),也是地球的自转轴。

(1) Axis (of the earth). The earth's Axis is its shortest diameter (PP'), about which it rotates in space.

(2)地极:地轴的两个端点。

(2) Poles (of the earth). The Poles are the extremities of the Axis of the earth.

(3)大圆:地球球面与通过其球心的平面的交线,它是球面上两点之间最短的距离。

(3) Great Circle. A Great Circle is the intersection of a spherical surface and a plane which passes through the center of the sphere. It is the shortest distance between two points on the surface of a sphere.

(4)小圆:地球球面与不通过其球心的平面的交线。

(4) Small Circle. A Small Circle is the intersection of a spherical surface and a plane which does NOT pass through the center of the sphere.

(5)子午线:通过地轴的任何一个平面都是子午圈平面,它与地球表面的交线是个椭圆,称为子午圈。子午线是半个子午圈,其两端是两极。图 1.1.2 中 PWP'的连线即为子午线。

(5) Meridian. Any plane through the earth's axis is the plane of the meridian circle, and its intersection with the earth's surface is an ellipse called the meridian circle. A Meridian is a semi-(Meridian) Circle on the earth's surface whose ends lie at opposite Poles. Meridians are shown by the successive positions of PWP' in Figure 1.1.2.

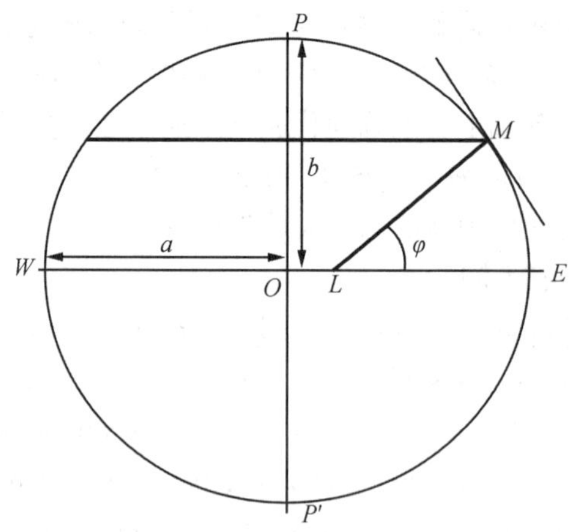

图 1.1.2 地球表面 M 点的纬度

Figure 1.1.2 The latitude of point M on the earth's surface

(6)本初子午线:也称为格林尼治子午线,指通过格林尼治天文台(在英国伦敦)的子午线。本初子午线也是 0°经线,东经和西经的起点。

(6) Prime Meridian. The Prime Meridian (also known as the Greenwich Meridian) passes through the Greenwich Observatory (London, UK). The Prime Meridian is the starting point (0°) for the measurement of Longitude, East and West from this Meridian.

(7)赤道:通过地球球心且与地轴垂直的平面为赤道平面,赤道平面与地球表面的交线为赤道,如图 1.1.2 中 *WE* 表示的圆,它将地球分为南、北两个半球。

(7) Equator. The plane through the center of the earth's sphere and perpendicular to the earth's axis is the equatorial plane, and the line of intersection between the equatorial plane and the earth's surface is the Equator, as shown by the circle represented by *WE* in Figure 1.1.2. The Equator divides the earth into two hemispheres, the north and the south.

1.1.2　地理坐标
1.1.2　Position on the Earth

参考椭球主要用作纬度(北/南)和经度(东/西)坐标系建立的基础。

A primary use of reference ellipsoids is to serve as a basis for a coordinate system of latitude (north/south) and longitude (east/west).

地球表面的一个位置可以通过参照赤道和本初子午线的平面来表示。图 1.1.2 显示了一个球体的子午线截面;点 *M* 的纬度是∠*MLE*(φ),其中 *L* 是垂直于地球表面 *M* 点的法线和赤道 *OE* 平面的交点。应该指出,在椭圆体中,*L* 点可能与 *O* 点(地心)不重合。

A position on the earth's surface may be expressed by reference to the planes of the Equator and the Prime Meridian. Figure 1.1.2 shows a Meridional section of a spheroid; the Latitude of point *M* is the angle *MLE* (φ), where *L* is the point of intersection of the perpendicular to the earth's surface at *M* and the plane of the Equator *OE*. It should be noted that in a spheroid, point *L* may not coincide with point *O* (center of the earth).

(1)纬度(φ):地球椭圆子午线上某点的法线与赤道面的夹角称为该点的地理纬度。自赤道起算,向北或向南度量到该点所在纬度圈,由 0°到 90°计量,向北度量的称为北纬,用 N 标示;向南度量的称为南纬,用 S 标示。

(1) Latitude (φ): The angle between the normal to a point on the earth's elliptical meridian and the equatorial plane is known as the geographic latitude of that point. From the Equator, it is measured northward or southward to the circle of latitude in which the point is located, measured from 0° to 90°; northward measurements are known as northerly latitudes, labeled N; southward measurements are southerly latitudes, labeled S.

(2)纬度圈:与赤道平行的等纬圈,除了赤道是大圆之外,其余均为小圆(参考图 1.1.1)。

(2) Parallels of Latitude: Planes parallel to the plane of the Equator are known as Parallels of Latitude (also see Figure 1.1.1). Except for the Equator itself, which is a Great Circle, they also comprise Small Circles.

(3)经度(λ):经度是格林子午线与该点所在的子午线在赤道上所夹的劣弧长(两者之间角度),由 0°到 180°计量。自格林子午线起算,向东度量的称为东经,用 E 标示;向西度量的称为西经,用 W 标示。如图 1.1.3 所示,*F* 点的经度是 *AB* 弧长也是∠*AOB*(在格林子午线以东)。

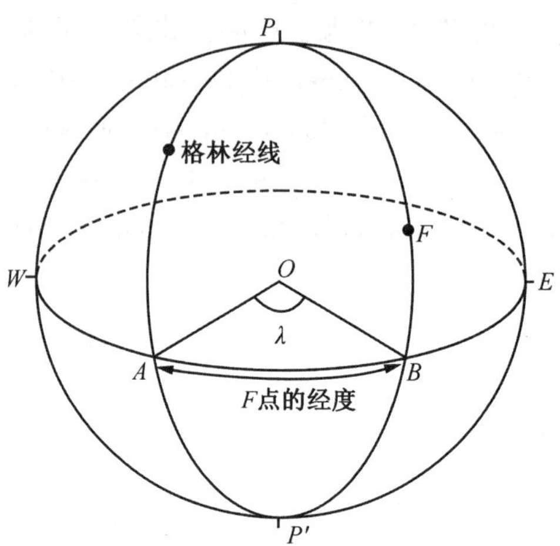

图 1.1.3 地球表面 F 点的经度

(3) Longitude (λ): Longitude is the length of the inferior arc (the angle between the two) between the Greenwich meridian and the meridian at the Equator where the point is located, measured from 0° to 180°. Measured eastward from the Green's meridian, it is called eastern longitude and is labeled E. Measured westward, it is called western longitude and is labeled W. As in Figure 1.1.3, the longitude of F is the arc AB = angle AOB (East of Greenwich meridian).

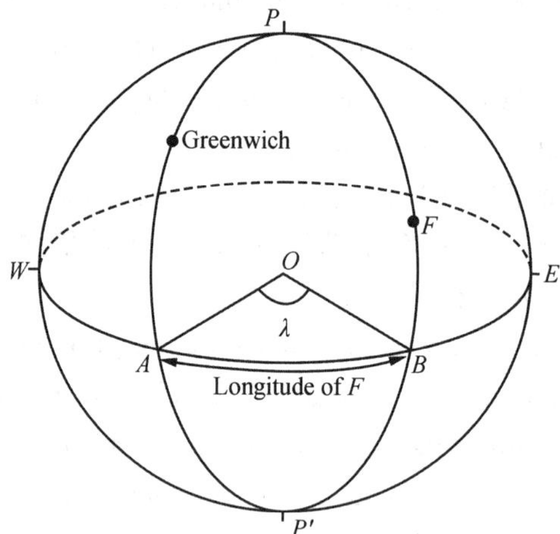

Figure 1.1.3 The longitude of point F on the earth's surface

从海图上看,大连老铁山西角的灯塔大约在赤道以北 38°43′40″,格林尼治以东 121°8′5″(WGS-84)。这可以表示为:

From the chart, Laotieshan Xijiao light house in Dalian approximate is at Latitude 38 degrees 43 minutes 40 seconds north of the Equator and at Longitude 121 degrees 8 minutes 5 seconds east of Greenwich (WGS-84). This may be expressed as:

(1) 38°43′40″N 121°08′05″E (传统写法);

(1) 38°43′40″N 121°08′05″E (for traditional use);

(2) 38°43′.66N 121°08′.09E (英版海图及中国常用的写法);

(2)38°43′.66N 121°08′.09E (accepted notation for admiralty charts, common usage in China);

(3)38°43.66′N 121°08.09′E (大多数美国和英国出版物中使用的可选的表示方法)。

(3)38°43.66′N 121°08.09′E (alternative notation used in most American and UK publications)。

1.1.3 纬差和经差

1.1.3 Difference of Latitude and Difference of Longitude

纬差($D\varphi$):两地之间的纬差是两条纬线之间的子午线弧线。当从一个地方前往另一个地方时,纬差根据目的地的纬度是出发地纬度的北面还是南面而被命名为北纬或南纬。

Difference of Latitude ($D\varphi$):The $D\varphi$ between two places is the arc of the Meridian between the two Parallels of Latitude. When proceeding from one place to another, $D\varphi$ is named North or South according to whether the Latitude of the destination is North or South of the Latitude of the place of departure.

经差($D\lambda$):两地之间的 $D\lambda$ 是赤道在两地子午线之间的劣弧长。当从一个地方前往另一个地方时,$D\lambda$ 根据目的地的经线在出发地经线的东面或西面而被命名为东经或西经。

Difference of Longitude ($D\lambda$):The $D\lambda$ between two places is the smaller arc of the Equator between their Meridians. When proceeding from one place to another, $D\lambda$ is named East or West according to whether the Meridian of the destination is East or West of the Meridian of the place of departure.

纬差和经差的计算:计算纬差和经差的规则如下:

Calculation of $D\varphi$ and $D\lambda$:The rule for finding the $D\varphi$ and $D\lambda$ is as follows:

$$D\varphi=\varphi_2-\varphi_1$$

$$D\lambda=\lambda_2-\lambda_1$$

式中:

Where:

φ_1、φ_2——起始点纬度和到达点纬度;

φ_1, φ_2——the latitude of departure point and the latitude of destination respectively;

λ_1、λ_2——起始点经度和到达点经度。

λ_1, λ_2——the longitude of departure point and the longitude of destination respectively.

计算中注意:

Cautions in the calculations:

(1)北纬、东经取正值(+),南纬、西经取负值(-);

(1)The North Latitude and East longitude are named positive or "+"; the South latitude and West longitude are named negative or "-";

(2)纬差和经差也有方向,北纬差和东经差取正值(+),南纬差和西经差取负值(-);

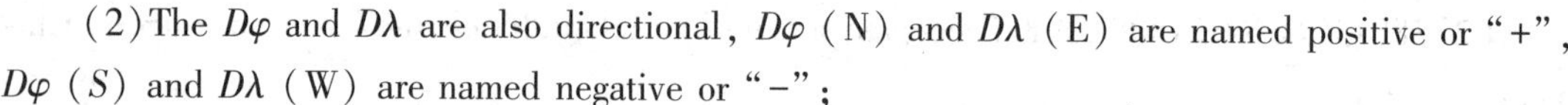

(2) The $D\varphi$ and $D\lambda$ are also directional, $D\varphi$ (N) and $D\lambda$ (E) are named positive or "+", $D\varphi$ (S) and $D\lambda$ (W) are named negative or "−";

(3)经差的绝对值不应大于180°,否则,应由360°减去该绝对值,并改变符号。

(3) The absolute value of $D\lambda$ should never exceed 180°, if so, the absolute value has to be subtracted from 360°, and reverse the name after subtraction.

1.2 方向

1.2 Directions on the Earth

方向是一个点相对于另一个点的位置。航海上将航向表示为与参考方向(通常为北或船首方向)的角度之差。这一部分将着重讲解航海上方向的定义和测量。

Direction is the position of one point relative to another. Navigators express direction as the angular difference in degrees from a reference direction, usually north or the ship's head. This part will focus on how directions in navigation are defined and measured.

1.2.1 方向的确定

1.2.1 Determination of Directions

为了更方便地说明,这里将地球看作圆球体,如图1.2.1所示。通过测者的眼睛A'并与重力方向重合的铅垂线称为测者铅垂线(AA')。垂直于测者铅垂线的平面被命名为测者地平平面。航行中只考虑其中两个特殊的测者地平平面:

See Figure 1.2.1, for simplicity the earth is assumed to be a sphere, the plumb line passing through the observer's eye A' and coinciding with the direction of gravity is called Observer's Plumb Line (AA'). The planes which make perpendicular to Observer's Plumb Line are named Horizons. Only two special horizons of these are taken into account in navigation:

(1)测者地面真地平平面:通过测者眼睛的地平平面,叫作测者地面真地平平面,见平面*NWSE*。

(1) Sensible Horizon: It is the horizon passing through the observer's eye, see plane *NWSE*.

(2)真地平平面(或天文地平平面):是指通过地心的地平平面,在天文航海中使用。

(2) True Horizon (or Celestial Horizon): It is the horizon passing through the center of the earth. This term is mostly used in Celestial Navigation.

实际上,地球表面两个点之间的真正方向是由它们之间的大圆给出的,它表示为子午线和大圆之间的角度。真正的北是子午线的北面。然而,人们常常感觉到的方向,是指在地文航海中的方向;测者的所有方向都是在测者地面真地平平面上定义的。

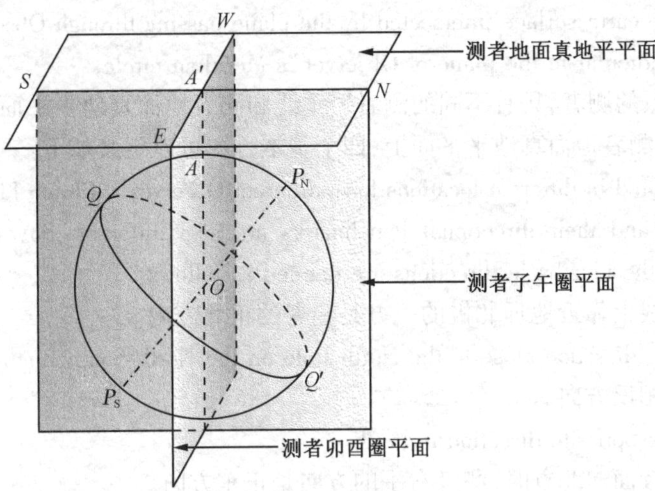

图 1.2.1 方向的确定

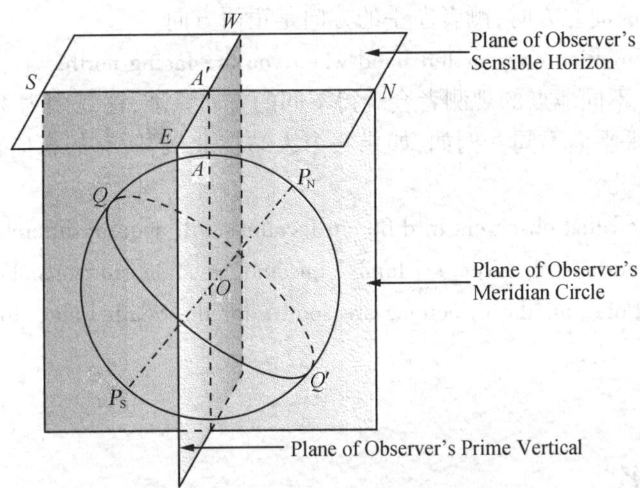

Figure 1.2.1 Determination of directions

Actually, the true direction between two points on the earth's surface is given by the Great Circle between them; it is expressed as the angle between the Meridian and Great Circle. True North is the northerly direction of the Meridian. However, often people sense the directions on a plane, especially in the subject of Terrestrial Navigation; all the directions for an observer are defined on the Observer's Sensible Horizon.

(1)南北线:是指测者地面真地平平面 *WSEN* 与测者子午圈平面 P_NAP_S 相交的直线 *SN*。

(1) North-South Line: It is the line (*SN*) of intersection between the plane of Observer's Meridian circle P_NAP_S and the plane of Observer's Sensible Horizon.

(2)东西线:测者地面真地平平面与测者卯酉圈平面的交线 *WE*。这里,卯酉圈平面是指,包含测者铅垂线,并与测者子午圈平面相垂直的平面。

(2) East-West Line: It is the line (*WE*) of intersection between the plane of Observer's Prime Vertical and the plane of Observer's Sensible Horizon. Herein, the prime vertical is the

Great Circle on the earth surface intersected by the plane passing through Observer's Plumb Line and making perpendicular to the plane of Observer's Meridian circle.

位于不同地点的测者,具有不同的测者铅垂线和测者地面真地平平面,其方向基准也各不相同。因此,在测者地面真地平平面上,四个基本方向可以定义如下:

Observers located in different locations have different Observer's Plumb Lines and Observer's Sensible Horizon, and their directional benchmarks are also different. So, on the Observer's Sensible Horizon, the four basic directions are defined as follows:

(1)北:南北线上靠近地理北极的一方是测者的正北方向。

(1)North:The direction close to the North Pole on the North-South Line.

(2)南:北的相反方向。

(2)South:The opposite direction to north.

(3)东:当测者面向北方时,测者右手的方向是正东方向。

(3)East:The direction on your right hand when you are facing north.

(4)西:当测者面向北方时,测者左手的方向是正西方向。

(4)West:The direction on your left hand when you are facing north.

需要注意的是,不同地点的观测者会获得不同的方向基准,这是因为不同观测者的铅垂线和测者地面真地平平面不同。例如,如果一个人站在北极,所有的方向都是南;而站在南极,所有的方向都是北。

It should be noted that observers in different locations will acquire different direction originations because of the various observer's Plumb Line and Sensible Horizons. For example, if one stands on the North Pole, all the directions are south; for the South Pole, all the directions are north.

1.2.2 方向的命名
1.2.2 Notation for Directions

1.2.2.1 圆周法
1.2.2.1 Circular Notation

圆周法方向按顺时针方向从000°到360°测量,并且总是以真北为基础,用3位数表示度数。例如,正北为000°(即360°),正东为090°,正南为180°,正西为270°。如今,它被广泛用于航海中描述方向。

It is measured clockwise from 000° to 360°, and ALWAYS expressed in 3-figure numbers in degrees on the basis of true north. For example, due north is 000°(ie 360°), due east is 090°, due south is 180° and due west is 270°. Nowadays, it is widely used on Navigation to describe directions.

1.2.2.2　半圆法
1.2.2.2　Semi-circular Notation

从真北或真南向东或向西测量,范围为 0°至 180°。它总是以“N”或“S”(起始点)和“E”或“W”(测量方向)作为后缀,这是描述的基本部分。例如,125°NW 表示从“N”到“W”的测量方向为 125°(与圆周符号 235°相同)。这种方法通常用于天文导航中表示天体的方位。

It is measured in 0° to 180° from the true north or true south towards the east or west. It is ALWAYS suffixed by “N” or “S” (the start points) and “E” or “W” (the measured direction) which are the essential parts of this description. For example, the direction of 125°NW means it is measured from “N” to “W” at 125° (the same to circular notation 235°). This method is normally used in Celestial Navigation to express the azimuth of a celestial body.

1.2.2.3　罗经点法
1.2.2.3　Compass-point Notation

如图 1.2.2 所示,这种方法将罗盘分为 32 个点(每个点为 11.25°),主要用于表示风和水流的大致方向。罗盘的 32 个点可分为 4 类:

See Figure 1.2.2, this is based on the division of the compass into 32 points(each division is 11.25°), and is mainly used to represent the approximate directions of winds and currents. The 32 compass points can be sorted to 4 types:

(1)基点:罗经点法以北、东、南、西四个基本方向为基点,即 N(000°),E(090°),S(180°),W(270°)。

(1)Cardinal points: The compass. point method is based on the four basic directions of north, east, south and west, N (000°), E (090°), S (180°), W (270°).

(2)隅点:将平分相邻基点之间的点称为隅点,即 NE(045°),SE(135°),SW(225°),NW(315°)。

(2)Inter-cardinal points: The points divide equally each adjacent two cardinal points, with NE being (045°), SE (135°), SW (225°), NW (315°).

(3)三字点:将平分相邻基点与隅点之间的点称为三字点,其命名规则为在基点名称之后加上隅点名称,即北北东(NNE)、东北东(ENE)、东南东(ESE)、南南东(SSE)、南南西(SSW)、西南西(WSW)、西北西(WNW)和北北西(NNW)等 8 个方向。例如,NNW 是基点 N 和隅点 NW 的组合,它对应圆周法表示为 337.5°,可通过公式 (360°+315°)/2 或 360°−22.5°得到。

(3)Intermediate points: The points divide equally the adjacent cardinal points and inter-cardinal points. The name of the first letter follows the name of cardinal point, and the remaining two letters correspond to the name of inter-cardinal point. Therefore, 8 intermediate points are NNE, ENE, ESE, SSE, SSW, WSW, WNW, and NNW. E.g., NNW is the point combining cardinal point N and inter-cardinal point NW, so its Circular Notation expression 337.5° can be get by the formula (360°+315°)/2 or 360°−22.5°.

图 1.2.2 罗经点

Figure 1.2.2 Compass points

(4)偏点:将平分相邻基点或隅点与三字点之间的 16 个点称为偏点。这些点以 N/W 或 NE/E 等形式表示,第一个名称(N 或 NE)对应基点或隅点,符号"/"后面的字母(W 或 E)对应从基点或隅点转向的方向。圆周率表示法的 N/W 可以用公式"360°−11.25°=348.75°"来表示,而 NE/E=045°+11.25°=056.25°。试着计算 SW/S,答案是 225°−11.25°=213.75°。

(4) By-points: The points divide adjacent cardinal point and intermediate point, or adjacent inter-cardinal point and intermediate point into half. Totally, there are 16 by-points on the compass card. These points are expressed in the form such as N/W, or NE/E, the first name (N or NE) corresponds to cardinal or inter-cardinal point, the letter behind the symbol "/" (W or E) corresponds to the direction turned from the cardinal or inter-cardinal point. The Circular Notation expression of N/W can be gotten by the equation "360°−11.25°=348.75°", but the NE/E=045°+11.25°=056.25°. Try to calculate the SW/S, the answer is 225°−11.25°=213.75°.

1.2.3 航向和方位

1.2.3 Course and Bearing

作为航海者,需要确定船舶在特定方向的移动路径,这里的方向多指"航向"。实际上有两种航海上常用的方向,分别是航向和方位。

The navigator's prime goal is to determine the track for the ship's movement in any particular direction. In simple terms, this direction is referred to as the "course", and there are two different ways to describe directions on the surface of earth: course and bearing.

1.2.3.1　定义

1.2.3.1　Definitions

(1)航向(*C*)指船舶行驶的或计划行驶的方向,用角度来表示,从000°顺时针度量到360°。严格地说,这一术语是相对水而言的,而非对地面。由于参考方向分别为真方向、磁方向、罗方向或陀罗方向,因此航向通常被指定为真航向、磁航向、罗航向或陀罗航向。

(1) Course (*C*) is the direction in which a vessel is steered or intended to be steered, expressed as angular distance from 000° (North), clockwise through 360°. Strictly, the term applies to direction through the water, not the direction intended to be made good over the ground. The course is often designated as true, magnetic, compass, or gyrocompass, as the reference direction is true, magnetic, compass, or gyrocompass, respectively.

(2)真航向(*TC*)是指测者所在的子午线和艏艉线之间的角度,以顺时针度量000°至360°。

(2) True course (*TC*) is measured by the angle between the Meridian through the vessel's position and the fore-and-aft line, clockwise from 000° to 360°.

(3)航向线(*CL*)指船舶航向的图形表示,艏艉线向船首方向的延伸线。

(3) Course line (*CL*) is the graphic representation of a ship's course, i.e. the ship's fore-and-aft line looking forward.

(4)船首向(*Hdg*)是指船的瞬时航向,用圆周法从000°到360°顺时针表示,当参考的基准是真北时,则称为真艏向。船首向容易与航向混淆。船首向随着船舶来回偏航而不断变化,这是由海浪、风和操舵误差等原因造成的。正因如此,船舶实际行驶的航迹(地面上的路径)弯弯曲曲的,在推算船的位置时,采用推算航迹(TMG),这是指从出发点指向到达点,在任何给定时间的单个合方向,如图1.2.3所示。

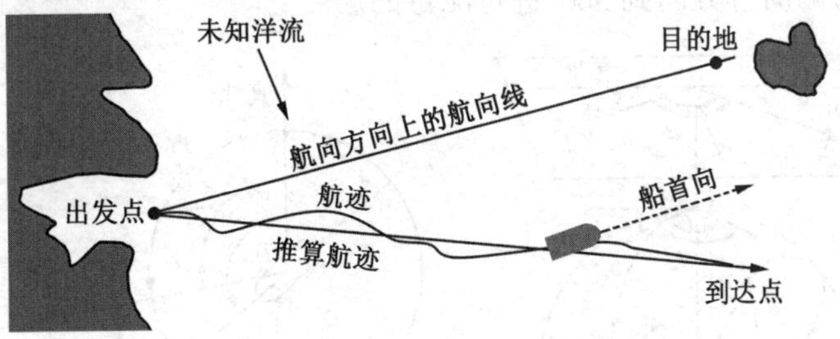

图1.2.3　航向线、推算航迹和船首向等图示

(4) Heading (*Hdg*) is the direction in which a vessel is pointed at any given moment, expressed as angular distance from 000°, clockwise through 360°. When this angle is referred to the *true meridian*, it is called a True Heading. It is easy to make heading confused with course. Heading constantly changes as a vessel yaws back and forth across the course due to sea, wind, and steering error. Because of this, the actual track of the ship (path over ground) is curved. When calculating the position of the ship, the track made good (TMG) is adopted, which is the single

resultant direction from the point of departure to the point of arrival at any given time (see Figure 1.2.3).

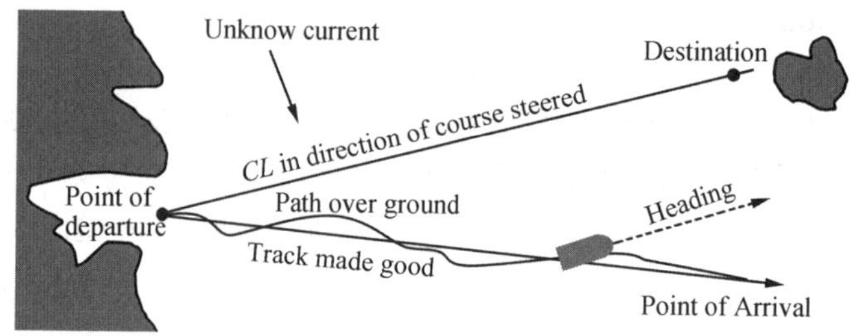

Figure 1.2.3 Course line, track made good and heading

(5)方位线(*BL*)是指测者真地平平面与物标方位圈平面 *AMN* 之间的交线,物标方位圈是通过观测者 *A* 和物体 *M* 的大圆,如图 1.2.4(a)所示。

(5) Bearing Line (*BL*) is the line of intersection between the plane of Observer's Sensible Horizon and the plane of object's bearing circle *AMN*, which is the Great Circle passing through the observer *A* and the object *M*, see Figure 1.2.4(a).

(6)方位(*B*)是指地面某点相对另一点的方向,用圆周法从000°到360°顺时针表示。方位因其度量所依据的北的基准不同,有真方位、磁方位、罗方位或陀罗方位之谓。物体的真方位(*TB*)是子午线与物体方向之间的夹角。

(6) Bearing (*B*) is the direction of one terrestrial point from another, expressed as angular distance from 000° (North), clockwise through 360°. The bearing is often designated as true, magnetic, compass, or gyrocompass according to the reference direction. The True Bearing (*TB*) of an object is the angle between the Meridian and the direction of the object.

(7)舷角(*Q*)以船首向为基准,分别向左或向右计量到物标方位线,计量范围000°到180°,向右计量为右舷角 Q_S,向左计量为左舷角 Q_P,如图 1.2.4(b)所示。有时,舷角是从000°(我船正前方)顺时针方向到360°进行测量的。

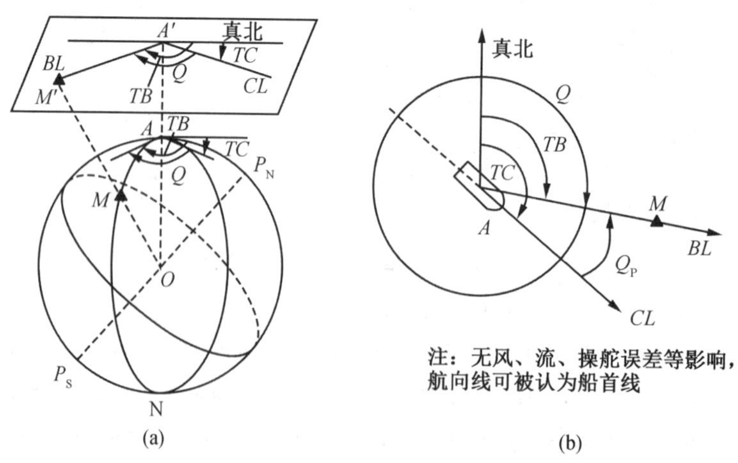

图 1.2.4 航向、方位和舷角

(7) Relative Bearing (Q): are normally stated relative to the ship's fore-and-aft line looking forward (i.e. from ship's heading) and are measured from the bow from 0° to 180° on each side. Starboard bearings are expressed as "Q_S" and port bearings expressed as "Q_P", see Figure 1.2.4 (b). Occasionally, Relative Bearing is measured relative to the ship's heading from 000° (dead ahead) clockwise through 360°.

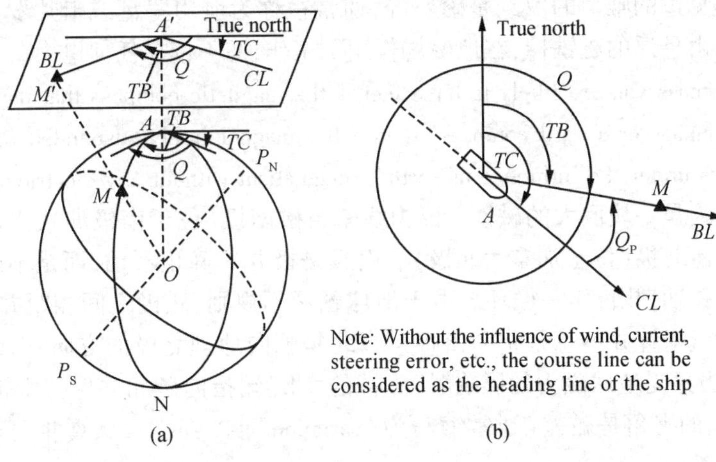

Figure 1.2.4　Course, bearing and relative bearing

(8)正横：当舷角 Q=090°或 $Q_{右}$=90°时，叫作物标的右正横；当 Q=270°或 $Q_{左}$=90°时，叫作物标的左正横，如果方位是大概的，那正横的表述一般是"ON THE BEAM" 或者 "ABEAM"。

(8) Broad on the beam: bearing 090° relative (broad on the starboard beam) or 270° relative (broad on the port beam). If the bearings are approximate, the expression ON THE BEAM or A-BEAM should be used.

关于舷角、真方位、真艏向(真航向)的转换关系如下：

To convert a relative bearing to a true bearing, add the true heading:

真方位=真艏向+舷角

True bearing=true heading+relative bearing

舷角=真方位-真艏向

Relative bearing=true bearing-true heading

注意：如果舷角为半圆法度量，舷角(Q)右为"+"，舷角(Q)左为"-"。

Note that if the relative bearing is semicircle, the relative bearing (Q) is "+" for the starboard Q, and is "-" for the port Q.

1.2.3.2　测量航向和方位的仪器

1.2.3.2　Instruments to Measure Course and Bearing

为了测量船上的角度并将船驶向所需的方向，需要使用罗经。船上使用的罗经包括磁罗经和陀螺罗经(俗称电罗经)。

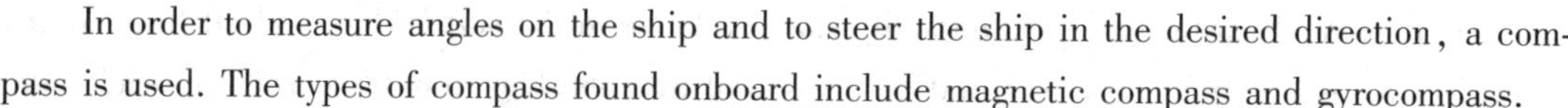

In order to measure angles on the ship and to steer the ship in the desired direction, a compass is used. The types of compass found onboard include magnetic compass and gyrocompass.

1.2.3.2.1 *磁罗经*

1.2.3.2.1 Magnetic Compass

你可能已经见过的唯一的罗经是磁罗经,通常被称为航用罗盘或卡片罗盘。它是一个在水平平面上自由悬浮的磁铁棒,在地磁场作用下工作,而不依靠任何电力。

The only compass you are likely to have met is the magnetic compass that usually is referred to as a marine compass or a card compass. It is a bar magnet freely suspended in the horizontal plane that operates under the influence of earth's magnetism without any electrical power supply.

地球可被认为是一块巨大的磁铁。磁力线来自磁南极(位于南极洲),沿着近似的半个大圆弧路径到达磁北极(位于加拿大北极)。而且磁极并非静止不动,而是不断地在一条基本未知的路径上移动,几百年一循环。由于地球磁场不规则,磁极之间相距并非 180°,所以自由悬浮的磁罗盘指针并不总是指向磁极。真北是朝向地理北极的方向,而磁北则指的是磁针的"北"端,当只受地球磁力的影响时,磁针的"北"端指向磁北并保持水平。正北(N_T)和磁北(N_M)之间的夹角是磁差(通常缩写为"variation"或"Var"),从真北向东或向西度量(如图 1.2.5 所示)。

The earth may be considered as a gigantic magnet. Magnetic lines of force emanate from the South Magnetic Pole (located in Antarctica). These lines of force follow approximate semi-Great Circle paths to the North Magnetic Pole (located in the Canadian Arctic). These Magnetic Poles are not stationary but are continually moving over a largely unknown path in a cycle of some hundreds of years. As the earth's magnetic field is irregular and Magnetic Poles are not 180° apart, a freely suspended magnetic compass needle does not always point towards the Magnetic Pole. True North is the direction towards the geographical North Pole. However, Magnetic North is the name given to the direction in which the "North" end of a magnetic needle, suspended so as to remain horizontal, would point when subject only to the influence of the earth's magnetism. The angle between True North (N_T) and Magnetic North (N_M) is Magnetic Variation (normally abbreviated to "variation" or "Var"), measured East or West from True North (see Figure 1.2.5).

磁差在不同的地方,其值不同,并且逐渐变化。

Variation has different values at different places and is gradually changing.

磁差随下列因素而变化:(1)因地而异;(2)因时而异;(3)地磁异常与磁暴。

The magnetic variation varies with the following factors:(1)place; (2) time; (3) Geomagnetic anomalies and magnetic storms.

某地的磁差可从航海图中找到,这些海图给出了某一年的磁差,同时也提供其长期的年度变化规律,这点必须考虑。如图 1.2.6 所示,2009 年的磁差为-4°15′(W)。这意味着,磁北指向 355°45′,而不是指向真北 000°。磁差的年变化为 8′(E)。因此,这一地区的磁差将在 2013 年减少到 3°43′W。

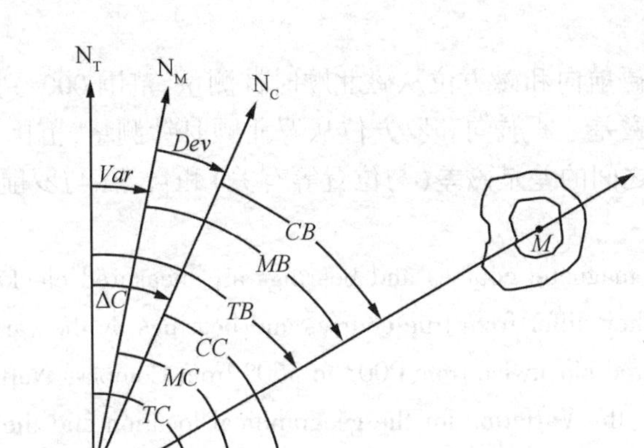

图 1.2.5　磁航向/方位以及罗航向/方位

Figure 1.2.5　Magnetic courses/bearings and compass courses/bearings

Its value at any place may be found from navigational charts which give the variation for a certain year, together with a note of its annual value of secular change for which allowance must be made. See Figure 1.2.6, the variation for the year 2009 is $-4°15'$ (West). This means, that the compass needle north-pole will point to 355°45′ instead of pointing to True North at 000°. The annual change of the magnetic variation is $+8'$ (East). So the variation in this region will decrease to 3°43′W in the year of 2013.

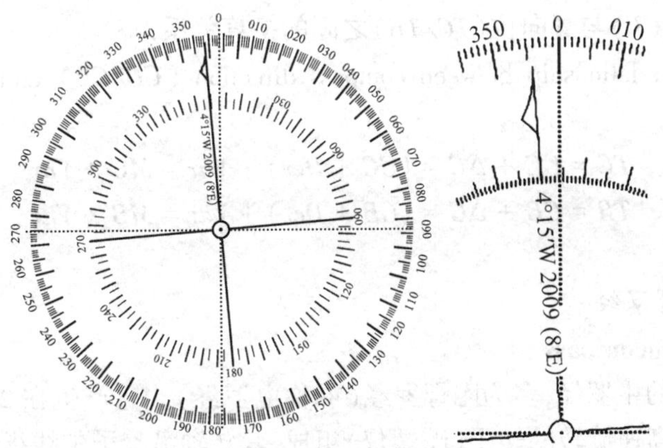

图 1.2.6　在航用海图上的罗经花及磁差表示

Figure 1.2.6　Compass Rose on navigational charts

如果将磁罗经放在船上，钢铁或电气设备的存在将导致磁罗经指针偏离磁北。磁北与最后指针所指的方向即罗北(N_C)之间的夹角，称为磁罗经自差(通常缩写为"deviation"或"Dev")，它从磁北向东或向西度量。

If a magnetic compass is put in a ship, the presence of iron, steel or electrical equipment will cause the magnetic compass to deviate from the Magnetic North. The angle between the Magnetic North and the direction in which the needle points (Compass North, N_C) is called Magnetic Deviation (normally abbreviated to "deviation" or "Dev"). It is measured East or West from Magnetic

North.

如图 1.2.6 所示,磁航向和磁方位从磁北顺时针测量,范围 000°到 360°。它们与真航向和真方位之间的差是磁差。罗航向和罗方位从罗北顺时针测量,范围 000°到 360°。它们分别与真航向和真方位之间的差是磁差(与位置等有关)和自差(与罗航向等有关)的代数和,称为罗经差(ΔC)。

See Figure 1.2.6, magnetic courses and bearings arc measured clockwise from 000° to 360° from Magnetic North. They differ from true courses and bearings by the variation. Compass courses and bearings are measured clockwise from 000° to 360° from Compass North. They differ from true courses and bearings by the Variation for the geographical location and the Deviation for the Compass Headings. The algebraic sum of deviation and variation is the Compass Error (ΔC).

在船上,磁罗盘由一张罗经刻度盘组成,罗经刻度盘底部附有磁针。磁针对准罗经刻度盘上标注的南北线。罗盘上刻有或标有一条表示艏艉线的线,称为"船首基线"。导航员可以很容易地从磁罗盘上读出船舶的航向,读出的位置是船首基线与罗经刻度盘外缘上标记的刻度线对齐的地方。

On ships, a magnetic compass consists of a compass card with magnetised needles attached to its underside. These are aligned to the north and south line that is marked on the card. A line indicating the fore-and-aft line of the ship, engraved or marked on the compass bowl, is called the "lubber line". Navigators can easily read the heading of a ship from a magnetic compass at a point where the lubber line is aligned to a scale marked on the outside edge of the compass card.

罗经向位(CC/CB)与真向位(TC/TB)之间的换算关系为:

The conversion relationship between compass direction (CC/CB) and true direction (TC/TB) is given by:

$$TC = CC + \Delta C = (CC + Dev) + Var = MC + Var$$
$$TB = CB + \Delta C = (CB + Dev) + Var = MB + Var$$

1.2.3.2.2 陀螺罗经

1.2.3.2.2 Gyrocompass

目前船上使用的主罗经,多为陀螺罗经(或称电罗经)。它产生在 20 世纪早期,它最简单的形式是由一个高速旋转的转子(陀螺仪)组成,其转轴沿着子午线指向真北。到了 20 世纪末 21 世纪初,陀螺罗经已成为非常精确、可靠的仪器,但需要供电和日常维护。有些船现在使用光纤陀螺仪(FOG)技术,具有很少的(如果有的话)可移动部件。

The main compass used by ships today, the gyrocompass, first made its appearance in the early part of the 20th century. In its simplest form it comprised a rapidly rotating wheel (Gyroscope), the rotation axis of which was made to point along the Meridian to True North. By the late 20th/early 21st centuries, gyrocompasses became extremely accurate, reliable instruments but requiring a power supply and routine maintenance; some now use Fibre Optic Gyro (FOG) technology with few, if any, moving parts.

陀螺罗经是一个复杂的仪器,有多种原因使其不能准确指向真北。当陀螺罗经作为准确的指向参考时,必须知道其误差,也即陀罗差(ΔG)。在磁罗经中,误差被命名为东或西,而陀螺仪的误差还可被命名为高或低,这取决于陀螺罗经指示方向高于或低于真实的方向。图 1.2.7 显示了这两种情况:如果已知物体 *M* 的真方位(*TB*)为 043°,陀罗方位(*GB*)为 045°,则陀罗差为高 2°,如图 1.2.7(a)所示;同样,如果陀罗方位(*GB*)为 041°,陀罗差则为低 2°,如图 1.2.7(b)所示。

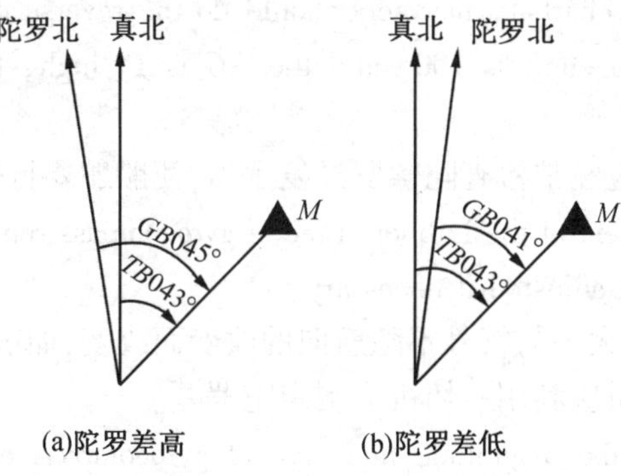

图 1.2.7　陀罗差高(低)

The gyrocompass is a complex instrument, and there are a number of reasons why it may not point exactly to true north. Any gyrocompass error (ΔG) must be established before the gyrocompass may be used as an accurate reference. Unlike the magnetic compass, where error is named east or west, the gyrocompass error is named high or low depending on whether the gyrocompass is indicating a direction higher or lower than the true. Figure 1.2.7 shows both situations: if the true bearing (*TB*) of an object *M* is known to be 043° and the gyrocompass bearing (*GB*) is 045°, then the gyrocompass is reading 2° high [Figure 1.2.7(a)]; similarly, if the gyrocompass bearing (*GB*) is 041°, the gyrocompass is reading 2° low [Figure 1.2.7(b)].

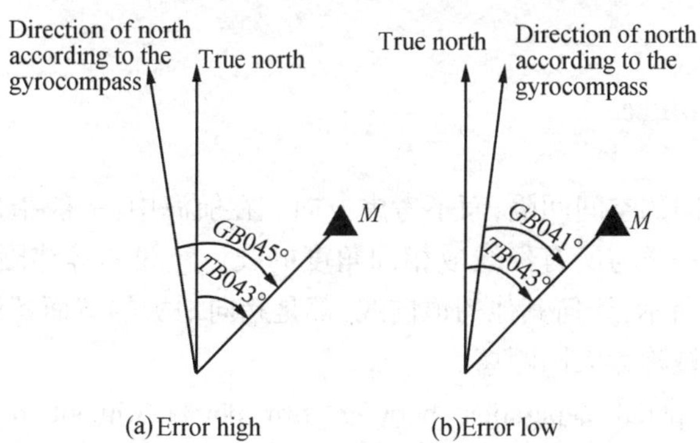

Figure 1.2.7　Gyrocompass error high (low)

为了获得真方位或真航向,当:

In order to obtain the true bearing or course:

(1)陀罗差高,须从观测到的方位或航向中减去陀罗差;

(1) Gyrocompass error high: it must be subtracted from the bearing or course observed;

(2)陀罗差低,须加陀罗差到观测的陀罗方位或航向上。

(2) Gyrocompass error low: it must be added to the gyrocompass bearing or course observed.

为了获得能够用来航行操舵的航向和方位,海员需将海图上的真航向或方位,转换成陀罗航向或方位,与上述操作反向即可,比如海图上 $TC=100°$,陀罗差高 1°,那么 $GC=101°$。

To obtain a gyrocompass bearing or course to set on the steering gyrocompass (given true course/bearing e.g., from charts), mariners should do the reverse operation with the above. For example, if the TC from a chart is 100° and the ΔG is 1° high, the GC to be steered should be 101°.

在船舶上,必要时,应经常检查陀螺罗经复示器,使船舶要行驶的航向与船首基线对齐。

On ships, the alignment of the Lubbers Line of gyrocompass repeaters to Ship's Head should be checked frequently and adjusted if necessary.

一般来说,陀罗差的大小与符号不随航向的改变而改变,而随着船舶航行的纬度与速度的变化而变化。航海人员应利用一切机会测定陀罗差。

Generally speaking, the magnitude and sign of gyrocompass error do not change with the change of course, but change with the change of latitude and speed of the ship. Seafarers should take every opportunity to measure gyrocompass error.

1.3 海上距离和速度

1.3 Nautical Distance and Speed

1.3.1 海上距离

1.3.1 Nautical Distance

距离是两个点之间的空间间隔,而不考虑方向。在航海中,一般指连接两个地方的恒向线的长度。恒向线是一条与所有经线成相同角度的线。经线和等纬圈也是特殊的恒向线。除此之外,如图 1.3.1 所示,任何其他的恒向线,都是趋向地极的球面螺旋线。而连接两个地方的大圆弧的长度则被称为大圆距离。

Distance is the spatial separation between two points without regard to direction. In navigation, it is the length of the rhumb line connecting two places. This is a line making the same angle with all meridians. Meridians and parallels which also maintain constant true directions may be considered special cases of the rhumb line. Any other rhumb line spirals toward the pole, forming a loxodromic curve, see Figure 1.3.1. Distance along the Great Circle connecting two points is customarily designated as Great-Circle distance.

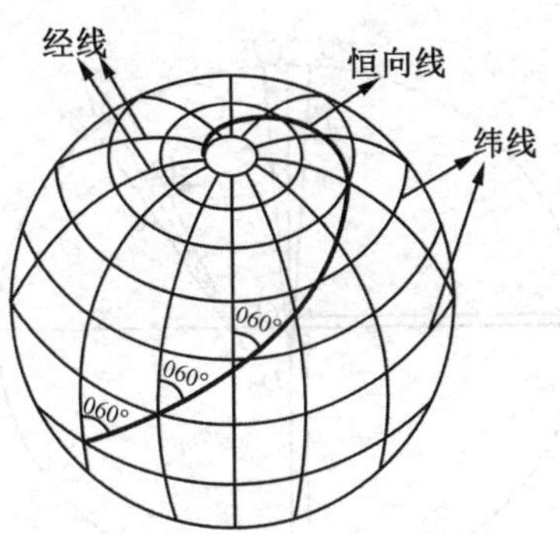

图 1.3.1　恒向线

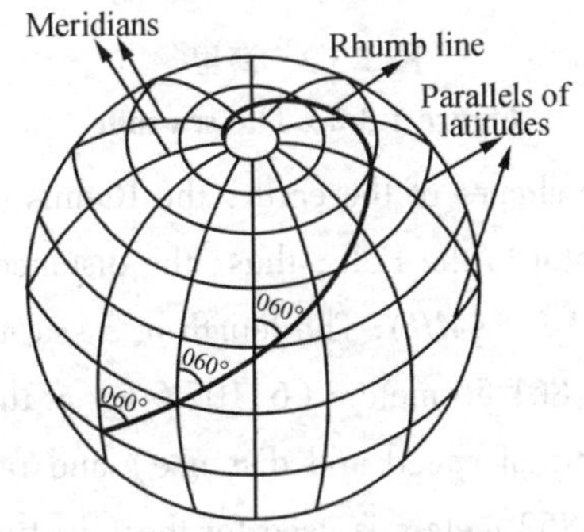

Figure 1.3.1　Rhumb line

一般距离的单位是码、海里或公里。“海里”不是指陆地距离单位——而是指海上的里程度量单位,海里,用符号“′”表示,如 16′即指 16 海里。海里是指地球椭圆子午线上纬度一分的弧长。而这一分的纬度在任何地方都指一个角度,该角度的中心不在地球的中心,而是在该处子午线的曲率中心。如图 1.3.2 所示,如果 *M* 是地球表面的位置,*C* 是 *M* 处的曲率中心,*AMB* 是该子午线 1′弧长,那么 *AMB* 就是 *M* 处 1 n mile 的长度。

The customary units of distance are yards, miles, or kilometers. The term “mile” does not refer to the land mile—it refers either to the sea mile or nautical mile, the symbol “′” is used for both, e.g., 16′ means 16 n mile. The sea mile is the length of a minute of arc measured along the meridian in the latitude of the position. A minute of latitude in any place is subtended by an angle, not at the center of the Earth, but at the center of curvature at that place. See Figure 1.3.2, if *M* is the place on the Earth’s surface, *C* is the center of circular curvature at *M*, and *AMB* is an arc of the Meridian subtending an angle of 1′, then *AMB* is the length of the sea mile at *M*.

由于地球形状不规则(两极略扁的椭球体),子午线的曲率半径随 *M* 点从赤道到极点而逐渐增大。因此,1′弧长所代表的距离也随之增大,如图 1.3.2 所示,弧 $EP_nF>AMB$。1 海里的长度从赤道的 1 842.94 m(6 046.4 ft)到两极的 1 861.56 m(6 107.5 ft)不等。为了避免在不同纬度上重新校准计程仪(船上用来计量速度和距离的仪器)和雷达装置等需要用到海里数据的仪器,这些仪器统一使用了 1 852 m 作为固定的海里长度,这就是国际海里,缩写“n mile”(或“nm”)。

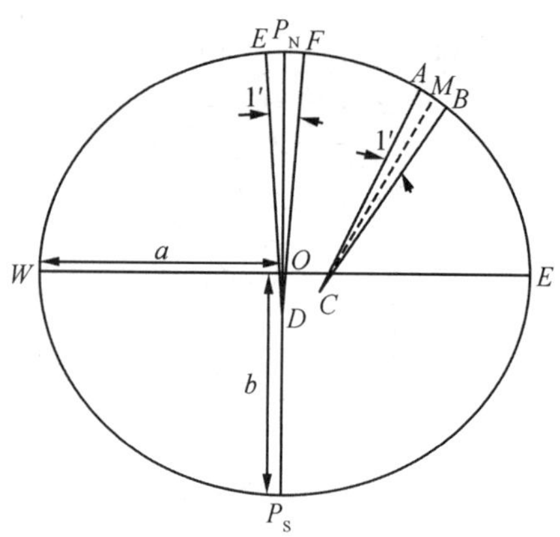

图 1.3.2 海里

Figure 1.3.2 The sea mile

Due to the irregularity to the shapes of the earth, the Radius of Curvature in the Meridian increases as M moves from the Equator to the Pole; thus, the distance subtended by 1′ of arc also increases (see Figure 1.3.2, arc $EP_nF > AMB$). The length of a sea mile varies from 1,842.94 meters (6,046.4 ft) at the Equator to 1,861.56 meters (6,107.5 ft) at the poles. In order to avoid recalibrating ship's Logs (the recorders of speed and distance) and radar sets in different latitudes a nautical mile of fixed length of 1,852 meters is used for these instruments. This is the International Nautical Mile, and its abbreviation is the term "n mile" (or "nm").

然而,当使用海图时,你将使用海里;1 n mile 等于纬度图尺上的 1′。

However, when you are using a chart you will be using sea miles; one sea mile is equivalent to one minute on the latitude scale.

另外在航海上常见的距离单位是"链",1 cab 约是 1/10 n mile,约 200 yd。进入锚地,一般用链表示与其他船舶之间的距离。1 cab 约为 100 拓(fathom),1 fm=6 ft=1.829 m。

Another unit which you will meet in navigation is the cable. This is taken as roughly 200 yards, or alternatively as a tenth of a nautical mile. Coming into an anchorage, for instance, the distance to go is called out in cables. 1 cable is about 100 fathom, 1 fathom=6 feet=1.829 meters.

航海中距离的两个组成部分是时间和速度。事实上,距离的数学表达式为 $D=vt$,其中 D 是距离,v 是速度,t 是时间。

Two components of distance in navigation are time and speed. Indeed, distance is expressed mathematically as $D=vt$, where D is distance, v is speed, and t is time.

1.3.2 速度
1.3.2 Speed

速度即运动速率,在航海上通常以节为单位进行度量。1 节就是 1 n mile/h。其缩写为"kn"(非"kt")。"节"源于抛绳记录航行距离时,等距打结以分节的标记。在一般航海实践中，使用 n mile 代替变化的海里引起的误差非常小(小于 0.50%)，因此 1 kn = 1 n mile/h。

Speed is defined as the rate of movement and in navigation is usually measured in knots. One knot is one International Nautical Mile (1,852 m) per hour. Its abbreviation is the term "kn" (NOT "kt"). The name "knot" originates from running out a log line with distances marked by knots tied in the line. In normal practice, the errors arising from using International Nautical Miles (n mile) instead of Sea Miles are very small (less than 0.50%), Thus 1 kn = 1 n mile/h.

需注意的是，航海中使用了两种速度。(1)对地速度(SOG)，也称为真实速度，是船舶相对于地面的速度，可通过测量船舶的已知航行距离所需的时间来计算。GPS 可提供 SOG 类型的速度读数，因为位置是相对于地面计算和测量的，且不受船舶周围水流的影响。(2)对水速度，是船舶相对于水的运动速度。对水速度是通过仪器测量的，这些仪器利用某种机械或电磁原理感知船只在水中的运动。

It is important to note that there are two kinds of speed used in nautical navigation. (1) Speed over the ground (SOG), also called true speed, is the vessel's speed relative to the surface of the earth and is calculated empirically by measuring the time required for a vessel to travel a known distance. GPS units provide speed reading of the SOG type because they are calculated relative to the earth's surface and are measured without being affected by the water surrounding the vessel. (2) Speed through the water is measured by instruments that sense the vessel's motion through the water, using some mechanical or electromagnetic principle.

1.3.3　速度的测量
1.3.3　Measurement of Speed

计程仪可用来记录船的速度和距离。常见的计程仪类型包括：回转式计程仪、水压式计程仪、电磁式计程仪、多普勒计程仪和声相关计程仪。前面三种均为相对计程仪，即能够记录相对水的速度(STW)，后面的两种计程仪只有在水深不太深时，可测出对地的速度(SOG)。

The instrument used to record the speed and distance covered by ship is the log. The following types of logs: impeller log, pitometer log, electro-magnetic log, Doppler speed log and acoustic correlation log have been equipped on most ships. The first three are used to measure the speed through the water (STW), the others can be used to measure the speed over the ground (SOG) when the depth of water is not very big.

除了上述直接测量船舶速度的方法外，另一种相当简单而有效的估算近似航速的方法适用于螺旋桨驱动船舶，那就是使用每分钟螺旋桨转速(RPM)求船速。对于具有较大吃水的船舶，采用非可变螺距的螺旋桨，其 RPM 与对水速度之间具有相当一致的关系。当一艘船投入使用时，她的海试内容应能提供速度与 RPM 之间的关系，如表 1.3.1 所示。该表提供了每一节速度所需的 RPM，放于驾驶台以备船舶在航时使用。在使用主机转速作为速度指示器时，必须考虑船舶的吃水情况、船污底情况和海洋状况，以获得较高的预测精度。

表 1.3.1 M/V "×××"转速表

RPM	速度(kn)		RPM	速度(kn)	
	满载	压载		满载	压载
120	14.0	14.7	80	10.3	11.2
110	13.2	14.0	70	9.2	10.2
100	12.3	13.0	60	8.2	9.2
90	11.4	12.4	50	7.2	8.2

In addition to the foregoing methods of direct measurement of vessel speed, another fairly simple yet effective means of estimating approximate speed long familiar to navigators of screw-driven ships is the use of shaft revolutions per minute (RPM). For all larger constant-draft vessels having nonvariable pitch propellers, there is a fairly consistent relationship between shaft RPM and speed through the water. When a ship is commissioned, one of her sea trials consists of the preparation of a graph showing speed versus RPM. From this graph, a revolution table (see Table 1.3.1) is prepared for use on the bridge while under way. It gives the RPM required for each knot of speed. In making use of engine revolutions as speed indicators, the draft of the ship, the condition of its bottom as to cleanliness, and the state of the sea must be considered for additional accuracy.

Table 1.3.1 M/V "×××" revolution table

RPM	Speed (kn)		RPM	Speed (kn)	
	Full loaded	Ballast		Full loaded	Ballast
120	14.0	14.7	80	10.3	11.2
110	13.2	14.0	70	9.2	10.2
100	12.3	13.0	60	8.2	9.2
90	11.4	12.4	50	7.2	8.2

1.4 助航标志

1.4 Aids to Navigation

航标是助航标志的简称,它是以特定的标志、灯光、音响或无线电信号等,供海员确定船位、航向,避离危险,使船舶沿着航道或预定航线安全航行的助航设施。航标包括视觉航标(如灯塔、灯桩、浮标等),声响航标(雾笛、雾号、雾钟等),雷达航标(雷达反射器和雷康),以及差分 GPS 航标和 AIS 航标等,并且它们之间还有一些分类方面的重叠。比如,许多浮标上配有灯、雾笛、雷达反射器,甚至 AIS 航标,一些雷康、雾号和 AIS 还会装于一些灯桩或灯塔之上,协助导航。

An aid to navigation, sometimes abbreviated and called a NAVAID or AtoN, is defined as any device external to a vessel intended to help mariners determine position and course, to warn of dangers or obstructions, or to mark the location of preferred routes. Collectively known as aids to navigation, they include visual aids (lighthouses, light beacons and buoys), aural aids (whistles, horns and bells), radar aids (reflectors and racons), as well as the DGPS (Differential Global Positioning System) and AIS (Automatic Identification System) aids. And there are considerable overlap in these categories. For example, many buoys have lights, whistles, reflectors even AIS attached to them, some racons, horns and or AIS may be mounted on light beacons or lighthouses to assist marine navigation.

本节主要讨论的现代视觉航标,安装在航海者需要导航的区域,并且在海图上有相关标识,包括固定在海岸或海底的永久性结构,例如灯塔、灯桩,以及一些浮动的助航标志,例如灯船和浮标。

The modern visual aids to be discussed in this section are those local to the area in which the navigator is operating and which appear on the chart. These include permanent structures attached to the shore or bottom, such as lighthouses, light beacons, as well as floating aids, such as light vessels and buoys.

1.4.1　固定航标

1.4.1　Fixed Aids

(1) 灯塔

(1) Lighthouse

它是一种比较高大、坚固,并能发出特定灯光的塔形建筑物,由塔身、塔基和发光器三部分组成。塔身具有显著的形状和颜色特征,顶部装有光力较强、射程较远的发光器。灯塔一般设置在显著的海岸、岬角、重要航道附近的陆地、岛屿上和港湾入口以及孤立危险物或其他有必要为海员提供导航的地方。现代灯塔通常是无人值守的,并配备了雷达信标、雾信号和其他导航无线电信号。

It is a relatively tall, sturdy, and can emit a specific light tower-shaped buildings, by the tower body, tower base and luminous device three parts. The tower body has a significant shape and color characteristics, the top is equipped with a stronger light force, longer-range luminous device. Lighthouses are generally placed on prominent shores, headlands, on land near important navigable channel, on islands, and at harbour entrances, as well as on isolated hazards or other places where it is necessary to provide navigation for mariners. The modern lighthouses are typically unmanned and equipped with radar beacons, fog signals and other navigational radio signals.

（2）灯桩

(2) Light beacon

这通常是打入海底的单桩或多桩结构，顶部装有照明灯。灯桩一般设置在航道附近的岛岸边，以及港口防波堤上。这种灯塔无人值守，射程也小于灯塔。

This is usually a single pile or multiple-pile structure driven into the bottom with a light at the top. Light beacons are generally located on the shore near navigable channels and on the head of breakwaters. It is not manned and the range is less than that of the lighthouse.

（3）立标

(3) Beacon

立标一般只有一根桩，桩顶标记为圆球或三角形标记。它通常位于浅水区或岩石、浅滩、水中孤石和通航航道中的小障碍物上。也有的立标设在岸上作为叠标或导标，用以引导船舶进出港口或测定罗经差和船舶运动性能。

This is generally only a single pile with top mark such as a ball or a triangular mark. It is usually located in shallow waters or on a rock, shoals, and isolated rock in water and minor obstacle in navigable channel. Some beacons are located ashore as leading marks or as marks for testing the compass error or the maneuverability of the ship.

1.4.2 浮动航标

1.4.2 Floating Aids

水上浮动航标是浮在水面上，用锚或沉锤、锚链牢固地系留在预定点海床上的航标，包括：

Floating navigation marks on water are navigation marks that float on the surface of the water and are firmly attached to the seabed at a predetermined point using anchors, sinkers, or anchor chains, including:

（1）灯船

(1) Light ship

灯船是一种特殊设计的船，与灯塔的用途相同。灯船一般设立在周围无显著陆标，又不便建造灯塔等的重要航道附近，以引导船舶进出港口和避险等。一般灯船在甲板高处装设有发光器、雾号和其他助航设施，其船身被漆成红色，标识有船名和标号，并且灯船在白天显示一个黑球，如图 1.4.1 所示。有人看守的灯船可靠性好，但维护费用高。

This is a specially designed vessel which serves the same purpose as the lighthouse. It is generally located at the place near important channel where there are no prominent landmarks around and where it's impracticable or impossible to construct a lighthouse at the desired location to guide ships in and out of ports and to avoid danger. Light ships are generally equipped with lights, fog signals and other navigational devices high above the deck, and the hull is usually painted red, marked with the ship's name and number, and displaying a black ball dayshape (see Figure 1.4.1). It is expensive to maintain as most light ships are manned.

图 1.4.1 灯船

Figure 1.4.1 Light ship (light vessel)

(2) 浮标

(2) Buoy

浮标是一种无人值守的浮动助航装置,牢牢固定在海床上,位于港口、航路和航道附近,以及靠近浅滩和障碍物等航行危险的水域。浮标通常装有发光器、音响设备、雷达信标和规定的顶标等。浮标通过使用颜色、形状、顶部标记、数字和光线特征来传达其目的并指示危险。这是最常用的导航辅助工具,但其经常受海流和潮汐的影响,实际位置以锚碇为中心在一定范围内移动,遇大风浪时可能移位或漂失,一般不能用来定位。配有发光器的浮标称为灯浮标。

This is an unmanned, floating aid to navigation securely anchored to the seabed, located in the vicinity of harbors, fairways and channels, and water areas in close proximity to hazards to navigation such as shoals and obstructions. Buoys are usually equipped with luminaries, sound equipment, radar beacons and prescribed top markers, etc. Buoys communicate their purpose and indicate danger through the use of colours, shapes, topmarks, numbers, and light characteristics. This is the most numerous aid to navigation, but buoys are often affected by currents and tides, the actual position of the anchor as the center of a certain range of movement, may be shifted or lost when encountering large winds and waves, generally can not be used to fix a ship's position. A buoy equipped with the light is called lighted buoy.

1.4.3 国际航标协会海上浮标系统和其他助航标志

1.4.3 IALA Maritime Buoyage System and Other Aids to Navigation

1.4.3.1 总述

1.4.3.1 General Information

浮标的形状和大小多种多样,作为最常用的导航辅助工具,浮标的历史由来已久。不同的国家都发展了各自的浮标系统。作为一个航海者,你必须熟悉世界各地航行中可能遇到的各种浮标系统。这不是个好主意,可能会带来不便或造成航行事故。在 20 世纪 70 年代中期之前,浮标系统标准化工作进展缓慢。直到国际航标协会(IALA)使得世界范围内基本接受了两个系统。这两个系统的规则非常相似,很容易合二为一,称为“国际航标协会海上浮标系统(MBS)”。这套规则允许国际航标协会(IALA)在区域基础上选择使用“左红或右红”的标准,即分成了 A 区和 B 区两个系统。其边界的确定如下:

Used in a variety of shapes and sizes, buoys as the most numerous aids to navigation have been around for a long time. Different nations have developed their own systems of buoyage. As a navigator, you must be familiar with the various systems of buoyage that you might encounter in your travel. That's not a good idea and may lead to accidents. Efforts toward standardization were made but achieved little success until the Mid-1970s, when an organization then known as the International Association of Lighthouse Authorities (IALA) developed and secured nearly two systems accepted worldwide. The rules for the two systems were so similar that it's easy to combine them into one, known as "The IALA Maritime Buoyage System (MBS)". This single set of rules allows Lighthouse Authorities the choice of using red to port or red to starboard, on a regional basis. The two regions are known as Region A and Region B. The boundaries of the buoyage regions were decided below:

(1)B 区域:包括美国和西半球其他地区,加上日本、韩国、菲律宾。

(1)Region B: the United States and the rest of the Western Hemisphere, plus Japan, Republic of Korea, and the Philippines。

(2)A 区域:除上述国家或区域之外的欧洲、非洲、大洋洲和亚洲的一些国家等。

(2)Region A: used in most of the world except the above.

鉴于航行环境的变化和电子助航设施的发展,2010 年起,国际航标协会(IALA)航标系统包括两个组成部分:海上浮标系统和其他固定和浮动的助航标志。这主要是基于物理分类的系统;然而,所有的标志都可以通过电子手段加以补充。“海上浮标系统和其他助航标志”制度,适用于所有固定、浮动和电子助航标志,用以标识:

In light of changes in the navigation environment and the further development of electronic aids to navigation, from 2010, the IALA Aids to Navigation system has two components: The Maritime Buoyage System and other aids to navigation comprised of fixed and floating devices. This is primarily a physical system; however, all of the marks may be complemented by electronic means. The Maritime Buoyage System and other aids to navigation provide rules that apply to all fixed, floating and electronic marks serving to indicate:

(1)指明可航水道的中央线和边侧界限;

(1)the centerline and lateral limits of navigable channels;

(2)天然危险物和其他障碍物(如沉船);

(2)natural dangers and other obstructions such as wrecks;

(3)登陆点、航向以及对海员有用的其他区域或特征;

(3)landfall, course to steer, and other areas or features of importance to the mariner;

(4)新危险物。

(4)new dangers.

海上浮标系统有六种类型的标志,可单独或组合使用。海员通过识别标志特征加以区分,如浮标的形状、颜色、顶标,以及闪烁(如果带灯)的节奏等。除了浮标区域 A 和 B 之间的侧面标志有所不同外,其他五种类型的标志在两个区域均相同。

Within the Maritime Buoyage System, there are six types of marks, which may be used alone or in combination. The mariner can distinguish between these marks by identifiable characteristics such as buoy shape, colour, topmarks, and if lighted, the rhythm of the flashes. Lateral marks differ between Buoyage Regions A and B, whereas the other five types of marks are common to both regions.

1.4.3.2 标志种类

1.4.3.2 Types of Marks

(1)侧面标志

(1)Lateral marks

侧面标志结合"浮标习惯走向"使用,通常用于界限明确的航道,该标志标明所要遵循航道的左舷和右舷。

Lateral Marks are generally used for well-defined channels with a "Conventional Direction of Buoyage", which indicates the port and starboard sides of the route to be followed.

浮标习惯走向是由局部走向(海员从海上驶近港口、河流、河口或其他水道时所采取的走向)或总体走向(原则上应是环绕大片陆地的顺时针方向)决定的。浮标习惯走向(如已确定)通常用红色箭矢符号标明,在《航路指南》中的特定区域有相应说明。

This is defined by either the Local Direction of Buoyage (used when approaching harbours, rivers, estuaries or other waterways from seaward), or a General Direction of Buoyage (created on the principle of a clockwise direction around land masses). The relevant Direction of Buoyage (if established) is normally shown on the chart with a large open arrow symbol and mentioned in Admiralty Sailing Directions (Pilots) for a particular area.

如图 1.4.2 所示,在 A 区,按箭头方向航行的船舶应将绿色浮标放在右舷,红色浮标置于左舷,即"左红右绿"。与浮标的一般走向相反而行的船舶则应将红色浮标置于右舷通过。

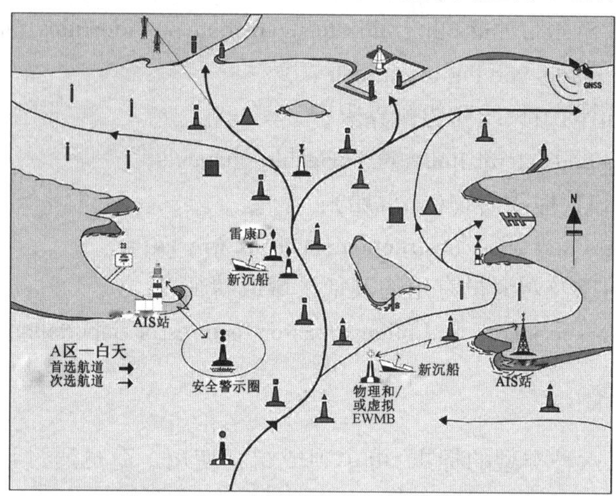

图 1.4.2　A 区域的浮标及其他助航标志

In Region A, see Figure 1.4.2, the ships moving in the direction of the arrow will have green buoys on the starboard side and red on the port side. The ships going opposite to the general direction of buoyage will keep red buoys on the starboard side.

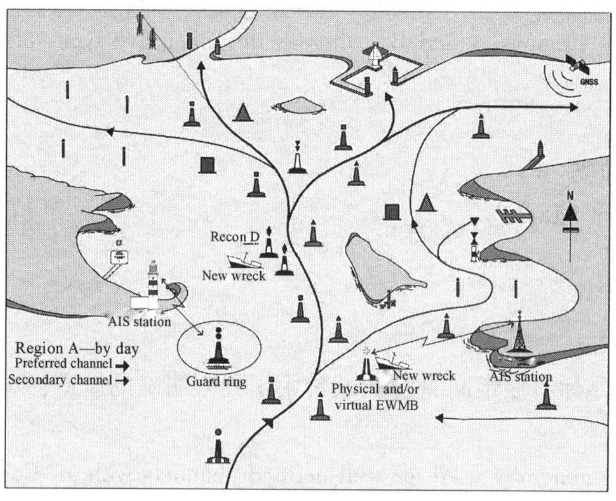

Figure 1.4.2　Examples of buoyage and other AtoN for Region A

在 B 区,当船舶进港时,应将绿色浮标置于左舷,当船舶出港时,应将红色浮标置于左舷。

In Region B, when a ship is entering harbour, the green buoys should be kept on the port side and when departing the red buoy should be kept on the port side.

在某些地方,有两条可航路线到达同一目的地。但是,如果这两条航道中,其中一个具有更好的水深或宽度的分支航道,被称为"推荐航道",这时,推荐航道侧面标志指明船只可以从哪一边通过。图 1.4.2 中 A 区域在航道的第一个分岔处,该标志为"推荐航道右侧标",表明推荐航道在其左侧。

At some places, there are two navigable passages available for arriving at the same destination. If, however, one of these two passages has better depth and width of available navigable water, then it is termed the "preferred channel", in which case preferred channel buoys are used to indicate the side from which the ships may pass. As shown in Figure 1.4.2, for Region A, there is a mark named "preferred channel to port side" at the first branch of the channel, which indicates the preferred channel is on its left side.

（2）方位标志

(2) Cardinal marks

方位标志结合罗经使用,用于指示海员可在何处找到最佳通航水域。从标记点开始,它们被放置在以隅点为界的四个象限(北、南、东、西)中的一个象限内。方位标志以其所在象限的名称命名。如果海员通过北方位标的北侧、东方位标的东侧、南方位标的南侧和西方位标的西侧,那么他就是安全的。

Cardinal marks are used in conjunction with the compass to indicate where the mariner may find the best navigable water. They are placed in one of the four quadrants (North, South, East and West) bounded by inter-cardinal bearings, from the point marked. Cardinal marks take their name from the quadrant in which they are placed. The mariner is safe if he passes N of a North mark, E of an East mark, S of a South mark and W of a West mark.

（3）孤立危险物标志

(3) Isolated danger marks

孤立危险物标志是指竖立或系泊在周围有可航水域、范围有限的孤立危险物之上的标志。例如,该标志可能伫立在某沉船、浅滩或小岛之上,周围尚有可航水域。

Isolated danger marks are placed or moored on top of isolated dangers with navigable water and limited range around it. For example, it may be moored on top of a wreck, a shoal or a small islet surrounded by navigable water.

（4）安全水域标志

(4) Safe water marks

安全水域标志用于指明在该标周围均有可航水域。这种标志可用作中线标志、航道中央标志或航道入口标志,或指明固定桥下最好的通过点。

Safe Water Marks are used to indicate that there are navigable waters all round a mark. Such a mark may be used as a centerline, mid-channel or landfall buoy, or to indicate the best point of passage under a fixed bridge.

（5）专用标志

(5) Special marks

专用浮标用于指示航行者特别关注的区域的边界,如锚地、军事演习区域和渔区等。

These buoys are used to indicate boundaries of areas that are of particular concern to the navi-

gator, such as anchorages, exercise areas, fish farms, etc.

(6)新危险物标志

(6) New danger marks

"新危险物"是指新发现的危险,不论自然的或是人工标志,可能尚未在海图和航海出版物中显示的,在信息充分公布之前,应使用适当的标志标识,例如侧面标志、方位标志、孤立危险物标志,或应急沉船示位标(EWMB)来标示新的危险。如果主管当局认为航行风险特别高,至少应重复其中一个标志。

"New dangers" are newly discovered hazards, natural or man-made, that may not yet be shown in nautical documents and publications, and until the information is sufficiently promulgated, should be indicated by marking a new danger by using appropriate marks such as lateral, cardinal, isolated danger marks, or equally using the emergency wreck marking buoy (EWMB). If the competent authority considers the risk to navigation to be especially high, at least one of the marks should be duplicated.

1.4.3.3 其他标志

1.4.3.3 Other Marks

其他标志包括灯塔、立标、光弧灯、导向线、大型浮标和辅助标志。这些视觉航标的目的是为海员提供导航信息,而不一定是关于航道边界或障碍物的信息。

Other marks include lighthouses, beacons, sector lights, leading lines, major floating aids, and auxiliary marks. These visual marks are intended to aid navigation as information to mariners, not necessarily regarding channel limits or obstructions.

(1)灯塔、立标和其他射程较小的标志是可在指定弧度上显示不同颜色和/或节奏的固定助航设备。立标也可能没有照明。

(1) Lighthouses, beacons and other aids of lesser ranges are fixed aids to navigation that may display different colours and/or rhythms over designated arcs. Beacons may also be unlighted.

(2)光弧灯在指定的光弧界限范围上显示不同的颜色和/或节奏。灯光的颜色可为海员提供方向性信息。

(2) Sector lights display different colours and/or rhythms over designated arcs. The colour of the light provides directional information to the mariner.

(3)导灯/叠标能够让船舶沿着固定灯标(导灯)或标志(导标)的连线的一部分航行,从而进行精确的船舶导航,在某些情况下也可使用单一的方向灯标。

(3) Leading lines/ranges allow ships to be guided with precision along a portion of a straight route using the alignment of fixed lights (leading lights) or marks (leading marks), in some cases a single directional light may be used.

(4)大型浮标包括灯船、灯浮标和大型助航浮标,一般用来标记近海的进港航路。

(4) Major floating aids include light vessels, light floats and large navigational buoys intended

to mark approaches from off shore.

(5)附加标志是用于协助导航或提供信息的其他标志。这些设备包括具有非侧面标志意义的辅助设备,用于定义明确的航道而不表明要遵循的航道的左舷和右舷,也可用来传送航行安全信息。

(5) Auxiliary marks are those other marks used to assist navigation or provide information. These include aids of non-lateral significance that are usually of defined channels and otherwise do not indicate the port and starboard sides of the route to be followed as well as those used to convey information for navigational safety.

(6)港口或港口标志,如防波堤、码头/码头灯、交通信号、桥梁标志和内河航道助航标志等。

(6) Port or harbor marks such as breakwater, quay/jetty lights, traffic signals, bridge marks and inland waterway aids to navigation.

1.5 海图

1.5 Nautical Charts

海图将球形地球的一部分表示在一个平面上。它显示水深、邻近陆地的海岸线、突出的地形特征、助航标志以及其他导助航信息。它是航海者绘制航线、确定位置、观察船舶与周围环境关系的工作区域。它帮助航海者避免危险并安全地到达目的地。

A nautical chart represents part of the spherical earth on a plane surface. It shows water depth, the shoreline of adjacent land, prominent topographic features, aids to navigation, and other navigational information. It is a work area on which the navigator plots courses, ascertains positions, and views the relationship of the ship to the surrounding area. It assists the navigator in avoiding dangers and arriving safely at his destination.

最早的海图是用羊皮手工绘制的,传统的海图经多代发展已为纸质印刷。现在由电子数据库和显示系统组成的电子海图正在使用中,并且正在取代许多船舶的纸质海图。电子海图并非只是纸质海图的数字化版本,它引入了全新的导航方法,其能力和局限性与纸质海图大不相同。电子海图符合国际海事组织的有关规定,即可具备替代纸质海图的条件。

Originally hand-drawn on sheepskin, traditional nautical charts have for generations been printed on paper. Electronic charts consisting of a digital data base and a display system are in use and are replacing paper charts aboard many vessels. An electronic chart is not simply a digital version of a paper chart; it introduces a new navigation methodology with capabilities and limitations very different from paper charts. The electronic chart is the legal equivalent of the paper chart if it meets certain International Maritime Organization specifications.

发生海上事故时使用的海图具有法律意义。在发生搁浅、碰撞和其他事故的情况下,海

图是还原事故和分配责任的关键记录,另外用于还原事故的海图也具有巨大的教学价值。

When a marine accident occurs, the nautical chart in use at the time would take on legal significance. In cases of grounding, collision, and other accidents, charts become critical records for reconstructing the event and assigning liability. Charts used in reconstructing the incident can also have tremendous training value.

1.5.1 海图投影

1.5.1 Chart Projection

因为制图者不能在不变形的情况下将球体转换到平面上,所以他必须将球体的表面投射到可展开的表面上。可展开的表面是可以被压平而形成平面的曲面,当然要满足一定的数学法则。这个过程被称为海图投影。如果球面上的点是从一个点投射出来的,则该投影称为透视投影。除了非常小的区域外,所有的投影都会包含一些失真。当地球表面不同部分的三个相同的圆形区域的轮廓分别从地球中心的一个起始点投射到平面图上时,它们的大小和形状是完全不同的(如图 1.5.1 中的例子)。

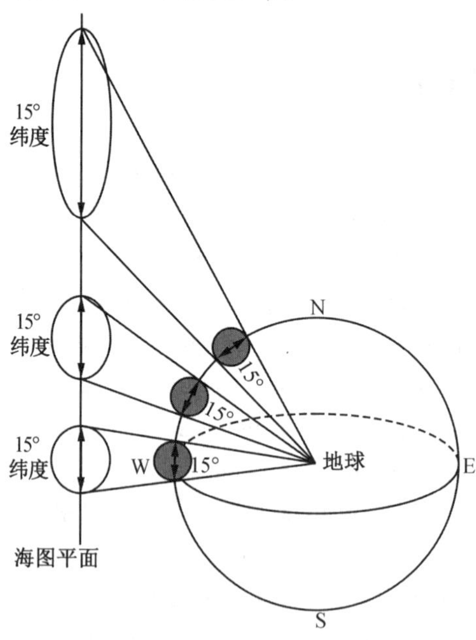

图 1.5.1 投影变形示意图

Because a cartographer cannot transfer a sphere to a flat surface without distortion, he must project the surface of a sphere onto a developable surface. A developable surface is one that can be flattened to form a plane and satisfy certain mathematical principles. This process is known as chart projection. If points on the surface of the sphere are projected from a single point, the projection is said to be perspective or geometric. Except over very small areas, all projections will contain some distortion. When the outlines of three identical circular areas from different parts of the earth's surface are each projected from a point of origin at the center of the earth on to a plane chart, they are represented by quite different sizes and shapes (see example in Figure 1.5.1).

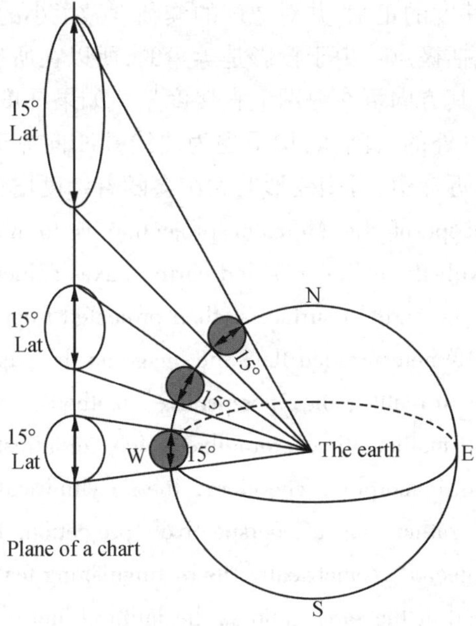

Figure 1.5.1　Example of distortion

投影变形一定会涉及四个相互关联的属性的一部分或全部:形状、方位、比例尺和面积。可以设计特定的投影方式消除变形或将这些变形的程度减少到微不足道,同时将其他变形保持在合理(可用)的范围内。因此,需要根据特定用途去选择不同的海图投影方式。

The distortion of a projection must involve some or all of the four interrelated properties: shape, bearing, scale and area. Projections can be devised which will eliminate or reduce to negligible proportions of these distortions, while keeping the others within reasonable (and thus usable) limits. The choice of projection for a chart is governed by the specific purpose for which the chart is intended.

对于航用海图,需要在其上面度量航向和方位,以便在实际航行中使用,或需要将实测的航向和方位绘制于海图之上。因此,航用海图的两个基本要求是:(1)具有等角的性质,或称为正形;(2)恒向线在图上表示为直线。最终航海上最常用的等角投影称为墨卡托投影。

For navigational charts, bearings and courses may be measured from the chart to be used at sea or plotted on the chart from measurements taken at sea. Therefore, the two basic requirements are: (1) correct angular relationships known as conformal; (2) rhumb lines represented as straight lines. At last, navigators most often use the conformal projection known as the Mercator projection.

墨卡托投影中采用类似的"透视"做法,是设想一个包裹在地球周围的圆柱体。该圆柱体和地球的轴线重合,它们的表面只在赤道接触;然后将地球表面从地球中心投射到该圆柱上(如图 1.5.2 所示)。展开圆柱面,圆柱体上的图网表示圆柱投影。实际上,仅靠这种"透视"不能形成墨卡托投影,还需要加入投影的数学法则,确保生成的图形是正形的或等角的,才能成为墨卡托投影。因此,"等角正圆柱投影"实际上是"数学"而不是"透视"投影。其等纬圈的变形可以从数学及几何上导出。它的特点是,经线和纬度圈都是随着纬度的增加而以相同的比例延展的。经线彼此平行,纬线也彼此平行。此外,在投影后,子午线将与等纬圈垂直。延展的倍数等于纬度的正割,并对地球的椭圆度做了小的修正。由于90°的正割是无穷大的,所以投影不能包括极点。由于投影是等角的,所以在所有方向和角度上延展是相同的。恒向线显示为直线,其方向可在海图上直接度量。如果纬度跨度很小,距离也可以直接测量出来。经线和赤道以外的大圆弧,均呈现为曲线并凹向赤道。很小的区域投影后基本保持其形状,除非它们靠近赤道,否则变形的大小会随着纬度增加而变大。

The "perspective" concept of the Mercator projection is to imagine a cylinder of paper wrapped around the earth, with the cylinder's and earth's axes coincident, and their surfaces in contact only at the Equator; the earth's surface is then projected from the earth's center onto the cylinder (see Figure 1.5.2). When unrolled flat, the image on the paper cylinder will represent a regular cylindrical projection. In reality, the "perspective" method is not used; instead the Mercator projection is produced by "mathematical" formulae which are adjusted to ensure that the resulting charts are conformal or orthomorphic. Therefore, the "Cylindrical Orthomorphic Projection" actually is a "mathematical" rather than a "perspective" projection. Its parallels can be derived mathematically as well as projected geometrically. Its distinguishing feature is that both the Meridians and parallels are expanded at the same ratio as the latitude increasing. The Meridians will be parallel to each other, and so will parallel of latitude. Also, Meridian will be perpendicular with parallel of latitude after projection. The expansion is equal to the secant of the latitude, with a small correction for the ellipticity of the earth. Since the secant of 90° is infinity, the projection cannot include the poles. Since the projection is conformal, expansion is the same in all directions and angles are correctly shown. Rhumb lines appear as straight lines, the directions of which can be measured directly on the chart. Distances can also be measured directly if the spread of latitude is small. Great Circles, except Meridians and the Equator, appear as curved lines concaved to the Equator. Small areas appear in their correct shape with increased size unless they are near to the Equator.

除了墨卡托投影,还有许多其他类型的投影用于航海上。例如,采用高斯投影、平面投影和日晷投影等,用于制作大比例尺图如港泊图。日晷投影的意义是:在该种投影的海图上,任何一个大圆都呈现为直线,因此采用这种方法制作的海图称为大圆海图。大圆海图最常用于规划两点之间的大圆弧航线。

Besides Mercator projection, many other types of projections are used in navigation. For example, Gauss projection, planimetric chart, and gnomonic projection are adopted to make a large-scale chart such as harbour charts. The usefulness of gnomonic projection rests upon the fact that any Great Circle appears on the map as a straight line, giving charts made on this projection the common name gnomonic charts. Gnomonic charts are most often used for planning the Great-Circle track between points.

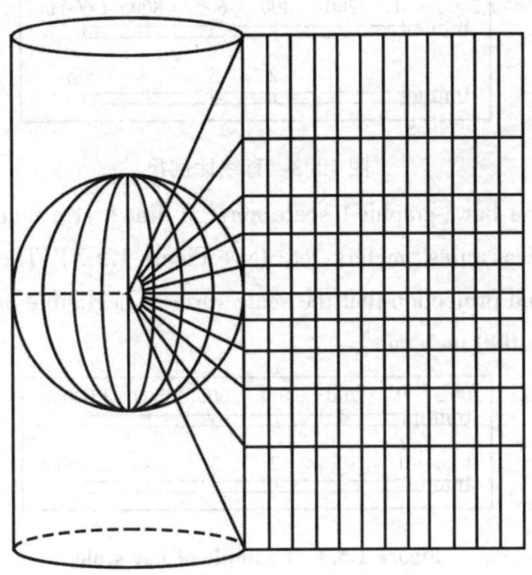

图 1.5.2　圆柱投影

Figure 1.5.2　Cylindrical projection

1.5.2　海图比例尺

1.5.2　Chart Scales

1.5.2.1　比例尺类型

1.5.2.1　Types of Scales

比例尺是图上任意线段长度和地面上相应的实际长度的比值。其表现形式多种多样。最常见的有：

The scale of a chart is the ratio of a given distance on the chart to the actual distance which it represents on the earth. It may be expressed in various ways. The most common ones are:

数字比例尺用分数或比例式表示。例如 1∶80 000 或 1/80 000，它表示在图上基准点处，一个单位长度等于地面上 8 万个相同单位的长度。这种比例尺有时称为基准比例尺或分数比例尺。

The representative fraction is expressed as a simple ration or fraction. For example, 1∶80,000 or 1/80,000 means that one unit (such as a meter) on the chart represents 80,000 of the same unit on the surface of the earth. This scale is sometimes called the natural or fractional scale.

一条线段或棒状的比例尺称为直线比例尺，其一般用比例图尺绘画在图上适当的地方，分成海里(链)、米等，如图 1.5.3 所示。直线比例尺只会出现在这种比例尺的海图上，即整张图的比例尺变化非常小，通常为 1∶75 000 或更大的比例尺。

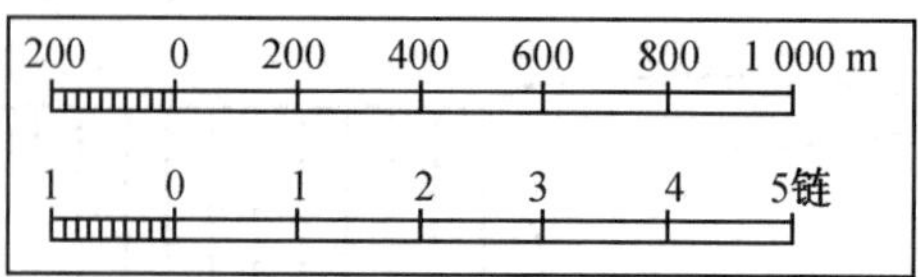

图 1.5.3 直线比例尺

A line or bar called a bar (graphic) scale may be drawn at a convenient place on the chart and subdivided into nautical miles, meters, etc.(see Figure 1.5.3). The bar scale will only appear on charts of such scale and projection that the scale varies a negligible amount over the whole chart (usually scales of 1 : 75,000 or larger).

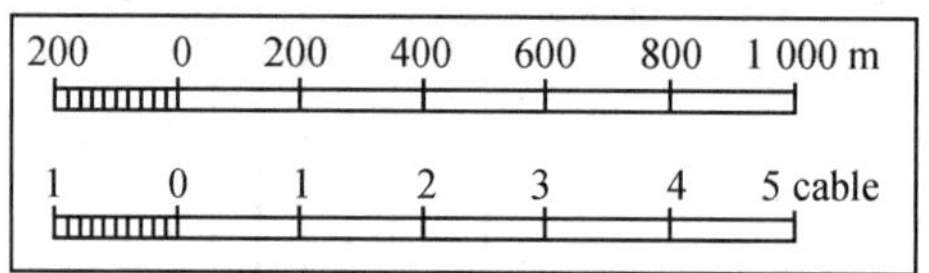

Figure 1.5.3 Example of bar scale

海图比例尺不仅决定着海图的精度,还决定着图上所绘制的资料的详细程度和海图作业的精度。比例尺越大,图上所绘制的资料就越详细、准确,海图的可靠性程度就越高,同时,作图误差小,海图作业的精度也越高。因此,船舶在航行时,应根据航区的特点,尽可能选择较大比例尺的海图,以便能够获得更详细的航海资料和提高海图作业的精度。

Chart scale not only determines the accuracy of chart, but also determines the detail of the data drawn on the chart and the accuracy of chart work. The larger the scale, the more detailed and accurate the data drawn on the chart, the higher the reliability of the chart, and the smaller the mapping error, the higher the accuracy of the chart operation. Therefore, when sailing, a large-scale chart should be selected as far as possible according to the characteristics of the navigation area, so that more detailed nautical data can be obtained and the accuracy of chart work can be improved.

1.5.2.2 基准比例尺和局部比例尺

1.5.2.2 Natural Scale and Local Scale

为了实现等角的特性,任何地方沿经线的比例尺都必须等于该处沿纬度的比例尺。现在,沿经线的比例尺不能统一,而必须根据沿纬度的比例尺进行调整。沿任意纬度的比例尺被定义为局部比例尺。

To achieve conformal properties, the scale along the Meridian at any place must be equal to the scale along the parallel at that place. The scale along the Meridian cannot now be uniform but must be adjusted to the scale along the parallels. The scale along any parallel is defined as local scale.

因此,一张海图在不同的纬度上有不同的局部比例尺,但在海图标题下只给出某一纬度上的一个比例尺。这个比例尺称为基准比例尺,该纬线所在的纬度称为基准纬度。也就是说,基准比例尺仅沿基准纬度正确。实际上,投影所覆盖的纬度是有限的,因此比例尺误差不会变得不可接受。

Therefore, one chart has different local scales at different parallels, but only one scale at certain latitude is given under the title of the chart. This scale is called the natural scale, and this latitude is called standard parallel. That is to say, the natural scale is correct only along the standard parallels. In practice, the latitude covered by the projection is limited so that the scale error does not become unacceptable.

在墨卡托图上,比例尺也随纬度而变化。这在一张覆盖南北方向相对较大距离的海图上是非常明显的。因此,在这样的海图上,应使用所求纬度附近的边界刻度来测量距离。

On a Mercator chart, the scale also varies with the latitude. This is noticeable on a chart covering a relatively large distance in a north-south direction. On such a chart the border scale near the latitude in question should be used for measuring distances.

1.5.3 海图识读
1.5.3 Chart Interpretation

海图为航海者提供了大量信息,包括:水深以及水下和水面的物标;陆地特征,主要是那些在水面航行的人特别感兴趣的特征;人造特征和海岸设施,重点还有那些有助于导航的设施;潮汐和海流信息;法律法规等。所有这些都通过使用符号、颜色、缩写和文字说明来表达。英国海道测量局(UKHO)出版的《5011 号海图》中包含了现行英版海图上用于显示数据的海图符号和缩写。中国人民解放军海军参谋部也根据 GB 12319—2022(海图国家标准)为中国海图用户出版了类似的航海出版物《中国海图图式》。航海者拿到海图后,应仔细查看。应阅读并理解海图上的所有解释性和警示性说明。

Nautical charts provide navigators with vast amounts of information including the depth of the water and objects under and on the surface; features of the land, primarily those of specific interest to those traveling the waters; man-made features and shore facilities, again with emphasis on those that assist in navigation; information on tides and currents; laws and regulations; and more. All this is conveyed through the use of symbols, colours, abbreviations, and written statements. Chart symbols and abbreviations employed to present data on modern admiralty charts are contained in a publication entitled Chart 5011 published by United Kingdom Hydrographic Office (UKHO). The People's Liberation Army Navy Staff also provides the similar nautical publication "Symbols, Abbreviations and Terms Used on Chinese Charts" for the users of Chinese charts based on GB 12319—2022 (a national standard for charting). When a navigator gets a nautical chart, it should be examined in detail. All explanatory and cautionary notes appearing on the chart should be read and understood.

1.5.3.1 海图标题栏和图廓注记

1.5.3.1 Chart Legend and Marginal Notes

阅读一张海图首先看的应该是海图标题栏。它是该图的说明栏,一般制图和用图的重要说明均印在此栏内,如图 1.5.4 所示。标题本身说明了海图覆盖的区域。其内容一般包括出版机关的徽志。海图的比例尺和投影方式显示在标题下方。海图将提供高程和深度基准,必要时还会提供基准转换说明。资料来源说明或图表将列出与测量日期配合使用的其他海图。

The chart legend (or title block) should be the first thing a navigator looks at when receiving a new edition chart. The chart legend is the description of the chart, and the important instructions for making and using the chart are printed in this block refer to Figure 1.5.4. The title itself tells what area the chart covers. Its contents include the logo of the publishing organization, the scale and projection appear below the title. The chart will give both height and depth datums and, if necessary, a datum conversion note. Source notes or diagrams will list the date of surveys and other charts used in compilation.

图 1.5.4 海图标题栏

Figure 1.5.4 Title block

海图图廓四周注记有许多与出版和使用海图有关的资料,称为图廓注记,包括:海图图号、发行和出版情况、小改正、图幅、邻接海图、对数图尺等内容。

Additional information on the charts appears between the neat line and the outer edge of a chart in the form of marginal notes. It includes the information about chart number, publication date and note, small correction, chart dimension, adjoining chart, logarithmic scale, etc.

1.5.3.2 高程和深度基准面

1.5.3.2 Height and Sounding Datum

海图上所标的山头、岛屿和明礁等高程的起算面称为高程基准面。除特殊情况外,我国沿海的海图高程基准面一般采用“1985 国家高程基准面”。英版海图采用平均大潮高潮面(以半日潮为主的海区)、平均高高潮面(以日潮为主的海区)或当地平均海面(在无潮海区)为高程基准面。

The datum for measuring the height of charted mountains, islands, and uncovered rocksare called height datum. Generally, “National 1985 height criterion” is taken as the height datum for measuring the charted height on Chinese charts, unless in special circumstances. For admiralty charts, the mean high water spring (for semi-diurnal tide area), mean higher high water (for diurnal tide area) or mean sea level (for non-tidal area) are normally taken as the height datum.

海图上标注的水深的起算面称为海图深度基准面,也是干出高度的起算面。海图基准面是某一潮汐状态下的计算高度或平均高度,而实际水深在任何物定时刻可能小于海图水深,对航海安全十分不利。海图基准面定得过低,自然可提高航海安全性,但也会给人以水深过浅的印象。其他国家出版的海图的测深基准面差别很大,但通常低于平均低水位。我国沿海系统测量区域采用理论最低潮面(旧称理论深度基准面)作为起算面,以原始数据作为远洋和国外航区的海图基准面。英版海图水深通常采用天文最低低潮面作为海图深度起算面。

All depths indicated on charts are reckoned from a selected level of the water, called the-sounding datum or chart datum; it is also the datum for measuring drying height on the chart. If the chart datum is a computed high or average height at some state of the tide, the depth of water at any particular moment may be less than shown on the chart, it will endanger the navigation nearby. A low chart datum will naturally improve navigational safety, but it will also give the impression that the water depth is too shallow. The sounding datum for charts published by other countries varies greatly, but is usually lower than mean low water. For Chinese charts, the theoretical lowest sea level is taken as the chart datum for the coastal area, and the original data is taken as the chart datum for the ocean and foreign sailing area. For admiralty charts, the level of lowest astronomical tide is taken as the chart datum.

1.5.3.3 颜色、符号和缩写

1.5.3.3 Colours, Symbols and Abbreviations

几乎所有的海图都使用颜色来区分不同类别的信息,如深水、浅水和陆地区域。深水区通常为白色(未着色),浅水区为蓝色,可能有两种颜色。白色和蓝色之间的浅水区深度将随海图的比例尺和使用而不同。潮间带区域是绿色的。大片陆地区域显示为黄色。深洋红色用于印刷的信息、罗经花和一些助航标志的符号。

Nearly all charts employ colour to distinguish various categories of information such as deep water, shoal water, and land areas. Deep-water areas usually are white (uncoloured), shoal areas are coloured blue; there may be two shades, and the shallow-water depth between white and blue will vary with the scale and use of the chart. Areas that cover and uncover with tidal changes are coloured green. Land areas are shown in a screened gold tint that appears as yellow. Dark magenta is used for printed information, compass roses, and some symbols for aids to navigation.

在海中航行,水深是航海者最关心的问题。这些在海图上都表示为小的罗马数字。大多数海图都有等深点的连线,称为等深线。其中之一将作为深水区(白色)和浅水区(蓝色)的边界。

In water areas, sounding (depth) is the item of greatest concern to navigators. These are shown as many small numbers in roman type. Most charts will have lines connecting points of equal depth called depth contours. One of them will serve as the boundary between deeper areas in white and shallower water tinted blue.

关于海底底质构成,如泥、沙子、贝壳、岩石、珊瑚等底泥组成的信息是海员锚泊时主要关注的内容。

Information on the composition of the bottom — mud, sand, shell, rock, coral, and so on — is of interest to mariners primarily when anchoring.

许多类型的符号被用来显示航行危险的位置(如沉船),可表明特定的危险是否任何时候都在水面之上,或淹没在水中(其上有净空高度),以及因潮汐变化覆盖和暴露的地带。

Many types of symbols are used to show the location of dangers to navigation (such as wrecks). These can indicate whether the particular hazard is above water at all times, submerged at all times (with the clearance over it), or covers and uncovers with tidal changes.

陆地的一般形状可以用等高线来表示,即连接相同的高程点的连线。

The general form of the land may be shown by the use of height contours, lines connecting points of equal elevation.

海上灯标主要以标身形状、颜色、光的节奏、名称和编号等进行区别。对于浮标,在其符号的位置圆(或点)上印上一个小的洋红色圆圈及灯焰,其标身形状、顶部标记、名称和编号都是明显可见的。对灯塔而言,其他的细节可以用“灯标注记”来表示,一般由书写在符号附近的容易理解的缩写来标识,比如★闪(3)20s125m18M代表的意思是:每 20 s 闪光 3 次,灯标高程 125 m,射程 18 n mile。为了便于识别灯的颜色,符号附近还印有字母缩写绿(G)、红(R)、黄(Y) 等(注意白光不使用字母缩写)。

Lights at sea are mainly distinguished by their shape of body, colour, rhythm of light, names and numbers, etc. For a light buoy symbol on a chart, a small magenta disc or flare is printed over the position circle (or dot) of the symbol, and its body shape, top-mark, name and number are obvious. But for a lighthouse, other details may be indicated by "light description", which is identified by readily understood abbreviations placed close to the symbol, such as ★闪(3)20s125m18M, it means: 3 flashes every 20 seconds, 125 meters above Mean High Water Spring (MHWS), visible for 18 nautical miles. To facilitate light colour identification, also a letter abbreviation — G, R, Y — is printed near the symbol (no letter abbreviation is used for a white light).

1.5.4 海图分类
1.5.4 Chart Cartography

按绘制图网的方法,即按地图投影方法的不同,海图又可分为墨卡托海图、高斯投影海图、大圆海图和平面图等。

According to the method of drawing the chart network, i.e. the difference in map projection methods, nautical charts can be further divided into Mercator charts, Gaussian projection charts, gnomonic charts and planimetric charts.

根据作用不同,海图可以分为航用海图和参考图两大类。

Charts are normally divided into two categories (nautical charts and thematic charts) as per different purposes for use.

参考图包括并不限于航路设计图、大圆海图、气候图、空白定位图等。

Thematic charts include but not limited to routing charts, gnomonic charts, meteorological charts, plotting diagram and sheets, etc.

航用海图用于拟定航线、进行航迹推算和定位等海图作业。航用海图按比例尺的大小,一般又可以分为:

Nautical charts are used for charting operations such as plotting courses, making track projections and positioning. According to the size of the scale, the charts can be divided into:

(1)总图
(1) General charts

其比例尺一般小于1∶3 000 000,包括世界大洋图和总图。由于比例尺较小,其信息量很少,除非是非常重要的地标或灯塔才印制在海图上。

The chart scale is less than 1∶3,000,000, consisting of world ocean charts and general charts. They are scarce in information due to its small scale, unless they are charted for very important landmarks or light houses.

(2)远洋航行图
(2) Ocean sailing charts

其比例尺一般在1∶1 000 000~1∶2 900 000。图上详细标有海上平台、显著地标的高程、雷达信标和重要的灯塔、灯船及浮标等。该图一般可用于远洋航行或作为航行参考图用。

The scale is between 1∶1,000,000 to 1∶2,900,000. More information related to offshore platforms, major heights of conspicuous landmarks, radar beacons, and important lighthouses or light vessels, buoys, etc, will be displayed for ocean sailing, and mainly regarded as reference chart.

(3) 近海航行图

(3) Offshore sailing charts

其比例尺一般在 1 : 200 000~1 : 990 000。除上述信息外,还将显示更多详细信息,如主要交通线、防波堤、码头、航道或锚地。

The scale is between 1 : 200,000 to 1 : 990,000. More detailed information will be displayed other than the above mentioned, such as major traffic lanes, breakwaters, piers, fairways, or anchorages.

(4) 沿岸航行图

(4) Coastal sailing charts

其比例尺一般在 1 : 100 000~1 : 190 000。周围区域的信息被详尽地显示出来,包括高密度的测深点和更相关的岸上物标。

The scale is between 1 : 100,000 to 1 : 190,000. The information in the surrounding area is thoughtfully displayed, including high density of sounding points and more relevant of ashore objects.

(5) 港湾图

(5) Harbour charts

其比例尺一般大于 1 : 100 000,包括港口、海港、码头、狭窄航道和航道等海图。随着比例尺的增加,将显示更准确的海图信息。

Generally, the scale of the harbour chart is larger than 1 : 100,000, including charts of port, harbour, pier, narrow channel and fairway, etc. More accurate charted information will be displayed as per the scale increasing.

1.5.5 电子海图及显示系统

1.5.5 Electronic Chart and Display System

1.5.5.1 电子海图

1.5.5.1 Electronic Chart

目前,有两种常用的电子海图数据:电子航海图(ENCs)和光栅海图(RNCs)。它们基于不同的计算机制图方式。

At present, there are two types of electronic charts available for commercial use. These are Electronic Navigational Charts (ENCs) and Raster Navigational Charts (RNCs). They are based on two different methods of creating computer graphics.

光栅海图是图像海图,基于像素(电脑和电视屏幕上的非常小的点)。光栅海图的显示不能按需显示，尽管其他信息可能会被覆盖。海图的物标特征不能被查询或探测报警。海图边界是可见的，当缩放或被其他信息覆盖时，海图显示信息可能变得杂乱无章。

RNCs are raster images, which are based on a grid of individual pixels (a pixel is a tiny dot on a computer or TV screen) that are generated on the computer screen to produce an image. Chart displays CANNOT be customised, although other information may be overlaid. Chart features CANNOT be interrogated or alarmed. Chart boundaries are visible and chart information may become cluttered when zoomed or overlaid with other information.

ENC实际上是官方电子海图矢量数据库，它根据存储在数据库中的信息使用数学算法来定义各种形状，如直线、曲线、矩形和其他符号。与RNC不同，ENC物标特征可以被查询，一些特征（如危险物和不安全水域）可以被警告。海图边界是无缝的，且具有缩放比例尺自动显示功能，避免显示信息的杂乱。

ENCs are "vector images" actually official databases, which use mathematical algorithms to define shapes such as lines, curves, rectangles and other symbols, based on the information stored in the database. Unlike RNC, ENC features CAN be interrogated and some features (dangers and unsafe waters) CAN be alarmed. Chart boundaries are seamless and zooming automatically features are shown to avoid confusion on display.

每个国家的海道测量机构负责为其管辖范围内的区域制作电子海图。为了消除格式上的差异，国际上有专门的ENC数据协调中心，以使海图制作标准化并协调一致，并符合国际海道测量组织（IHO）的原则。国际海道测量组织（IHO）特别出版物S-63由国际海道测量组织（IHO）数据保护安全工作组开发，用于对ENC数据进行商业加密和数字签名。海图数据是根据国际海道测量组织（IHO）专门出版物S-57中规定的标准组织的，并按照国际海道测量组织（IHO）专门出版物S-52中规定的显示格式显示，以确保不同系统之间数据呈现的一致性。未来关于ENC的标准定义在国际海道测量组织（IHO）出版物S-100中。

The Hydrographic Office in each country is responsible for the production of electronic charts for the area under their jurisdiction. To remove any differences in format, an organisation called IC-ENC (International Center for Electronic Navigational Charts) was setup to standardise and harmonise chart production to the principles of the IHO (International Hydrographic Organisation). IHO Special Publication S-63 developed by the IHO Data Protection Security Working Group is used to commercially encrypt and digitally sign ENC data. Chart data is captured based on standards stated in IHO Special Publication S-57, and is displayed according to a display format stated in IHO Special Publication S-52 to ensure consistency of data rendering between different systems. The future standard for ENCs will be defined in IHO Publication S-100.

1.5.5.2 显示系统

1.5.5.2 Display Systems

电子海图（ENCs和RNCs）有三种类型的显示系统。

Three types of display systems are available for use with electronic charts (both ENCs and

RNCs).

电子海图显示与信息系统(ECDIS)能够将ENC数据和来自船舶定位系统的数据以及来自其他设备的传感器数据,集成到一台计算机中的船载电子导航系统。ECDIS由计算机硬件、电子海图数据和软件组成。计算机硬件是一台能够与其他设备/仪器联网的PC机,可连接驾驶台和其他区域的设备或传感器,如罗经、GPS、雷达、回声测深仪、计程仪、AIS和自动操舵仪、电子海图等,如图1.5.5所示。ECDIS应符合国际海事组织(IMO)的性能标准,并有符合条件的备用配置,才可被认为符合2002年国际海事组织(IMO)《SOLAS公约》第V章第19条的关于设备配备的要求。ECDIS还应符合国际电工委员会(IEC)制定的ECDIS测试标准IEC 61174。

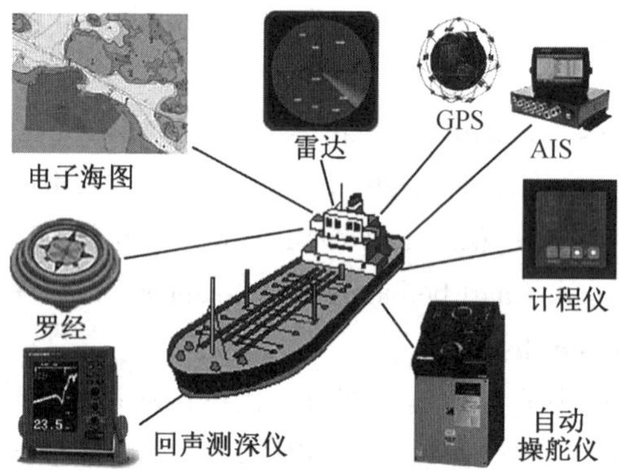

图1.5.5 ECDIS部件

Electronic Chart Display and Information System (ECDIS) is a shipboard electronic navigation system that is capable of combining data from shipboard positioning systems, sensors from other equipment and ENCs into one computer. ECDIS consists of computer hardware, electronic chart data and software. The computer hardware is a PC networked to other equipment/instrument on the bridge and divices or sensors in other areas of the ship such as the ship's compass, GPS, radar, echo sounder, speed log, AIS and autopilot, in addition to the electronic chart, see Figure 1.5.5. ECDIS complies with the IMO performance standards and which, with adequate back-up arrangements, can be accepted as complying with carriage requirements of Chapter V Regulation 19 of the 2002 IMO SOLAS Convention. And the consequent test standards for ECDIS have been developed by the International Electrotechnical Commission (IEC) in International Standard IEC 61174.

光栅海图显示系统(RCD)是通过使用RNC来显示航线规划和监控信息的导航信息系统。该系统不能提供ECDIS的全部功能,只能与适当的最新纸质海图一起结合使用。

Raster Chart Display Systems (RCD) is a navigation information system that displays route planning and monitoring information by using RNCs. This system does not provide full use of ECDIS, and can only be used with appropriate up-to-date paper charts.

电子海图系统(ECS)是一种通用术语,适用于以电子格式显示海图的设备,其不满足《SOLAS公约》的要求,不得用作最新正式海图的替代品。然而,ECS可以合法地与纸质海图一起使用,并且使用过程中加以训练可以促进航行安全,提高对周围环境的情景感知。

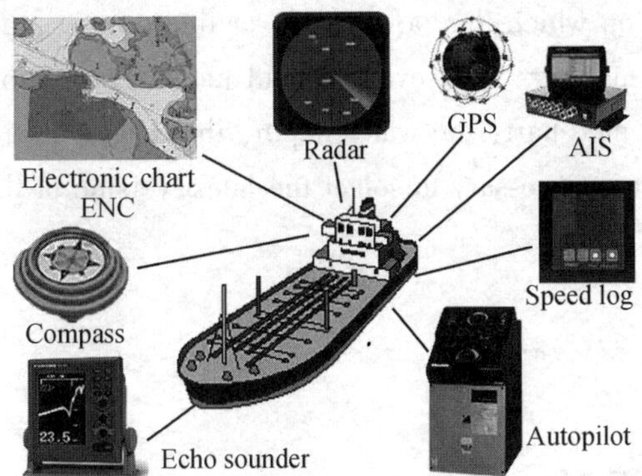

Figure 1.5.5　ECDIS components

Electronic Chart System (ECS) is a generic term for equipment that displays charts in electronic format, which do NOT satisfy IMO SOLAS requirements, and may NOT be used as a substitute for up-to-date official charts. However, an ECS may legally be used alongside paper charts and can improve navigational safety and situational awareness provided care is exercised in its use.

1.5.6　海图作业及其注意事项
1.5.6　Chart Works and Precautions

不论是纸质航海图,还是电子航海图,都是为了记录船舶的位置,确保船舶在海图上划定的计划航线上安全航行。作为海员,应及时通过航迹推算、陆标定位、天文定位、卫星定位等方法定出船位,在纸质航海图上借助分规、三角板以及平行尺等进行相应的标绘,也即要进行海图作业。通过海图作业,绘制航线、确定船位,用以判断船舶的航迹和计划航线的相对位置关系,从而为船舶安全航行提供参考。

Both paper and electronic navigation charts are used to determine the position of the ship and ensure the safe navigation of the ship on the planned route delineated on the chart. As a mariner, the ship position should be determined by dead reckoning, landmark positioning, astronomical positioning, satellite positioning and other methods in time, and the corresponding plotting should be carried out on the paper navigation chart with the help of the marine divider, triangular plates and parallel rulers, that is, chart works should be carried out. Through the chart works, the planning path is drawn and the position of the ship is determined to judge the relative position relationship between the ship's track and the planned path, so as to provide reference for the safe navigation of the ship.

另外注意海图都有可能是不完整的、存在误差的,要么是由于其所依据的海洋实测不完善,要么是由于随后地形或海底的变迁。因此,海员必须根据海图的比例尺、水深、测量日期和出版日期等因素来评估和判断海图的可信度。在使用时,需选择最新版大比例尺的海图进行定位导航。

Note also that charts are likely to be incomplete and inaccurate, either due to incomplete

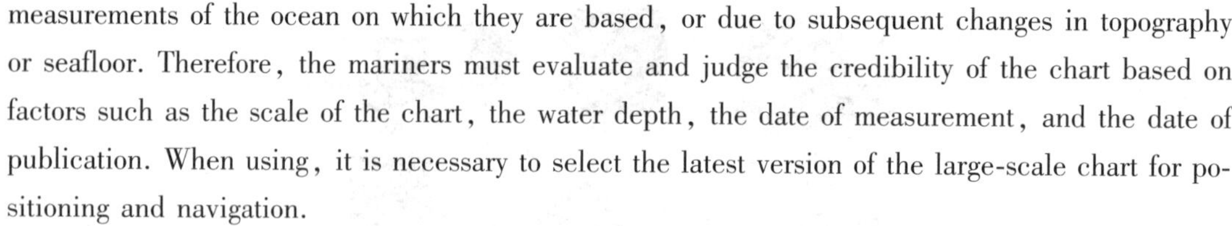

measurements of the ocean on which they are based, or due to subsequent changes in topography or seafloor. Therefore, the mariners must evaluate and judge the credibility of the chart based on factors such as the scale of the chart, the water depth, the date of measurement, and the date of publication. When using, it is necessary to select the latest version of the large-scale chart for positioning and navigation.

1.6 航海出版物

1.6 Nautical Publications

安全航行是船舶驾驶员的首要任务。从所有相关航海出版物中获取信息是安全航行的基础,因为从中可了解到与船舶航行有关的危险物、设施、注意事项和方法。可以从以下两个方面考虑:

Safe navigation is the prime task for a ship's deck officer. It is important to be aware of the hazards, facilities, precautions and methods used for a ship's navigation by obtaining information from all relevant publications. This can be achieved by covering the following two subject areas:

(1)首要考虑的是出发港到目的地之间的航线。船舶要选择最佳路线,并在之上绘制航线,了解航线附近危险,并监控整个沿航线航行的过程。因此,每艘船舶都需要配备一整套海图,涵盖从泊位到泊位的整个航线。此外,还需要航海出版物提供更详细的资料,说明航线的优劣,以及进入其他国家港口所需的程序。

(1) The primary consideration is the route a vessel must take between the departure and destination. To choose the best route requires the charts on which to lay the track and monitor progress and provide information concerning hazards. Therefore, each ship requires a set of nautical charts which cover the entire route from berth to berth. In addition, publications are needed to provide detailed information on the pros and cons of each route and the procedures required to enter a country's harbors.

(2)其次考虑的是海上水文气象条件,以及对恶劣情况的充分警告。

(2) A vessel needs information on sea and weather conditions and sufficient warning of adverse conditions.

不同的船舶对航海出版物的配备要求不同,并且要求每艘船舶必须配备覆盖其航线的改正到最新的航海出版物。下面列举一些满足《SOLAS 公约》第Ⅴ章要求常见的航海出版物。

Different ships have different requirements for the carriage of publications, and every vessel must have up-to-date publications which cover the intended passage. The following nautical publications satisfy the requirements of SOLAS Chapter Ⅴ.

1.6.1 航海天文历
1.6.1 Nautical Almanac

天文历是书或表格,包含了一个日历年的太阳和月亮的升起和落下时间、月亮的相位、恒星和行星的位置等信息。《航海天文历》载有用于获取船只位置和计算日出和日落时间等的天文数据。

An almanac is a book or table containing a calendar year, data on the rising and setting times of the sun and moon, the phases of the moon, the positions of the planets and stars. Nautical Almanac contains astronomical data used to obtain the positions of ships and calculate times of sunrise and sunset, etc.

1.6.2 世界大洋航路(NP136)
1.6.2 Ocean Passages for the World（NP136）

《世界大洋航路》由英国海道测量局出版,是介绍世界主要大洋航线的书籍,可供机动船和帆船拟定大洋航线时参考。书中介绍了气象和其他影响航线拟定的因素和经常被选用的大量航线的航行要点及这些航线的航程。

Published by the UKHO, Ocean Passage for the World is for planning worldwide passages for power-driven and sailing vessels. The book describes the meteorological and other factors influencing the routes, the main notes of the route and the distance of the routes that are often used.

1.6.3 航路指南
1.6.3 Admiralty Sailing Directions（Pilot Books）

英版《航路指南》共计 70 多卷,补充了航用海图上的信息。它们涵盖了全球沿海地区,为航海者拟定航线和海区航行提供指导。另外,该套书还提供关于各国港口和港口设施、要求和限制的补充资料。《航路指南》的新版本定期出版。其间,重要更新信息通过《航海通告》周版第Ⅳ部分发布以用于改正。

The Admiralty Sailing Directions, also known as pilot books, are published in more than 70 volumes that supplement the information given on navigational charts. They cover coastal areas of the entire globe and provide guidance to navigators on planning and conducting coastal passages, with additional information on the facilities, requirements and restrictions in the ports and harbours of various countries. New Editions of Admiralty Sailing Directions are published on a regular basis. Navigationally significant information for these publications is issued via the Admiralty Notices to

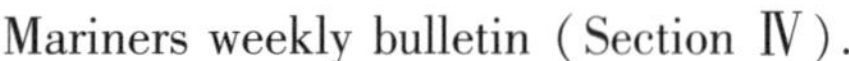

Mariners weekly bulletin (Section Ⅳ).

1.6.4 进港指南
1.6.4 Guide to Port Entry

《进港指南》每两年出版一次,由英国航运指南公司出版,提供全面的港口信息、计划和泊位图。

Guide to Port Entry is published every two years by the Shipping Guides LTD. of United Kingdom, with comprehensive port information, plans and mooring diagrams.

该书包括四册,两册为正文港口资料说明(TEXT),两册为港口及泊位平面图(PLAN)。每一册 TEXT 搭配 PLAN 组成一套,按照国家名称首字母 A~K 为一套,L~Y 为另一套。该书覆盖了世界上众多的港口地图平面图、码头泊位示意图,用来介绍港口各种设施情况和要求,如进港航道情况、锚地、泊位分布、引航制度、通信和信号要求、进港手续、装卸设备、工班、物资供应以及代理业务等。

This book consists of four hardback volumes—two of port data text, two of port plans. According to the first letters of the names of nations, they are divided into two sets of A to K (text+plans) and L to Y (text+plans). The book covers the plans of many ports and the diagrams of terminals and berthing in the world, which is used to introduce the various facilities and requirements of ports, such as the conditions of channels, anchorage, berth distribution, pilot, communication and signaling requirements, port entry procedures, loading and unloading equipment, working classes, material supply and agency business, etc.

1.6.5 灯标表
1.6.5 Admiralty List of Lights and Fog Signals (ALL)

英版《灯标雾号表》(ALL)一般称为《灯标表》,由英国海道测量局(UKHO)出版,共计十几卷覆盖全球。《灯标表》包括所有灯标、助航标志、带灯的构筑物、灯船、雷康、灯浮标、其他浮动航标(高度超过 8 m)和雾号的详细信息。该书每年出版一次,并通过周版的《航海通告》(第Ⅴ部分)更新。

The Admiralty List of Lights and Fog Signals (ALL) is commonly known as the List of Lights and consists of a dozen volumes covering the entire globe. The British Admiralty (UKHO) produces List of Lights with details of all known lights, navigational marks, light-structures, light vessels, RACONS, light buoys, floating navigation marks (exhibiting light at heights exceeding 8 m) and fog signals. They are published annually and kept up-to-date by weekly editions of the Admiralty Notices to Mariners (Section Ⅴ).

1.6.6　无线电信号表(NP281~286)
1.6.6　Admiralty List of Radio Signals（ALRS, NP281 to 286）

英版《无线电信号表》(ALRS)介绍了海岸无线电台(国际通信),无线电助航标志、卫星导航系统、标准时、法定时、无线电时号和电子定位系统,无线电天气服务、海上安全信息(MSI)播发、全球范围的航海电传(NAVTEX)和安全网(SafetyNET)信息,气象观测站一览表,全球海上遇险与安全系统(GMDSS),引航服务、船舶交通管理(VTS)和港口业务等资料。该书每年出版一次,并通过周版的《航海通告》(第Ⅵ部分)更新。新刊物每年出版一次,其中包含该资料信息的所有更改。

The Admiralty List of Radio Signals (ALRS) presents information on coastal radio stations (international communications), radio aids to navigation, satellite navigation systems, standard time, legal time, radio time signals and electronic positioning systems, radio weather services, Maritime Safety Information (MSI) broadcasts, worldwide nautical teletype (NAVTEX) and SafetyNET information, a list of meteorological observation stations, global maritime distress and safety systems (GMDSS), pilotage services, vessel traffic services (VTS) and port operations information. This is published on a yearly basis and kept up-to-date by the weekly editions of Admiralty Notices to Mariners (Section Ⅵ). New Editions are published annually containing all changes to information held.

1.6.7　海员手册(NP100)
1.6.7　Mariner's Handbook（NP100）

英版《海员手册》由英国海道测量局(UKHO)以纸质和电子形式出版,是海员的综合参考书。它包括但不限于下列资料:海图上的基本海事资料汇编;操作规程;潮汐、海流和海洋特性;基本气象;冰区航行、航行的危险和限制;以及国际航标协会(IALA)的浮标系统。

The Mariner's Handbook, published by UKHO in both paper and electronic format, is the comprehensive reference book for seafarers. It includes but not limited to the following information: a compendium of essential maritime information on charts; operations and regulations; tides, currents and characteristics of the sea; basic meteorology; navigation in ice, hazards and restrictions to navigation; and the IALA Buoyage system.

1.6.8 航海图书总目录(NP131)
1.6.8 Catalogue of Admiralty Charts and Publications (NP131)

该出版物通常被称为“海图总目录”,由英国海道测量局(UKHO)每年出版一次。其主要用于:

This publication is commonly known as the “chart catalogue” and is published by the British Admiralty (UKHO) on an annual basis. It's used to:

(1)抽选航用海图;

(1)Select navigational charts;

(2)抽选航海书表;

(2)Select nautical publications;

(3)查验船上所存海图和图书是否适用;

(3)Check the validity of navigational charts on board;

(4)获得海图授权代理商/分销商和航海通告(ANM)供应。

(4)Get the Admiralty Authorised Chart Agents/Distributors and ANM supplies.

1.6.9 潮汐表
1.6.9 Admiralty Tide Tables

英国海道测量局(UKHO)每年出版英版《潮汐表》(ATTs),基本涵盖了全球所有的可航行水域,以潮汐计算为目的。该书将世界港口分为两类:

The Admiralty Tide Tables (ATTs), published by the UKHO annually, provides coverage of all the navigable waters on earth. The world ports, for the purpose of tidal calculations, have been divided into two types:

(1)主港:直接给出高潮和低潮对应的时间和高度;

(1)Standard ports, for which times and heights of high and low water are given;

(2)附港:参照主港,根据提供的潮时和潮高差进行附港潮汐的推算。

(2)Secondary ports, for which time differences are given with reference to standard ports.

《潮汐表》含有当年 12 个月的数据(每年 1 月至 12 月)、230 多个主港和 6 000 多个附港的潮汐数据,并由每周出版的《航海通告》对其更新。

The ATTs contain data for 12 months (January to December for each year), for over 230 standard ports and over 6,000 secondary ports and are updated by the weekly editions of Admiralty Notices to Mariners.

1.6.10　航海通告
1.6.10　Admiralty Notices to Mariners（ANM）

英版《航海公告》(ANM)用于改正船上配有的由英国海道测量局(UKHO)出版的英版海图和出版物。一旦英国海道测量局(UKHO)得知海图和出版物中涉及的信息有变化,即会将这些变化通过编制航海通告的形式发送给相关单位。

Admiralty Notices to Manners are used to update the admiralty charts and publications carried onboard. As soon as the UKHO is notified of any changes or additions to the information included in the charts or publications, they distribute it to the seafaring community by issuing these notices.

通常,ANM每周出版一次,其中包含影响航行安全的重要信息的多个部分。重要事项包括设置和更换助航设备,发现和排除水中的危险和障碍,改变海底结构,对海港、航道和锚地的深度的改正,特殊海域的变化,各种界限和航行规则的改变,公布航海图和出版物的信息,航行警告和其他与航行有关的信息。其他的《航海通告》如《航海通告年度摘要》《航海通告累积表》等也应作为通告的补充资源。

Usually, ANMs are published weekly, which contain several sections for important information affecting navigational safety. The important matters include the establishment and changes of navigational aids, discovery and removal of dangers and obstructions in water, changes of submarine structures, corrections to depths in harbours, channels and anchorages, changes of special sea areas, changes in various limits and regulations of navigation, publishing information about nautical charts and publications, navigational warnings and other information related to navigation. Other kinds of ANMs such as Annual Summary of Admiralty Notices to Mariners, Cumulative List of Admiralty Notices to Mariners etc. also may be used onboard as the additional resources.

1.6.11　IMO船舶定线制
1.6.11　IMO’s Ship’s Routing

本出版物的主要目的是向负责设计、维护和管理定线制系统的组织和政府机构提供指导,而定线制系统主要为国际航行船舶所使用。

The primary purpose of this publication is to provide guidance to the organizations or government agencies responsible for the planning, maintenance and management of the routing systems used by international ships.

1.6.12 航路设计图
1.6.12 Routing Charts

航路设计图由英国海道测量局(UKHO)出版,覆盖世界海洋的13个海域。它们包括156张图表,因为每年每个月为每个海域提供一张图表。这些墨卡托投影图作为规划海洋航线的主要参考图,并与世界大洋航路(NP136)一起搭配使用。

Routing Charts are provided by UKHO for 13 sea areas covering the ocean of the world. They include 156 sheets of charts because one sheet is provided for each month of the year for each of the sea areas. These Mercator projection charts, as the main reference charts for the planning ocean routes, are used in conjunction with the Ocean Passage for the World (NP136).

1.6.13 电子图书资料
1.6.13 Electronic Publications

目前,航海图书资料已经出现了电子化的趋势,而且电子图书资料可以取代相应的纸质图书资料在船上按要求配备。例如常见的有电子《潮汐表》、电子《灯标表》、《无线电信号表》等,这些电子图书可以按照分区购买,查询和更新都非常方便,是航海图书未来发展的一个趋势。

Currently, nautical publications have appeared the trend of electronic, and electronic nautical publications can replace the corresponding paper publications on board, according to the requirement of the related standards. For example, Admiralty Toaltide tables, Admiralty Digital List of Lights, Admiralty Digital Radio Signals, etc., these electronic publications can be purchased according to the required areas, related query and update is very convenient, it will be a trend in the development of nautical publications.

1.7 潮汐与潮汐表
1.7 Tides and Tide Tables

潮汐即海面周期性的升降运动。其中,海面上升的过程称为涨潮,海面下降的过程称为落潮,海面升到最高,称为高潮;海面降到最低,称为低潮。船舶航行在海图水深和船舶吃水接近的水域时,及时得知潮汐资料对船舶安全航行非常重要。因此,在本部分中,我们将讨论潮汐的成因和求取潮高的方法。

Tide is the periodic vertical rise and fall of the level of the ocean, in which the process of rise is called rising tide or flood tide, of the fall called falling or ebb tide, the highest level reached is called high water or high tide yet the lowest level fallen to called low water or low tide. Knowing the height of tide at times is very important to vessels safety in areas where the charted depth is close to their draft. Thus, in this part we will discuss the causes of tides and the methods to find the height of tide.

1.7.1 潮汐相关术语
1.7.1 The Terms Regarding the Tides

潮汐的成因是天体的引潮力,主要是月亮和太阳。天体引潮力是地球和天体之间的引力以及惯性离心力的向量和。

The cause of tides is the tide-producing force of the heavenly bodies, mainly the moon and the sun. The tide-producing force is the combination of the gravitational and centrifugal forces between the earth and the heavenly bodies.

1.7.1.1 潮汐类型
1.7.1.1 The Types of Tide

潮汐根据性质可以分为四种类型:

Tides can be divided into four types according to their properties:

(1)正规半日潮:在一个太阴日内发生两次高潮和低潮。两次高潮和两次低潮的高度都相差不大,而涨落潮时也很接近。

(1) Normal semi-diurnal tide. In this type of tide, there are two high and two low waters each tidal day with relatively small inequality in the consecutive high and low water heights, and in the rising and falling times.

(2)正规日潮:在半个月中有连续7天以上是日潮,即在一个太阴日内只发生一次高潮和一次低潮,而在其余日子则为半日潮。

(2) Normal diurnal tide. In this type of tide, the diurnal tide that there are only a single high and a single low water each tidal day occurs continuously for more than 7 days each half month, and the semi-diurnal tide occurs in the other days.

(3)不正规半日潮混合潮:它基本上还具有正规半日潮的特性,但在一个太阴日内相邻的高潮或低潮的潮位相差很大,涨潮时和落潮时也不等。

(3) Abnormal semi-diurnal mixed tide. This type of tide is the same as the normal semi-diurnal tide in the numbers of the low and high waters but is characterized by a large inequality in the high-water heights, low-water heights, or in both, and in the rising and falling times.

(4)不正规日潮混合潮:在半个月中,日潮的天数不超过7天,其余天数为不正规半日潮。

(4) Abnormal diurnal mixed tide. In this type of tide, the diurnal tide occurs in less than 7 days each half month, the abnormal semi-diurnal tide occurs in the other days.

1.7.1.2 潮汐术语

1.7.1.2 Tide Terms

在前文中,我们已介绍了一些潮汐术语,为了预测潮汐,接下来再多介绍一些潮汐术语,如图 1.7.1 所示。

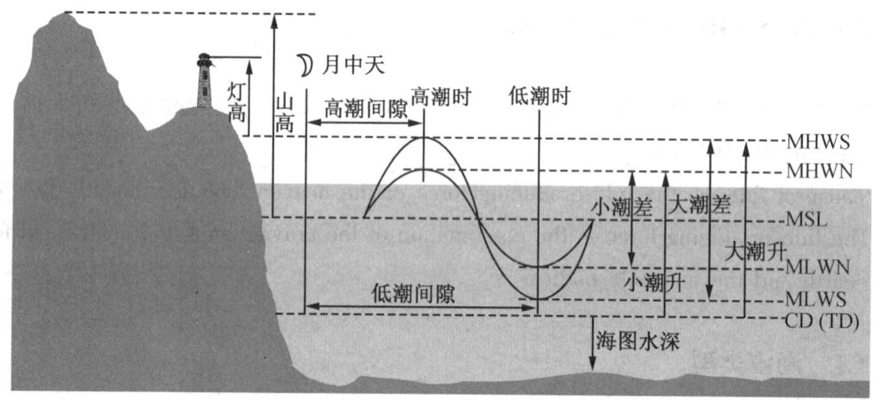

图 1.7.1 潮汐图解

In the previous text, we have introduced some of the tide terms, here in the following we will present some more as shown in Figure 1.7.1 for the sake of tide prediction.

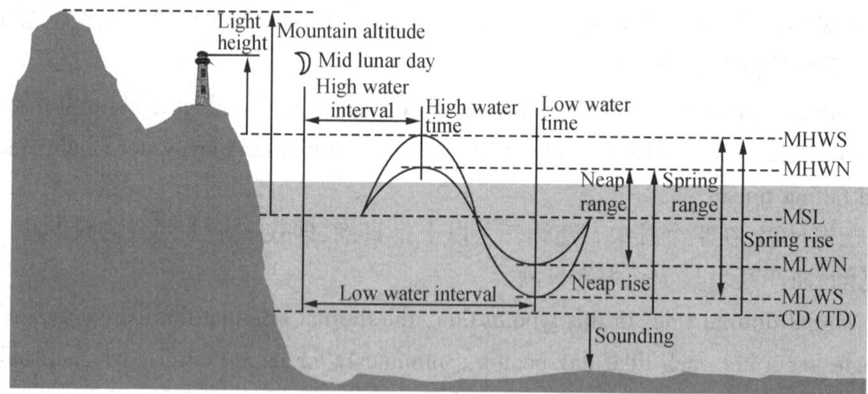

Figure 1.7.1 Tidal diagram

(1) 平均海面:根据长期潮汐观测记录算得的某一时期的海面平均高度。

(1) Mean sea level (MSL or M.L): the mean height of the water surface found from the long period observations.

(2) 海图基准面:计算海图深度的起算面。

(2) Chart datum (CD): a reference plane for charted soundings.

(3)潮高基准面:计算潮高的起算面,一般即为海图深度基准面。若一些海域两者不一致,则海员计算水深时应对这一差值进行相应的订正。

(3) Tidal datum (TD): a reference plane for measurement of tide height. It is generally the same as the chart datum. However, the chart datum is different from the tidal datum for some areas. Therefore, mariners must make corresponding correction to this difference when calculating the depth of water.

(4)涨潮时间:从低潮时到高潮时的时间间隔。

(4) Duration of rise: the interval from low water to high water.

(5)落潮时间:从高潮时到低潮时的时间间隔。

(5) Duration of fall: the interval from high water to low water.

(6)潮差:相邻高、低潮潮高之差。

(6) Tide range: the difference in the consecutive low and high water heights.

(7)大潮升:从潮高基准面到平均大潮高潮面的高度。

(7) Spring Rise (SR): the height measured from tidal datum to the plane of mean high water springs.

(8)小潮升:从潮高基准面到平均小潮高潮面的高度。

(8) Neap Rise (NR): the height measured from tidal datum to the plane of mean high water neap.

(9)高高潮:在一个太阴日中发生的两次高潮中潮高较高的高潮。

(9) Higher high water (HHW): the higher of two successive high waters in a tidal day where diurnal inequality is present.

(10)低高潮:在一个太阴日中发生的两次高潮中潮高较低的高潮。

(10) Lower high water (LHW): the lower of two successive low waters in a tidal day where diurnal inequality is present.

(11)高低潮:在一个太阴日中发生的两次低潮中潮高较高的低潮。

(11) Higher low water (HLW): the higher of two successive low waters in a tidal day where diurnal inequality is present.

(12)低低潮:在一个太阴日中发生的两次低潮中潮高较低的低潮。

(12) Lower low water (LLW): the lower of two successive low waters in a tidal day where diurnal inequality is present.

(13)回归潮:当月球赤纬最大时(此时月球在北回归线或南回归线附近)的潮汐称为回归潮。此时,日潮不等现象最显著。

(13) Tropic tide: the tide occurring when the moon is near the tropic of Cancer or Capricorn. Then tidal diurnal inequality is most conspicuous.

(14)分点潮:当月球赤纬最小时的潮汐称为分点潮。此时潮汐日潮不等现象最小。

(14) Equinoctial tide: the tide occurring when the moon is near the Celestial Equator. Then the tidal diurnal inequality is minimal.

(15)潮龄:由朔望至实际大潮发生的时间间隔称为潮龄。潮龄一般为1~3天。

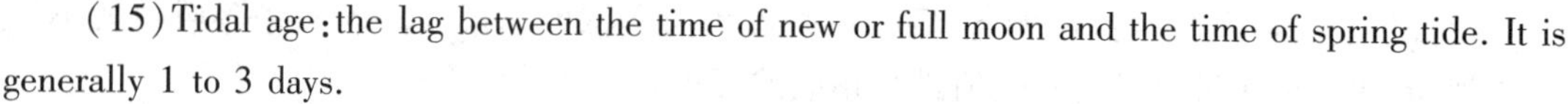

(15) Tidal age: the lag between the time of new or full moon and the time of spring tide. It is generally 1 to 3 days.

1.7.2 英版《潮汐表》与潮汐推算

1.7.2 Admiralty Tide Tables and Tide Prediction

英版《潮汐表》共有八卷,每年出版,书号为NP201~NP208,包括世界各主要港口的潮汐资料。

Admiralty Tide Tables (ATT) are published in eight volumes annually and assigned Admiralty publication numbers as NP201 to NP208 and include tidal information about the world's major ports.

(1)各卷主要内容

(1) The contents of the tables

英版《潮汐表》每卷分为三个主要部分:

Each volume of Admiralty tide tables is divided into three main parts:

第一部分为一些主港提供每日涨潮时间和涨潮高度的预报。

Part Ⅰ gives daily predictions of the times and heights of high and low water for a selection of standard ports.

第二部分包含用以预报附港潮汐的潮时差和潮高差,以便用这些资料求取更多附港的潮时和潮高。

Part Ⅱ contains the time and height differences which are to be applied to the standard port predictions, in order to derive predictions at a much larger number of secondary ports.

第三部分列出所有已知港口的调和常数数据,以便利用简化的调和常数法预报潮汐。

Part Ⅲ lists the principal harmonic constants for all those ports where they are known, intended for use with the Simplified Harmonic Method (SHM).

(2)潮汐推算

(2) Tide prediction

①主港高低潮的潮高和潮时

①Times and heights of high and low waters at standard ports

这些内容可从潮汐表第一部分表格直接查得。具体程序是首先利用主港索引查到所求港潮汐预报资料在表中的页数,然后翻到此页获取潮汐信息。需要注意的是,应确保表列区时与船时是一致的。

All these can be directly found in Part 1 of tables. The procedure to do so is first find on which pages the information for the port is listed from the Index to standard ports, then turn to these pages to get the information. Care should be taken to ensure that the time zone shown is the actual one in use on that date.

②附港高低潮的潮高和潮时

②Times and heights of high and low waters at secondary ports

计算公式

Formulae

附港高(低)潮时=主港高(低)潮时+高(低)潮时差 (1.7.1)

TH (TL) at secondary port=TH (TL) at standard port + TDH (TDL) (1.7.1)

附港潮高=主港潮高-主港平均海面季节改正+潮高差+附港平均海面季节改正 (1.7.2)

HH (HL) at secondary port=[HH (HL)-SC in MSL] at standard port+ HDH (HDL)+SC in MSL at secondary port (1.7.2)

其中,TH 和 TL 分别为高、低潮时,HH 和 HL 为高度,TDH 和 TDL 为时间差,HDH 和 HDL 为高、低潮时的高度差。

Here, TH and TL are the times of high and low waters respectively, HH and HL are the heights, TDH and TDL are the time differences and HDH and HDL are the height differences of high and low waters.

在计算时,首先在"地理索引"中查取附港的编号。根据编号,在第二部分"用以预报附港潮汐的潮时差和潮高差"表中查取该附港的主港、潮时差、潮高差,然后查取主港高低潮的潮时与潮高,再利用主附港的潮时差和超高差资料计算得到附港高低潮的潮时与潮高。计算应采用一定的格式,如英版《潮汐表》预测部分所采用的格式。

The procedure to find the times and heights of high and low waters is first to find the number of the secondary port from Geographical Index and obtain, based on the number, the time and height differences and the standard port of the secondary in Part Ⅱ of the table, then find the times and heights of high and low waters of the standard port and apply the two differences to the times and heights found here to obtain the times and heights of high and low waters at the secondary port. The calculations should be made in certain format, such as the one used in the section of prediction according to Admiralty Tide Tables.

1.7.3 电子潮汐表

1.7.3 Digital Tide Tables

(1) Admiralty TotalTide 程序

(1) Admiralty TotalTide Program

Admiralty TotalTide 是一个运行于计算机上的潮汐预测程序,可以在全球范围内快速、准确提供 7 000 多个港口的潮汐数据和 3 000 多个地方的潮流数据。它使用与英版《潮汐表》相同的预测算法和调和常数,并已设计为满足《SOLAS 公约》的相关要求。

The Admiralty TotalTide is a PC-based tidal prediction program providing fast, accurate tidal height and tidal stream predictions for over 7,000 ports and more than 3,000 tidal stream stations worldwide. It uses the same prediction algorithms and Harmonic Constants as the Admiralty Tide

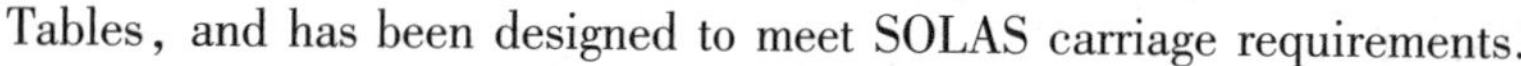

Tables, and has been designed to meet SOLAS carriage requirements.

该程序可以提供多个港口连续 7 天的潮汐和潮流预报。目前,TotalTide 可以与大多数电子海图显示与信息系统连接,显示潮汐和潮流信息。

Tidal heights for multiple ports may be calculated for up to 7 consecutive days. Presently, TotalTide can be interfaced to most ECDIS equipments for the display of tidal height and tidal streams.

(2) EasyTide 服务

(2) EasyTide Service

EasyTide 是一个基于网络的潮汐预报服务,专为满足休闲市场的需要而设计,提供全球 7 000 多个港口的潮汐数据以及许多其他有用的信息。海员可以通过登录网站 http://easytide.ukho.gov.uk 免费获得当天和未来 6 天的天气预报。Admiralty EasyTide 包括一个增强的选项,只需少量费用,就可以获取其他日期的潮汐预报,也可以获得其他信息,包括:月相、日出和日落时间、大潮和小潮数据以及全球范围服务。

EasyTide is a web-based tidal prediction service specifically designed to meet the need of the leisure market, which provides tidal data for over 7,000 ports worldwide together with a host of other useful information. Mariners can get free predictions for the current day and the next consecutive 6 days by logging in the website http://easytide.ukho.gov.uk. Admiralty EasyTide includes an enhanced option which, for a small fee, enables you to select the date of your prediction and obtain other useful information including: Lunar phases, Times of Sunrise and Sunset, Springs and Neaps data and Worldwide Coverage.

第 2 章 货物基础知识

Chapter 2 | Basic Knowledge of Cargoes

大多数船舶从事货物运输，以满足世界不同地区的生产和生活的需求。因此，航海主要以货物运输为目的。了解有关货物的知识是航海的必要技能。

Most ships are engaged in the transportation of cargoes to meet the requirement of production and living needs of different parts of the world. Therefore, the main purpose of navigation is for transporting cargoes. Knowing knowledge about goods is a necessary skill for navigation.

2.1 货物种类

2.1 Types of Cargoes

按照货物形态和装运方式，货物一般可分为以下几种：

According to the form of the cargoes and the mode of shipment, the cargoes can generally be divided into the following types:

2.1.1 杂货

2.1.1 General Cargo

杂货是指具有一定形式的包装货物、裸装货物、货物运输单元、同包装货物一起运输的散装货物及需专门运输的特殊货物，主要包括：

General cargoes are certain types of packaged cargoes, bared cargoes, cargo transport units, bulk cargoes transported together with packaged cargoes, and special cargoes that need to be trans-

ported exclusively. Mainly includes:

2.1.1.1 包装货物

2.1.1.1 Packaged Cargo

(1) 包装危险品

(1) Dangerous cargoes in package

危险货物是指可以危害人、其他生物、财产或环境的固体、液体或气体。它们通常受到化学规定的约束。危险货物通常具有放射、易燃、易爆、腐蚀、氧化、窒息等性质,也包括具有压缩气体和液体、热物质等物理条件的货物,还包括在特定环境中呈现出一定危险性的物质或化学品。

Dangerous goods are solids, liquids, or gases that can harm people, other living organisms, property, or the environment. They are often subject to chemical regulations. Dangerous goods include materials that are radioactive, flammable, explosive, corrosive, oxidizing, asphyxiating, also included are physical conditions such as compressed gases and liquids or hot materials, including all goods containing such materials or chemicals, or may have other characteristics that render them hazardous in specific circumstances.

根据危险货物存在的危害或最主要的危害,本规范适用的物质(包括混合物和溶液)和物品被划分为1~9个类别。

Substances (including mixtures and solutions) and articles subject to the provisions of this Code are assigned to one of the classes 1 to 9 according to the hazards or the most predominant of the hazards they present.

(2) 包装液体货

(2) Liquid cargo in package

包装液体货指非危险品的包装液体或半流质货,多以桶装形式运输,如桶装的酒类、动植物油、蜂蜜、肠衣、化工产品、酱菜等。该类货物的包装有大小铁桶、木桶、塑料桶、鼓形桶等。单件重量不一,在运输中会发生渗漏,若垛形系固不牢及堆垛不紧凑将会发生倒塌和移动。

Non-dangerous cargoes packaging liquid or semi-liquid goods, are mostly in barrel form, such as barrels of alcohol, animal and vegetable oil, honey, casings, chemical products, pickles and so on. The goods are packed in large and small iron drums, wooden barrels, plastic drums, drum-shaped barrels, etc. The weight of each piece varies, and leakage will occur during transportation. If the shape is not secure and the stacking is not compact, collapse and movement will occur.

(3) 气味货

(3) Smelling cargo

气味货指能散发某种异味的货物。气味货有的是货物自身具有强烈的气味,如烟叶、辣椒干、棕榈粉、樟脑、化妆品、香料等。有的是因含其他成分而有特殊异味,如各种皮类、丝绸等内含樟脑,以防虫害。

Smelling cargoes are the cargo that can emit a cartain smell. The smelling goods have the strong smell of the goods themselves, such as tobacco leaves, dried peppers, palm powder, camphor, cosmetics, spices, etc. Some have special odors due to other ingredients, such as various kinds of skin, silk which contains camphor to prevent pests.

(4) 易碎品

(4) Fragile cargo

易碎品指受挤压、撞击而易于破碎的货物,如玻璃及其制品、陶瓷制品、各种瓶装或罐装货物等,通常为箱装。

Fragile cargoes are easily crushed by crushing or impacting, such as glass and its products, ceramic products, various bottled or canned goods, etc., usually in cases.

本类货物主要是自身易于损坏,应选择合适的舱位,防止受到其他货物的挤压和碰撞。

This type of cargo is mainly susceptible to damage and should be selected to prevent it from being crushed and collided by other cargo.

(5) 食物食品

(5) Food cargo

食物食品指各种食品、谷物及饲料,如糖果、奶粉、花生、瓜子、茶叶、调味品、罐头、粮食、药品等。由于本类多为供人食用的食品及原料,因而无论是舱位的卫生条件还是与其他货物的相容关系都应予以充分考虑。

Food cargoes are various foods, grains and feeds, such as candy, milk powder, peanuts, sunflower seeds, tea, condiments, canned food, grain, medicines, etc. Since this category is mostly food and raw materials for human consumption, both the sanitary conditions of the cabin and the compatibility with other goods should be fully considered.

(6) 清洁货物

(6) Clean cargo

清洁货物指不允许混入杂质或被沾染的货物,如滑石粉、焦宝石、纸浆、镁砂、生丝等。本类货物一般对其他货物不会造成危害,但应防止被其他货物所沾染或掺混。

Clean cargoes are not allowed to be mixed with impurities or contaminated, such as talcum powder, coke gems, pulp, magnesia, raw silk, etc. This type of cargo generally does not pose a hazard to other goods, but should be prevented from being contaminated or blended by other goods.

(7) 贵重货物

(7) Valuable cargo

贵重货物指价格昂贵或具有特殊使用价值的货物,如精密仪器、高价商品、历史文物、展

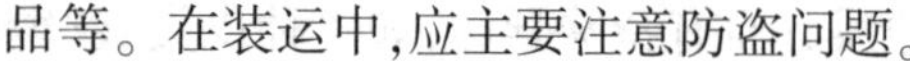

品等。在装运中,应主要注意防盗问题。

Valuable cargoes are expensive or have special use value, such as precision instruments, high-priced goods, historical relics, exhibits, etc. In the shipment, the main issue should be the anti-theft problem.

(8) 普通货物

(8) General cargo

普通货物是指件杂货中除上述货类以外的其他货物,它们在运输中通常无特殊要求。

In addition to the above-mentioned goods in the general cargoes, they usually have no special requirements in transportation.

2.1.1.2 裸装货物

2.1.1.2 Bared Cargo

(1) 木材类

(1) Timber cargo

木材类是指散装运输的原木、锯材(成材)及制材(木材制品)。原木是采伐后经修整的不同长度和直径的圆材;锯材是指将原木经过加工,锯成各种不同用途的板条、方木、圆木及其他形状的木料;制材则为经过加工而成为有特殊用途的木材,如胶合板、复合板、软木砖等。

Timber cargoes refer to logs, sawn timber (materials) and timber (wood products) shipped in bulk. Logs are rounds of different lengths and diameters that have been trimmed after harvesting; sawn timber refers to slats, squares, logs and other shapes of wood that have been processed and sawn into various uses; timber has become a special-purpose wood, such as plywood, composite panels, cork bricks, etc.

木材具有体积大,积载因数大,吸湿、可燃等特点,运输中应注意它们对船舶营运及安全的影响。

Wood has the characteristics of large volume, large stowage factor, moisture absorption, flammability, etc., and attention should be paid to their impact on ship operation and safety during transportation.

(2) 裸装钢材类

(2) Iron and steel

本类包括各种类型的无包装成件金属类货物,按形状可分为以下几种:

This category includes various types of unpackaged metal goods, which can be divided into the following types according to their shapes:

①板型材:厚度不一,如钢板、镀锌钢皮(白铁皮)、镀锡钢皮(马口铁)等。

①Plate profiles: different thickness, such as steel plate, galvanized steel (white iron), tinned steel (tinplate), etc.

②型钢材:按截面和外表形状不同,其可分为圆钢、方钢、角钢、扁钢、槽钢等,它们各具有不同用途。

②Steel type:according to its cross section and external shape, it is divided into round steel, square steel, angle steel, flat steel, channel steel, etc., each of which has different purposes.

③管钢材:其按制造方法不同分为无缝钢管和有缝钢管。它们的口径不一,且有的具有较粗管头。

③Pipe steel: it is divided into seamless steel pipe and seamed steel pipe according to different manufacturing methods. They have different calibers and some have thicker tubes.

④铸锭类:指各种金属铸锭等块状货物,如生铁块、铝锭、铅块等。

④Ingot:refers to various metal ingots and other block goods, such as pig iron, aluminum ingots, lead blocks and so on.

⑤丝卷类:指各种细长金属丝线,一般以卷型方式运输,如铁丝、盘圆、电线、电缆等。

⑤Silk coil type:refers to a variety of elongated metal wire, generally transported in a roll type, such as wire, coil, wire, cable and so on.

⑥其他钢材类:形状未包含在上述范围内的钢材类制品,如铸铁盖板等。

⑥Other steel grades:steel products that are not included in the above range, such as cast iron covers.

金属类货物具有积载因数小、长型材长度大,易锈蚀和易变形等特点,装运时应注意它们对船舶稳性和强度的影响,并确保货物质量。

Metal goods have the characteristics of small stowage factor, large length of long profile, easy rust and easy deformation. Attention should be paid to their influence on the stability and strength of the ship and ensure the quality of the goods.

(3)散货

(3) Bulk cargo

散货指非整船运输的未加包装的块状、颗粒状、粉末状的货物,如散装谷物、矿石、化肥、水泥等。杂货船运输的固体散货的若干特性与专用船运输时方式相同。

Bulk cargo refers to the unpackged cargo shaped in block, granular or powder that are not shipped in whole ships, such as bulk grain, ore, fertilizer, cement, etc. The characteristics of solid bulk cargo transported by a general cargo ship are the same as those for a special ship.

2.1.1.3　货物运输单元

2.1.1.3　Cargo Transport Unit

(1)车辆

(1) Vehicle

车辆指可在公路及铁路上运行的各种车辆,如拖车、公路列车及组合体、机车、客车或货

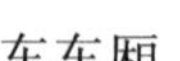

车车厢。

Vehicle refers to a variety of vehicles that can operate on roads and railways, such as trailers, road trains and assemblies, locomotives, buses or trucks.

(2)集装箱和货运箱

(2) Container or freight box

集装箱和货运箱指非集装箱船装运的各种类型集装箱及用于装运小件货物以便利装卸的货箱。

Container or freight box refers to various types of containers shipped by non-container ships and containers used to carry small items for convenient loading and unloading.

(3)货盘及货物组件

(3) Pallet and cargo components

货盘指各种以托盘形式运输的货物;货物组件指将若干包件或散件组合在一起所构成的搬运单位。

A pallet refers to a variety of goods that are transported in the form of pallets; a cargo component is a handling unit that combines several packages or parts.

(4)散装容器和罐柜

(4) Bulk containers and tanks

散装容器和罐柜指非永久性固定于船上,允许使用机械装卸。其结构设备满足一定要求的容器及罐柜,用来装载气体、液体或固体。

Bulk containers and tanks refer to containers and tanks that are not permanently fixed to the ship and allow the use of mechanical loading and unloading. The structural equipment meets certain requirements and is used to load gas, liquid or solid.

(5)重质货件

(5) Heavy cargo

重质货件指积载因数小而重量较大的货件,如通常每卷重量超过 10 t 的卷钢。

Heavy cargo refers to a shipment with a small stowage factor and a large weight, such as a coil that typically weighs more than 10 tons per roll.

(6)重大件货

(6) Awkward and lengthy cargo

重大件货指尺寸、体积或重量较大的货件,如起重设备、变压器、车辆、桥梁构件等。

Awkward and lengthy cargo refers to shipments of larger size, volume, or weight, such as lifting equipment, transformers, vehicles, bridge components, etc.

货物单元具有重量大、体积或尺寸大、形状各异、装卸困难、需特别固定等特点,在装运中需根据各自特征谨慎处理,以确保船舶安全和货物完整。

Cargo units have the characteristics of large weight, large size or volume, different shapes, difficult loading and unloading, and need to be specially fixed. They must be handled carefully according to their respective characteristics during shipment to ensure the safety of the ship and the integrity of the cargo.

2.1.2 固体散货
2.1.2 Solid Bulk Cargo

固体散货指除液体或气体外,由粉末、颗粒、球状、块状等构成的不加包装而直接装运的货物,如粮谷、矿石、煤炭、水泥、化肥、饲料等。

Solid bulk cargoes mean any cargoes, other than liquid or gas, consisting of a combination of particles, granules or any large pieces of material generally uniform in composition, which is loaded directly into the cargo spaces of a ship without any intermediate form of containment, such as grain, ore, coal, cement, fertilizer, feed, etc.

根据《IMBSC 规则》,固体散货分为三类货物:

According to IMBSC Code, solid bulk cargoes are divided into three types of cargoes:

2.1.2.1 A 类——易流态化或动态分离的货物
2.1.2.1 Group A—Cargoes Which May Liquefy or Undergo Dynamic Separation

固体流态化指较细颗粒物质与流动的流体接触,使颗粒物质呈类似于流体的状态。

Solid liquefy means that the finer particulate matter is in contact with the flowing fluid, rendering the particulate matter in a fluid-like state.

易流态化货物的流态化指该类物质在外在因素的作用下,产生流态的趋势及可能性。它是易流态化货物最显著及最主要的特征。

The liquefy of cargoes which may liquefy refers to the trend and possibility of generating fluidity under the influence of external factors. It is the most significant and most important feature of easily fluidized cargo.

易流态化货物指由至少一部分细颗粒的混合物构成且含有一定水分的物质。当水分含量超过一定比例时,在海上运输过程中,受到外界各种力的作用,水分逐渐渗移而形成货物表面流态化从而导致货物移动。这类货物往往在装载时可能呈干燥的颗粒状,但却可能含有相当的水分,由于航行中出现的沉积和震动作用使之流态化。

The cargo which may liquefy refers to a material composed of a mixture of at least a part of fine particles and containing a certain amount of water. If the moisture content exceeds a certain proportion, in the course of marine transportation, the water is gradually absorbed and formed by the external force, the surface of the cargo is fluidized to cause the cargo to move. Such goods tend

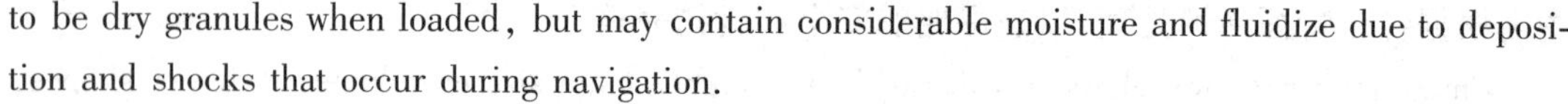

to be dry granules when loaded, but may contain considerable moisture and fluidize due to deposition and shocks that occur during navigation.

易流态化货物大致分成两类。一类是积载因数为0.33~0.57 m^3/t 的各种精矿,如铁精矿、铅精矿、镍精矿、铜精矿、锌精矿、黄铁矿、硫化锌(闪锌矿)等。另一类是具有与精矿性质类似的其他物质,包括含有足够水分的细颗粒状物质、散装草泥、散装鲜鱼和据报能形成流态化的煤炭(细颗粒状)、煤泥(含水粉砂,颗粒粒度一般小于1 mm)、焙烧黄铁矿、氟石等物质。

Cargoes which may liquefy are roughly divided into two categories. One type is various concentrates with a stowage factor of 0.33 to 0.57 m^3/t, such as iron concentrate, lead concentrate, nickel concentrate, copper concentrate, zinc concentrate, pyrite, zinc sulfide. Others are other substances that are similar in nature to concentrates, including fine particulate matter containing sufficient moisture, bulk grass mud, bulk fresh fish, and coal that is reported to form fluidized (fine particles shape), slime (aqueous silt, particle size is generally less than 1 mm), roast pyrite, fluorite and other substances.

易动态分离货物指由含有一定的细颗粒物和一定水分的物质,如果装船时含水量超过其适运水分限,则可能发生动态分离。

Cargoes which may undergo dynamic separation mean cargoes which contain a certain proportion of fine particles and a certain amount of moisture, and may undergo dynamic separation if shipped at a moisture content in excess of their transportable moisture limit.

动态分离指在固体物质上方形成液体浆液(水和细小固体)的现象,从而产生自由液面效应,严重影响船舶的稳性。

Dynamic separation means the phenomenon of forming a liquid slurry (water and fine solids) above the solid material, resulting in a free surface effect which may significantly affect the ship's stability.

2.1.2.2 B类——具有化学危险性的货物
2.1.2.2 Group B—Materials Possessing Chemical Hazards

具有化学危险的货物指由于自身的化学性质而在运输中会产生危险的固体散装货物。这类货物可分成两类。

Materials possessing chemical hazards is a solid bulk cargo that poses a hazard during transport due to its own chemical nature. This type of goods can be divided into two categories.

(1)已列入《IMDG规则》的固体散货

(1) Solid bulk cargoes that have been included in IMDG Code

此类货物以包装形式和散装形式运输。因本身的化学性质,它们都属于危险货物。它们具有相同的分类号。但是,由于其运输方式的不同,有关安全运输的要求存在一定差别。它们都应该遵守不同的规则条款。属于《IMDG规则》中的固体散货类别有:

Such cargoes are transported in both package and bulk form. They are classified as dangerous cargoes because of their own chemical properties. They have the same classification number. However, due to the different modes of transportation, there are certain differences in the requirements for safe transportation. They should comply with different rules. This type of solid bulk cargo belongs to the category in the IMDG Code:

第4.1类:易燃固体,如硫黄。本类物质具有易被火花和火焰等外部火源点燃、易于燃烧、受摩擦时易引起燃烧或助燃等特性。

Class 4.1: Flammable solids, like sulfur. This kind of material has the characteristics of being easily ignited by an external fire source such as sparks and flames, easy to burn, and easily causing combustion or combustion during friction.

第4.2类:易自燃物质,如干椰肉、种子饼、氧化铁、金属屑等。本类物质具有易自热并自燃的共同特性。

Class 4.2: Substances liable to spontaneous combustion, like dried copra, cardamom, iron oxide, metal shavings, etc. This type of substance has the common characteristics of being self-heating and spontaneous combustion.

第4.3类:遇水放出易燃气体的物质,如废铝、锌渣、硅铁等。本类物质具有遇水产生可燃气体的共同特性。

Class 4.3: Substances which, in contact with water, emit flammable gases, such as waste aluminum, zinc slag, ferrosilicon, etc. This type of substance has the common characteristics of producing flammable gas in contact with water.

第5.1类:氧化剂,如硝酸铝、硝酸铵、硝酸钙、硝酸镁等。本类物质尽管本身不一定可燃,但与其他物质接触时其产生的氧气或发生的类似反应会增加燃烧的危险和强烈程度。

Class 5.1: Oxidizing substances, such as aluminum nitrate, ammonium nitrate, calcium nitrate, magnesium nitrate, etc. Although this material is not necessarily flammable by itself, the oxygen produced by it or the similar reaction occurring when it comes into contact with other substances increases the danger and intensity of combustion.

第6.1类:有毒物质。本类物质如被吞咽、吸入或与皮肤接触,易造成死亡或严重损伤。

Class 6.1: Toxic substances. This type of substance is prone to death or serious injury if swallowed, inhaled or in contact with the skin.

第7类:放射性物质。该类物质指含有放射性核素的任何物质,且托运货物的放射性强度和总量大于《IMDG规则》要求的数值。本类物质能释放出大量射线。

Class 7: Radioactive material. This substance refers to any substance containing radionuclides, and the radioactive intensity and total amount of the consignment are greater than the values required by the IMDG Code. This class of substances can release a large amount of radiation.

第8类:腐蚀性物质。本类物质具有在原来形态下在某种程度上严重损伤活体组织的共同特性。

Class 8: Corrosive substances. This type of substance has the common characteristics of seri-

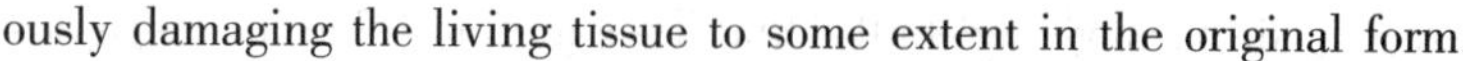

ously damaging the living tissue to some extent in the original form.

第 9 类：其他危险货物，如鱼粉、蓖麻子肥等。

Class 9：Miscellaneous dangerous substances and articles, such as fish meal, castor seed fertilizer, etc.

（2）仅在散装运输时具有危险的货物（MHB）

（2）Materials hazardous only in bulk（MHB）

未列入《IMDG 规则》，但在散装运输中易产生危险而应予以特别关注的固体散货属于仅在散装运输时具有危险的货物（Materials Hazardous only in Bulk，MHB），能减少舱内含氧量的物质、易自热物质、潮湿时会产生危险的物质等均属于此类。此类货物包括煤、木炭、油焦炭、沥青球、木屑片、锯末、动物肥、直接还原铁、磷铁、锰硅合金、锑矿、铬矿、钒土矿、生石灰、氟石等。

Solid bulk cargoes that are not listed in IMDG Code, but which are subject to special hazards in bulk transport, should be given special attention to materials that are only dangerous in bulk transport（Material Hazardous only in Bulk, MHB）. Substances that can reduce oxygen in the tank, substances that are prone to self-heating, and substances that are dangerous when wet are of this type. Such goods include coal, charcoal, oil coke, asphalt balls, wood chips, sawdust, animal fertilizer, direct reduced iron, ferrophosphorus, manganese silicon alloy, antimony ore, chrome ore, vanadium ore, quicklime, fluorite and the like.

2.1.2.3 C 类——既不易流态化又无化学危险的固体散货（C 类货物既不属于 A 类，也不属于 B 类）

2.1.2.3 Group C—Bulk Materials Which are Neither Liable to Liquefy and to Possess Chemical Hazards（Group C Consists of Cargoes Which are Classified as Neither Group A nor Group B）

此类物质通常称为普通固体散货。虽然它们当中有的与 A 类散货同名，但其块状较大或含水量较低而不易流态化；有的与 B 类散货同名，但已经某种化学处理或因某些物质含量较小而不具有特别危险性；某些物质虽自身尚具有一定毒性或腐蚀性，但较 B 类散货其危险性大为减小。其具体包括水泥、滑石粉、石膏、黏土、硼砂、白云石、苜蓿粉、碳酸钡、重烧镁、盐、沙子、糖等。

Such materials are often referred to as ordinary solid bulk cargoes. Although some of them have the same name as the Group A bulk cargo, they are larger in block size or lower in water content and less fluidized; some have the same name as Group B bulk cargo, but have some chemical treatment or some smaller substance content and not particularly dangerous; some substances are inherently toxic or corrosive, but they are much less dangerous than Group B bulk cargoes. Specifically, it includes cement, talcum powder, gypsum, clay, borax, dolomite, strontium powder, barium carbonate, burnt magnesium, salt, sand, sugar, etc.

2.1.3 散装谷物
2.1.3 Bulk Grain

除《IMSBC 规则》所规定的三类固体散货外,还有一类非常重要的散货是散装谷物。散粮指包括小麦、玉米、燕麦、稞麦、大麦、大米、豆类,及由其加工的与谷物在自然状态下具有相同特征的制成品。

In addition to the three types of solid bulk cargoes specified in the IMSBC Code, one of the most important bulk cargoes is bulk grain. Bulk grains include wheat, maize, oats, rye, barley, rice, pulses, and processed by them which have the same characteristics as a grain in its natural state.

谷物的散装运输比包装运输更具有优越性。散装运输能够节省包装费用、提高船舶载货能力和装卸效率、减少装卸费用。因此,大宗谷物一般均采用散装方式运输。然而,考虑到散装谷物的自身特性,必须采取一定的措施才能确保船舶安全。

Bulk transportation of grain is superior to packaging transportation. Bulk transportation can save packaging costs, improve cargo loading capacity and loading and unloading efficiency, and reduce loading and unloading costs. Therefore, bulk grain is generally transported in bulk. However, given the nature of bulk grain, certain measures must be taken to ensure ship safety.

散装谷物的性质包括:

The properties of bulk cereals include:

(1)呼吸性
(1) Respiratory

谷物靠呼吸作用获得能量来维持生命,呼吸作用使谷物中的水和二氧化碳含量增加并产生热量。呼吸强度受粮谷的水分、温度、空气成分、籽粒状态等因素影响,其中水分是最重要的因素。在一定范围内,粮谷水分含量增大,呼吸作用将大大加强。干燥谷物的呼吸作用极为微弱,当水分超过安全水分时,呼吸强度骤然增强。在温度 0~50 ℃范围内,呼吸强度随温度上升而增强,适宜温度为 20~40 ℃。空气中氧含量充足,呼吸强度大。新粮、瘪粒、破碎粒、表面粗糙的籽粒等呼吸作用较强。

Grains rely on respiration to gain energy to sustain life, and respiration increases the amount of water and carbon dioxide in the grain and produces heat. Respiratory intensity is affected by factors such as moisture, temperature, air composition, and status of the grain. Water is the most important factor. Within a certain range, the grain moisture increases, the breathing will be greatly enhanced. Dry grain respiration is extremely weak, and when the moisture exceeds safe moisture, the respiration intensity suddenly increases. In the temperature range of 0 to 50 ℃, the respiration intensity increases with temperature, and the suitable temperature is 20 to 40 ℃. When the oxygen content in the air is sufficient, the respiration intensity is high. New grains, glutinous grains, bro-

ken grains, and rough-surfaced grains have strong respiration effects.

(2) 发热性

(2) Febrile

谷物发热的主要原因是粮谷自身、微生物、虫害呼吸作用产生热量积聚的结果。由于谷物导热性能较差,所产生的热量很难散发。同时,粮温增高又为生物体的旺盛呼吸创造了条件,这样就会产生舱内谷物自身促进发热的现象。

The main cause of fever in cereals is the result of heat accumulation by the grain itself, microbes, and insect respiration. Due to the poor thermal conductivity of the grain, the heat generated is difficult to dissipate. At the same time, the increase in grain temperature creates conditions for the vigorous breathing of the organism, which will result in the phenomenon that the grain itself promotes fever.

为保证谷物运输质量,应抑制谷物发热,如通过降低谷物水分及温度来限制其呼吸作用、谷物熏蒸减小虫害和微生物影响等。

In order to ensure the quality of grain transport, grain heat should be inhibited, such as reducing the moisture and temperature of the grain to limit its breathing, grain fumigation to reduce pests and microbial effects.

(3) 吸湿和散湿性

(3) Moisture absorption and dissipate

谷物能吸收外界水分和向外散发水分。当谷物比较干燥而外界空气湿度较大时,谷物会吸收水分使其含水量增大。在一定温、湿度条件下,这会增强呼吸作用,利于霉菌、害虫繁殖,引起发热、发芽、霉变、虫害。当外界空气湿度较小时,谷物会向周围散发水分。船舶在航行中应进行正确通风,以防外界潮湿高温空气进入舱内。

Grains absorb outside moisture and emit moisture. When the grain is relatively dry and the outside air humidity is relatively high, the grain will absorb water and increase the water content. Under certain temperature and humidity conditions, it will enhance the respiration, which is beneficial to mold and pest reproduction, causing fever, germination, mildew and insect pests. When the outside air humidity is small, the grain will emit moisture to the surroundings. The ship should be properly ventilated during navigation to prevent outside humid high temperature air from entering the cabin.

(4) 吸附性

(4) Adsorption

谷物易感染或吸附异味和有害气体的特性被称为吸附性。一经感染,异味和有害气体散发很慢,或不能散失,会影响谷物的食用性,甚至使谷物不能被使用。为防止谷物感染异味而影响质量, 装货前应做好货舱准备工作。

The characteristic that cereals are susceptible to infection or adsorption of odors and harmful gases is called adsorption. Once infected, it is very slow, or can not be lost, it will affect the consumption or even use. In order to prevent the grain from infecting the odor and affecting the quality, the cargo hold should be prepared before loading.

（5）易受虫害作用

(5) Vulnerable to pests

谷物易感染害虫。害虫不仅蛀食谷物，引起重量损失和质量降低。另外，害虫在蛀食、呼吸、排泄和变态等生命活动中，散发热量和水分，促使结露、生芽、霉变。其产生的分泌物、粪便、尸体、皮屑等还会污染粮谷。谷物的主要害虫是米象、谷象等，谷物还常遭鼠咬吞食。为防止虫害作用，谷物和货舱应用药物熏蒸。

Grains are susceptible to pests. They not only feed on grains, but also cause weight loss and quality degradation. In addition, the pests emit heat and moisture during life activities such as foraging, breathing, excretion and metamorphism, causing condensation, sprouting, and mildew. The resulting secretions, feces, corpses, dander, etc. can also contaminate the grain. The main pests of cereals are rice elephants, valley elephants, etc., and they are often swallowed by rats. To prevent pests, the fumigation of the grain is applied to the grain and cargo compartment.

（6）下沉性

(6) Sinkage

下沉性指装于船舱内的散装谷物，在受船舶摇摆、振动等作用下，谷物间的空隙逐渐缩小引起谷物表面下沉的特性。谷物的下沉一方面导致舱内谷物重心下降，另一方面使初始呈满载状态货舱内出现一个空当，形成可自由流动的谷物表面。谷物的下沉性与颗粒大小、形状、积载因数、表面状态、含水量等因素有关。

Sinkage refers to the bulk grain contained in the hold, under the action of the ship's rocking and vibration, the gap between the grains gradually shrinks, causing the surface of the grain to sink. The sinking of the grain results in a decrease in the center of gravity of the grain in the tank and, on the other hand, an empty space in the cargo tank that is initially fully loaded, forming a free-flowing grain surface. The sinking of grain is related to particle size, shape, stowage factor, surface state, water content and other factors.

（7）散落性

(7) Shifting

散装谷物在船舶摇摆、振动等产生的外力作用下能自动松散流动的特性称为散落性。

The characteristic that the bulk grain can automatically loosely flow under the external force generated by the ship's rocking, vibration, etc. is called the shifting.

2.1.4 散装液体货物
2.1.4 Liquid Bulk Cargo

2.1.4.1 原油
2.1.4.1 Crude Oil

原油,又称石油原油,是直接从油井中开采出来的一种具有特殊气味的、有色的、黏稠的可燃性矿物油,为多种烃类(烷烃、环烷烃、芳香烃)的复杂混合物。在常温常压下,碳原子 $C_1 \sim C_4$ 的烃类呈气态,存在于天然气中; $C_5 \sim C_{15}$ 的烃类是液态,是石油的主要成分; C_{16} 以上的烃类为固态。

Crude oil, also known as petroleum crude oil, is special, odorous, viscous, flammable mineral oil that is directly extracted from oil wells and is a complex mixture of hydrocarbons (alkanes, naphthenes, aromatics). At normal temperature and pressure, the hydrocarbons of carbon atoms C_1 to C_4 are in a gaseous state and exist in natural gas; the hydrocarbons of C_5 to C_{15} are liquid and are the main components of petroleum; and the hydrocarbons of C_{16} and above are solid.

石油的性质因产地而异,密度为 0.8~1.0 g/cm³,黏度范围很宽,凝固点差别很大(30~60 ℃),沸点范围为常温到 500 ℃以上,可溶入多种有机溶剂,不溶于水,但可与水形成乳状液。组成石油的化学元素主要是碳(83%~87%)、氢(7%~14%),其余为硫(0.06%~0.8%)、氮(0.02%~1.7%)、氧(0.08%~1.82%)及微量金属元素(镍、钒、铁等)。由碳氢化合物形成的烃类构成石油的主要组成部分,占 95%~99%。含硫、氧、氮的化合物对石油产品有害,在石油加工中应尽量除去。

The nature of petroleum varies from place to place, density is 0.8 to 1.0 g/cm³, viscosity range is wide, freezing point is very different (30 to 60 ℃), boiling point range is from normal temperature to above 500 ℃, and it can be dissolved into various organic solvents, insoluble in water, but can form an emulsion with water. The chemical elements that make up petroleum are mainly carbon (83% to 87%), hydrogen (7% to 14%), and the rest are sulfur (0.06% to 0.8%), nitrogen (0.02% to 1.7%), and oxygen (0.08% to 1.82%) and trace metals (nickel, vanadium, iron, etc.). Hydrocarbons formed from hydrocarbons constitute the main component of petroleum, accounting for 95% to 99%. Compounds containing sulfur, oxygen and nitrogen are harmful to petroleum products and should be removed as much as possible in petroleum processing.

不同产地的石油中,各种烃类的结构和所占比例相差很大,但主要属于烷烃、环烷烃、芳香烃三类。通常以烷烃为主的石油称为石蜡基石油;以环烷烃、芳香烃为主的称环烃基石油;介于两者之间的称中间基石油。原油经过加工可以提炼出汽油、煤油、柴油、润滑油和其他化工产品。

Among the oils of different origins, the structure and proportion of various hydrocarbons vary greatly, but mainly belong to three types of alkanes, cycloalkanes and aromatic hydrocarbons. The

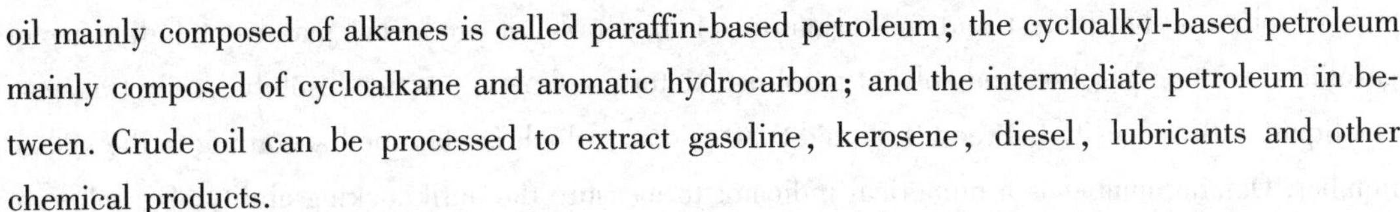

oil mainly composed of alkanes is called paraffin-based petroleum; the cycloalkyl-based petroleum mainly composed of cycloalkane and aromatic hydrocarbon; and the intermediate petroleum in between. Crude oil can be processed to extract gasoline, kerosene, diesel, lubricants and other chemical products.

2.1.4.2　成品油

2.1.4.2　Oil Product

在油田经过脱盐、脱水的原油，送往炼油厂，进行分馏和加工，才能得到各种石油产品。所谓分馏是指通过不断地加热和不断地冷凝，将石油分离成不同沸点的蒸馏产物的过程。炼油厂通常把产品分为“白油”和“黑油”两大类。一般来说，白油是直馏轻质馏分，又称清油；黑油是重质馏分。在分馏塔内，轻质馏分的蒸气上升较高，在塔的上部冷凝成液体，通常称为蒸馏油，其沸点较低，如汽油、煤油、轻柴油等。重质馏分的蒸气在较低的高度冷凝，通常称为蒸余油，其沸点较高，如燃料油、渣油、沥青等。因此，可从分馏塔不同的高度得到不同的馏分。主要产品依次为石油气、汽油、煤油、柴油、重油。

The crude oil that has been desalted and dehydrated in the oil field is sent to the refinery for fractionation and processing to obtain various petroleum products. Fractionation refers to the process of separating petroleum into distillation products of different boiling points by continuous heating and continuous condensation. Refineries usually divide their products into two categories: “white oil” and “black oil”. In general, white oil is a straight-run light fraction, also known as clean oil; black oil is a heavy fraction. In the fractionation column, the light fraction has a higher vapor rise and condenses into a liquid at the upper part of the column, commonly referred to as distillate fuel, which has a lower boiling point such as gasoline, kerosene, light diesel oil, etc. Vapor is condensed at a lower level, commonly referred to as residual fuel or residual oil, which has a higher boiling point, such as fuel oil, residual oil, bitumen, and the like. Therefore, different fractions can be obtained from different heights of the fractionation column. The main products are petroleum gas, gasoline, kerosene, diesel, heavy oil.

(1) 汽油

(1) Petrol or gasoline

汽油是石油产品中比重最轻、最易挥发的油品，主要包括车用汽油、航空汽油和溶剂汽油。车用汽油是一种不溶于水的、密度在 0.65～0.80 g/cm^{3}之间的油状透明液体，按辛烷值的高低分牌号。辛烷值是衡量汽油在汽缸内抗爆震燃烧能力的一种数字指标。其值高表示抗爆性好，常用的辛烷值有研究法辛烷值和马达法辛烷值。车用汽油按照马达法辛烷值可分为66、70、76、80、85 五个牌号；按照研究法辛烷值可分为90、93、95、97、99 等牌号。牌号越高，表示抗爆震性能越好。为了提高汽油的抗爆震性能，通常在油内掺入烷基铅作抗爆剂，如四乙基铅、四甲基铅等。纯净的汽油为无色透明的液体。由于四乙基铅等有剧毒，为表示有毒，将掺入剧毒添加剂的车用汽油染成黄色或红色，以引起注意。

Gasoline is the lightest and most volatile oil in petroleum products, mainly including motor gasoline, aviation gasoline and solvent gasoline. Motor gasoline is a water-insoluble, oily transparent liquid with a density between 0.65 and 0.80 g/cm^3, which is classified according to the octane number. Octane number is a numerical indicator to measure the antiknocking ability of gasoline in the cylinder. The high value indicates good antiknock performance. The commonly used octane number has research octane number and motor octane number. According to the motor octane number, motor gasoline can be divided into five grades of 66, 70, 76, 80, and 85; according to the research method, the octane number can be divided into 90, 93, 95, 97, and 99 grades. The higher the grade, the better the antiknock performance. In order to improve the antiknock performance of gasoline, alkyl lead is usually incorporated into the oil as an antiknock additive such as tetraethyl lead or tetramethyl lead. Pure gasoline is a colorless and transparent liquid. Due to the high toxicity of tetraethyl lead, it is toxic, and the gasoline used in the highly toxic additives is dyed yellow or red to attract attention.

(2) 煤油

(2) Kerosene

煤油是一种无色透明液体,密度约为 0.80 g/cm^3,闪点在 40 ℃左右(作为航空燃料的煤油闪点为 38 ℃)。其在低温下着火性能较差,使用时比汽油安全。其按用途可分灯用煤油、拖拉机用煤油、航空用煤油和重质煤油。煤油除了作为燃料外,还可作为机器洗涤剂以及医药工业和油漆工业的溶剂。灯用煤油比汽油重,比柴油轻,用于点灯照明,作为汽灯和煤油炉的燃料。灯用煤油严防汽油混入,以免点火时引起火灾。混入柴油会降低煤油的质量。

Kerosene is a colorless transparent liquid with a density of about 0.80 g/cm^3 and a flash point of around 40 ℃ (the kerosene flash point of aviation fuel is 38 ℃). It has poor ignition performance at low temperatures and is safer to use than gasoline. According to the use, it can be divided into kerosene for lamps, kerosene for tractors, kerosene for aviation and heavy kerosene. In addition to being used as a fuel, kerosene can also be used as a solvent for machine detergents and the pharmaceutical and paint industries. The lamp kerosene is heavier than gasoline and lighter than diesel. It is used for lighting and is used as fuel for steam lamps and kerosene stoves. Use lamp kerosene to prevent gasoline from entering, so as to avoid fire when ignition. Mixing diesel will reduce the quality of kerosene.

(3) 柴油

(3) Diesel

柴油主要作为柴油发动机的燃料,分为轻柴油和重柴油。

Diesel is mainly used as fuel for diesel engines which is divided into light diesel and heavy diesel.

①轻柴油:供各种柴油汽车、拖拉机、各种高速柴油机(1 000 r/min 以上)等作燃料用。凝点指在规定的冷却条件下油品停止流动的最高温度。其按凝点的高低分为+10、0、-10、

-20、-35、-50 六个牌号，分别表示其凝点不高于+10 ℃、0 ℃、-10 ℃、-20 ℃、-35 ℃、-50 ℃。牌号越高，凝点越低。

①Light Diesel Oil: for a variety of diesel vehicles, tractors, various high-speed diesel engines (1,000 r/min or more) for fuel. The freezing point is the highest temperature at which the oil stops flowing under the specified cooling conditions. According to the high and low points of the freezing point, the scores of +10, 0, -10, -20, -35, -50 indicate that the freezing point is not higher than +10 ℃, 0 ℃, -10 ℃, -20 ℃, -35 ℃, -50 ℃. The higher the grade, the lower the freezing point.

②重柴油：供各种中低速柴油机(1 000 r/min 以下)作燃料用。其按凝点的高低分为10、20、30 三个牌号，分别表示其凝点不高于 10 ℃、20 ℃、30 ℃。牌号越高，凝点越高。

②Heavy Diesel Oil: it is used as fuel for various medium and low speed diesel engines (below 1,000 r/min). According to the level of the freezing point, it is divided into three grades of 10, 20, and 30, which indicate that the freezing point is not higher than 10 ℃, 20 ℃, and 30 ℃. The higher the grade, the higher the freezing point.

(4) 燃料油

(4) Fuel oil

燃料油又叫锅炉油，是原油蒸馏出汽油、煤油、柴油后在 350 ℃以上并经精制除杂直接蒸馏得到的油品。其密度为 0.940~0.995 g/cm^3。其主要供船舶、工业和工厂锅炉作燃料用。黏度是衡量流体流动性的指标，指液体受外力作用移动时，分子间产生的内摩擦力大小的量度。其按黏度的大小分为 20、60、100、200 四个牌号。牌号越大，黏度越大。

Fuel oil is also called boiler oil. It is obtained by distilling out gasoline, kerosene and diesel at 350 ℃ and refined by direct distillation. The density is 0.940 to 0.995 g/cm^3. Fuel oil is mainly used on ships, industrial and factory boilers. Viscosity is an indicator of the fluidity of a fluid as a measure of the amount of internal friction generated between molecules when the liquid is moved by an external force. According to the size of the viscosity, it is divided into four grades of 20, 60, 100 and 200. The larger the grade, the greater the viscosity.

(5) 润滑油

(5) Lubricating oil

润滑油是提取了汽油、煤油、柴油后剩下的重质油，采取减压蒸馏法制成的液体油品。其主要用于机械设备的摩擦部位，起润滑作用。在运输过程中，应严防混入水分和杂质，混入水分极易乳化而无法分离，使机械锈蚀、润滑性变坏；混入杂质会擦伤和磨损机械，失去润滑作用。

Lubricating oil is a heavy oil that has been extracted from gasoline, kerosene, and diesel, and is made into a liquid oil by vacuum distillation. It is mainly used for the friction parts of mechanical equipment to provide lubrication. In the process of transportation, water and impurities are strictly prevented from being mixed, and the water is easily emulsified and cannot be separa-

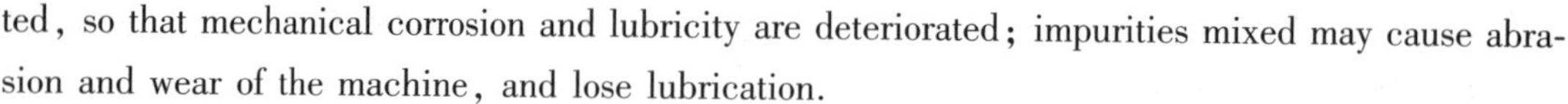

ted, so that mechanical corrosion and lubricity are deteriorated; impurities mixed may cause abrasion and wear of the machine, and lose lubrication.

2.1.4.3 液化气

2.1.4.3 Liquefied Gas

液化气主要包括液化石油气、液化天然气、液化化学气。

Liquefied gas mainly includs liquefied petroleum gas, liquefied natural gas, liquefied chemical gas.

液化石油气的主要成分是丙烷。

The main component of liquefied petroleum gas is propane.

液化天然气的主要成分是甲烷。

The main composition of liquefied natural gas is methane.

液化化学气的成分是碳氢化合物,还有氧化丙烯和聚氯乙烯。

The composition of liquefied chemical gas is hydrocarbon, as well as propylene oxide and polyvinyl chloride.

2.1.4.4 散装液体化学品

2.1.4.4 Bulk Liquid Chemical Cargo

美国海岸警卫队(USCG)按化学反应性将散装液体化学品分为5类:

The US Coast Guard (USCG) divids the bulk liquid chemical cargoes into five categories based on chemical reactivity:

(1)0类:指几乎不发生反应的物质,但在某种条件下能与4类物质反应,如饱和烃。

(1) Class 0: it refers to a substance that hardly reacts, but can react with Class 4 of substances under certain conditions, such as saturated hydrocarbons.

(2)1类:仅与4类物质反应的液体化学品,如芳香烃、烯烃、醚、酯。

(2) Class 1: liquid chemicals that react only with Class 4 of substances, such as aromatic hydrocarbons, olefins, ethers, and esters.

(3)2类:不能与0类和1类物质反应,或本来物质不能互相反应的液体化学品,但能与3类和4类物质反应,如醇、酮、聚合物。

(3) Class 2: liquid chemicals that cannot react with Class 0 and Class 1 substances, or that are not reactive with each other, but can react with Class 3 and Class 4 substances, such as alcohols, ketones, and polymers.

(4)3类:能与2类和4类物质反应,且本来化学品能相互反应,如有机酸、液氨、环氧衍生物。

(4) Class 3: it can react with Class 2 and Class 4 substances, and the original chemicals can react with each other, such as organic acids, liquid ammonia, and epoxy derivatives.

(5)4 类:可以相互反应,并能与所有其他的化学品反应,如无机酸、强碱、磷、硫。

(5)Class 4:It can react with each other and react with all other chemicals, such as inorganic acids, strong bases, phosphorus, sulfur.

《国际散装运输危险化学品船舶结构与设备规则》(《IBC 规则》)所涵盖的散装化学品货物指在 37.8 ℃温度下蒸气压力绝对值不超过 0.28 MPa 的危险化学品或有害液体物质(NLS)的散装货物。

The bulk chemical cargoes are bulk cargoes of dangerous chemicals or noxious liquid substances (NLS) which having a vapor pressure not exceeding 0.28 MPa absolute at a temperature of 37.8 ℃, covered by International Code for the Construction and Equipment of Ships Carrying Dangerous Chemicals in Bulk (IBC Code).

《MARPOL 公约》附则Ⅱ"防止散装有毒液体物质污染规则",将有害液体物质分为以下 4 大类:

Noxious liquid substances shall be divided into four categories in Annex Ⅱ Regulations for the Control of Pollution by Noxious Liquid Substances in Bulk of MARPOL as follows:

(1)X 类:X 类指在清舱或排压载水工作中排放入海后将会对海洋资源或人类健康造成严重危害的有害液体物质,因此有必要严禁将此类物质排入海洋环境。

(1) Category X: noxious liquid substances which, if discharged into the sea from tank cleaning or deballasting operations, are deemed to present a major hazard to either marine resources or human health and, therefore, justify the prohibition of the discharge into the marine environment.

(2)Y 类:Y 类指在清舱或排压载水工作中排放入海后将会对海洋资源或人类健康造成严重危害或对舒适性或其他合法利用海洋造成损害的有害液体物质,因此有必要对排入海洋环境的此类物质的质量加以限制。

(2) Category Y: noxious liquid substances which, if discharged into the sea from tank cleaning or deballasting operations, are deemed to present a hazard to either marine resources or humans health or cause harm to amenities or other legitimate uses of the sea and therefore justify a limitation on the quality and quantity of the discharge into the marine environment.

(3)Z 类:Z 类指在清舱或排压载水工作中排放入海后将会对海洋资源或人类健康造成较小的危害的物质,因此有必要对排入海洋环境的此类物质的质量加以限制。

(3) Category Z: noxious liquid substances which, if discharged into the sea from tank cleaning or deballasting operations, are deemed to present a minor hazard to either marine resources or human health and therefore justify less stringent restrictions on the quality and quantity of the discharge into the marine environment.

(4)其他物质(OS):在清舱或排压载水工作中,经评估后发现不属于 X 类、Y 类或 Z 类,将其排入海中后不会对海洋资源或人类健康造成危害或不会对舒适性或其他合法利用海洋造成损害的物质,因此排放含有 OS 类物质的舱底污水、压载水其他残余物或混合物不受《MARPOL 公约》附则Ⅱ要求的约束。

(4)Other substances (OS):substances which have been evaluated and found to fall outside

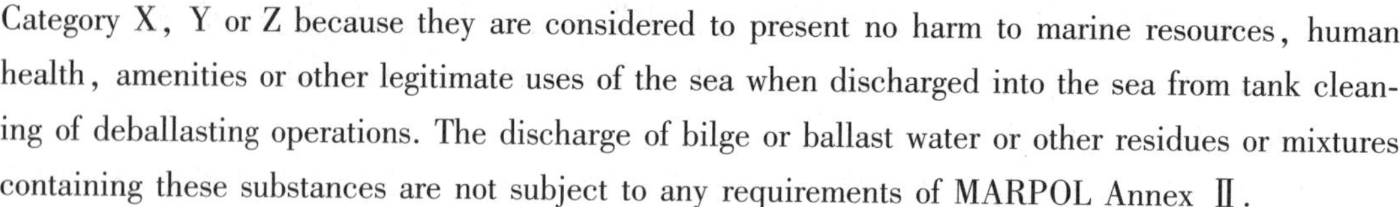

Category X, Y or Z because they are considered to present no harm to marine resources, human health, amenities or other legitimate uses of the sea when discharged into the sea from tank cleaning of deballasting operations. The discharge of bilge or ballast water or other residues or mixtures containing these substances are not subject to any requirements of MARPOL Annex Ⅱ.

2.1.5 特殊货物
2.1.5 Special Cargo

(1) 木材
(1) Timber

海运的木材货物属于散货范畴。其种类较多,按木材形状及加工程度分,有原木、成材和木材制品。原木形体长大,长度约为6~8 m,运输量最多。木材积载因数较大,在1.3~2.3 m^3/t,极易吸收水分和散发水分。干燥的木材易燃烧。湿材、新伐材及某些树种木材具有一定的气味。由于木材在露天储存时表面衍生物的呼吸作用,会使封闭货舱内缺氧,木材表层的腐败可产生有毒气体氰化氢(HCN)和易燃的沼气(CH_4),这会对船舶安全和人员健康带来不利影响。

Wood is a bulk cargo transported by sea. There are many types, such as logs, timber and wood products according to the shape and processing degree of wood. The log body grows up to a length of about 6 to 8 m and has the largest amount of transportation. The wood has a large stowage factor of 1.3 to 2.3 m^3/t, which is easy to absorb moisture and emit moisture. Dry wood is easy to burn. It has a certain odor for wet materials, freshly cut wood and certain tree species. Due to the respiration of surface derivatives in the open storage of wood, the lack of oxygen in the closed cargo compartment, the corruption of the surface of the wood can produce toxic gases hydrogen cyanide (HCN) and flammable biogas (CH_4), for ship safety and personnel health to adversely affect.

(2) 冷藏货物
(2) Refrigerated cargoes

冷藏货物指要求在低于常温的条件下运输、保管的易腐性货物。这类货物在常温条件下经过较长时间的保管和运输,微生物作用、呼吸作用和化学作用等,会使其成分发生分解、变化而腐败,以致失去使用价值。在易腐性货物中多数为动物性食品和植物性食品,冷藏运输的目的是使货物在运输期间不致变质、过热或腐烂。

Refrigerated cargoes are perishable cargoes that are required to be transported and stored under conditions below normal temperature. Such goods are stored and transported under normal temperature conditions for a long period of time, due to the action of microorganisms, respiration and chemistry, their components may be decomposed, changed and corrupted, resulting in loss of use value. Most of the perishable goods are animal foods and vegetable foods. The purpose of refrigerated

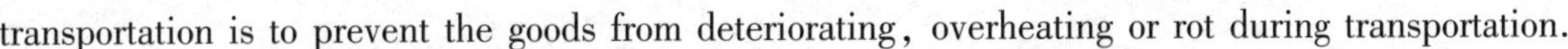

transportation is to prevent the goods from deteriorating, overheating or rot during transportation.

(3)货物运输单元

(3) Cargo transport unit

货物运输单元指车辆(公路车辆、拖车)、铁路货运车、集装箱、平台、托盘、可移动罐柜、中型散装容器、包装组件、成组货件、重质货件等。未永久性固定在船上的货物装卸设备或部件,也应视为货物运输单元。

Cargo transport unit refers to vehicles (road vehicles, trailers), railway freight cars, containers, platforms, pallets, removable tanks, medium bulk containers, packaging components, group shipments, heavy goods, etc. Cargo handling equipment or components that are not permanently attached to the ship shall also be considered as cargo transport units.

根据船舶为其货物运输单元所配备的货物系固系统情况,货物运输单元可分成三类:标准货物、半标准货物和非标准货物。标准货物指船上配备有为其特定种类设计并批准的货物系固系统的货物运输单元,如格栅式集装箱船装载的集装箱、钢材专用船装载的卷钢等;半标准货物指船上装备有能适应于具有有限种类的货物系固系统的货物运输单元,如滚装船上装载的车辆、拖车等;非标准货物指需进行单独积载和系固布置的货物。

According to the cargo securing system provided by the ship for its cargo transport unit, the cargo transport units are divided into three categories: standard cargo, semi-standard cargo and non-standard cargo. Standard cargo means a cargo transportation unit equipped with a cargo securing system designed and approved for its specific type, such as a container loaded by a grid container ship, a coil loaded by a steel special ship, etc.; semi-standard cargo means that the ship is equipped with energy adapted to cargo transport units with a limited variety of cargo securing systems, such as vehicles loaded on ro-ro ships, trailers, etc.; non-standard cargoes are those that require separate stowage and securing arrangements.

2.2 货物积载与系固

2.2 Cargo Stowage and Security

2.2.1 货物运输单元特性

2.2.1 The Feature of Cargo Transport Unit

就货物安全积载与系固而言,以下特性应给予适当考虑。

For the safe stowage and security of cargo, the following characteristics should be given due consideration.

（1）变形或压实

(1) Deformation or self-compaction

某些货物在航行中会产生变形或自压实，造成系索松动而引起货物移动。船舶应及时做好加固工作。

Some cargoes will be deformed or self-compacted during navigation, causing the ropes to loosen and causing the cargoes to move. The ship should be secured in time.

（2）低摩擦性

(2) Low friction

对于金属类货物单元，当将其积载于各层甲板上时，仅产生较小摩擦力。除沿船宽方向紧密积载的情况外，若在积载时未采取填加衬垫增大摩擦的措施，就难以牢固系固。

For metal cargo units, when they are stowed on each deck, only a small amount of friction is generated. Except for the tight stowage along the width of the ship, if the stowage is not filled, the friction is increased, the measures are difficult to firmly secure.

（3）尺寸及形状的特殊性

(3) Special dimensions or forms of cargo

某些货物运输单元因其自身尺寸和形状，当积载于船上某一位置上时，难于适当系固或仅凭系索难以系牢。需采取特别措施方能保证其运输安全。在此类货物选择舱位时，尺寸和形状是应首要考虑的因素之一。

Some cargo transport units, due to their size and shape, are difficult to securely fasten or simply rely on the lanyard when it is stowed on a certain position on the ship. Special measures are required to ensure safe transportation. Size and shape are one of the primary considerations when selecting a class for this type of cargo.

（4）重量及其分布

(4) Weight and its distribution

货物运输单元的重量及其分布会影响装载位置、衬垫方案、系固计划及船舶稳性等方面。

The weight and distribution of the cargo transport unit affect the loading position, the cushioning scheme, the securing plan and the stability of the ship.

（5）货物危险性

(5) Danger of the cargo

某些货物运输单元自身或其内容属于危险和有害货物，如装运固体、液体或气体的移动式罐柜或容器等。

Some cargo transport units themselves or their contents are dangerous and hazardous goods, such as mobile tankers or containers that carry solids, liquids or gases.

2.2.2 货物衬垫
2.2.2 Dunnage of Cargo

货物运输单元衬垫的主要作用包括：

The following are considered important purposes in respect of the dunnage of cargo units:

(1)保证船舶局部强度。

(1) Sufficient dunnage is always needed to ensure the local strength.

(2)增大货件与甲板间、货件与货件间的摩擦。

(2) Increase the friction coefficient between the cargo and deck, as well as between the cargo items themselves.

若货物与甲板或结构间或货物运输单元间摩擦力较小，就存在滑动的危险，为此，需在它们之间使用适当材料，如软板或衬垫，来增大摩擦力。

Where friction between the cargo and the ship's deck or structure or between cargo transport units is insufficient to avoid the risk of sliding, suitable material such as soft boards or dunnage should be used to increase friction.

(3)防止货物倾斜和滑动。

(3) Prevent cargo unit form tipping and sliding.

2.2.3 货物系固
2.2.3 Securing of Cargo

2.2.3.1 系固设备
2.2.3.1 Securing Devices

(1)"固定系固设备"指整体的，即焊接在船体结构上的，或非整体的，即焊接在船体结构上的固定点和支撑物，包括舱壁、强肋骨、支柱等上的眼板、带环螺栓等，甲板上的象脚装置、集装箱配件、地令等。

(1) "Fixed securing devices" means securing points and supports either integral, i.e., welded into the hull structure, or non-integral, i.e., welded onto the hull structure, including padeyes, eyebolts on bulkheads, web frames, stanchions etc.; elephant-feet fittings, container fittings, apertures, etc. on decks.

(2)"便携式固定设备"指用于捆绑、固定或支撑货物单元的便携式装置，如链条、钢丝绳、杆、松紧器(花篮螺丝、紧链器)、集装箱堆放装置、集装箱甲板固定装置、集装箱联锁装置、桥锁、支架和千斤顶等。

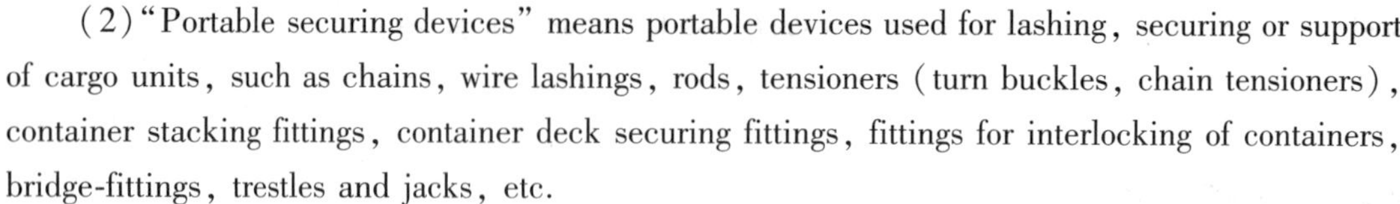

(2)"Portable securing devices" means portable devices used for lashing, securing or support of cargo units, such as chains, wire lashings, rods, tensioners (turn buckles, chain tensioners), container stacking fittings, container deck securing fittings, fittings for interlocking of containers, bridge-fittings, trestles and jacks, etc.

2.2.3.2 系固设备的强度

2.2.3.2 Strength of the Securing Devices

(1)破断强度

(1)BS

破断强度指构件、材料和元件不能再支撑或承受载荷的值。制造厂家至少应提供该设备的以千牛(kN)为单位的标准破断强度资料。

The breaking strength means the point at which the component, material or element can no longer support or sustain the load. Manufacturers of securing equipment should at least supply information on the nominal breaking strength in kilonewtons (kN).

(2)最大系固负荷

(2)MSL

最大系固负荷是用于定义将货物固定到船上设备时所允许的负荷能力。最大系固负荷对于系固设备,就像安全工作负荷对于起重设备一样。

Maximum securing load is a term used to define the load capacity for a device used to secure cargo to a ship. Maximum securing load is to secure devices as safe working load is to lifting tackle.

不同系固设备的最大系固负荷如表 2.2.1 所列。

表 2.2.1 不同系固设备的最大系固负荷

系固设备	最大系固负荷
卸扣、眼环、扭锁、绑扎拉杆、D 形扣、绑扎桥、低碳钢花篮螺丝	50%破断强度
纤维绳	33%破断强度
钢丝绳(第一次使用)	80%破断强度
钢丝绳(重复使用)	30%破断强度
钢带(第一次使用)	70%破断强度
链条	50%破断强度

The *MSLs* for different securing devices are given in Table 2.2.1.

Table 2.2.1　The *MSLs* for different securing devices

Securing devices	*MSL*
Shackles, ring plates, twist locks, lashing rods, D-rings, bridge fittings, turn buckles of mild steel	50% of breaking strength
Fibre rope	33% of breaking strength
Wire rope (single use)	80% of breaking strength
Wire rope (re-useable)	30% of breaking strength
Steel band (single use)	70% of breaking strength
Chains	50% of breaking strength

应当注意的是,当多个设备串联使用时(如一根钢丝绳连接卸扣到眼环),*MSL* 取其中最小者。

It should be noted that when the components of a lashing device are connected in series (for example, a wire to a shackle to a ring plate), the minimum *MSL* in the series shall apply to that device.

(3) 计算强度

(3) Calculated strength

在使用平衡计算方法评估系固设备强度时,应使用安全因数 F_s 来考虑设备间的受力不均匀或由于设备组装不当或其他原因导致的能力降低的可能性。*MSL* 使用安全因数推导出计算强度(*CS*),相关的计算公式如下。

When using balance calculation methods for assessing the strength of the securing devices, a safety factor F_s is used to take account of the possibility of uneven distribution of forces among the devices or reduced capability due to the improper assembly of the devices or other reasons. This safety factor is used in the formula to derive the calculated strength (*CS*) from the *MSL* and shown in the relevant method used.

$$CS = \frac{MSL}{F_s} \tag{2.2.1}$$

尽管考虑到这样一个安全因数,但为了使各系固设备有一致的弹性变形,也应选用材料和强度相近的系固设备。

Notwithstanding the introduction of such a safety factor, care should be taken to use securing elements of similar material and length in order to provide a uniform elastic behaviour within the arrangement.

2.2.3.3 可移动系固设备的正确使用
2.2.3.3 Correct Application of Portable Securing Devices

正确使用可移动系固设备应考虑以下因素：

The following factors should be taken into account for the correct application of portable securing devices:

(1)航次时间。

(1)Duration of the voyage.

(2)航经的地理区域,尤其是可移动系固设备最低安全使用温度。

(2)Geographical area of the voyage with particular regard to the minimum safe operational temperature of the portable securing devices.

(3)可预见的海况。

(3)Sea conditions which may be expected.

(4)船舶尺度及设计特征。

(4)Dimensions, design characteristics of the ship.

(5)航行中可预计的静外力和动外力。

(5)Expected static and dynamic forces during the voyage.

(6)包括车辆在内的货物单元的形式和包装。

(6)Type and packaging of cargo units including vehicles.

(7)包括车辆在内的货物单元计划积载方案。

(7)Intended stowage pattern of the cargo units including vehicles.

(8)货物单元和车辆的重量和尺寸。

(8)Mass and dimensions of the cargo units and vehicles.

2.2.4 货物积载与系固安全操作规则
2.2.4 Code of Safe Practice for Cargo Stowage and Securing

为了解决由于船舶不当积载和系固产生的问题和风险,国际海事组织(IMO)于1991年通过并于2002年修改了《货物积载与系固安全操作规则》(以下简称《规则》)。《规则》列入经修改的《1974年SOLAS公约》后由建议性改成强制性。《规则》共有7章和13个附录。《规则》目的是为货物的安全积载和系固提供一个国际标准。

In order to deal with the problems and hazards arising from improper stowage and securing of certain cargoes on ships, the International Maritime Organization (IMO) adopted in 1991 and amended in 2002 the Code of Safe Practice for Cargo Stowage and Securing (hereinafter reffered to as the Code). The Code has been included in the revised Convention on the Safety of Life at Sea (1974) and changed from the advisory code to compulsory code. The Code includes 7 chapters and 13 annexes. The purpose of this Code is to provide an international standard to promote the safe stowage and securing of cargoes.

《规则》的主要内容包括：

Contents of the Codes：

2.2.4.1 总则

2.2.4.1 General

（1）适用范围

(1) Application

《规则》适用于船舶装载的货物(除固体散货、液体散货和甲板木材以外)，特别是实践已经证明在积载与系固方面具有困难的货物。

The Code applies to cargoes carried on board ships (other than solid and liquid bulk cargoes and timber stowed on deck) and, in particular, to those cargoes whose stowage and securing have proved in practice to create difficulties.

（2）相关术语的定义

(2) Definitions of the terms used

对《规则》使用的货物运输单元、中型散装集装箱(IBC)、移动式罐柜、公路罐车公路车辆、公路拖车、滚装船、单位载荷等相关术语给出了定义。

For the purposes of the Code, definitions of the terms such as cargo unit, intermediate bulk container (IBC), portable tank, road tank-vehicle, road vehicle, roll-trailer, ro-ro ship, unit load, are given.

（3）力

(3) Forces

力一般是由作用于船轴的横向、纵向和垂向力组成，必须通过适当的积载和系固来防止货物移动。

Forces are generally composed of transverse, longitudinal, and vertical forces acting on the ship's axis, which have to be absorbed by suitable arrangements for stowage and securing to prevent cargo shifting.

施加的横向力与船的稳心高度成正比。

The transverse forces exerted increase directly with the metacentric height of the ship.

不适当的稳心高度可能由以下原因引起：

An undue metacentric height may be caused by：

①船舶设计不当；

①improper design of the ship；

②货物分配不当；

②unsuitable cargo distribution;

③燃料和压载分布不合理。

③unsuitable bunker and ballast distribution.

货物的分布应使船舶的稳心高度超过要求的最小值,并且在可行的情况下,在可接受的上限内,以最大限度地减少作用在货物上的力。

Cargo should be so distributed that the ship has a metacentric height in excess of the required minimum and, whenever practicable, within an acceptable upper limit to minimize the forces acting on the cargo.

除上述力外,甲板上的货物还受到风压力和波溅力。船舶操纵(航向和航速)不当会使船舶与货物受力增加。

In addition to the forces referred to above, cargo carried on deck may be subjected to forces arising from the effects of wind and green seas. Improper ship handling (course or speed) may create adverse forces acting on the ship and the cargo.

使用《货物系固手册》(如果有的话)中所载的适当计算方法可以对货物受力进行估算。

The magnitude of the forces may be estimated by using the appropriate calculation methods as contained in the Cargo Securing Manual, if provided.

虽然减摇装置可以改善船舶航行性能,但在规划货物的积载与系固时,不应考虑该装置的影响。

Although the operation of anti-roll devices may improve the behaviour of the ship in a seaway, the effect of such devices should not be taken into account when planning the stowage and securing of cargoes.

(4)货物的特性

(4) Behaviour of cargoes

从货物的安全积载角度,规则给出了货物单元的相关特性,包括变形、自压实、低摩擦性等性质及对货物的影响。

From the perspective of the safe stowage of goods, the rules give the relevant characteristics of the cargo unit, including deformation, self-compaction, low friction and other properties and impact on the cargo.

(5)货物移动可能的因素

(5) Possible factors influencing cargo shifting

估计货物移动可能的因素包括:货物的尺寸和物理特性;货物在船上的积载位置和形式;船舶对特殊货物的适运性;船上系固设备的适用性;航线上预计的天气和海况;预计的船舶航行计划;船舶稳性状况;航行区域以及航行持续时间。

When estimating the risk of cargo shifting, the following should be considered: dimensional and physical properties of the cargo; location of the cargo and its stowage on board; suitability of the ship for the particular cargo; suitability of the securing arrangements for the particular cargo;

expected seasonal weather and sea conditions; expected ship behaviour during the intended voyage; stability of the ship; geographical area of the voyage; and the duration of the voyage.

应根据下述因素确定合理的积载与系固方法以及系固设备所受到的力。船长只有在认为可以安全运输的前提下,方可接受货物装载。

These criteria should be taken into account when selecting suitable stowage and securing methods and whenever reviewing the forces to be absorbed by the securing equipment. Bearing in mind the above criteria, the master should accept the cargo on board his ship only if he is satisfied that it can be safely transported.

①《货物系固手册》。

①Cargo Securing Manual.

②船上系固设备。

②Securing Devices on board.

③特殊的货物运输单元。

③Special cargo transport units.

④货物信息。

④Cargo information.

2.2.4.2 货物安全积载与系固的一般原则

2.2.4.2 Principles of Safe Stowage and Securing of Cargoes

(1)集装箱、公路车辆箱驳、铁路挂车中货物应适当填装与系固,以防止航行过程中对船舶的损伤及对船员和海洋的伤害。

(1) Cargo carried in containers, road vehicles, shipborne barges, railway wagons and other cargo transport units should be packed and secured within these units so as to prevent, throughout the voyage, damage or hazard to the ship, to the persons on board and to the marine environment.

(2)为防止货物的移动、倾覆、晃动、倒塌,船长对货物积载与系固方案的制定和监督尤为重要。货物的配置应保证船舶稳性在一定限度内以尽量减小过大加速度的不利影响。货物配载尚应考虑船体结构的强度情况。

(2) It is of utmost importance that the master takes great care in planning and supervising the stowage and securing of cargoes in order to prevent cargo from sliding, tipping, racking, collapsing, etc. The cargo should be distributed so as to ensure that the stability of the ship throughout the entire voyage remains within acceptable limits so that the hazards of excessive accelerations are reduced as far as practicable. Cargo distribution should be such that the structural strength of the ship is not adversely affected.

(3)应特别注意,货物与系固设备之间的受力应尽可能均匀。如出现不均匀情况,需进行相应改进。货物系固装置和设备应具有足够的剩余强度,以允许在其使用寿命期间正常磨损。

(3) Particular care should be taken to distribute forces as evenly as practicable between the

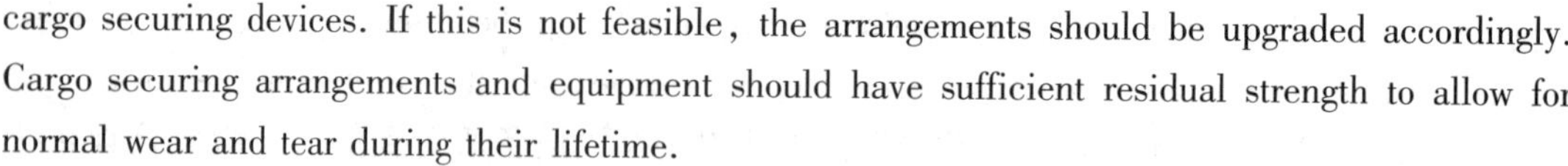

cargo securing devices. If this is not feasible, the arrangements should be upgraded accordingly. Cargo securing arrangements and equipment should have sufficient residual strength to allow for normal wear and tear during their lifetime.

(4)如果货物与船舶甲板或结构物、货物运输单元之间的摩擦不足以避免滑动危险,则应使用适当防滑材料(如软板或衬垫)增大摩擦力。

(4)Where friction between the cargo and the ship's deck or structure or between cargo transport units is insufficient to avoid the risk of sliding, suitable material such as soft boards or dunnage should be used to increase friction.

(5)防止不当积载与系固的主要方法是加强装载监督和检查。在可行的情况下,航行中应定期检查货舱以确保货物、车辆和运输单元安全。船长应确保进入任何封闭空间前,对大气进行充分评估以避免缺氧或易燃有毒气体存在,以确保人员安全。

(5) The principal means of preventing the improper stowage and securing of cargoes is through proper supervision of the loading operation and inspections of the stow. As far as practicable, cargo spaces should be regularly inspected throughout the voyage to ensure that the cargo, vehicles and cargo transport units remain safely secured. The atmosphere in any enclosed space may be incapable of supporting human life through lack of oxygen or it may contain flammable or toxic gases. The master should ensure that it is safe to enter any enclosed space.

(6)在装载货物、货物运输单元或车辆之前,船长应考虑的因素包括:载货处所甲板应尽可能清洁、干燥且无油脂;货物、货物运输单元或车辆处于适装状态并已有效系固;船上已备有所需要的系固设备且性能良好;在切实可行的范围内,货物运输单元和车辆内或车辆上的货物应妥善积载并固定在该单元或车辆上。

(6)The master should ensure, prior to loading of any cargo, cargo transport unit or vehicle that:the deck area for their stowage is, as far as practicable, clean, dry and free from oil and grease; the cargo, cargo transport unit or vehicle appears to be in suitable condition for transport, and can be effectively secured; all necessary cargo securing equipment is on board and in good working condition; and cargo in or on cargo transport units and vehicles is, to the extent practicable, properly stowed and secured on to the unit or vehicle.

2.2.4.3 标准货物的积载与系固

2.2.4.3 Standardized Stowage and Securing Systems

从货物安全积载的角度出发,规则给出了货物单元的相关特征,包括变形、自压实、低摩擦性等特性,以及对货物的影响。

From the perspective of the safe stowage of goods, the code give the relevant characteristics of the cargo unit, including deformation, self-compaction, low friction and other properties and impact on the cargo.

2.2.4.4　半标准货物的积载与系固

2.2.4.4　Semi-standardized Stowage and Securing Systems

运载公路车辆、公路拖车和汽车等特殊货物的滚装船，应根据预期运行情况，按照安全准则设置间距足够大的系固点。

Ro-ro ships intended for the carriage of certain specific cargoes such as road vehicles, systemized cargo-carrying roll-trailers and automobiles, etc., should be provided with securing points spaced sufficiently close to each other for the intended operation of the ship in accordance with the guidelines for securing arrangements.

装载标准货物的滚装船应提供安全积载准则以确保车辆及其货物的安全。应特别考虑积载高度、密度以及货物重心高度的影响。除非道路车辆符合预定航程并具有满足国际海事组织(IMO)相关决议要求的系固点，否则船长不应接受车辆在其船上运输。

Ro-ro ships carrying systemized cargo should be provided with arrangements for the safe stowage and securing of the vehicle and its cargo. Special consideration should be given to the height of the stow, the compactness of the stow and the effects of a high center of gravity of the cargo. The master should not accept a road vehicle for transport on board his ship unless satisfied that the road vehicle is apparently suitable for the intended voyage and is provided with at least the securing points specified in accordance with the guidelines to resolution of IMO.

2.2.4.5　非标准货物的积载与系固

2.2.4.5　Non-standardized Stowage and Securing

《规则》本章及附录就《规则》第3章和第4章未包括的货物的积载与系固(特别是难以在船上积载与系固的货物)提出了一般性建议。需要注意，附录所列货物清单并非详尽无遗，因为若这些货物未得到妥善堆装和系固，可能会导致其他危险。

This chapter and the annexes of this Code provide advice of a general nature for the stowage and securing of cargoes not covered by chapters 3 and 4 of this Code and particularly specific advice for the stowage and securing of cargoes which have proved to be difficult to stow and secure on-board ships. The list of cargoes given in the annexes should not be regarded as exhaustive, as there may be other cargoes which could create hazards if not properly stowed and secured.

《规则》附录中给出的指导意见为有关货物固有问题提供了保障措施，其他的积载与系固方法也可提供同等水平的安全性。任何替代方法必须提供至少与《规则》前言中所列决议、通告和准则所述的安全保障水平相当。

The guidance given in the annexes of this Code provides for certain safeguards against the problems inherent in the cargoes covered. Alternative methods of stowage and securing may afford the same degree of safety. It is imperative that any alternative method chosen should provide a level of securing safety at least equivalent to that described in the resolutions, circulars and guidelines

listed in the foreword to this code.

2.2.4.6 恶劣天气条件下应采取的措施
2.2.4.6 Actions Which May be Taken in Heavy Weather

船长尽可能仔细制订航线计划以避开天气和海况恶劣的海区，是减小过大加速度的方法之一。

One way of reducing excessive accelerations is for the master, as far as possible and practicable, to plan the voyage of the ship carefully so as to avoid areas with severe weather and sea conditions.

避免过大加速的措施有：改变航向、改变航速或两者结合；滞航；尽早避开不利的天气和海况；根据船舶实际稳性情况加排压载水。

Measures to avoid excessive accelerations are: alteration of course or speed or a combination of both; heaving to; early avoidance of areas of adverse weather and sea conditions; and timely ballasting or deballasting to improve the behavior of the ship, taking into account the actual stability conditions.

2.2.4.7 仅在货物移动时应采取的措施
2.2.4.7 Actions Which May be Taken Once Cargo Has Shifted

这些措施包括：改变航向以减小加速度；降低航速以减小加速度和振动；监测船舶的水密度；对货物重新堆装或系固，如可能增设摩擦材料；绕航以寻求避风或避开恶劣海况。只有在确保船舶稳性的前提下方可打排压载水。

The following actions may be considered: alterations of course to reduce accelerations; reductions of speed to reduce accelerations and vibration; monitoring the integrity of the ship; restowing or resecuring the cargo and, where possible, increasing the friction; diversion of routes in order to seek shelter or improved weather and sea conditions. Tank ballasting or deballasting operations should be considered only if the ship has adequate stability.

2.2.5 非标准货物的积载
2.2.5 Stowage of Non-standardized Cargo

2.2.5.1 集装箱
2.2.5.1 Container

对于在非为运输集装箱而专门设计和装备的船舶甲板上装载集装箱时，其积载和系固应注意以下事项：

Safe stowage and securing of containers on deck of ships which are not specially designed and fitted for the purpose of carrying containers should consider the following items:

（1）积载

(1) Stowage

①装载于船上甲板或舱口的集装箱最好沿船首尾方向积载。

①Containers carried on deck or on hatches of such ships should preferably be stowed in the fore-and-aft direction.

②集装箱不应超出船舷。当集装箱悬在舱口或甲板之上时，应提供足够支撑。

②Containers should not extend over the ship's sides. Adequate supports should be provided when containers overhang hatches or deck structures.

③留有为积载和系固需要而便于人员走进的空间。

③Containers should be stowed and secured so as to permit safe access for personnel in the necessary operation of the ship.

④集装箱的积载应能保证其甲板或舱口盖的局部强度。

④Containers should at no time overstress the deck or hatches on which they are stowed.

⑤底层集装箱，当不是放在堆码位置上时，应积载在足够厚度的木材上，其排列方式能将堆放载荷均匀地转移到堆放区上。

⑤Bottom-tier containers, when not resting on stacking devices, should be stowed on timber of sufficient thickness, arranged in such a way as to transfer the stack load evenly on to the structure of the stowage area.

⑥在堆积集装箱时，应选择适当的紧锁装置、锥体或类似的堆积辅助装置。

⑥When stacking containers, use should be made of locking devices, cones, or similar stacking aids, as appropriate, between them.

（2）系固

(2) Securing

①所有集装箱都应有效系固，防止滑动和倾斜。承载集装箱的舱盖应适当系固在船上。

①All containers should be effectively secured in such a way as to protect them from sliding and tipping. Hatch covers carrying containers should be adequately secured to the ship.

②系索用钢丝绳或链条或具有等效强度和特性的材料为宜。

②Lashings should preferably consist of wire ropes or chains or material with equivalent strength and elongation characteristics.

③集装箱的系固可采用图 2.2.1 中的三个方法之一或其他等效方法。

③Containers should be secured using one of the three methods recommended in Figure 2.2.1 or methods equivalent thereto.

④木横支架长度不超过 2 m。

④Timber shoring should not exceed 2 m in length.

⑤钢丝夹应当适量涂抹油脂,并拉紧到钢丝绳的自由端明显受到挤压力,如图 2.2.1 所示。

⑤Wire clips should be adequately greased, and tightened so that the dead end of the wire is visibly compressed, see Figure 2.2.1.

⑥应尽可能使系锁受到均匀的拉力。

⑥Lashings should be kept, when possible, under equal tension.

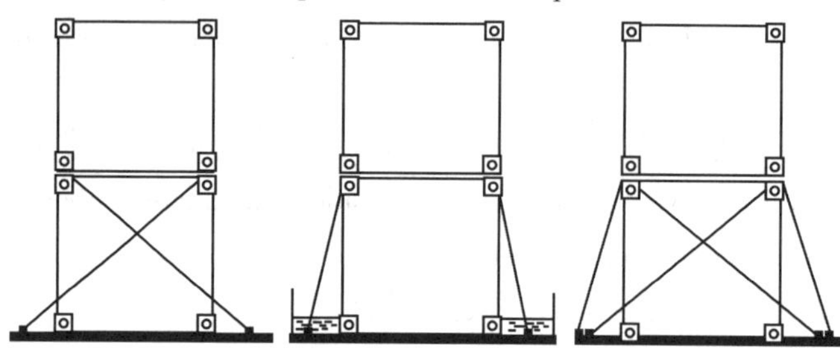

图 2.2.1　集装箱的系固

Figure 2.2.1　Securing of container

2.2.5.2　移动式罐柜

2.2.5.2　Portable Tanks

移动式罐柜指非永久性固定在船上,容积为 450 L 及以上且外壳装有外部稳定构件和运输货物所必备的维修工具和结构性设备的罐柜,可用于装运液体、固体或气体货物。装载气体的移动式罐柜的容积应在 1 000 L 以上。

A portable tank means a tank which is not permanently secured on board the vessel and has a capacity of more than 450 L or more and a shell fitted with external stabilizing members and items of service equipment and structural equipment necessary for the transport of liquids, solids or gases. The capacity for portable tanks for gases is more than 1,000 L.

移动式罐柜应能在不拆卸罐柜结构的情况下装满和卸空,并能在装有货物时直接装上或卸下船舶。

Portable tanks should be capable of being loaded and discharged without the need of removal of their structural equipment and be capable of being lifted onto and off the ship when loaded.

(1) 积载

(1) Stowage

①无论是在甲板上积载还是在舱内积载时,移动式罐柜和容器均应沿船首尾方向。

①Tanks should be stowed in the fore-and-aft direction on or under deck.

②积载后,移动式罐柜和容器的外端应不超出船舷。

②Tanks should be stowed so that they do not extend over the ship's side.

③移动式罐柜积载后,应能使得作业人员安全接近。

③Tanks should be stowed so as to permit safe access for personnel in the necessary operation of the ship.

④积载应能保证甲板和舱口的局部强度;舱盖应固定在船上,防止其翻倒。

④At no time should the tanks overstress the deck or hatches; the hatch covers should be so secured to the ship that tipping of the entire hatch cover is prevented.

⑤未装满的移动式罐柜,其内液体的晃动所产生的压力可使箱体受损时,应禁止装运。

⑤Portable tanks should not be offered for shipment in an ullage condition liable to produce an unacceptable hydraulic force due to surge within the tank.

⑥移动式罐柜用于运输危险货物时,应当按照《国际危规》的规定进行认证,该认证必须由主管机关或其授权机构完成。

⑥Portable tanks for the transport of dangerous goods should be certified in accordance with the provisions of the IMDG Code by the competent approval authority or a body authorized by that authority.

（2）系固

(2) Security

①对系固角的要求:防滑目的时应不大于25°,防倾倒目的时应不小于45°~60°。

①The lashing angles against sliding should not be greater than 25° and against tipping not less than 45° to 60°.

②移动式罐柜的底部结构为非木材或其他低摩擦系数材料时,必要时应在移动式罐柜与甲板间以木料衬垫来增大摩擦系数。

②Whenever necessary, timber should be used between the deck surface and the bottom structure of the portable tank in order to increase friction. This does not apply to tanks on wooden units or with similar bottom material having a high coefficient of friction.

③货件上的系固点应具有适当强度并做出明显标志。

③Securing points on the tank should be of adequate strength and clearly marked.

④若移动式罐柜上无系固点,则系索应环绕其一周,并使两端系固在罐柜同一侧。

④Lashings attached to tanks without securing points should pass around the tank and both ends of the lashing should be secured to the same side of the tank.

⑤当货件积载于甲板或舱口部位上并在其上进行系固时,应考虑甲板或舱口部件的结构强度。

⑤The structural strength of the deck or hatch components should be taken into consideration when tanks are carried thereon and when locating and affixing the securing devices.

2.2.5.3 移动式容器

2.2.5.3 Portable Receptacles

(1) Stowage

(1)积载

①容器最好在甲板上或舱内纵向积载。

①The receptacles should preferably be stowed in the fore-and-aft direction on or under deck.

②容器应予以衬垫,避免直接与钢制甲板接触。除非容器已装入框架内而成为一个组件,否则,在积载容器时应根据需要用木楔制动。液化气容器应直立存放。

②Receptacles should be dunnaged to prevent their resting directly on a steel deck. They should be stowed and chocked as necessary to prevent movement unless mounted in a frame as a unit. Receptacles for liquefied gases should be stowed in an upright position.

③容器在直立积载时,应紧密积载,用合适、坚固的木材制作木架围住。木架下部应垫起,避免与钢制甲板接触。木架内的容器应予固定,以避免移动。木架体应用木楔和系锁固定,以免移动。

③When the receptacles are stowed in an upright position, they should be stowed in a block, cribbed or boxed in with suitable and sound timber. The box or crib should be dunnaged underneath to provide clearance from a steel deck. The receptacles in a box or crib should be braced to prevent movement. The box or crib should be securely chocked and lashed to prevent movement in any direction.

④圆筒应在横向垫木上纵向积载。如可行,在货堆下预先横向放置两根或更多钢丝绳,绕经货堆,系在对侧的系固点上。钢丝绳应用紧固装置收紧,以便货堆密实。在装货期间,为防止圆筒滚动,可使用木楔挤紧。

④Cylinders should be stowed fore-and-aft on athwartships dunnage. Where practicable, the stow should be secured by using two or more wires, laid athwartships prior to loading, and passed around the stow to securing points on opposite sides. The wires are tightened to make a compact stow by using appropriate tightening devices. During loading, wedges may be necessary to prevent cylinders rolling.

⑤装箱中的圆筒,若可行,圆筒应直立积载,若阀口位于顶部,应将护盖盖紧。圆筒应用钢带或类似装置系缚在集装箱底的系固点上,以抵预期航次之严酷。若圆筒不能在封闭集装箱中直立装载,则应装载在顶开门或框架上的集装箱内。

⑤Cylinders should, whenever practicable, be stowed upright with their valves on top and with their protective caps firmly in place. Cylinders should be adequately secured, so as to withstand the rigours of the intended voyage, by means of steel strapping or equivalent means led to lashing points on the container floor. When cylinders cannot be stowed upright in a closed container, they should be carried in an open top or a platform-based container.

(2)系固

(2) Security

甲板上或舱内容器的系固如下:①容器应按所指示位置系固;②可能时,可利用容器上的提升装置进行系固;③系锁应定期检查和定期重新收紧。

Securing of receptacles stowed on or under deck should be as follows: ①lashings should be positioned as shown; ②where possible, the hoisting devices on receptacles should be used to lash them; ③the lashings should be checked and retightened at regular times.

2.2.5.4　滚动(轮载)货物

2.2.5.4　Wheeled-based (Rolling) Cargoes

轮载货物是指所有装有轮子或履带的货物,包括用于装运其他货物的巴士、拖拉机、运土设备和轮式拖车,但不包括挂车和公路列车。

Wheel-based cargoes are all cargoes which are provided with wheels on tracks, including those which are used for the stowage and transport of other cargoes, except trailers and roadtrains, but including buses, tractors, earth-moving equipment, rolltrailers, etc. but except trailers and road trains.

以下是轮载(滚动)货物积载与系固的一般要求:

General recommendations for the stowage and securing of wheeled-based (rolling) cargoes are listed hereunder:

(1)积载滚装货物的处所应干燥、清洁且无油脂。

(1) The cargo spaces in which wheel-based cargo is to be stowed should be dry, clean and free from grease and oil.

(2)滚装货物上应设有合适的且做出明显标志的系固点或设有足够强度的等效装置。

(2) Wheel-based cargoes should be provided with adequate and clearly marked securing points or other equivalent means of sufficient strength to which lashings may be applied.

(3)没有系固点的滚装货物应将可使用系锁的地方做出明显标志。

(3) Wheel-based cargoes which are not provided with securing points should have those places, where lashings may be applied, clearly marked.

(4)无橡胶轮的或履带下表面无摩擦力增加层的滚装货物,应装载在垫木或其他增加摩擦力的材料上,如软板、橡胶垫等。

(4) Wheel-based cargoes, which are not provided with rubber wheels or tracks without friction-increasing lower surface, should always be stowed on wooden dunnage or other friction-increasing material such as soft boards, rubber mats, etc.

(5)滚装货物装载在积载位置上时,应使用刹车或止动装置(如有的话)。

(5) When in stowage position, the brakes of a wheel-based unit, if so equipped, should be set.

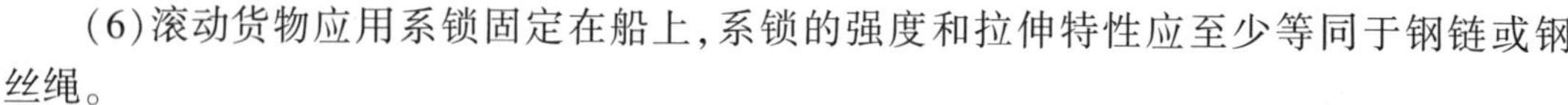

(6)滚动货物应用系锁固定在船上,系锁的强度和拉伸特性应至少等同于钢链或钢丝绳。

(6) Wheel-based cargoes should be secured to the ship by lashings made of material having strength and elongation characteristics at least equivalent to steel chain or wire.

(7)若可能,不能满舱满载的滚装货物,应紧靠船舷积载,或积载在设有足够系固点的处所,或在货物处所集中积载。

(7) Where possible, wheel-based cargoes, carried as part cargo, should be stowed close to the ship's side or in stowage positions which are provided with sufficient securing points of sufficient strength, or be block-stowed from side to side of the cargo space.

(8)若可能,为防止没有足够系固点滚装货物的横向移动,这些货物应靠船舷紧凑积载,或由所装载集装箱等其他货件阻挡。

(8) To prevent any lateral shifting of wheel-based cargoes not provided with adequate securing points, such cargoes should, where practicable, be stowed close to the ship's side and close to each other, or be blocked off by other suitable cargo units such as loaded containers, etc.

(9)若可能,为防止滚装货物移动,这些货物应沿船长方向而不沿横向积载。若滚装货物不得不横向积载,则必须加具有足够强度的系索。

(9) To prevent the shifting of wheel-based cargoes, it is, where practicable, preferable to stow those cargoes in a fore-and-aft direction rather than athwartships. If wheel-based cargoes are inevitably stowed athwart-ships, additional securing of sufficient strength may be necessary.

(10)滚装货物的轮子应用木楔塞牢制动。

(10) The wheels of wheel-based cargoes should be blocked to prevent shifting by wedges.

(11)装载在滚装组件内的货物应充分系固在积载底板上,若有合适设施还应系固到其边板上。设置在滚装组件上的杆件、臂状物或转塔等外部活动部件,应锁牢或系固在其位置上。

(11) Cargoes stowed on wheel-based units should be adequately secured to stowage platforms or, where provided with suitable means, to its sides. Any movable external components attached to a wheel-based unit, such as derricks, arms or turrets should be adequately locked or secured in position.

2.2.5.5 机车、变压器等重货

2.2.5.5 Heavy Cargo Items Such as Locomotives, Transformers, etc.

(1)货物资料

(1) Cargo information

应向船长提供有关任何待运重型货物的详尽信息,以便能正确规划其积载和系固。该资料至少包括:总重、带有图纸/图片说明的主要尺寸和形状(如可能)、重心位置、基座面积及特定基座的防护措施、提升点和吊货位置、系固点及其强度等详情。

The master should be provided with sufficient information on any heavy cargo offered for shipment so that he can properly plan its stowage and securing; the information should at least include the following: gross mass; principal dimensions with drawings or pictorial descriptions, if possible; location of the center of gravity; bedding areas and particular bedding precautions if applicable; lifting points or slinging positions; and securing points, where provided, including details of their strength.

(2)积载位置

(2) Location of stowage

积载位置的选择,应顾及船舶加速度的典型分布:较小加速度发生在船中和甲板下方;较大加速度发生在船尾和甲板上方。

When considering the location for stowing a heavy cargo item, the typical distribution of accelerations on the ship should be kept in mind: lower accelerations occur in the midship sections and below the weather deck; and higher accelerations occur in the end sections and above the weather deck.

①为了保证局部构件不受损伤,在甲板或舱盖上装载重件时,应用足够强度的木材或钢梁将重件重量传递到船舶结构上。

①To ensure that the local components are not damaged, when heavy items are loaded on the deck or hatch cover, timber or steel beams of sufficient strength shall be used to transfer the weight of the heavy items to the ship structure.

②重件货物最好纵向积载。

②Heavy items should preferably be stowed in the fore-and-aft direction.

③当重件货物在甲板上积载时,如可能应考虑具体航次"上风舷"的不利影响。

③When heavy items are to be stowed on deck, the expected "weather side" of the particular voyage should be taken into account if possible.

④在开敞集装箱、ISO 货盘或带有/适用于集装箱船的框架箱中装载重件货,应按《规则》本章的规定进行积载和系固,但在此类集装箱中,货物的积载和系固须遵循国际海事组织(IMO)、国际劳工组织(ILO)、联合国欧洲经济委员会(UNECE)有关货物运输单元包装的准则。

④While the stowage and securing of open containers, ISO platforms or platform-based containers (flatracks) on a container ship or a ship fitted or adapted for the carriage of containers should follow the information of this chapter in this Code, but the stowage and securing of the cargo in such containers should be carried out in accordance with the IMO, ILO, UNECE Guidelines for packing of cargo transport units.

⑤所使用的国际标准框架箱应系合适的类型,具有足够的强度,并且系固点可承受足够大的负荷。

⑤The ISO standard platform, etc., used should be of a suitable type with regard to strength and MSL of the securing points.

⑥尽可能均匀分布货件的重量。

⑥The weight of the heavy cargo item should be properly distributed.

⑦必要时,装载在国际标准框架箱内的重件货不仅要系在框架箱内还应系固在邻近箱上或船舶的固定构件上。

⑦Where deemed necessary, the heavy cargo items carried on ISO platforms or platform-based containers, should not only be secured to the platforms or platform-based containers, but also to neighboring platforms, or to securing points located at fixed structure of the ship.

(3)系固

(3) Securing

①除了货件底部为木支架或橡胶胎等类似摩擦系数大的材料外,在积载处所表面与货件装置底部应尽可能使用木材衬垫以增大摩擦。

①Whenever possible, timber should be used between the stowage surface and the bottom of the unit in order to increase friction. This does not apply to items on wooden cradles or on rubber tyres or with similar bottom material having a high coefficient of friction.

②保持最佳系固角,防滑目的时为25°,防倾倒目的时为45°~60°。

②The optimum lashing angle against sliding is about 25°, while the optimum lashing angle against tipping is generally found between 45°and 60°.

③若重件是在加了润滑油的滑板上或以降低摩擦力的其他方法拖到位置上,防滑系索的数量相应增加。

③If a heavy cargo item has been dragged into position on greased skid boards or other means to reduce friction, the number of lashings used to prevent sliding should be increased accordingly.

④因条件所限,仅可以较大系固角系固时,则必须用木支柱、焊接配件或其他可行方法防止滑动,但任何焊接应按规定的热工程序进行。

④If, owing to circumstances, lashings can be set at large angles only, sliding must be prevented by timber shoring, welded fittings or other appropriate means. Any welding should be carried out in accordance with accepted hot work procedures.

⑤伸出舷外的重货件应另外增加系索,使其作用于纵向和垂向方向上。

⑤Items projecting over the ship's side should be additionally secured by lashings acting in longitudinal and vertical directions.

⑥货物上的系固点应具有适当的强度,且具有明显的标志。应注意,为公路或铁路货物运输设计的系固点可能不适用于船舶。

⑥If lashings are to be attached to securing points on the item, these securing points should be of adequate strength and clearly marked. It should be borne in mind that securing points designed for road or rail transport may not be suitable for securing the items on board ship.

⑦货件上无适合系固点时,系索应绕货物一周,并使两端系固在货件的同一侧。

⑦Lashings attached to items without securing points should pass around the item, or a rigid part thereof, and both ends of the lashing should be secured to the same side of the unit.

⑧正确使用钢丝绳、夹具。绳夹的鞍座部分应装在动载段，U 形螺栓应装在静载段或缩短端段。

⑧Connecting elements and tightening devices should be used in the correct way. The saddle portion of the clip should be applied to the live load segment and the U-bolt to the dead or shortened end segment.

2.2.5.6　Coiled Sheet Steel

2.2.5.6　成卷钢板

通常，成卷钢板即卷钢每卷毛重在 10 t 以上。本节只给出卷钢的卧式积载方法，因为立式装载方法通常不存在系固问题。

Normally, coils of sheet steel have a gross mass in excess of 10 tonnes each. This section deals only with coiled sheet steel stowed on the round. Vertical stowage is not dealt with because this type of stowage does not create any special securing problems.

(1) 积载

(1) Stowage

①卷钢应从底层堆起，且底部为横向放置的垫木。

①Coils should be given bottom stow and, whenever possible, be stowed in regular tiers from side to side of the ship.

②卷钢应存放在横向铺设的垫木上。卷钢的轴线应与船首尾方向一致，紧凑堆积，最下层在装载时为防滚移，可用木楔塞住。

②Coils should be stowed on dunnage laid athwartships. Coils should be stowed with their axes in the fore-and-aft direction. Each coil should be stowed against its neighbor. Wedges should be used as stoppers when necessary during loading and discharging to prevent shifting.

③每排最后一卷放在邻近的两卷上边。该卷质量将起到固定该排其他卷材的作用。

③The final coil in each row should normally rest on the two adjacent coils. The mass of this coil will lock the other coils in the row.

④如有必要，上层卷材应压在下层卷材接缝处。

④If it is necessary to load a second tier over the first, then the coils should be stowed in between the coils of the first tier.

⑤在最高一层卷钢中，钢卷之间的任何空当应加以适当填塞。

⑤Any void space between coils in the topmost tier should be adequately secured.

(2) Securing

(2) 系固

①一般情况下，最高一层的最后 3 排应进行系固。

①In general, the last 3 rows of the highest level should be secured.

②建议采用奥林匹克系固法或成组系固法。

②It is recommended to use the Olympic lashing method or the group lashing method.

③对无外包装的顶层不宜使用成组系固法,顶层最后一排应使用垫木填塞和钢丝绳系固,钢丝绳应从一侧到另一侧拉紧,使用附加钢丝绳拉到舱壁。

③For the top layer without outer packaging, it is not advisable to use the group securing method. The last row of the top layer should be secured with a padding and wire rope. The wire rope should be tightened from one side to the other and pulled to the bulkhead with an additional wire rope.

④卷材铺满整个舱室底面积并有良好的支撑,除用于固定的卷材外,不再需要用系索固定。

④The coil covers the entire floor area of the cabin and has good support. It is no longer required to be fixed with a lanyard except for the fixed coil.

⑤系索通常为具有足够强度和防止利刃损坏保护的钢丝绳。

⑤The lanyard is typically a wire rope that has sufficient strength and protection against sharp edge damage.

2.2.5.7 金属重件

2.2.5.7 Heavy Metal Products

金属重件指金属制成的重货件,如棒材、管材、盘条、板材和线材卷等。海上运输金属重件会给船舶造成下述危险:

Heavy metal products include any heavy item made of metal, such as bars, pipes, rods, plates, wire coils, etc. The transport of heavy metal products by sea exposes the ship to the following principal hazards:

- 若积载中产生超过船体许用应力或甲板允许负荷,则船舶结构将承受超限压力。
- Overstressing of the ship's structure if the permissible hull stress or permissible deck loading is exceeded.
- 由于稳性高度过大造成横摇周期过短,船舶结构将承受超限应力。
- Overstressing of the ship's structure as a result of a short roll period caused by excessive metacentric height.
- 货物因系固不当而移动,则会导致船舶稳性丧失或船体受到损坏。
- Cargo shifting because of inadequate securing resulting in a loss of stability or damage to the hull or both.

由此可见,金属重件的积载和系固非常重要。

It can be seen from the above that the stowage and securing of heavy metal products are very important.

(1)积载

(1) Stowage

①积载金属重件货物的处所应干净、干燥、无油脂。

①The cargo spaces in which heavy metal products are to be stowed should be clean, dry and free from grease and oil.

②货物重量的分布应避免使船体受到过大应力。

②The cargo should be so distributed as to avoid undue hull stress.

③积载中,不得超过甲板和船底的许用负荷。

③The permissible deck and tank top loading should not be exceeded.

④货件应从船舶一舷向另一舷密实积载,货件间不留空当,必要时用木块塞紧。

④Cargo items should be stowed compactly from one side of the ship to the other leaving no voids between them and using timber blocks between items if necessary.

⑤在可能和可行时,货件表面应保持平整。

⑤Cargo should be stowed level whenever possible and practicable.

⑥对于薄板和小包货件,纵向和横向交替积载的效果较好,层次间应使用足量的干垫木或其他材料以增加摩擦力。

⑥In the case of thin plates and small parcels, alternate fore-and-aft and athwartships stowage has proved satisfactory. The friction should be increased by using sufficient dry dunnage or other material between the different layers.

⑦管材、铁轨、型钢和钢坯等应沿纵向积载,以避免货物移动对船舷造成损伤。

⑦Pipes, rails, rolled sections, billets, etc., should be stowed in the fore-and-aft direction to avoid damage to the sides of the ship if the cargo shifts.

⑧线材卷应平放积载,使每卷与邻卷相靠。上层线材卷应压缝叠装在下层卷上。

⑧Wire coils should be stowed flat so that each coil rests against an adjacent coil. The coils in successive tiers should be stowed so that each coil overlaps the coils below.

⑨对像桶一样卧式积载的线材垛系固时,应特别注意,若顶层未系固则货堆中部的线材卷会因为船舶的运动而被下边的货件挤出货堆。

⑨When securing wire coils stowed on their sides in several layers like barrels, it is essential to remember that, unless the top layer is secured, the coils lying in the stow can be forced out of the stow by the coils below on account of the ship's motions.

(2)系固

(2)Securing

①货物表面应予以系固。每根系索应相互独立地对货物表面施加垂向压力,不得留有未受力的货件。

①The surface of the cargo should be secured. Whenever the surface of the cargo is to be secured, the lashings should be independent of each other, exert vertical pressure on the surface of the cargo, and be so positioned that no part of the cargo is unsecured.

②撑柱应由牢固、无裂纹的木材制成,其尺寸应足以抵御加速度力。船舶的每根肋骨应设一个撑柱,但间隔不应小于1 m。

②The shoring should be made of strong, non-splintering wood and adequately sized to with-

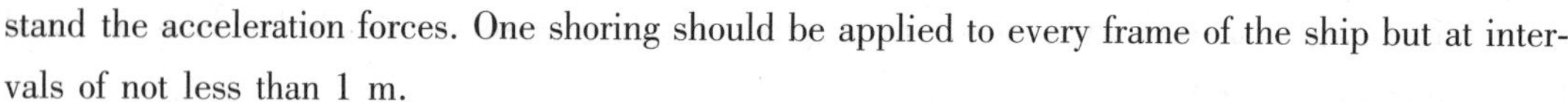

stand the acceleration forces. One shoring should be applied to every frame of the ship but at intervals of not less than 1 m.

③货件尤其最高一层的货件,可在其上部装载其他货物或用钢丝绳、木楔或其他材料系固。

③The cargo, and especially the topmost layer, can be secured by having other cargo stowed on top of it, or lashing by wire, chocking off or similar means.

④当金属重件的积载没有从一舷铺满到另一舷时,应特别注意对其进行充分系固。

④Whenever heavy metal products are not stowed from side to side of the ship, special care should be taken to secure such stowages adequately.

⑤线材卷应密实积载,用牢固的系固装置系固。如果线材卷之间存在空隙或者货舱的侧面或末端有缝隙,应对其进行充分系固。

⑤Wire coils should be tightly stowed together and substantial securing arrangements should be used. Where voids between coils are unavoidable or where there are voids at the sides or ends of the cargo space, the stow should be adequately secured.

2.2.5.8 锚链

2.2.5.8 Anchor Chains

船舶和海上结构物的锚链通常以捆装或散装形式运输。只要在装载过程中采取一定的安全措施,锚链可以成捆地直接装载在积载处所,或沿着船舶整舱长度,或部分舱长纵向积载,而不需做进一步处理。

Anchor chains for ships and offshore structures are usually carried in bundles or in continuous lengths. Provided certain safety measures are followed prior to, during and after stowage, anchor chains may be lowered directly onto the place of stowage in bundles without further handling or stowed longitudinally either along the ship's entire cargo space or part thereof.

(1)积载锚链的货舱应清洁和无油脂。

(1)Cargo spaces in which chains are stowed should be clean and free from oil and grease.

(2)锚链只应装载在覆有永久木质铺板的,覆有足够厚度垫木层的,或覆有其他增加摩擦力材料的表面上。锚链不得直接在金属表面上积载。

(2) Chains should only be stowed on surfaces which are permanently covered either by wooden ceiling or by sufficient layers of dunnage or other suitable friction-increasing materials. Chains should never be stowed directly on metal surfaces.

(3)成捆锚链可直接吊装到积载处,而不需要做进一步处理,吊索应留在锚链上,另用钢丝绳绕在锚链捆上系妥。

(3)Chains in bundles, which are lifted directly onto their place of stowage without further handling, should be left with their lifting wires attached and should preferably be provided with additional wires around the bundles for lashing purposes.

(4)不必用垫木等增加摩擦力的材料来隔开锚链层,因为锚链捆会相互夹持。

(4) It is not necessary to separate layers of chain with friction-increasing material such as dunnage because chain bundles will grip each other.

(5)在可能和可行时,每层锚链的积载应在接近船舷处开始或结束。应注意保证货堆的密实。

(5) Stowage of each layer of chain should, whenever possible and practicable, commence and terminate close to the ship's side. Care should be taken to achieve a tight stow.

(6)锚链捆的最高一层应用系索系在船舶两舷舱壁上。锚链捆可用系索独立或成组系固。

(6) The top layer of chain bundles should be secured to both sides of the ship by suitable lashings. Bundles may be lashed independently or in a group, using the lifting wires.

(7)根据预计的气候和海况、航次长短和特性及锚链上层货物的性质,每一货堆的顶层应利用具有足够强度的系索系固,系索在货堆上的间距要适当,以便固定住整个货堆。

(7) Bearing in mind the expected weather and sea conditions, the length and nature of the voyage and the nature of the cargo to be stowed on top of the chain, the top layer of each stow should be secured by lashings of adequate strength crossing the stow at suitable intervals and thus holding down the entire stow.

2.2.5.9　散装废金属

2.2.5.9　Metal Scrap in Bulk

散装废金属指因尺寸、形状和质量而难以紧密积载的金属废料,但不包括金属钻屑、刨屑和切屑等金属废料,后者应以《IMSBC 规则》规定运输。

Metal scrap in bulk is the metal scrap which is difficult to stow compactly because of its size, shape and mass, but does not apply to metal scrap such as metal borings, shavings or turnings, the carriage of which is addressed by IMSBC.

运输废金属对船舶的危害为:

The hazards involved in transporting metal scrap include:

(1)因货堆移动造成船舶横倾。

(1) Shifting of the stow which in turn can cause a list.

(2)个别重件移动会戳穿水线下船侧外板而致使船舱严重进水。

(2) Shifting of individual heavy pieces which can rupture the side plating below the waterline and give rise to serious flooding.

(3)舱底板或甲板间底板超负荷。

(3) Excessive loading on tank tops or 'tween-decks.

(4)稳性高度过大造成剧烈横摇。

(4) Violent rolling caused by excessive metacentric height.

装货前,舱壁下部护条应用厚实垫木保护以防舱壁受损,避免沉重锐利的废料与船侧板接触。只用木板防护的空气管、测深管、污水井及压载水管应做相应保护。

Before loading, the lower battens of the spar ceiling should be protected by substantial dunnage to reduce damage and to prevent heavy and sharp pieces of scrap coming in contact with the ship's side plates. Air and sounding pipes, and bilge and ballast lines protected only by wooden boards, should be similarly protected.

装货时,应注意第一批装入货物的落放高度不至于造成舱底受损。如果轻的和重的废金属在同一舱内装载,则应先装重废金属。废金属不得装载在金属屑或类似废料上部。废金属应落实、均匀积载,不留空当,不留悬空面。

When loading, care should be taken to ensure that the first loads are not dropped from a height which could damage the tank tops. If light and heavy scrap is to be stowed in the same cargo space, the heavy scrap should be loaded first. Scrap should never be stowed on top of metal turnings, or similar forms of waste metal. Scrap should be compactly and evenly stowed with no voids or unsupported faces of loosely held scrap.

废金属重件若移动会造成船侧板或端舱壁损坏,因而应在上面加压载或用系索系固。因废料的性质,使用撑木一般无效。应注意避免舱底板和甲板超负荷。

Heavy pieces of scrap, which could cause damage to the side plating or end bulkheads if they were to move, should be overstowed or secured by suitable lashings. The use of shoring is unlikely to be effective because of the nature of the scrap. Care should be taken to avoid excessive loading on tank tops and decks.

2.2.5.10 挠性中型散装容器

2.2.5.10 Flexible Intermediate Bulk Containers

挠性中型散装容器指容量不大于 3 m^3 (3 000 L),用于装运固体的挠性移动式包装,使用机械装卸,应对其进行一次使用或多次使用检测,以验证其在运输和承载应力方面的可靠性。

A flexible intermediate bulk container (FIBC) means a flexible portable packaging to be used for the transport of solids with a capacity of not more than 3 m^3 (3,000 L) designed for mechanical handling and tested for its satisfactory resistance to transport and bearing stresses in a one-way type or multi-purpose design.

(1) 积载

(1) Stowage

①如可行,积载处所应是矩形的并且没有障碍物。

①The cargo spaces should, where practicable, be rectangular in shape and free of obstructions.

②积载处所应清洁、干燥、无油污和铁钉。

②The stowage space should be clean, dry and free from oil and nails.

③当挠性中型散装容器仅在舱口下舱位积载时,应在货物两侧及前后两端用其他货物

或物料阻挡,以使其得到充分的支撑。

③When FIBCs are stowed in the hatchway only, the space in the wings and the forward and aft end of the cargo space should be loaded with other suitable cargo or blocked off in such a way that the FIBCs are adequately supported.

④以船宽与该货物挠性中型散装容器之商作为横向积载的容器数,余数即为空当。积载时应从两舷向中间逼近,使空当居于舱口中央。

④The width of the ship divided by the width of the FIBC will give the number of FIBCs which can be stowed athwartships and the void space left. If there is a void space, the stowage of the FIBCs should start from both sides to the center, so that any void space will be in the center of the hatchway.

⑤挠性中型散装容器堆积应尽可能紧凑,空当应塞牢。

⑤FIBCs should be stowed as close as possible against each other and any void space should be chocked off.

⑥装妥第一层后,以后各层应以相同的方法积载,使其覆盖住下边的挠性中型散装容器。若后层有空当,也应留在舱口中央,并予以塞牢。

⑥The next layers should be stowed in a similar way so that the FIBCs fully cover the FIBCs underneath. If in this layer a void space is left, it should also be chocked off in the center of the hatchway.

⑦若舱口间有足够空间可在其下货面上装载另一层容器,则应确定舱口围板能否作为围壁,如果不能则需采取措施防止挠性中型散装容器积堆移动到船舶两侧。否则挠性中型散装容器应自舱口围板的一侧装载至另一侧。在这两种情况下,空当均应留在中央部位予以塞牢。

⑦When there is sufficient room in the hatchway on top of the layers underneath to stow another layer, it should be established whether the coamings can be used as bulkheads. If not, measures should be taken to prevent the FIBCs shifting to the open space in the wings. Otherwise, the FIBCs should be stowed from one coaming to another. In both cases, any void space should be in the center and should be chocked off.

(2)系固

(2) Securing

①在舱内仅用二层甲板间舱或底舱的部分空间装载挠性中型散装容器时,应采取措施以防止移动,用格板或胶合板抵住容器后使用钢丝绳从一侧到另一侧系牢。

①In cases where only a part of a 'tween-deck or lower hold is used for the stowage of FIBCs, measures should be taken to prevent the FIBCs from shifting. These measures should include sufficient gratings or plywood sheets placed against the FIBCs and the use of wire lashings from side to side to secure the FIBC cargo.

②航行中,应定期或在恶劣天气前后对系固用的钢丝绳和胶合板进行检查,必要时应重新收紧。

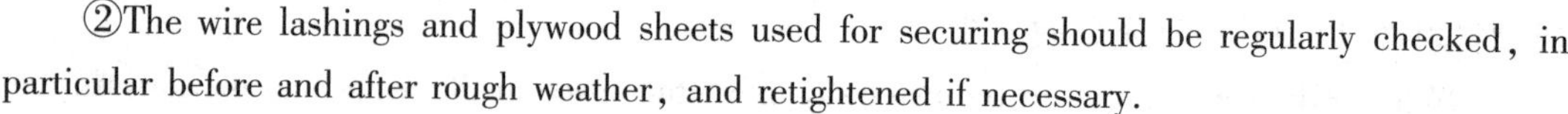

②The wire lashings and plywood sheets used for securing should be regularly checked, in particular before and after rough weather, and retightened if necessary.

2.2.5.11 舱装原木

2.2.5.11 The Under-deck Stowage of Log

为保证甲板下木材货物的安全运输,以下部分提出了为安全装运而采取的积载和其他安全运营措施建议。

The purpose of this subsection is to recommend safe practices for the under-deck stowage of logs and other operational safety measures designed to ensure the safe transport of such cargoes.

(1)装载准备工作

(1)Prior to loading

①了解装货舱位及待装原木的特点,如装货舱位的构造(长、宽、深)、容积、原木的长度、体积(原木平均值)以及设备装载原木的能力等。

①Each cargo space configuration (length, breadth and depth), the cubic bale capacity of the respective cargo spaces, the various lengths of logs to be loaded, the cubic volume (log average), and the capacity of the gear to be used to load the logs should be determined.

②根据上述资料,提前制订积载计划,以最大限度地利用可用空间;甲板下的积载能力越大,甲板上的载货越安全。

②Using the above information, a pre-stow plan should be developed to allow the maximum utilization of the available space; the better the under-deck stowage, the more cargo can safely be carried on deck.

③检查货舱及相关设备,以查明舱内构件、骨架和设备的情况是否会影响货物的安全运输。如有损坏,应以适当方式修复。

③The cargo spaces and related equipment should be examined to determine whether the condition of structural members, framework and equipment could affect the safe carriage of the log cargo. Any damage discovered during such an examination should be repaired in an appropriate manner.

④检查舱底水吸口滤网,保持清洁、有效,防止碎片进入污水排放系统。

④The bilge suction screens should be examined to ensure they are clean, effective and properly maintained to prevent the admission of debris into the bilge piping system.

⑤舱底井应无树皮、木屑等异物。

⑤The bilge wells should be free of extraneous material such as wood bark and wood splinters.

⑥确认污水泵处于随时可用状态。妥善的维护和操作对船舶安全至关重要。为防止污水管系堵塞,船上尚应配备足够功率和扬程的移动式排水泵。

⑥The capacity of the bilge pumping system should be ascertained. A properly maintained and operating system is crucial for the safety of the ship. A portable dewatering pump of sufficient capacity and lift will provide additional insurance against a clogged bilge line.

⑦货舱舷侧护板、管道护罩等用于保护内壳的设施,应在其原有位置上。

⑦Side sparring, pipe guards, etc., designed to protect internal hull members should be in place.

⑧船长应确保任何高压载水阀门的开闭情况在航海日志中正确记载。考虑到高压载水舱须便于装卸及《1966 年国际载重线公约》第 22 条 1 款规定须在舷外排水管道安装阀门,船长需确保泵阀关闭并得到适当监控,以防止水意外进入压载舱内而造成船舶横倾、甲板货物移动甚至船舶倾覆。

⑧The master should ensure that the opening and closing of any high ballast dump valves are properly recorded in the ship's log. Given that such high ballast tanks are necessary to facilitate loading and bearing in mind regulation 22(1) of the International Convention on Load Lines, 1966, which requires a screw-down valve fitted in gravity overboard drain lines, the master should ensure that the dump valves are properly monitored to preclude the accidental readmission of water into these tanks. Leaving these tanks open to the sea could lead to an apparently inexplicable list, a shift of deck cargo, and potential capsize.

(2)装载期间

(2) During loading operations

①舱内尽量装满装实,以移除尽可能多的空当。按上轻下重的原则,应将最重的原木首先装入货舱,以增大货舱内装载量并尽可能降低货物重心,这样,则有利于甲板木材的装载。

①The logs should be stowed compactly, thereby eliminating as many voids as is practicable. The amount and the vertical center of gravity of the logs stowed under deck will govern the amount of cargo that can be safely stowed on deck. In considering this principle, the heaviest logs should be loaded first into the cargo spaces.

②原木在舱内一般纵向堆装,较长者应装在舱的前、后区域。若纵向长度间有空当,应在原木长度允许的情况下尽可能用横向积载的原木填满空当。

② Logs should generally be stowed compactly in a fore-and-aft direction, with the longer lengths towards the forward and aft areas of the space. If there is a void in the space between the fore and aft lengths, it should be filled with logs stowed athwartships so as to fill in the void across the breadth of the spaces as completely as the length of the logs permits.

③若舱内仅能纵向积载一根原木,任何前后空当均应以横向积载的原木填入。

③Where the logs in the spaces can only be stowed fore-and-aft in one length, any remaining void forward or aft should be filled with logs stowed athwartships so as to fill in the void across the breadth of the space as completely as the length of the logs permits.

④横向空当应在装货过程中逐层填入。

④Athwartship voids should be filled tier by tier as loading progresses.

⑤原木粗端应首尾向交替放置,以达到较平坦的积载效果,但内底舷弧过大者除外。

⑤Butt ends of the logs should be alternately reversed to achieve a more level stowage, except

where excess sheer on the inner bottom is encountered.

⑥若舱宽大于舱口宽度,应从装货高度至 2 m 始将纵向原木滑入舱口两侧舱位,以尽可能避免货堆呈金字塔形。

⑥If the cargo hold width is greater than the hatch width, longitudinal logs should be slid into the compartments on both sides of the hatch starting from a loading height of 2 meters to avoid forming a pyramid-shaped cargo stack as much as possible.

⑦当货物堆至约甲板下 1 m 时,应减小每吊原木的尺寸,以便其全在余下空间积载。

⑦When the logs are stowed to a height of about 1 m below the forward or aft athwartship hatch coaming, the size of the lift of logs should be reduced to facilitate stowing of the remaining area.

(3)航行期间

(3) During the voyage

①时常检测船舶的横倾角和横摇周期。

①The ship's heeling angle and rolling period should be checked, in a seaway, on a regular basis.

②楔子、纱头、锤子和活动泵(如有)应放在易取处。

②Wedges, wastes, hammers and portable pump, if provided, should be stored in an easily accessible place.

③船长或负责船员应注意下舱安全:确定货舱的通风方式(自然或机械风);测定不同高度处氧气含量;对于进入封闭空间的人,如怀疑通风不足,则需戴自给式呼吸机。

③The master or a responsible officer should ensure that it is safe to enter an enclosed cargo space by: ensuring that the space has been thoroughly ventilated by natural or mechanical means; testing the atmosphere of the space at different levels for oxygen deficiency and harmful vapor where suitable instruments are available; and requiring self-contained breathing apparatus to be worn by all persons entering the space where there is any doubt as to the adequacy of ventilation or testing before entry.

2.2.5.12 成组货物

2.2.5.12 Unit Load

成组货物是指将若干包装货放置或堆叠在托盘等装载板上,并通过捆扎、收缩包装或其他合适的方式过行系固的货物;或放置在货箱等保护性外包装里的货物;或作为一吊并永久性系固在一起的货物。

Stowage of unit load means that a number of packages are either placed or stacked, and secured by strapping, shrink-wrapping or other suitable means, on a load board such as a pallet; or placed in a protective outer packaging such as a pallet box; or permanently secured together in a sling.

(1)积载处所应清洁、干燥并无油脂。

(1)The cargo spaces of the ship in which unit loads will be stowed should be clean, dry and free from oil and grease.

(2)甲板,包括舱底板,应是水平的。

(2)The decks, including the tank top, should be flush all over.

(3)货物积载处所最好在水平和垂直方向上都是矩形的,船首尾货舱应增设支架,将积载区域形状尽可能形成一规则的方形体。

(3)The cargo spaces should preferably be of a rectangular shape, horizontally and vertically. Cargo spaces of another shape in forward holds or in ‘tween-decks should be transformed into a rectangular shape both athwartships and longitudinally by the use of suitable timber.

(4)成组货物与船舶之间不应有任何空当,以防货物倾斜。

(4)The unit loads should be stowed without any void space between the loads and the ship's sides to prevent the unit loads from racking.

(5)如必要,成组货物积载后应能从货堆的所有面上系固。

(5)The unit loads should be stowed in such a way that securing, if needed, can be performed on all sides of the stow.

(6)货物重叠堆积时,应注意货盘强度和货物形状及特性。

(6)When unit loads have to be stowed on top of each other, attention should be paid to the strength of pallets and the shape and the condition of the unit loads.

(7)系固时的注意事项

(7)Precautions during fastening

应确保货物块状堆积,不留空当。

Block stowage should be ensured and no void space be left between the unit loads.

①一边不靠的系固

①Securing when stowed athwartships

当成组货物在底舱或二层甲板内沿舱壁从一舷到另一舷堆装时,应将格板或胶合板垂直靠置于成组货物堆的外侧。需用钢丝绳从一舷到另一舷进行系固,确保格板或胶合板紧密贴靠货堆。此外,可在货堆上方沿舱壁不同间距处设置钢丝绳,并与水平放置的钢丝绳相连,以进一步收紧货堆。

When unit loads are stowed in a lower hold or in a ‘tween-deck against a bulkhead from side to side, gratings or plywood sheets should be positioned vertically against the stack of the unit loads. Wire lashings should be fitted from side to side keeping the gratings or plywood sheets tight against the stow. Additionally, lashing wires can be fitted at different spacing from the bulkhead over the stow to the horizontally placed wire lashings in order to further tighten the stow.

②两边不靠的系固

②Stowage in a wing of a cargo space and free at two sides

若成组货物积载于舱内一舷的前部或后部即两边不靠积载并存在两个货移方向，应紧贴货堆未紧固侧垂直安置格板或胶合板。钢丝绳应从舷侧绕过货堆至另一侧系固在舱壁上。另外，需在货堆角隅处安装格板或胶合板以防止角隅处货物因系固而损坏。

When unit loads are stowed in the forward or after end of a cargo space and the possibility of shifting in two directions exists, gratings or plywood sheets should be positioned vertically to the stack faces of the unit loads of the non-secured sides of the stow. Wire lashings should be taken around the stow from the wings to the bulkhead. Where the wires can damage the unit loads (particularly on the corners of the stow), gratings or plywood sheets should be positioned in such a way that no damage can occur on corners.

③三边不靠的系固

③Stowage free at three sides

货物沿船舷一侧积载，即三边不靠积载，因而具有三个货移方向，应紧贴货堆系固而垂直安置格板或胶合板。在货堆角隅处，应特别注意防止系索损坏货物。应结合各侧格板或胶合板在不同高度上使用钢丝绳收紧货堆。

When unit loads are stowed against the ship's sides in such a way that shifting is possible from three sides, gratings or plywood sheets should be positioned vertically against the stack faces of the unit loads. Special attention should be paid to the corners of the stow to prevent damage to the unit loads by the wire lashings. Wire lashing at different heights should tighten the stow together with the gratings or plywood sheets at the sides.

④可以铝质撑柱或足够强度的板条代替格板或胶合板。

④Instead of gratings or plywood sheets, other possibilities are the use of aluminium stanchions or battens of sufficient strength.

2.3 货物运输管理

2.3 Cargo Care When En route

货物的航行管理对于安全运输货物起着至关重要的作用，是海运货物的非常重要的一环。

The navigation management of cargoes plays a vital role in the safe transport of cargoes and is a very important part of shipping cargoes.

2.3.1　货物管理的主要项目
2.3.1　Main Items of Cargo Management

(1)检查货物的状况
(1) Check cargo condition

航行途中经常下舱检查货物的状态,如货物是否移动、温度变化是否影响货物质量、是否汗湿及变质等。如果任何影响货物质量的因素在持续发展,应采取必要的防范措施。

During the voyage, the condition of the cargo should be often checked such as whether the cargo shifts, whether the temperature changes affect the quality of the cargo, whether it is wet or deteriorated, etc. If any factors affecting the quality of the cargo are continuously developed, necessary precautions should be taken.

(2)测量并排除舱内污水
(2) Measure and exclude bilge

经常测量污水沟或污水井内的污水并及时排除,防止污水过多而浸湿舱内货物。当污水突然增多时,应查明原因并采取相应措施。

Frequently measure the remaining bilge in bilge wells and eliminate them in time to prevent excessive bilge and soak the cargo in the hold. When the bilge suddenly increases, the cause should be identified and appropriate measures taken.

(3)测定并排除舱内有害气体
(3) Measure and elimination of harmful gases in the hold

某些货物(如杂货)在运输中易产生有害气体,引起舱内缺氧、货物自燃、腐烂变质等,应定期检测并采取适当方式予以排除。

Some cargoes are likely to generate harmful gases during transportation, causing lack of oxygen in the hold, spontaneous combustion of the cargo, deterioration of the cargo, etc., which should be regularly tested and taken out in an appropriate manner.

(4)测定舱内温、湿度,防止舱内出汗
(4) Measure hold temperature and humidity to prevent sweat in the hold

通过测定舱内温度和湿度的情况,结合外界气候条件,做好货舱通风工作,以防汗湿舱内货物。

By measuring the temperature and humidity in the hold, combined with the external climatic conditions, the cargo hold is ventilated to prevent the cargoes sweat.

(5)做好恶劣天气的防范工作

(5)Prepare for the bad weather

根据气象变化情况,在大风浪等恶劣天气到来之前认真检查货物状况,做好必要的货物加固、通风设备紧固、货舱盖的密闭等防范工作。

According to the changes in meteorological conditions, carefully check the condition of the cargoes before the arrival of bad weather such as heavy winds and waves, and do the necessary precautions such as reinforcement of the cargoes, fastening of ventilation equipment, and sealing of the cargo compartment cover.

(6)保证消防设备的有效状态

(6)Keep the fire equipment in an effective state

货物在运送过程中,由于各种意外原因可能会引起火灾,这就要求船舶的消防设备处于随时可用状态,以便尽快扑灭火灾,减少货物损失。

During the transportation of the cargoes, fires may occur due to various accidents. This requires the ship's fire-fighting equipment to be ready for use in order to extinguish the fire as soon as possible and reduce the loss of the cargoes.

2.3.2 货舱通风

2.3.2 Ventilation of Hold

很多货物索赔是由在航行途中的货损造成的。很多货损是由"船舶出汗"或者"货物出汗"引起的。货舱的适当有效的通风可以减少汗湿。

A great number of cargo claims are made for merchandise which has been damaged in transit. Much of this damage is caused by either "ships sweat" or "cargo sweat" and could be effectively reduced by prudent ventilation of cargo spaces.

当空气温度降低到露点之下时,空气中的多余水蒸气液化成水滴,就会形成"汗"。水滴可以沉积在船的结构上或货物上。水滴凝结在船体结构上时,被称为"船舶出汗",之后汗水可能流到货物上。货物的温度较低而外界温度较高,由于不恰当的通风导致外界空气进入货舱内,水滴在货物上形成,这称为"货物出汗"。

Sweat is formed when water vapor in the air condenses out into water droplets once the air is cooled below its dew point. The water droplets may be deposited onto the ship's structure or onto the cargo. In the former, it is known as "ships sweat" and this may run or subsequently drip onto the cargo. When the water droplets form on cargo, this is known as "cargo sweat" and will occur when the temperature of the cargo is cold and the incoming air is warm.

为了避免汗水以及汗水的危害性的影响,必须频繁地比较货舱内的空气和外界空气的干湿球温度。如果外部空气的温度低于货舱内的空气露点,则很可能发生出汗的现象。这种情况导致“船舶出汗”,并且通常在从温暖地区航行至干冷地区时出现。同样,如果货舱(或货物)中的空气温度低于进入空气的露点,则可能再次出汗,从而产生“货物出汗”。这可能是由寒冷地区航行至暖湿地区时出现。

To avoid sweat and its damaging effects, it is imperative that “wet and dry” bulb temperatures of the air entering and the air contained within the cargo compartment, are taken at frequent intervals. If the temperatures of the external air is less than the dew point of the air already inside the space, sweating could well occur. Such conditions give rise to “ships sweat” and is commonly found on voyages from warm climates towards colder destinations. Similarly, if the temperature of the air in the cargo compartment (or the cargo) is lower than the dew point of incoming air, sweating could again occur, giving rise to “cargo sweat”. This would be expected on voyages from cold places towards destinations in warmer climates.

如果货舱已经出汗或者即将出汗,应该禁止从外界通风,直到外界的空气适合通风。然而,往往无差别的通风比断绝通风后果更加严重。值得注意的是,通风筒随风向的角度不同时,货舱内的通风速率差别较大。航向和风向的角度也会影响货舱的通风效率。当下风舷的通风筒转向上风,而上风舷的通风筒转向下风,通风换气量最大,称为对流循环通风,如图2.3.1所示。

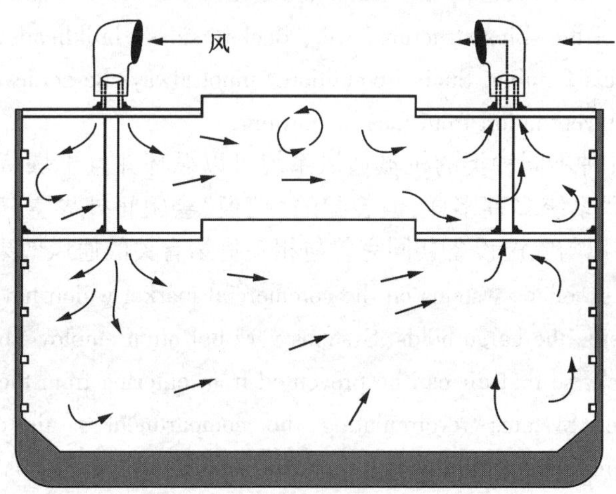

图 2.3.1 对流循环通风

If cargo sweat is being experienced or likely to occur, ventilation from the outside air should be stopped until more favourable conditions are obtained. However, it should be noted that indiscriminate ventilation often does more harm than no ventilation whatsoever. It is also of concern that variation in the angles of ventilators away from the wind can cause very different rates of air flow within the compartment. The angle at which the ship's course makes with the wind also affects the general flow of air to cargo compartments. In general, the greatest air flow occurs when the lee ventilators are trimmed on the wind and the weather ventilators are trimmed away from the wind. This is known as through ventilation, as shown in Figure 2.3.1.

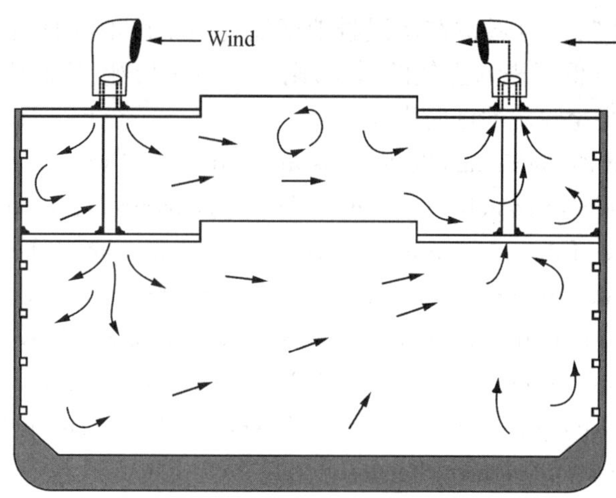

Figure 2.3.1 Through ventilation

机械通风——如果货舱空气的露点温度小于船体结构的温度，例如甲板、舷侧、舱壁和货物，货舱就没有出汗的风险。如果没有风扇或鼓风机等机械通风的方式，这种情况一般不会出现。

Forced ventilation—if the dew point temperature in the cargo compartment can be retained below the temperature of the ships structure, i.e., decks, sides, bulkheads and the cargo, there would be no risk of sweat forming. Such a condition cannot always be achieved without some form of mechanical (forced) ventilation from fans or blowers.

目前，布面上有几种不同种类的机械通风系统可以循环并且干燥货舱。当外界空气不适合通风时，机械通风系统多种多样，但装配的“挡板”会阻止外界空气进入货舱以及二层舱。系统“再循环”可以与除湿设备共同完善与相关货物有关的通风效果。

There are several excellent systems on the commercial market which have the ability to circulate and dry the air inside the cargo holds. Systems vary but often employ “baffle” plates fitted in the hold and tween decks so that air can be prevented from entering from the outside when conditions are unfavourable. Systems re-circulating the compartment's air can also operate in conjunction with dehumidifying equipment to achieve satisfactory conditions pertinent to relevant cargo.

衬垫——一般是指由大副负责的厚度约 35~40 mm 的木板条。衬垫可以单层铺设或以纵横交错的双垫板形式铺设，以便为货物的下面提供通风通道。衬垫使货堆四周都可以通风，减小了货物发生汗湿的可能性。衬垫应该是清洁的，并且不应该沾染有可能污染货物的油污。

Dunnage—timber slats of a thickness of about 35 to 40 mm which are ordered in bundles by the Ship's Chief Officer. The purpose of dunnage, which can be laid either singularly or in a criss-cross double dunnage pattern, is to provide an air gap to the underside of the cargo. This allows ventilation around all sides of the cargo stow. This is again to effectively reduce the risk of sweat damage to cargo. Dunnage should be in a clean condition and not oily or greasy as this could cause contamination to sensitive cargoes.

污染——容易受到污染的货物，例如茶、面粉、烟草等应远离具有浓烈气味的货物。如果船舶已经装载过类似于丁香或者肉桂这类的刺激性的货物，那么在装载下一批货载前应该对货舱进行除臭。不能将不洁货物和清洁货物装载于同一舱室内。通常不洁货物包括油脂、油漆、动物油产品等，而清洁货物包括食品、纺织品等。很明显，两类货物中都会有一些货物会有些例外。

Contamination—cargoes which taint easily, e.g., tea, flour, tobacco, etc. should be kept well away from strong smelling cargoes. If a pungent cargo has been carried previously, i.e., cloves or cinnamon, the compartment should be deodorized before loading the next cargo. Dirty cargoes should never be carried in the same compartment as clean cargoes. A general comparison of dirty cargoes would include such commodities as oils, paints or animal products, whereas clean cargoes would cover the likes of foodstuffs or fabrics. Obviously, some notable exceptions in each of the two classes are to be found.

货物隔票——相同货物拆成不同票运输时，两票货物中间需要一定的隔票是非常重要的。根据货物的类型，使用不同的隔票材料。常见的隔票材料包括彩色洗涤、防水油布、粗麻布、纸张、垫料、粉笔、绳纱或聚乙烯薄片。隔票的目的是便于区别货物，以免混淆。

Separation of cargoes—it is often a requirement when separate parcels of the same cargo are carried together that a degree of separation between the units is essential. The type of goods being shipped will reflect the type of separation method employed. Examples of separation materials include colour wash, tarpaulins, burlap, paper sheeting, dunnage, chalk marks, rope yarns or polythene sheets. The idea of separation is to ensure that the cargo parcels, although maybe looking the same, are not allowed to become inadvertently mixed.

防盗——很多货物容易引起小偷的注意，例如烈酒、啤酒、烟草和贵重的货物。为了减少损失，这类货物应该严格理货，从装到卸的整个装运过程应该封锁。船上的值班人员应该联合岸上的值班人员和安保人员共同完成货物的防盗工作。

Pilferage—certain cargoes always attract thieves. Notable items include spirits, beer, tobacco or high value small items. To reduce losses, such cargoes should be tallied in and tallied out. Lock-up stow should be provided throughout the voyage from the onset of loading to the time of discharge. Shore watchmen and security personnel should be used whenever it is practical and good watch-keeping practice should be the order of the day.

第 3 章　船舶基础知识

Chapter 3 | Basic Knowledge of Ships

3.1　船舶基本结构

3.1　Basic Structure of Ships

船舶是能够用作水上运输或作业的交通工具。随着科学技术的不断发展,新技术、新观念不断被应用到造船领域,船舶的种类和结构一直在变化。

A ship is a vehicle that is capable of being used as a means of transportation or working on water. With the continuous development of science and technology, new technologies and concepts are applied to the field of shipbuilding, the types and structures of ships are changing all the time.

3.1.1　船舶基本组成

3.1.1　Basic Components of Ships

船舶是由主船体、上层建筑及其他附属设备所组成。以上甲板为界,船舶下部分为主船体,船舶上部分为上层建筑。船舶主要部位如图 3.1.1 所示。

A ship consists of main hull, superstructure and other Auxiliary equipment. Taking the upper deck as the boundary, the part of a ship below the upper deck is called main hull, and the part above the upper deck is called superstructure. The main components of a ship are shown in Figure 3.1.1.

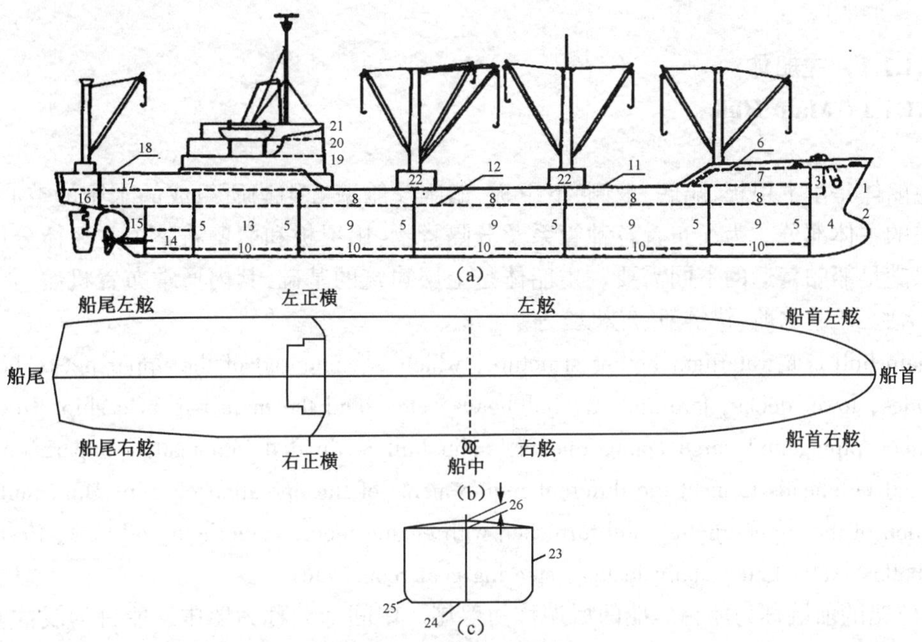

图 3.1.1　船舶主要部位

1—艏柱；2—球鼻艏；3—锚链舱；4—艏尖舱；5—水密横舱壁；6—艏楼甲板；7—艏楼；8—甲板间舱；9—货舱；10—双层底；11—上甲板；12—下甲板；13—机舱；14—轴隧；15—艉尖舱；16—舵机舱；17—艉楼；18—艉楼甲板；19—艇甲板；20—驾驶甲板；21—罗经甲板；22—桅屋；23—舷侧；24—船底；25—舭部；26—梁拱

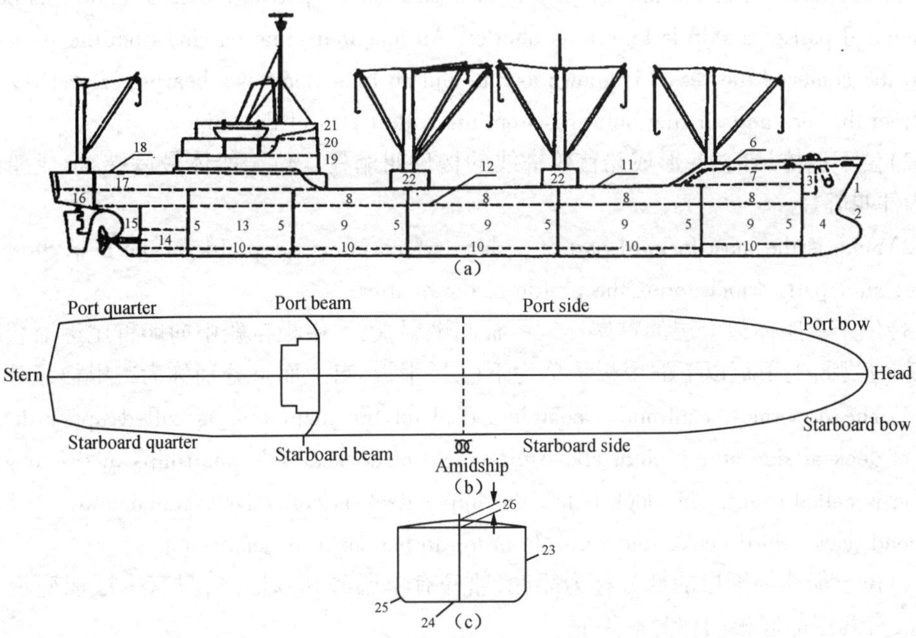

Figure 3.1.1　Main components of a ship

1—Stem; 2—Bulbbous bow; 3—Chain locker; 4—Forepeak tank; 5—Transverse watertight bulkhead; 6—Forecastle deck; 7—Forecastle; 8—Tween deck hold; 9—Cargo hold; 10—Double bottom; 11—Upper deck; 12—Lower deck; 13—Engine room; 14—Pipe tunnel; 15—Afterpeak tank; 16—Steering gear room; 17—Poop; 18—Poop deck; 19—Boat deck; 20—Bridge deck; 21—Compass deck; 22—Mast house; 23—Broadside; 24—Bottom; 25—Bilge; 26—Camber

3.1.1.1 主船体
3.1.1.1 Main Hull

主船体是由上甲板、船底、舷侧、下甲板、艏艉及舱壁等结构所组成的水密的空心结构，为船舶的主体部分。为了布置各种管系及分隔货物，用甲板和舱壁将整个主船体分成数个舱室以满足船舶营运的不同需要。主船体是上层建筑的基础，其内通常布置机舱、货舱、油舱、淡水舱、压载水舱、锚链舱、舵机舱等。

Main hull is a watertight hollow structure, which is composed of the upper deck, bottoms, broadsides, lower decks, fore and aft, bulkheads, etc., and the main part of a ship. To arrange the various piping and cargo compartments, main hull is divided into many compartments with decks and bulkheads to meet the different requirements of the operation of ship. Main hull is the foundation of the superstructure and furnished with engine room, cargo hold, oil tank, fresh water tank, ballast water tank, chain locker, steering gear room, etc.

(1)船的前端称为船首。船的后端称为船尾。中间部分称为船中。船首的线性弯曲部分称为艏舷。船尾的线性弯曲部分称为艉舷。经过船首、船尾，将船体分成左右对称两部分的直线叫艏艉线或纵中线。在最大船宽处垂直于艏艉线的方向叫正横。

(1)The forward end of the ship is called head. The aft end of the ship is called stern. The middle of the vessel is called amidship. The forward rounded part of a ship is known as bow. The after rounded part of a ship is known as quarter. An imaginary line passing from the stem to stern through the center of the vessel is known as fore and aft line. Beam is a bearing projected at a right angle from the fore and aft line outwards from the widest part of the ship.

(2)位于船体最前端，形成船首轮廓线的构件叫艏柱。位于船体最后端，形成船尾轮廓线的构件叫艉柱。

(2)Stem is the most forward part of a ship, which forms the profile of the bow. Stern post is the most after part, which forms the profile of the quarter.

(3)位于主船体最上层的首尾连续甲板叫上甲板，上甲板自船中向船首尾逐渐翘起的垂直高度叫舷弧，上甲板以下的甲板统称为下(层)甲板，自上而下分别称为二甲板、三甲板等。

(3)The uppermost continuous complete deck of the main hull is called upper deck. The height of deck at side at any point above the height of deck at side amidships in the longitudinal direction is called sheer. The deck below the upper deck is collectively called lower deck. There are second deck, third deck, and so on from top to bottom in the main hull.

(4)位于船体最下层的部分称为船底，船底有单层底和双层底，只有一层船底板的称为单层底，有两层船底板的称为双层底。

(4)Lowest part of the main hull refers to bottom. There are two kinds of bottom: single bottom and double bottom. Single bottom has only one bottom plating, and double bottom has two bottoms.

(5)沿船长方向将船内空间分隔成若干舱室的竖壁称横舱壁，最前端的水密横舱壁称为艏尖舱舱壁，又称防撞舱壁。沿船宽方向将船内空间分隔成若干舱室的竖壁称纵舱壁。最后端的水密横舱壁称为艉尖舱舱壁。

(5) The vertical wall that divides the space inside a ship into several compartments in the longitudinal direction is called transverse bulkhead. Fore peak bulkhead is the most forward watertight bulkhead, and also called collision bulkhead. The vertical wall that divides the space inside a ship into several compartments in the transverse direction is called longitudinal bulkhead. After peak bulkhead is the most after watertight bulkhead.

(6)两侧直立部分叫舷侧,位于船底中心线的沿首尾方向的船底板叫平板龙骨。舷侧与船底交会处的圆弧部分叫舭部。甲板在中间拱起的高度叫梁拱。

(6) The vertical part on both sides of a ship is known as broadside. The bottom plate running fore and aft on the bottom center line is known as plate keel. The rounded portion which connects the bottom with broadsides is known as bilge. The height of the deck at its center above the height of deck at side in the transverse direction is know as camber.

3.1.1.2 上层建筑
3.1.1.2 Superstructure

上层建筑是在上甲板上,由一舷伸至另一舷的或其侧壁板离舷侧板向内不大于船宽 B 的4%围蔽建筑物。上层建筑是水密空心结构,由两边侧壁、前端壁、后端壁、甲板和内部隔壁组成。为了满足船员或旅客工作、生活、储藏等需要,上层建筑内通常布置船员或旅客房间、驾驶台、厨房、配餐间、餐厅、休息室、洗衣间、烘干室、储藏室等。上层建筑位于上甲板之上,包括艏楼、桥楼和艉楼。因此,上层建筑又称为船楼。

Superstructure is an enclosed structure on the upper deck, extending from side to side of the ship, or with the side plating not more than 4% of the breadth (B) inboard of the shell plating. Superstructure is a watertight hollow structure, which is composed of both side platings, front bulkheads, aft bulkheads, decks and internal bulkheads, etc. In order to meet the requirements of crews or passengers, such as working, living, storage and so on, superstructure is usually equipped with crew or passenger room, navigation bridge, galley, pantry, mess room, lounge, laundry, storage room, etc. Superstructure is above the upper deck and consists of forecastle, bridge and poop. Therefore, superstructure is also called erection.

(1)艏楼:位于船首部的上层建筑。艏楼的作用是减小船首部上浪,改善船舶航行条件。艏楼内的舱室可作为储藏室。

(1) Forecastle: is the superstructure at the head of a ship. Forecastle is used for reducing shipping water on deck and enhancing navigation safety. Compartments in the forecastle are used as store room.

(2)艉楼:位于船尾部的上层建筑。艉楼的作用是可减小船尾上浪,保护机舱,并可布置船员住舱及其他舱室。

(2) Poop: is the superstructure in the aft of a ship. Poop is used for reducing shipping water on deck, protecting the engine room, and arranging crew rooms and other accommodation.

(3)桥楼:位于船中部的上层建筑。桥楼的作用是布置驾驶室和船员居住处所。

(3)Bridge:is the superstructure in the middle of a ship. Bridge is used for arranging wheel house and crew accommodation.

甲板室是在上甲板上,宽度小于船宽92%的围蔽建筑物。桅柱建在上面的甲板室称为桅屋。因为在甲板室两侧外面的甲板是露天的,所以有利于甲板上的操作和便于前后行走。

Deckhouse is an enclosed structure on the upper deck, with a width less than 92% of the breadth. Deckhouse into which the mast is built is called mast house. Because the deck outside the deckhouse is exposed to weather and sea, it is conducive to working on this deck and easy to walk back and forth.

通常不严格区分时,上甲板以上的各种围蔽建筑物,统称为上层建筑。上层建筑包括船楼和甲板室两种形式。

Generally speaking, all the enclosed structures on the upper deck are collectively called superstructure. Superstructure includes erection and deckhouse.

3.1.1.3 附属设备

3.1.1.3 Auxiliary Equipment

附属设备主要包括主机、辅机及其配套、电器、各种管系、甲板设备(锚设备、系泊设备、舵设备、装卸设备、系固设备)、安全设备(包括消防设备、救生设备)、通信设备、导航设备及生活设施配套设备等。

Auxiliary equipment mainly includes main engine, auxiliary engines and their supporting facilities, electrical appliances, various piping, deck equipment (anchor gear, mooring gear, rudder and steering gear, cargo gear, securing devices), safety equipment (including fire fighting equipment, life saving appliance), communication equipment, navigation equipment and supporting equipment for life facilities, etc.

船上的设备和船舶结构一样,通常应通过船级社的检验并获得许可证。主要设备的作用如下:

The equipment on board, as well as ship structures, should be normally inspected and licensed by the classification society. The functions of the major equipment are as follows:

(1)推进装置:包括主机、传动设备、轴系、推进器等。推进器对水产生推力,使船舶克服阻力以一定航速航行。通常把推进船舶的机械统称为主机。

(1)Marine propulsion device:includes main engine, transmission equipment, shafting, propeller, etc. The thrust of a propeller against the water causes the ship to overcome resistance and travel at a certain speed. The machinery used to propel a ship generally refers to main engine.

(2)辅助装置:包括供全船使用的船舶电站、辅锅炉、泵站和空气压缩系统等,以便供应船舶航行、作业和生活设施的需要。通常把主机以外的其他辅助的机械设备统称为辅机。

(2)Auxiliary devices:includes the power station for the whole ship, auxiliary boiler, pump station, air compression system, etc., to supply the needs of navigation, working and living facilities. Other auxiliary mechanical equipment other than main engine generally collectively refers to auxiliary engine.

(3)锚设备:主要有锚、锚链、锚链筒、制链器、锚机、锚链管、锚链舱和弃链器等。抛锚后,船舶拖着锚链使锚爪抓底,以抵御风、流等对船舶的作用力,最终使船舶被系留在指定水域。

(3) Anchor gear: includes anchor, anchor chain, hawse pipe, chain stopper, windlass, chain pipe, chain locker, chain releaser, etc. After anchoring, the ship pulls the anchor chain to make the anchor flukes dig into the sea bed, so as to resist the wind, current and other forces on the ship, and finally fixes the ship in the designated waters.

(4)系泊设备:主要有缆绳、导缆装置、挽缆装置、绞缆机、卷缆设备和系泊属具等。系泊设备使用缆绳形成系固力,以抵御风、流、潮汐等对船舶的作用力,最终使船舶被系固于某终端。

(4) Mooring gear: includes mooring rope, fairlead, bitt, mooring winch, hawser reel, mooring fitting, etc. Mooring gear use ropes to form the mooring force to resist the wind, current, tide and other forces on the ship so that the ship is finally secured to a certain terminal.

(5)舵设备:主要有舵装置、舵机、转舵装置、操舵装置的控制装置等。舵设备是船舶在航行中保持和改变航向及旋回运动的主要工具。

(5) Rudder and steering gear: includes rudder, steering engine, rudder actuator, steering gear control system, etc. Rudder and steering gear are the main devices for ships to keep and change the course and turn motion during navigation.

(6)消防设备:主要有灭火器、固定式灭火系统、固定式探火和失火报警系统、消防员装备、紧急逃生呼吸装置、国际通岸接头、通风系统、脱险通道、通用应急报警和有线广播系统等。消防设备可用于预防、探测、消灭船上火灾,以保障海上人命、船舶、货物和环境的安全。

(6) Fire fighting equipment: includes fire extinguisher, fixed fire extinguishing system, fixed fire detection and fire alarm system, fire fighter's outfit, emergency escape breathing device, international shore connection, ventilation system, mean of escape, general alarm and public address system, etc. Fire fighting equipment may be used for preventing, detecting and putting out a fire on board, so as to ensure the safety of life, ship, goods and environment at sea.

(7)救生设备:主要有救生艇、救生筏、救生圈、救生衣、抛绳设备、求救信号弹、通用应急报警和有线广播系统等。救生设备可用于救助落水人员或在船舶遭遇海难时弃船自救。

(7) Life saving appliance: includes lifeboat, liferaft, lifebuoy, lifejacket, line throwing appliance, distress flares, general alarm and public address system, etc. Life saving appliance may be used for rescuing man overboard or abandoning ship and self rescuing in case of shipwreck.

(8)通信设备:主要有 MF/HF 通信设备、VHF 通信设备、NAVTEX 接收机、SART 设备、卫星通信设备等。通信设备用于海上遇险、安全和搜救活动以及常规通信的综合通信系统。

(8) Communication equipment: includes MF/HF communication equipment, VHF communication equipment, NAVTEX receiver, SART equipment, satellite communication equipment, etc. Communications equipment is an integrated communication system for maritime distress, safety and search and rescue operations, and conventional communication.

(9)导航设备:主要有雷达、电子海图显示与信息系统、磁罗经、陀螺罗经、测深仪、计程

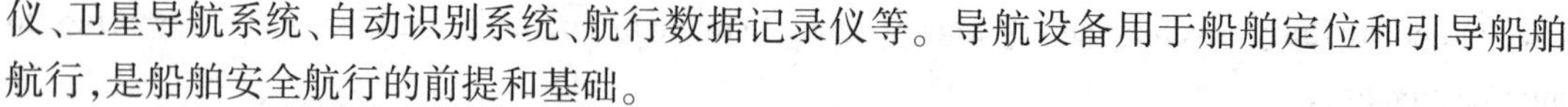

仪、卫星导航系统、自动识别系统、航行数据记录仪等。导航设备用于船舶定位和引导船舶航行，是船舶安全航行的前提和基础。

(9) Navigation equipment: includes radar, electronic chart display and information system, magnetic compass, gyrocompass, depth sounder, log, satellite navigation system, automatic identification system, voyage data recorder and so on. Navigation equipment is used for locating and guiding ships, which is the premise and foundation of safety navigation of ships.

3.1.2 船舶主船体结构
3.1.2 Main Hull Structure

主船体由船体外板、船底结构、舷侧结构、甲板结构、舱壁结构、艏艉结构等组成。为了保证船体水密、强度和刚性，除正确选用船体结构钢材外，还应合理地布置它们，以最大限度地发挥它们的效力。按照构件的排列方式，船体结构可分为横骨架式、纵骨架式和混合骨架式三种形式。

Main hull is composed of outer hull plate, bottom structure, side structure, deck structure, bulkhead structure, fore and aft end structure and so on. In order to ensure the watertightness, strength and rigidity of ships' hull, in addition to the correct selection of steel for hull structure, they should also be reasonably arranged to maximize their effectiveness. According to the arrangement of framing, hull framing system consists of transverse framing system, longitudinal framing system, combined or mixed framing system.

(1) 横骨架式船体结构是在上甲板、船底和舷侧结构中，横向构件数目多、排列密，而纵向构件数目少、排列疏的船体结构。

(1) Transverse framing system is adopted in upper deck, bottom and side structures, which consists of many small closely spaced transverse members, and few large widely spaced longitudinal members.

(2) 纵骨架式船体结构是在上甲板、船底和舷侧结构中，纵向构件数目多、排列密，而横向构件数目少、排列疏的船体结构。

(2) Longitudinal framing system is adopted in upper deck, bottom and side structures, which consists of many small closely spaced longitudinal members, and few large widely spaced transverse members.

(3) 混合骨架式船体结构是在上甲板和船底采用纵骨架式结构，而在舷侧采用横骨架式结构。

(3) Combined or mixed framing system is that longitudinal framing system is adopted in upper deck and bottom structures, and transverse framing system is adopted in side structure.

3.1.2.1 船体外板

3.1.2.1 Outer Hull Plate

船体外板又称为船壳板,包括舷侧板和船底板。外板由一块块钢板焊接而成。钢板的长边通常沿船长方向布置,许多块钢板依次端接后成为一长条板,称为列板,如图 3.1.2 所示。若干个列板组成外板。

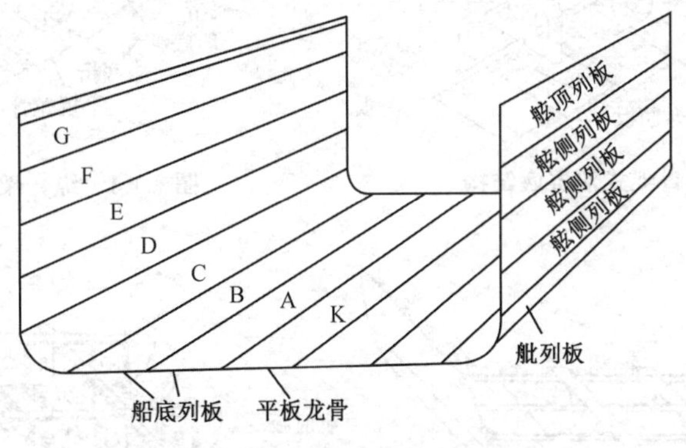

图 3.1.2 船壳板的列板

Outer hull plate is also called shell plating, which includes side shell plating and bottom shell plating. Outer hull plate is composed of many steel plates welded together. The long edges of steel plates are usually laid out in longitudinal direction, thus many steel plates are butted successively to form a strip, which called strake, see Figure 3.1.2. So shell plating is composed of lots of strakes.

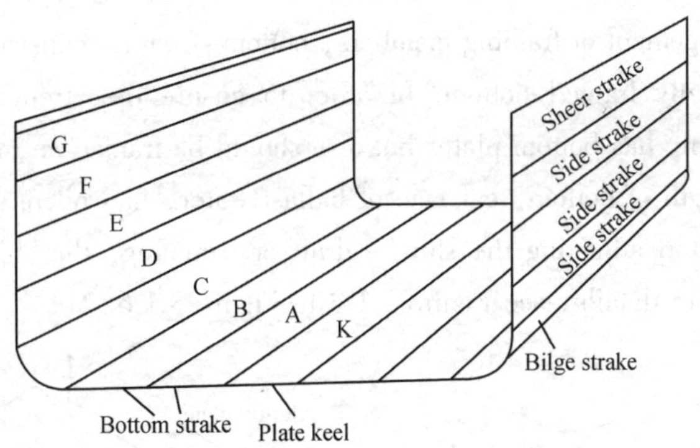

Figure 3.1.2 Strakes of shell plating

3.1.2.2 船底结构

3.1.2.2 Bottom Structure

船底结构有单层底结构和双层底结构两种类型,按骨架排列方式又可分为横骨架式和纵骨架式两种形式。为了保证船底结构强度,只有船底板还是远远不够的,还需要设置强有力的骨架。为了增加船底强度,装载压载水、燃油或滑油,提高船舶抗沉性和调节船舶的吃水和纵倾，通常船舶采用双层底结构。具体如图 3.1.3 至图 3.1.6 所示。

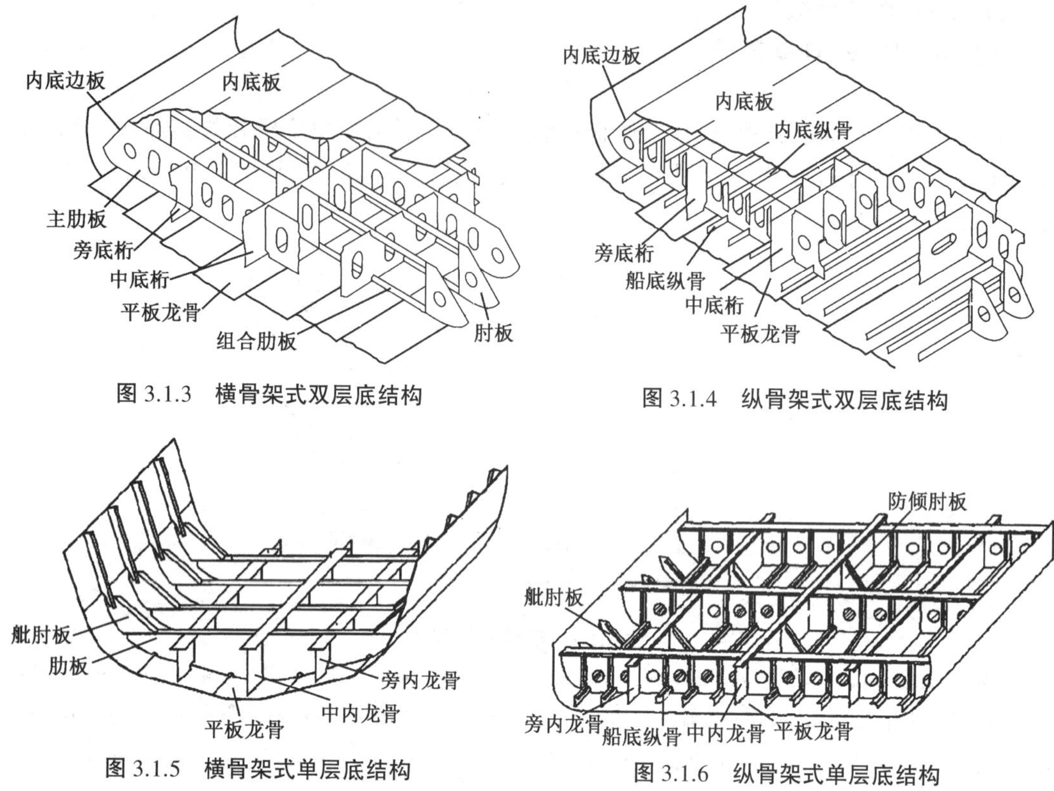

图 3.1.3　横骨架式双层底结构

图 3.1.4　纵骨架式双层底结构

图 3.1.5　横骨架式单层底结构

图 3.1.6　纵骨架式单层底结构

There are two kinds of bottom structure: single bottom structure and double bottom structure. According to the arrangement of framing members, bottom structure consists of transversely framed bottom and longitudinally framed bottom. In order to ensure the strength of bottom structure, bottom structure not only has bottom plates but also should be framed and reinforced. For the sake of increasing the strength of bottom, carriage of ballast water, fuel oil or lubricating oil, limiting the extent of flooding and adjusting the ship's draft or trimming, the ship is usually fitted with double bottom. For more details, see Figure 3.1.3 to Figure 3.1.6.

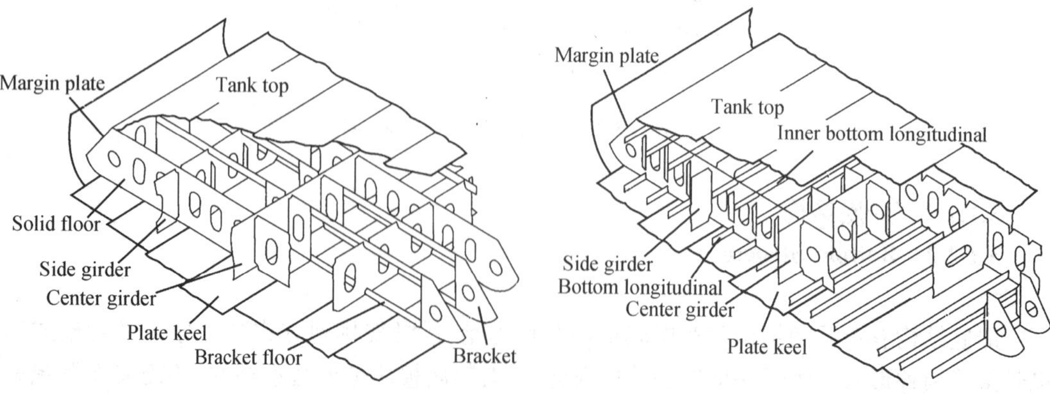

Figure 3.1.3　Transversely framed double bottom

Figure 3.1.4　Longitudinally framed double bottom

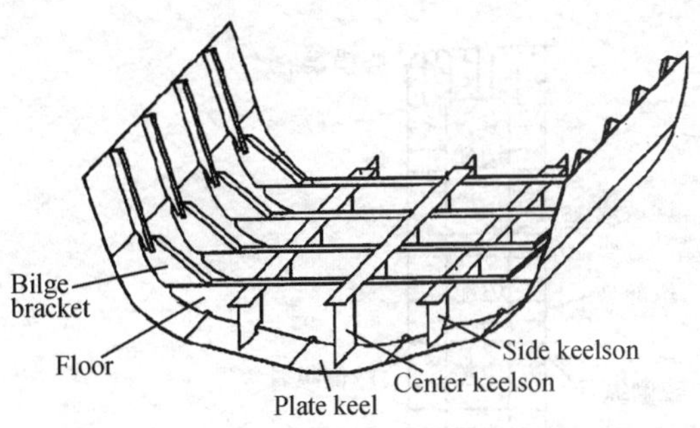

Figure 3.1.5　Transversely framed single bottom

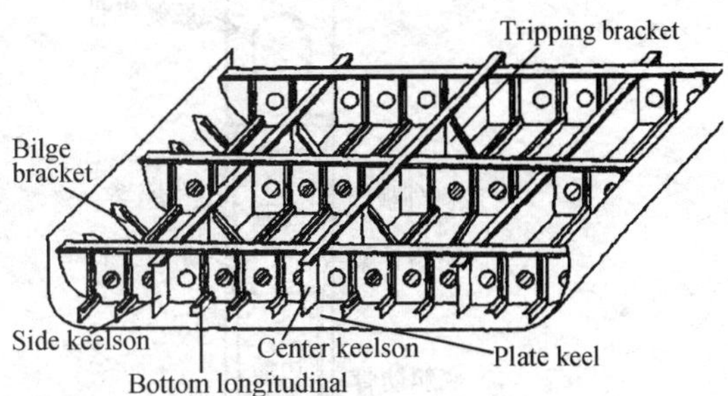

Figure 3.1.6　Longitudinally framed single bottom

3.1.2.3　舷侧结构

3.1.2.3　Side Structure

舷侧结构有单舷侧结构和双舷侧结构两种类型，如图 3.1.7 和图 3.1.8 所示。舷侧结构按骨架排列方式又可分为横骨架式和纵骨架式两种形式。通常船舶采用单舷侧、横骨架式结构。集装箱船和大型油船一般采用双舷侧结构。为了保证舷侧结构强度，只有舷侧外板还是远远不够的，还需要设置强有力的骨架。

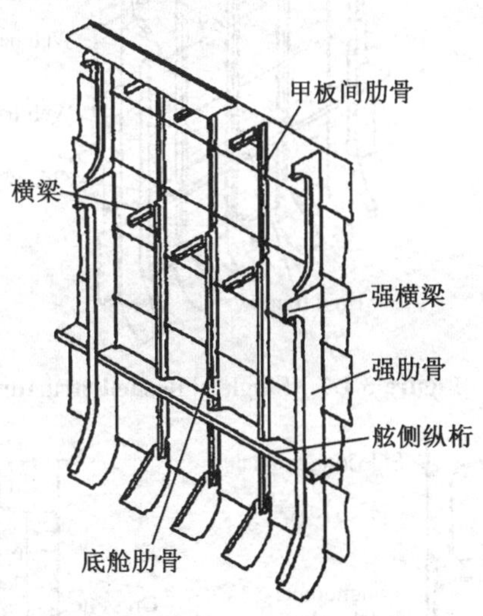

图 3.1.7　单舷侧结构

There are two kinds of side structure: single side shell structure and double side shell structure, see Figure 3.1.7 and Figure 3.1.8. According to the arrangement of framing members, side structure consists of transversely framed side shell and longitudinally framed side shell. The ship is usually fitted with single side shell and transversely framed side shell. Container ships and large oil tankers generally adopt double side shell structure. In order to ensure the strength of side structure, side structure not only has side plates but also should be framed and reinforced.

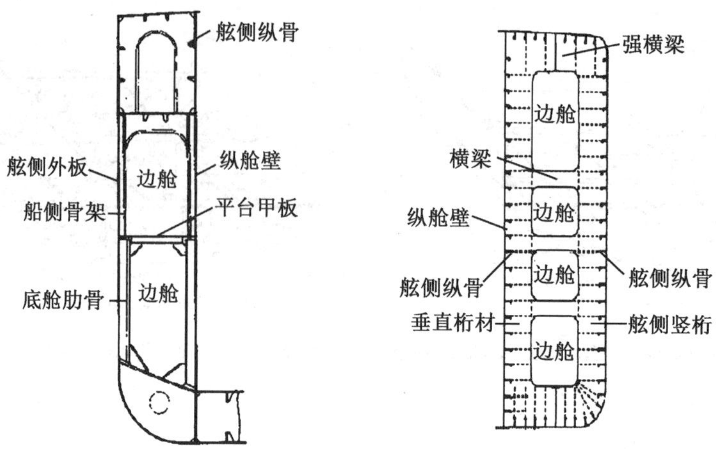

图 3.1.8 双舷侧结构

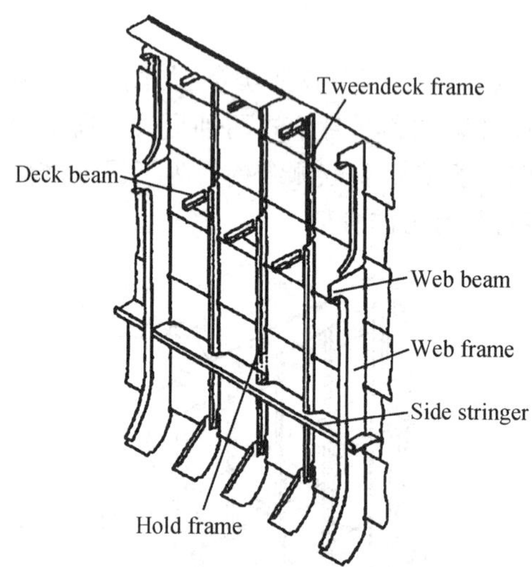

Figure 3.1.7 Single side shell structure

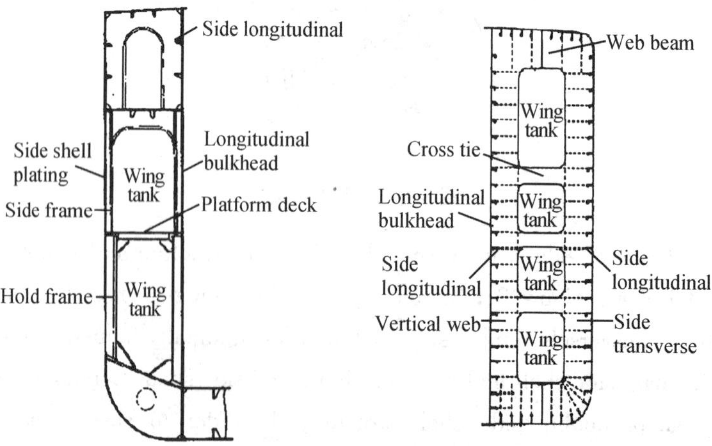

Figure 3.1.8 Double side shell structure

3.1.2.4　甲板结构

3.1.2.4　Deck structure

甲板结构有单甲板结构和双甲板结构两种类型,一般船舶采用单甲板结构。甲板结构按骨架排列方式可分为横骨架式和纵骨架式两种形式,如图 3.1.9 和图 3.1.10 所示。上甲板主要承受总纵弯曲,下甲板主要承受货物载荷。因此,一般上甲板采用纵骨架式结构,下甲板采用横骨架式结构。为了保证甲板结构强度,只有甲板板还是远远不够的,还需要设置强有力的骨架。

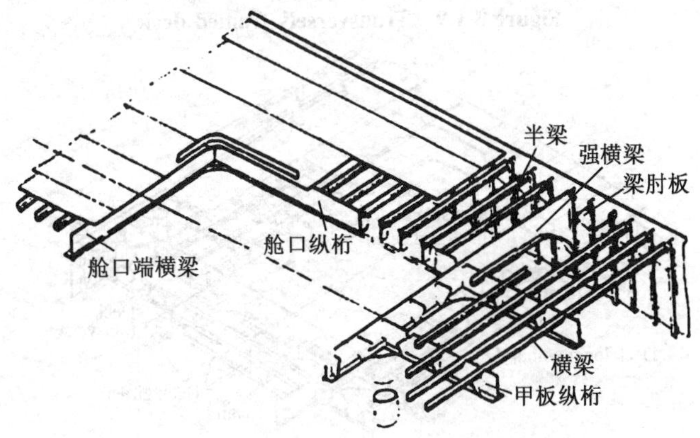

图 3.1.9　横骨架式甲板结构

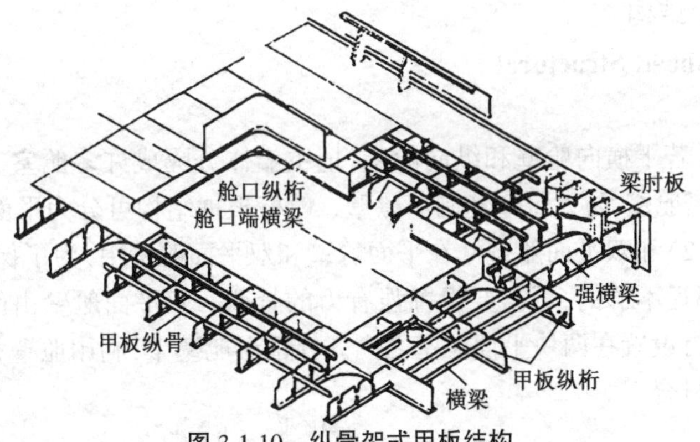

图 3.1.10　纵骨架式甲板结构

There are two kinds of deck structure: single deck structure and double deck structure. The ship is commonly fitted with single deck structure. According to the arrangement of framing members, deck structure consists of transversely framed deck and longitudinally framed deck, see Figure 3.1.9 and Figure 3.1.10. Upper deck mainly bears the longitudinal bending, while lower deck mainly bears the cargo load. Therefore upper deck is longitudinally framed, and lower deck is transversely framed. In order to ensure the strength of deck structure, deck structure not only has deck plates but also should be framed and reinforced.

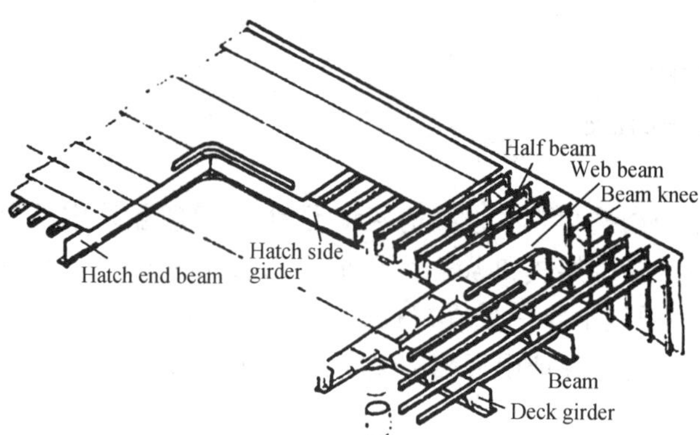

Figure 3.1.9 Transversely framed deck

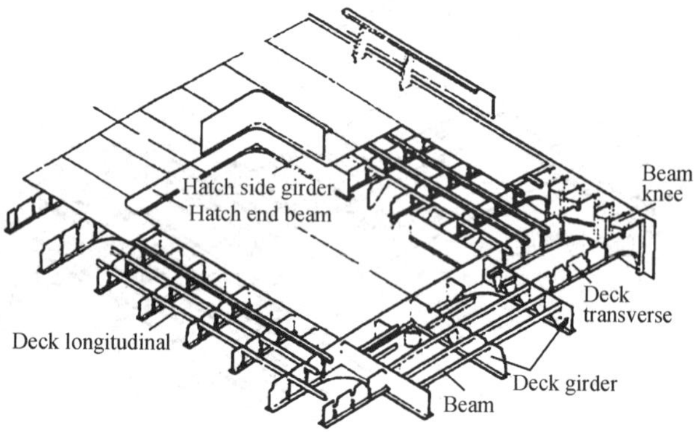

Figure 3.1.10 Longitudinally framed deck

3.1.2.5 舱壁结构

3.1.2.5 Bulkhead Structure

主船体设置了若干横向舱壁和纵向舱壁，把主船体分隔成许多舱室。舱壁根据作用可分为水密舱壁、油密舱壁、防火舱壁和制荡舱壁。舱壁根据结构可分为平面舱壁(图 3.1.11)、槽形舱壁(图 3.1.12)和双平面舱壁。在平面舱壁和双平面舱壁中，为了保证舱壁结构强度，只有舱壁板还是远远不够的，还需要设置强有力的骨架。双平面舱壁由两块平面舱壁组合而成，扶强材和桁材设置在两块平面舱壁之内。在槽形舱壁中，利用舱壁板的折曲代替扶强材的作用，做到板材合一。

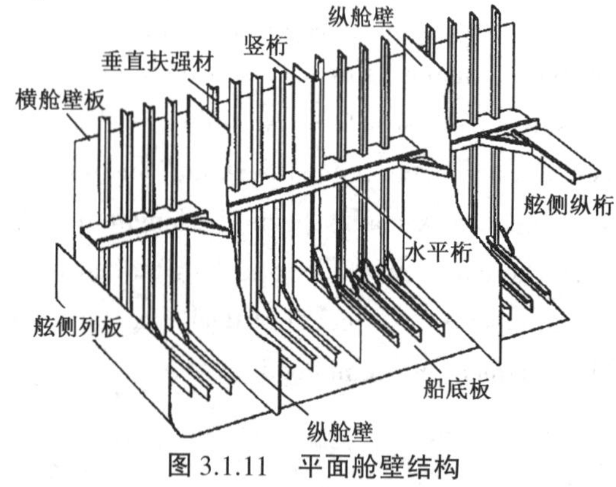

图 3.1.11 平面舱壁结构

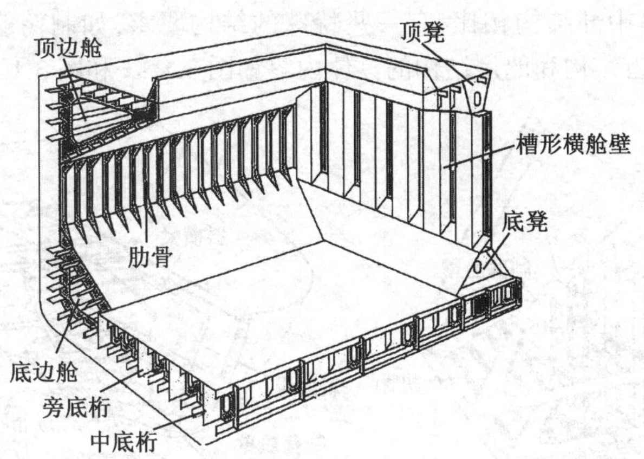

图 3.1.12　槽形舱壁结构

Main hull is divided into several compartments by a number of transverse and longitudinal bulkheads. According to the difference of the function, bulkheads are divided into watertight bulkhead, oiltight bulkhead, fire proof bulkhead and swash bulkhead. Bulkheads are divided into plane (plain) bulkhead (see Figure 3.1.11), corrugated bulkhead (see Figure 3.1.12) and double plate bulkhead as per the difference of the structure. In order to ensure the strength of bulkhead structure, plane bulkhead structure and double plate bulkhead structure not only have bulkhead plates but also should be framed and reinforced. Double plate bulkhead has double plates with stiffeners and girders inside for supporting the bulkhead. In the corrugated bulkhead, corrugated plate is used to dispense with stiffeners, so the plates and stiffeners are integrated.

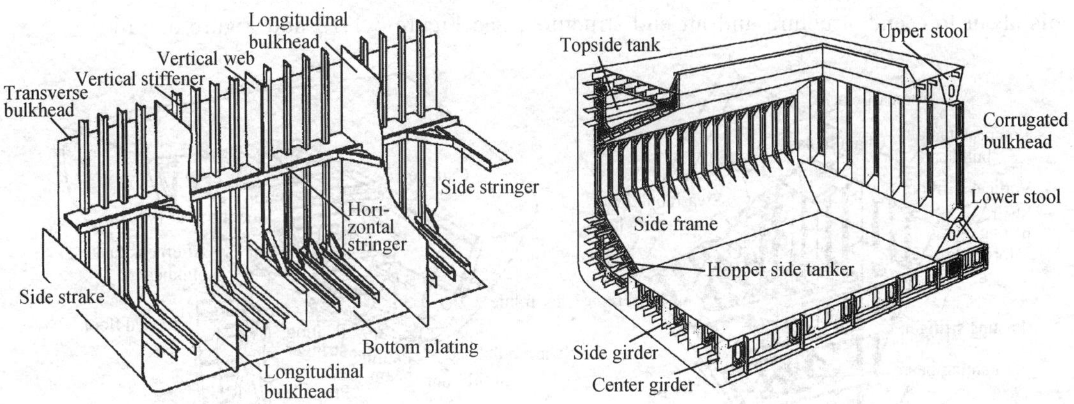

Figure 3.1.11　Plane bulkhead structure　　**Figure 3.1.12　Corrugated bulkhead structure**

3.1.2.6　艏艉结构

3.1.2.6　Fore and Aft end Structure

船舶的艏部和艉部受总纵弯曲作用较小，而受局部作用力较大，如艏部的碰撞力、砰击力、拍底力，艉部的舵力、螺旋桨振动力等。因此，艏艉部多采用横骨架式结构，并做特别加强。艏艉结构与船体中部结构相比,有一些特殊的结构要求,如制荡舱壁、强胸结构、球鼻艏、艉突出体等。船首结构和船尾结构的具体内容如图 3.1.13 和图 3.1.14 所示。

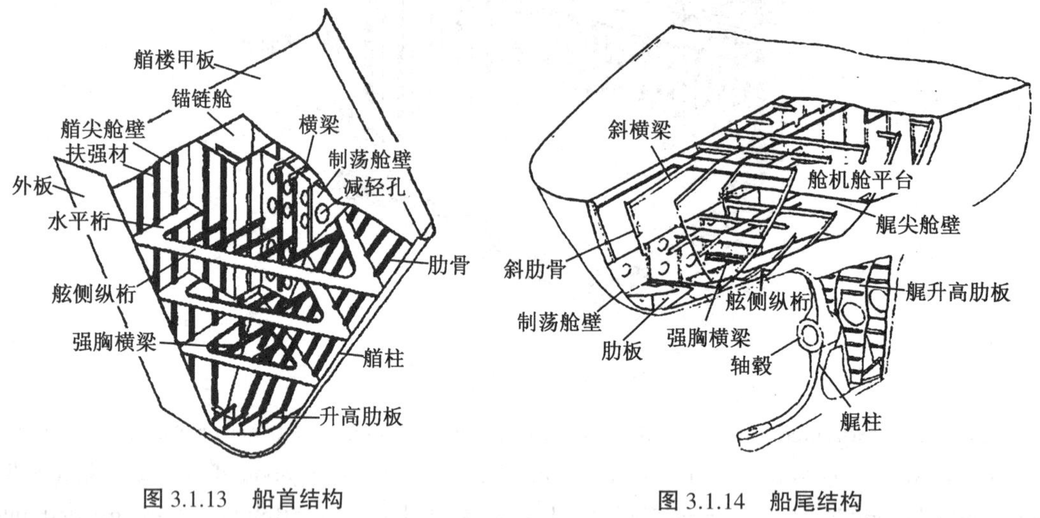

图 3.1.13　船首结构

图 3.1.14　船尾结构

Fore end and aft end of the ship suffer a small longitudinal bending, but are subjected to a great local force, such as collision force, slamming force and pounding force on the bow, rudder force and propeller vibration force at the stern, etc. Therefore the ship is commonly fitted with transversely framed structure at the fore and aft end and specially stiffened. Compared with the middle hull structure, there are some special structural requirements in fore and aft structure, such as swash bulkhead, panting arrangement, bulbous bow, overhanging structure, etc. For more details about fore end structure and aft end structure, see Figure 3.1.13 and Figure 3.1.14.

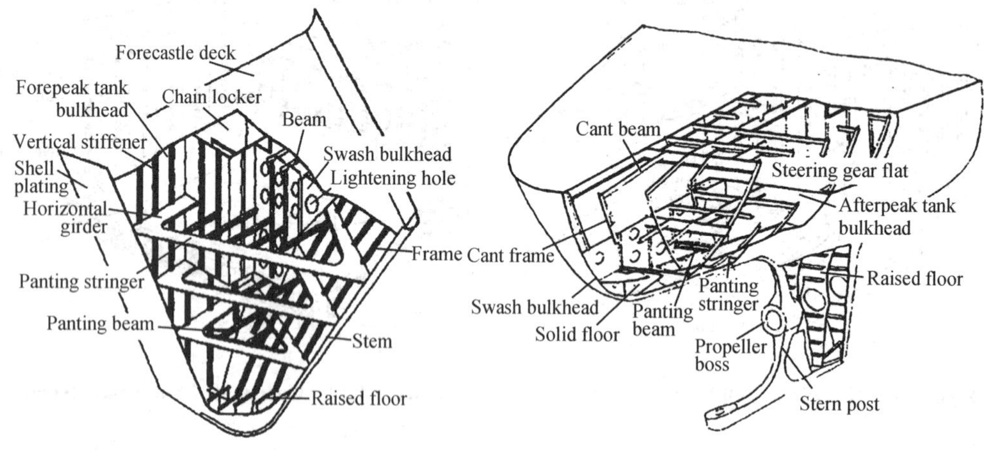

Figure 3.1.13　Fore end structure

Figure 3.1.14　Aft end structure

3.1.3　船舶上层建筑结构
3.1.3　Superstructure Structure

根据船舶种类、大小的不同,上层建筑甲板的层数及命名方法均有所不同。有的船舶从上甲板向上按 A、B、C……的方式命名各层甲板,有的船舶则按各层甲板的功能不同而命名,如起居甲板、艇甲板、驾驶甲板、罗经甲板、艏楼甲板、艉楼甲板等。

According to the different types and sizes of the ship, the number of tiers and naming methods of superstructure decks are different. Deck is named A, B, C…… up from upper deck to the top-most deck in some ships, while in other ships deck is named according to different functions of each deck, such as promenade deck, boat deck, bridge deck, compass deck, forecastle deck, poop deck, etc.

根据上甲板以上的建筑物的布置,上层建筑有如下六种形式:

According to the layout of the structure on the upper deck, there are six types of superstructure as follows:

①三岛式:艏楼、桥楼和艉楼分离,形如三座岛屿。

①Three island type: forecastle, bridge and poop are separated, which looks like three islands.

②长艏楼式:艏楼与桥楼连接。

②Long forecastle type: forecastle and bridge are combined.

③长艉楼式:艉楼与桥楼连接,在现代大多数艉机型船中得到了广泛采用。

③Long poop type: poop and bridge are combined, which is widely used by stern-engined ships in the modern.

④长桥楼式:仅设置桥楼而无艏楼和艉楼。

④Long bridge type: the ship only set bridge but no forecastle and poop.

⑤连续上层建筑式:艏楼、艉楼与桥楼连接,在上甲板上增加一层或多层连通甲板。

⑤Continuous superstructure type: forecastle, poop and bridge are combined, and one or more complete decks are set on the upper deck.

⑥平甲板式:无船楼,仅在机舱口设置小范围甲板室。

⑥Flush deck type: the ship doesn't have erection, but only arrange low deckhouse around machinery openings.

"育鲲"轮驾驶甲板布置及上层建筑形式如图 3.1.15 和图 3.1.16 所示。

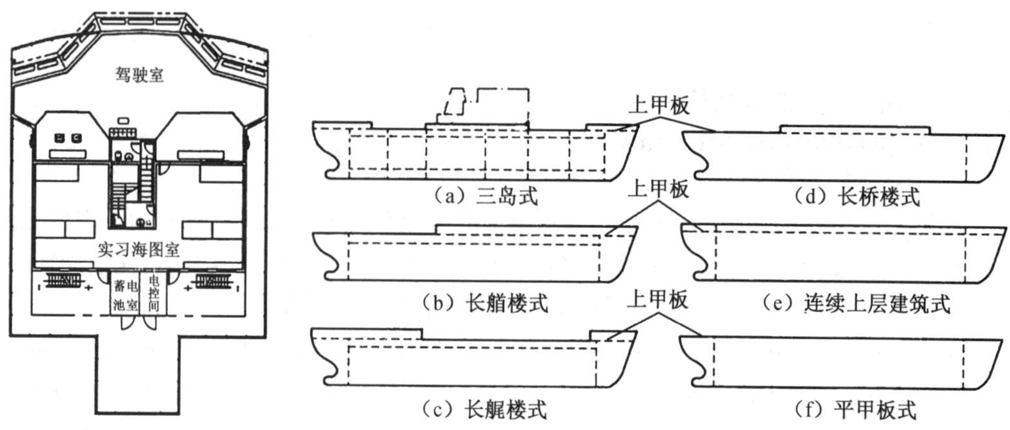

图 3.1.15 “育鲲”轮驾驶甲板布置

图 3.1.16 上层建筑形式

Arrangement of bridge deck and forms of superstructure on “YU KUN” are shown in Figure 3.1.15 and Figure 3.1.16.

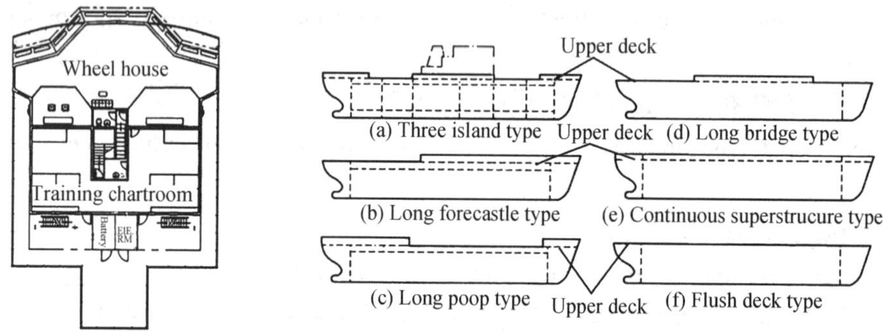

Figure 3.1.15 Arrangement of bridge deck on “YU KUN”

Figure 3.1.16 Forms of superstructure

船楼可为甲板的开口提供保护，特别是船楼的舱壁能承受甲板上浪，增加船舶储备浮力。上层建筑对外入口应设置钢制水密门，并能在任何一面都可操作。船楼的结构与主船体结构很相似，也是由侧壁、端壁、甲板、内部隔壁及其骨架、支柱等组成，如图 3.1.17 所示。根据参与船体总纵弯曲的有效程度，船楼可分为强力上层建筑和轻型上层建筑。强力上层建筑参与船体总纵弯曲，轻型上层建筑不参与船体总纵弯曲。强力上层建筑的板厚和骨架尺寸一般大于轻型上层建筑。因此，强力上层建筑甲板及侧壁一般为纵骨架式，轻型上层建筑甲板及侧壁一般为横骨架式。船楼的前后端壁的下方应设置舱壁、隔壁、支柱或其他强力构件，使其得到可靠的支撑，保持结构的连续性。

Erection provides protection for the openings through decks, particularly bulkheads of the erection are to withstand the force of any seas shipped, which increases the reserve buoyancy. Access openings of the erection shall be provided with steel watertight door, which can be operated on any side. Erection structure, which consists of side platings, bulkhead platings, deck platings, internal diaphragm platings and their framing members, pillars and so on, is similar to main hull structure, see Figure 3.1.17. According to the effectiveness of suffering the longitudinal bending of the hull, erection is divided into effective superstructure and non-effective superstructure. Effective superstructure bears the longitudinal bending, while non-effective superstructure doesn't. The thickness of plates and the size of framing members of effective superstructure are generally larger than that of non-effective superstructure. Therefore, deck structure and side platings structure of effective superstructure are generally longitudinally framed, while effective superstructure are generally transversely framed. Bulkheads, diaphragms, pillars or other strengthening members are arranged under the fore and aft ends of erections for support and ensuring effective continuity of structure.

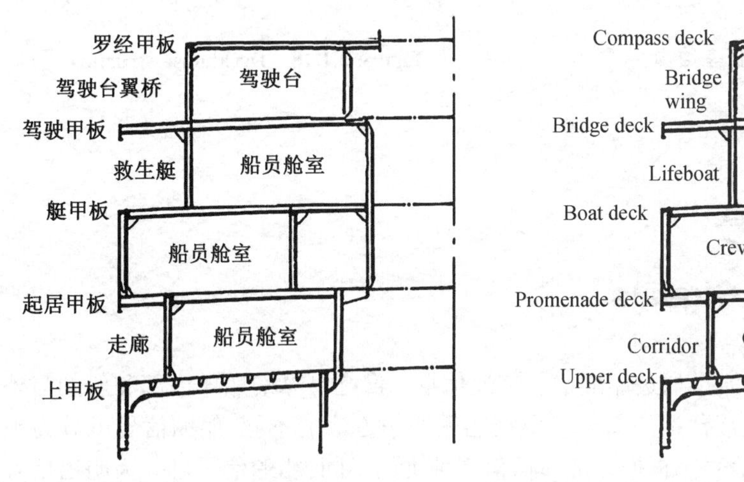

图 3.1.17 船楼结构　　Figure 3.1.17 Erection structure

甲板室的结构与上层建筑结构很相似,如图 3.1.18 所示。甲板室可为甲板的开口提供保护,如机舱棚用于保护机舱在露天甲板上的开口。甲板室由围壁、甲板、内部隔壁及其骨架、支柱等构成。为减轻船舶重量,围壁和甲板都用较薄的板材,但均有骨架加强。甲板室可分为强力甲板室和轻型甲板室。强力甲板室参与船体总纵弯曲,轻型甲板室不参与船体总纵弯曲。甲板室的前后端壁的下方应设置舱壁、隔壁、支柱或其他强力构件,使其得到可靠的支撑,保持结构的连续性。

Deckhouse structure is similar to erection structure, see Figure 3.1.18. Erection provides protection for the openings through decks, such as machinery space openings in the exposed deck are protected by machinery casings. Deckhouse consists of boundary bulkhead platings, deck platings internal diaphragm platings and their framing members, pillars and so on. In order to reduce the ship's weight, boundary bulkheads and decks are made of thinner plates, but are reinforced with and framing members. Deckhouse is divided into effective deckhouse and non-effective deckhouse. Effective deckhouse bears the longitudinal bending, while non-effective deckhouse doesn't. Bulkheads, diaphragms, pillars or other strengthening members are arranged under the fore and aft ends of erections for support and ensuring effective continuity of structure.

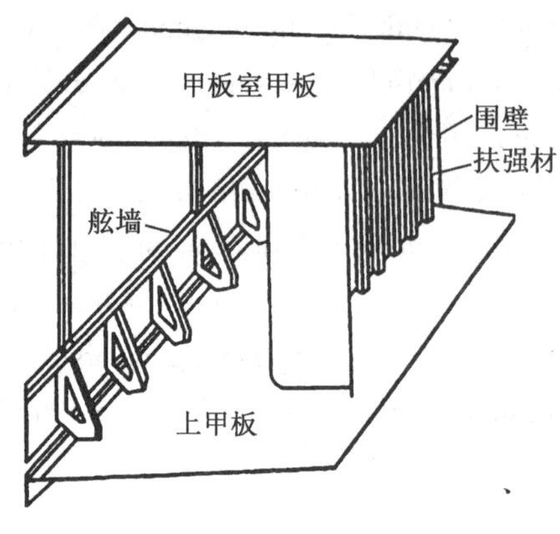

图 3.1.18 甲板室结构

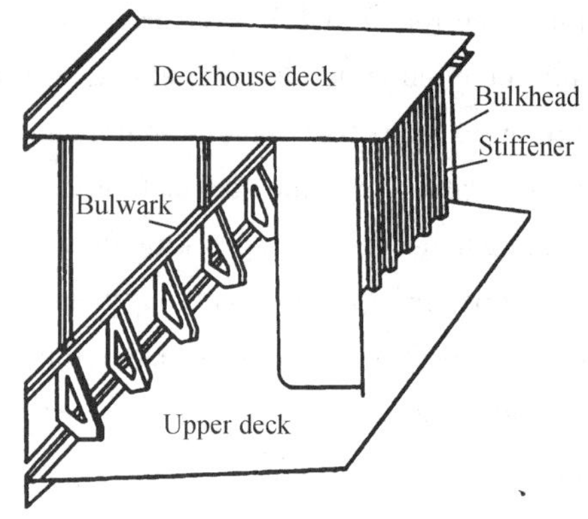

Figure 3.1.18 Deckhouse structure

3.2 船舶信号

3.2 Nautical Signals

信号是信息的载体。海员通过船舶信号传递信息。健全可靠的船舶内部和船舶与外界通信是船舶安全航行和正常营运的需要。根据船舶通信方法的不同,船舶信号可分为视觉信号、声响信号和无线电信号。根据船舶通信信文种类的不同,船舶信号可分为明语信号和码语信号;船舶码语信号又可分为单字母信号、双字母信号和三字母信号。根据船舶信号的用途不同,船舶信号可分为船舶避碰信号、船舶应变信号、船舶遇险信号、船舶救生信号和船舶安全信号等。

The signal is the carrier of information. The mariner transmits information through nautical signals. Sound and reliable internal and external communication is necessary for safety navigation and normal operation of ships. According to different methods of communication, nautical signals are divided into visual signals, sound signals and radio signals. Nautical signals are divided into plain language signals and code language signals as per different types of information. Code language signals consist of single-letter signals, double-letter signals and three-letter signals. On the basis of the different purpose, nautical signals involve collision avoidance signals, emergency alarm signals, distress signals, life saving signals, safety signals and so on.

3.2.1　船舶视觉信号
3.2.1　Visual Signals

船舶视觉信号是在视觉范围内的近距离通信方式,包括旗号通信信号、灯光通信信号、手旗或手臂通信信号。船舶视觉信号设备有闪光信号灯、国际信号旗、国旗、区旗、手旗等。不同大小的船舶应配备的船舶视觉信号设备不一致。其中,闪光信号灯有手提式、旋转座架式、桅顶式,如图 3.2.1 所示;国际信号旗、国旗、区旗和手旗有 1 号、2 号等不同规格。国际信号旗 1 套共 40 面,包括字母旗 26 面,数字旗 10 面,代旗 3 面,回答旗 1 面,如图 3.2.2 所示。手旗一般为字母“O”“P”信号旗套在木柄上制成。

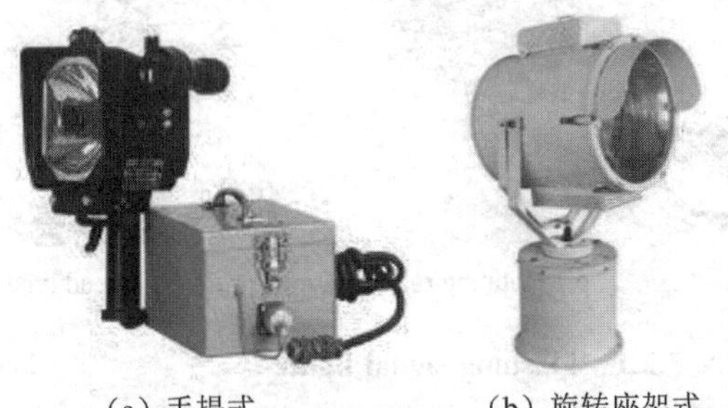

(a) 手提式　(b) 旋转座架式　(c) 桅顶式

图 3.2.1　船舶闪光信号灯

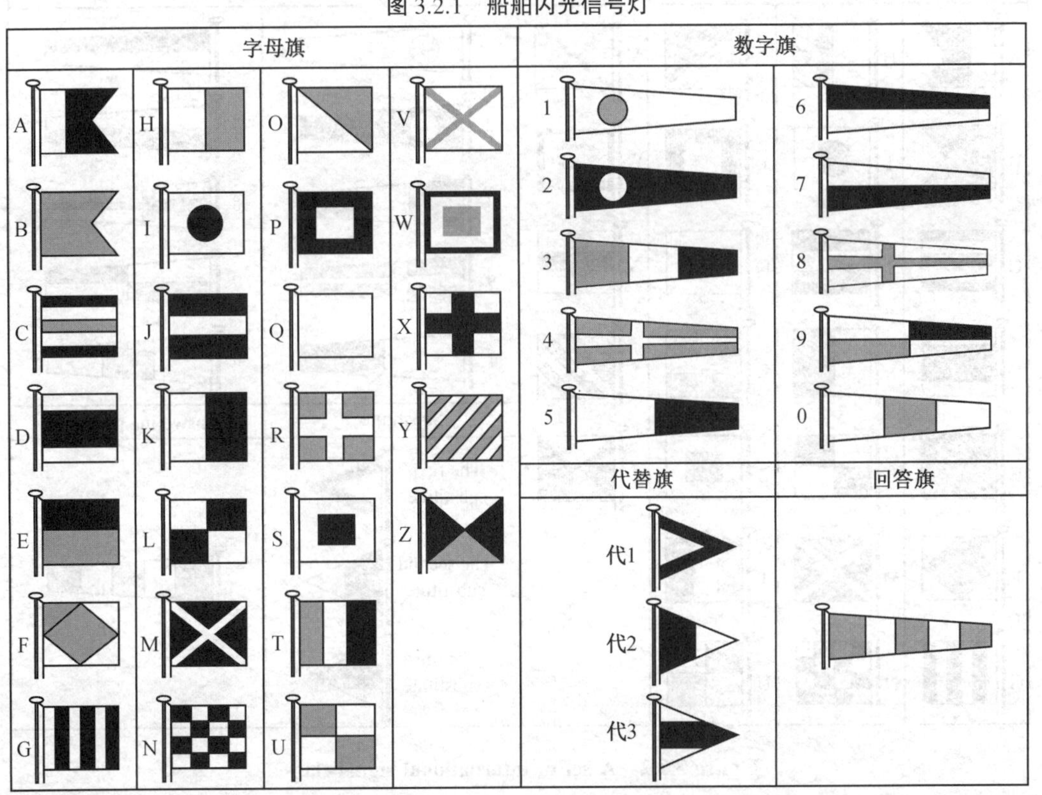

图 3.2.2　1 套国际信号旗

Visual signals are methods of short distance communication in visual range, including flag signals, flashing light signals, and hand-flags or arms signals. Equipments for visual signals involve flashing signal lights, international signal flags, national flags, regional flags, hand-flags, etc. Different sizes of vessels shall be equipped with different equipment for visual signals. There are three types of flashing signal lights: portable, rotating rack and masthead type, see Figure 3.2.1; international signal flags, national flags, regional flags and hand-flags come in different sizes, such as flag 1, flag 2, etc. A set of international signal flags consists of 26 alphabetical flags, 10 numeral pendants, 3 substitutes and 1 answering pendant, see Figure 3.2.2. Hand-flags are commonly made of signal flag O or signal flag P with wooden stick.

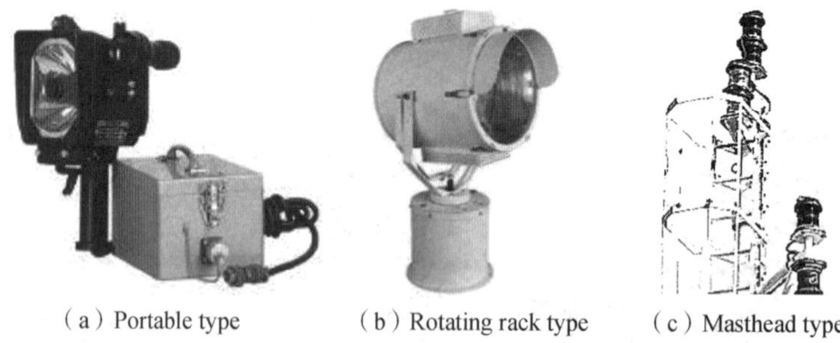

(a) Portable type　　(b) Rotating rack type　　(c) Masthead type

Figure 3.2.1　Flashing signal lights

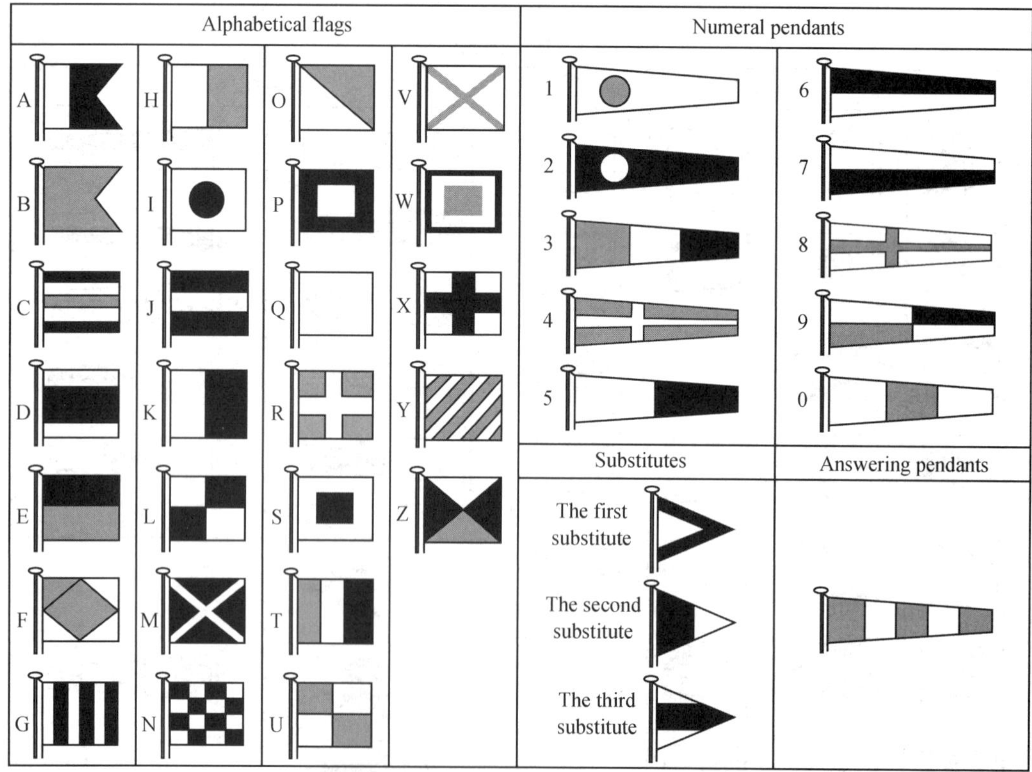

Figure 3.2.2　A set of international signal flags

为了使得在海上通信各方之间明语沟通障碍时仍能够通信,国际海事组织(IMO)实施《国际信号规则》,通信各方可利用码语进行通信,即采用国际共同约定的且能代表一定实际意义的信号码代替明语通信。船舶视觉信号可用明语和码语两种信文通信。视觉通信中应尽可能首先使用明语。当存在语言隔阂时,可用码语通信。其中,旗号通信采用信号旗进行信号传递,灯光通信采用闪光信号灯进行莫尔斯信号传递,手旗或手臂通信采用手旗进行或手臂进行莫尔斯信号传递,如表 3.2.1 所示。

表 3.2.1　字母和数字的莫尔斯符号

字母	莫尔斯符号	字母	莫尔斯符号	数字	莫尔斯符号
A	·—	N	—·	1	·————
B	—···	O	———	2	··———
C	—·—·	P	·——·	3	···——
D	—··	Q	——·—	4	····—
E	·	R	·—·	5	·····
F	··—·	S	···	6	—····
G	——·	T	—	7	——···
H	····	U	··—	8	———··
I	··	V	···—	9	————·
J	·———	W	·——	0	—————
K	—·—	X	—··—		
L	·—··	Y	—·——		
M	——	Z	——··		

In order to make communication possible whenever communication difficulties in plain language between communication parties at sea, IMO implements the International Code of Signals, which propose the code language may be used by parties, that is, the internationally agreed signal code that can represent a certain practical meaning is used instead of plain language communication. Visual signals are used in plain language and code language. Visual communication should be in plain language first as far as possible. Code language is used to communicate when language difficulties exist. Among them, flag signaling is any method of communication by signal flags, flashing light signaling is any method of communication using Morse symbols by flashing signal lights, and hand-flags or arms signaling is any method of communication using Morse symbols by hand-flags or arms, see Table 3.2.1.

Table 3.2.1 Morse symbols of alphabet and numerals

Alphabet	Morse symbols	Alphabet	Morse symbols	Numerals	Morse symbols
A	·—	N	—·	1	·————
B	—···	O	———	2	··———
C	—·—·	P	·——·	3	···——
D	—··	Q	——·—	4	····—
E	·	R	·—·	5	·····
F	··—·	S	···	6	—····
G	——·	T	—	7	——···
H	····	U	··—	8	———··
I	··	V	···—	9	————·
J	·———	W	·——	0	—————
K	—·—	X	—··—		
L	·—··	Y	—·——		
M	——	Z	——··		

此外,《国际信号规则》对部分信号码做了规定,包括单字母信号码、双字母信号码和三字母信号码。现代航海中仅单字母信号码较为常用。

Besides, the International Code of Signals stipulates some letter signals, including single-letter signals, two-letter signals and three-letter signals. Single-letter signals are very commonly used in modern navigation.

(1)单字母信号码:26 个英文字母除 R 外,每一个字母都表达一个意义,如表 3.2.2 所示。

(1) Single-letter signals: 26 English letters in addition to letter R, each letter expresses a meaning, see Table 3.2.2.

表 3.2.2 单字母信号码意义

字母	意义
A	我下面有潜水员;请慢速远离我
B	我正在装、卸或载运危险货物
C	是(肯定或"前组信号的意义应理解为肯定的")
D	请让开我;我操纵困难
E	我正在向右转向
F	我操纵失灵;请与我通信
G	我需要引航员 在渔场附近由正在作业的渔船使用时,它的意思是"我正在收网"

续表

字母	意义
H	我船上有引航员
I	我正在向左转向
J	请远离我,我船失火,并且船上有危险货物,或我船正在泄漏危险货物
K	我希望与你通信
L	你应立即停船
M	我船已停,并已没有对水速度
N	不(否定或"前组信号的意义应理解为否定的")
O	有人落水
P	在港内,本船将要出海,所有人员应立即回船 在海上,当由渔船使用时,意为"我的网缠在障碍物上";也可以用声号表示"我需要一名引航员"
Q	我船没有染疫,请发给进口检疫证
S	我船正在向后推进
T	请让开我;我正在对拖作业
U	你正在临近危险中
V	我需要援助
W	我需要医疗援助
X	中止你的意图,并注意我发送的信号
Y	我正在走锚
Z	我需要一艘拖船 在渔场附近由正在作业的渔船使用时,它的意思是"我正在放网"

Table 3.2.2 Meaning of single-letter signals

Alphabet	Meaning
A	I have a diver down; keep well clear at slow speed
B	I am taking in, or discharging, or carrying dangerous goods
C	Yes (affirmative or "The significance of the previous group should be read in the affirmative")
D	Keep clear of me; I am maneuvering with difficulty
E	I am altering my course to starboard
F	I am disabled; communicate with me
G	I require a pilot When made by fishing vessels operating in close proximity on the fishing grounds it means: "I am hauling nets"
H	I have a pilot on board

Continued

Alphabet	Meaning
I	I am altering my course to port
J	I am on fire and have dangerous cargo on board, keep well clear of me, or I am leaking dangerous cargo
K	I wish to communicate with you
L	You should stop your vessel instantly
M	My vessel is stopped and making no way through the water
N	No (negative or "The significance of the previous group should be read in the negative")
O	Man overboard
P	In harbour—All persons should report on board as the vessel is about to proceed to sea At sea—It may be used by fishing vessels to mean:"My nets have come fast upon an obstruction"; may also be used as a sound to mean:"I require a pilot"
Q	My vessel is"healthy" and I request free pratique
S	I am operating astern propulsion
T	Keep clear of me; I am engaged in pair trawling
U	You are running into danger
V	I require assistance
W	I require medical assistance
X	Stop carrying out your intentions and watch for my signals
Y	I am dragging my anchor
Z	I require a tug When made by fishing vessels operating in close proximity on the fishing grounds it means:"I am shooting nets"

(2)双字母信号码:两个英文字母构成,表达一个意义。

(2)Two-letter signals:consist of 2 English letters, which express a meaning.

(3)三字母信号码:以"M"字母为首的三个英文字母构成,表达一个意义,

(3)Three-letter signals:consist of 3 English letters beginning with "M", which expresses a meaning.

如果庆祝船籍国或港口国的重大节日、迎接贵宾、举办船舶首航或者其他重要活动,船舶应悬挂满旗。船舶悬挂满旗的方法为:习惯按两面字母旗和一面三角旗(数字旗、代替旗或回答旗)的顺序重复连接起来,通常这个顺序需要按旗子的颜色均匀分布,以便所有的黄色、红色或蓝色信号旗不会在一起。满旗绳从船首旗杆经过桅顶直至船尾旗杆;在桅顶悬挂船籍国国旗。"育鲲"轮挂满旗如图 3.2.3 所示。

In case of celebrating major festivals in the country of registration or port state, welcoming very important persons, holding maiden voyage or other important activities, ships should be fully dressed. The method of full-dress ship is:it is a good practice to follow a sequence of two alphabetical and one pendant (numeral pendant, substitute or answering pendant), repeated over and over, generally this sequence needs an even distribution of the colors of the flags, so that all the yellow or red or blue signal flags aren't together. The dressing line starts from the jack staff to the masthead and thence to the ensign staff; the National ensign is hoisted at the masthead. Fully dressed "YU KUN" is shown in Figure 3.2.3.

图 3.2.3 "育鲲"轮挂满旗

Figure 3.2.3 Fully dressed "YU KUN"

3.2.2 船舶声响信号

3.2.2 Sound Signals

船舶声响信号是在听觉范围内的近距离通信方式,可通过气笛、号笛、雾角、号钟或其他声响器具发送莫尔斯信号传递信息,或利用强力扬声器明语或语音拼读喊话传递信息。船舶声响信号可用明语和码语两种信文通信。由于声响器具的特性,发送的莫尔斯声响信号必须缓慢。此外,海上误用声响信号会造成严重混乱,因此在雾中应尽量少用声响信号。在现代航海中,莫尔斯声响信号通信较少使用。在利用强力扬声器喊话时,字母和数字有专门的语音拼读,详见字母拼读表和数字拼读表。

Sound signals are methods of short distance communication in hearing range, passing Morse signals by means of siren, whistle, foghorn, bell, or other sound apparatus, or using plain language or phonetic spelling by voice over a loud hailer. Sound signals are used in plain language and code language. Owing to the nature of the apparatus, sound signaling is necessarily slow. Moreover, the misuse of sound signaling is of a nature to create serious confusion at sea. Sound signaling in fog should therefore be reduced to a minimum. Sound signalling passing Morse signals are rarely used in modern navigation. While using voice over a loud hailer, both letters and figures have special phonetic spelling, see letter-spelling table and figure-spelling table for details.

3.2.3 船舶无线电信号

3.2.3 Radio Signals

船舶无线电信号是利用无线电波在空中传播信号的较远距离通信方式,包括无线电报通信信号、无线电话通信信号、无线电传通信信号、无线传真通信信号、电子邮件通信信号等。目前无线电报通信已被淘汰。根据船舶无线电通信设备的组成,船舶无线电信号可分为地面通信信号和卫星通信信号。目前,地面通信包括 MF/HF 通信、VHF 通信、NAVTEX 通信和 SART 通信等;卫星通信信号包括 Inmarsat 通信、COSPAS-SARSAT 通信和 VSAT 通信等。国际海事组织(IMO)对于不同海区航行的船舶无线电通信设备的配备要求不同。船舶最常用的无线电通信为 VHF 无线电话通信,任何海区航行的船舶均应配备 1 台 VHF 无线电话设备。无线电话信号可用明语和码语两种信文通信。无线电通信中应尽可能首先使用明语。当存在语言隔阂时,可用码语通信。在无线电话通信时,字母和数字有专门的语音拼读,详见字母拼读表(如表 3.2.3 所示)和数字拼读表(如表 3.2.4 所示)。无线电话中听到下列任何一个字母或数字开始的信息均是有关船舶安全的。

表 3.2.3 字母拼读表

字母	代码	发音	字母	代码	发音
A	Alfa	**AL** FAH	N	November	NO **VEM** BER
B	Bravo	**BRAH** VOH	O	Oscar	**OSS** CAH
C	Charlie	**CHAR** LEE	P	Papa	PAH **PAH**
D	Delta	**DELL** TAH	Q	Quebec	KEH **BECK**
E	Echo	**ECK** OH	R	Romeo	**ROW** ME OH
F	Foxtrot	**FOKS** TROT	S	Sierra	SEE **AIR** RAH
G	Golf	GOLF	T	Tango	**TANG** GO
H	Hotel	HOH **TELL**	U	Uniform	**YOU** NEE FORM
I	India	**IN** DEE AH	V	Victor	**VIK** TAH
J	Juliett	**JEW** LEE **ETT**	W	Whiskey	**WISS** KEY
K	Kilo	**KEY** LOH	X	X-ray	**ECKS** RAY
L	Lima	**LEE** MAH	Y	Yankee	**YANG** KEY
M	Mike	MIKE	Z	Zulu	**ZOO** LOO

注:黑体字的音节应重音读出。

表 3.2.4　数字拼读表

数字	代码	发音	数字或标点	代码	发音
0	NADAZERO	NAH-DAH-ZAY-ROH	6	SOXISIX	SOK-SEE-SIX
1	UNAONE	OO-NAH-WUN	7	SETTESEVEN	SAY-TAY-SEVEN
2	BISSOTWO	BEES-SOH-TOO	8	OKTOEIGHT	OK-TOH-AIT
3	TERRATHREE	TAY-RAH-TREE	9	NOVENINE	NO-VAY-NINER
4	KARTEFOUR	KAR-TAY-FOWER	小数点	DECIMAL	DAY-SEE-MAL
5	PANTAFIVE	PAN-TAH-FIVE	句号	STOP	STOP

注:每个音节轻重相同。

Radio signals are methods of long distance communication, passing signals by radio waves in the air, including radiotelegraphy signals, radiotelephony signals, radioteletype signals, radio facsimile signals, E-mail signals, etc. Radiotelegraphy is now obsolete. According to the composition of marine radio communication equipment, radio signals are divided into terrestrial communication signals and satellite communication signals. At present, terrestrial communication system involves MF/HF communications, VHF communications, NAVTEX communications, SART communications and so on; Satellite communication system involves Inmarsat communications, COSPAS-SARSAT communications, VSAT communications and so on. According to the IMO regulations, in different sea areas the requirements for marine radio communications equipment are different. The most common radio communication on ships is the VHF radiotelephony. Every ship in any sea area shall be provided with a VHF radio installation. Radio signals are used in plain language and code language. Radio communication should be in plain language first as far as possible. Code language is used to communicate when language difficulties exist. While using radiotelephony both letters and figures have special phonetic spelling, see letter-spelling table (see Table 3.2.3) and figure-spelling table for details (see Table 3.2.4). Any message which you hear prefixed by one of the following words concerns SAFETY:

Table 3.2.3　Letter-spelling table

Letter	Code word	Pronunciation	Letter	Code word	Pronunciation
A	Alfa	**AL** FAH	N	November	NO **VEM** BER
B	Bravo	**BRAH** VOH	O	Oscar	**OSS** CAH
C	Charlie	**CHAR** LEE	P	Papa	PAH **PAH**
D	Delta	**DELL** TAH	Q	Quebec	KEH **BECK**
E	Echo	**ECK** OH	R	Romeo	**ROW** ME OH
F	Foxtrot	**FOKS** TROT	S	Sierra	SEE **AIR** RAH
G	Golf	GOLF	T	Tango	**TANG** GO
H	Hotel	HOH **TELL**	U	Uniform	**YOU** NEE FORM

Continued

Letter	Code word	Pronunciation	Letter	Code word	Pronunciation
I	India	**IN** DEE AH	V	Victor	**VIK** TAH
J	Juliett	**JEW** LEE **ETT**	W	Whiskey	**WISS** KEY
K	Kilo	**KEY** LOH	X	X-ray	**ECKS** RAY
L	Lima	**LEE** MAH	Y	Yankee	**YANG** KEY
M	Mike	MIKE	Z	Zulu	**ZOO** LOO

Note: the boldfaced syllables are emphasized.

Table 3.2.4 Figure-spelling table

Figure	Code word	Pronunciation	Figure or mark	Code word	Pronunciation
0	NADAZERO	NAH-DAH-ZAY-ROH	6	SOXISIX	SOK-SEE-SIX
1	UNAONE	OO-NAH-WUN	7	SETTESEVEN	SAY-TAY-SEVEN
2	BISSOTWO	BEES-SOH-TOO	8	OKTOEIGHT	OK-TOH-AIT
3	TERRATHREE	TAY-RAH-TREE	9	NOVENINE	NO-VAY-NINER
4	KARTEFOUR	KAR-TAY-FOWER	Decimal/poing	DECIMAL	DAY-SEE-MAL
5	PANTAFIVE	PAN-TAH-FIVE	Full stop	STOP	STOP

Note: each syllable should be equally emphasized.

(1) MAYDAY:遇险,表示一艘船舶、飞机或其他交通工具受到重大而紧迫的危险,要求立即援助。

(1) MAYDAY: distress, indicates that a ship, aircraft, or other vehicle is threatened by grave and imminent danger and requests immediate assistance.

(2) PAN-PAN:紧急,表示呼叫台有很紧急的电信要发送,关系到一艘船舶、飞机或其他交通工具的安全或人员的安全。

(2) PAN-PAN: urgency, indicates that the calling station has a very urgent message to transmit concerning the safety of a ship, aircraft, or other vehicle, or the safety of a person.

(3) SECURITE:安全,表示呼叫台将要发送有关航行安全的电信或发出重要的气象警告。

(3) SECURITE: safety, indicates that the station is about to transmit a message concerning the safety of navigation or giving important meteorological warnings.

3.2.4 船舶避碰信号

3.2.4 Collision Avoidance Signals

船舶避碰信号包括船舶的号灯与号型、船舶的声响和灯光信号。这些信号有助于船舶驾驶人员海上避碰。

Collision avoidance signals include lights and shapes, sound and light signals. These signals aid the officer in charge of a navigational watch to avoid collisions at sea.

3.2.4.1　号灯和号型

3.2.4.1　Lights and Shapes

《国际海上避碰规则》对船舶的号灯与号型的适用范围、号灯的种类与能见距离、各类船舶的号灯与号型以及号灯与号型的位置及技术细节等做了规定，如表 3.2.5 所示。船舶驾驶人员可通过船舶的号灯和号型识别船舶种类、大小、动态和工作性质等。在航机动船显示的号灯如图 3.2.4 所示。船舶的各种号型（均为黑色）如图 3.2.5 所示。

表 3.2.5　船舶各种号灯的灯色、水平光弧和最小能见距离

号灯类别	灯色	水平光弧	最小能见距离/n mile			
			$L\geqslant 50$ m	$20\leqslant L<50$ m	$12\leqslant L<20$ m	$L<12$ m
桅灯	白	225°；正前方至左右舷正横后 22.5°	6	5	3	2
舷灯	左红，右绿	112.5°；正前方至该舷正横后 22.5°	3	2	2	1
艉灯	白	135°；正后方至左右舷各 67.5°	3	2	2	2
拖带灯	黄	135°；正后方至左右舷各 67.5°	3	2	2	2
环照灯	红绿白黄	360°	3	2	2	2
闪光灯	白黄	360°	闪频≥120 次/分			

注：L 为船长。

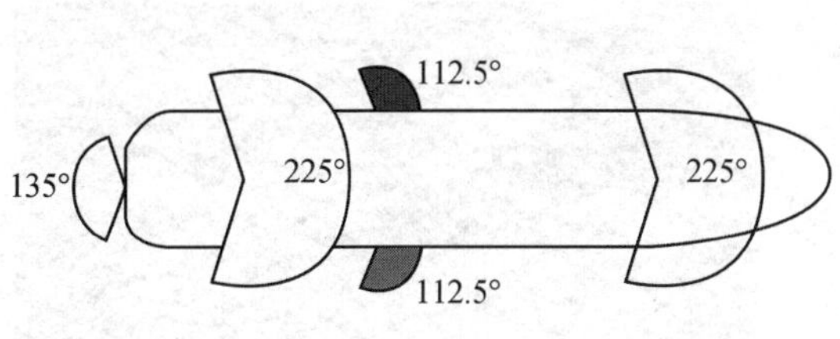

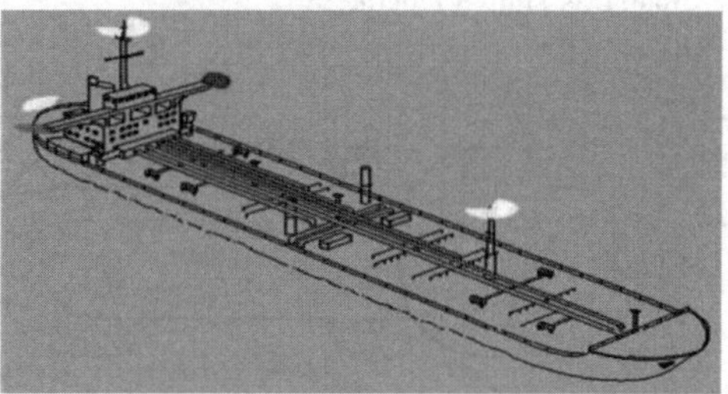

图 3.2.4　在航机动船显示的号灯

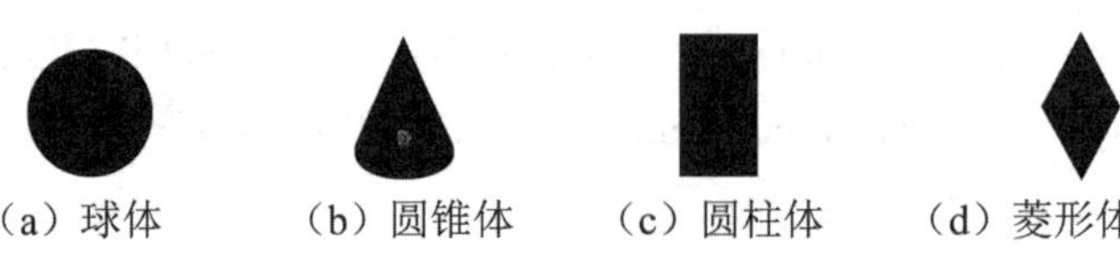

图 3.2.5　船舶的各种号型(均为黑色)

The COLREGs stipulate the application of lights and shapes, types and visibility of lights, lights and shapes for various vessels, as well as the positioning and technical details of signal lights and shapes, see Table 3.2.5. The officer in charge of a navigational watch may identify the type, size, dynamic state and the nature of work of a vessel by lights and shapes exhibited. Lights for a power-driven vessel underway are shown in Figure 3.2.4. Shapes for vessels (all are black) are shown in Figure 3.2.5.

Table 3.2.5　Color, arc of horizon and minimum range of lights

Types of lights	Color	Arc of horizon	Minimum range/n mile			
			$L \geq 50$ m	$20 \leq L < 50$ m	$12 \leq L < 20$ m	$L < 12$ m
Masthead light	White	225°; from right ahead to 22.5° abaft the beam on either side	6	5	3	2
Sidelights	Red(P.S.) Green(S.S.)	112.5°; from right ahead to 22.5° abaft the beam on its respective side	3	2	2	1
Sternlight	White	135°; 67.5° from right aft on each side	3	2	2	2
Towing light	Yellow	135°; 67.5° from right aft on each side	3	2	2	2
All-round light	Red/Green/ White/Yellow	360°	3	2	2	2
Flashing light	White/Yellow	360°	A frequency of 120 flashes or more per min.			

Note: L is ship's length.

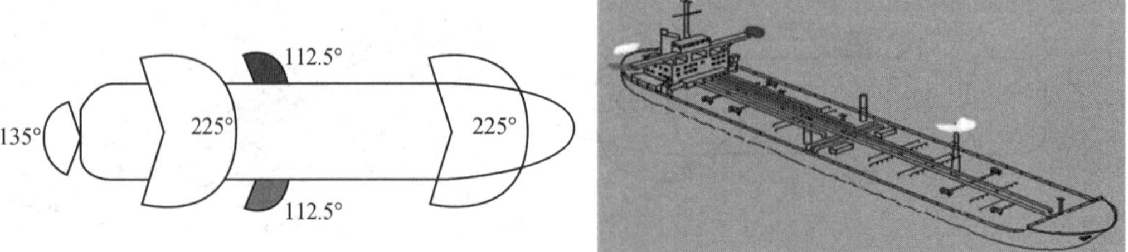

Figure 3.2.4　Lights for a power-driven vessel underway

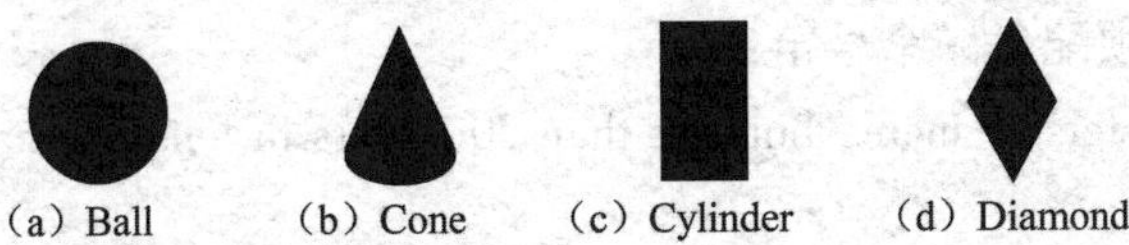

Figure 3.2.5 Shapes for vessels (all are black)

3.2.4.2 声响和灯光信号
3.2.4.2 Sound and Light Signals

《国际海上避碰规则》对船舶的声响设备的配置要求、船舶在互见中和能见度不良情况下应施放各种船舶的声号和灯光信号以及声号器具的技术细节等做了规定。船舶的声响和灯光信号与船舶号灯与号型作用相似。船舶驾驶人员可通过声响和灯光信号识别船舶种类、大小、动态、工作性质和警告等。船舶声响设备如图 3.2.6 所示,其中(a)为号笛,(b)为号钟,(c)为号锣。

The COLREGs stipulate the equipment requirements of sound signals, sound and light signals for various vessels in sight of another and restricted visibility, as well as the technical details of sound signal appliances. The function of sound and light signals is similar to that of lights and shapes. The officer in charge of a navigational watch may identify the type, size, dynamic state, the nature of work and warning of a vessel by sound and light signals exhibited. Equipment for Sound signals are shown in Figure 3.2.6, wherein (a) is a whistle, (b) is a bell, (c) is a gong.

图 3.2.6 船舶声响设备

Figure 3.2.6 Equipment for sound signals

船舶应配备的声号设备根据船长 L 规定了四个等级:

Four classes of equipment for sound signals shall be equipped according to the length of a vessel:

①$L \geqslant 100$ m,须配备一个号笛、一个号钟和一个号锣;

①A vessel of 100 meters or more in length shall be provided with a whistle, a bell and a gong;

②100 m$>L \geqslant 20$ m,须配备一个号笛、一个号钟;

②A vessel of 20 meters or more, but less than 100 meters in length, shall be provided with a whistle, and a bell;

③20 m>L≥12 m，须配备一个号笛；

③A vessel of 12 meters or more, but less than 20 meters in length, shall be provided with a whistle;

④L<12 m，不要求备有上述声响器具，但至少应配备能发出有效声响的其他设备，如雾角和手摇铃等。

④A vessel of less than 12 meters in length shall not be obliged to carry the sound signaling appliances prescribed above. But if she does not, she shall be provided with some other means of making an efficient sound signal, such as a horn, handbell.

用作显示操纵行动灯光信号的号灯是一盏环照白灯，能见距离至少为 5 n mile。如需招引他船注意，任何船舶都可以发出灯光或声响信号，但这种信号应不致被误认为《国际海上避碰规则》其他条款所准许的任何信号，或者可用不致妨碍任何船舶的方式把探照灯的光束朝着危险的方向。任何招引他船注意的灯光，应不致被误认为是任何助航标志的灯光。为此目的，应避免使用诸如频闪灯这样高亮度的间歇灯或旋转灯。

The light used for maneuvering signals is all-round white, visible at a minimum range of 5 n mile. If necessary to attract the attention of another vessel, any vessel may make light or sound signals that cannot be mistaken for any signal authorized elsewhere in the COLREGs, or may direct the beam of her searchlight in the direction of the danger, in such a way as not to embarrass any vessel. Any light to attract the attention of another vessel shall be such that it cannot be mistaken for any aid to navigation. For the purpose, the use of high-intensity intermittent or revolving lights, such as strobe lights, shall be avoided.

3.2.5 船舶应变信号
3.2.5 Emergency Alarm Signals

如表 3.2.6 所示，船舶应变信号是通过通用应急报警系统以船舶号笛或者气笛以及附加电铃或电喇叭或其他等效报警系统发出的通用应急报警信号和其他应变信号。除了船舶号笛外，船舶通用应急报警系统必须能在船舶驾驶台和其他重要位置操作。全船所有起居处所及船员通常工作场所均能听到该系统的信号。该信号在启动后应能连续发出直至人工关闭或被公共广播系统的信息暂时打断。公共广播系统可作为通用应急报警系统的补充，但不能播发船舶应变信号，仅用于发布指令、说明应变信号内容。船舶通用报警信号为七个或以上的短声继以一长声。根据船舶应急演习或实际的紧急情况的不同，船舶应变信号可主要分为：

As shown in Table 3.2.6, emergency alarm signals are the general emergency alarm signal and other emergency alarm signals sounded by general emergency alarm system on the ship's whistle or siren and additionally on an electrically operated bell or klaxon or other equivalent warning system. The general emergency alarm system shall be capable of operation from the navigation bridge and, except for the ship's whistle, also from other strategic points. The system shall be throughout all the accommodation and normal crew working spaces. The signal shall continue to function after it has been triggered until it is manually turned off or is temporarily interrupted by a message on the public address system. The public address system is used as a supplement to the general emergency alarm system, but it cannot sound emergency alarm signals and is only used to broadcast instructions and explain the content of the signal. The general emergency alarm signal consists of seven or more short blasts followed by one long blast. According to the emergency drills or real emergency situation, other emergency alarm signals are mainly divided into:

(1)消防应变信号:一般为短声 1 min;前部失火为短声 1 min 接一长声,中部失火为短声 1 min 接二长声,后部失火为短声 1 min 接三长声,机舱失火为短声 1 min 接四长声,生活区失火为短声 1 min 接五长声。

(1)Fire alarm signal:commonly short blasts for one minute; short blasts for one minute and 1 long blast for the fore part, short blasts for one minute and 2 long blasts for the middle part, short blasts for one minute and 3 long blasts for the aft part, short blasts for one minute and 4 long blasts for the engine room, short blasts for one minute and 5 long blasts for the accommodation area.

(2)弃船(救生)应变信号:一般为七短声继以一长声。

(2)Abandon ship alarm signal (boat drill signal):commonly 7 short blasts and 1 long blast.

(3)溢油应变信号:一般为一短声、二长声继以一短声。

(3)Oil spill signal:1 short blast, commonly 2 long blasts and 1 short blast.

(4)人员落水应变信号:一般为三长声;右舷落水为三长声继以一短声,左舷落水为三长声继以二短声。

(4)Man overboard alarm signal:commonly 3 long blasts; 3 long blasts and 1 short blast for MOB on the starboard side, 3 long blasts and 2 short blasts for MOB on the port side.

(5)堵漏(进水)应变信号:一般为二长声继以一短声。

(5)Flooding signal:commonly 2 long blasts and 1 short blast.

(6)警报解除信号:一般为一长声。

(6)Alarm dismissal signal:commonly 1 long blast.

表 3.2.6　船舶应变信号

船舶应变种类	应变信号
消防	· · · · · · · · · 1 min;接 — 前部失火,接 — — 中部失火,接 — — — 后部失火,接 — — — — 机舱失火,接 — — — — — 生活区失火
弃船(救生)	· · · · · · · —
溢油	· — — ·
人员落水	— — — · 右舷落水, — — — · · 右舷落水
堵漏(进水)	— — ·
警报解除	—

Table 3.2.6 Emergency alarm signals

Types	Signals
Fire alarm signal	· · · · · · · · · · 1 min;add — fore,add — — middle,add — — — aft,add — — — — E.R.,add — — — — — — accommodation
Abandon ship alarm signal	· · · · · · · · —
Oil spill signal	· — — ·
Man overboard alarm signal	— — — · MOB starboard,— — — · · MOB port
Flooding signal	— — ·
Alarm dismissal signal	—

3.2.6 船舶遇险信号
3.2.6 Distress Signals

如图 3.2.7 所示,船舶遇险信号是船舶在遇险并需要救助时,应使用或显示的信号。不论是一起或分别使用或显示下列信号,均表示遇险需要救助。

As shown in Figure 3.2.7, distress signals are signals that a ship shall use or exhibit when she is in distress and requires assistance. The following signals, used or exhibited either together or separately, indicate distress and need of assistance.

(1)每隔约 1 min 鸣炮或燃放其他爆炸信号一次。

(1)A gun or other explosive signal fired at intervals of about a minute.

(2)以任何雾号器具连续发声。

(2)A continuous sounding with any fog-signalling apparatus.

(3)以短的间隔,每次鸣放一个抛射红星的火箭或信号弹。

(3)Rockets or shells, throwing red stars fired one at a time at short intervals.

(4)任何通信方法发出莫尔斯码 · · · — — — · · · (SOS)的信号。

(4) A signal made by radiotelegraphy or by any other signalling method consisting of the group · · · — — — · · · (SOS) in the Morse Code.

(5)无线电话发出"Mayday"语言的信号。

(5)A signal sent by radiotelephony consisting of the spoken word "Mayday".

(6)《国际信号规则》中表示遇险的信号 N.C.。

(6)The International Code Signal of distress indicated by N.C.

(7)由一面方旗放在一个球体或任何类似球体的上方或下方所组成的信号。

(7)A signal consisting of a square flag having above or below it a ball or anything resembling a ball.

(8)船上的火焰(如从燃着的柏油桶、油桶等发出的火焰)。

(8)Flames on the vessel (as from a burning tar barrel, oil barrel, etc.).

图 3.2.7　船舶遇险信号

Figure 3.2.7　Distress signals

(9)火箭降落伞或手持式的红色突耀火光。

(9)A rocket parachute flare or a hand-flare showing a red light.

(10)放出橙色烟雾的烟雾信号。

(10)A smoke signal giving off orange-coloured smoke.

(11)两臂侧伸,缓慢而重复地上下摆动。

(11)Slowly and repeatedly raising and lowering arms outstretched to each side.

(12)通过在下列频道或频率上发出的数字选择性呼叫(DSC)发出的遇险警报:

(12)A distress alert by means of digital selective calling (DSC) transmitted on:

①甚高频第70信道;或

①VHF channel 70; or

②中频/高频 2 187.5 kHz、8 414.5 kHz、4 207.5 kHz、6 312.5 kHz、12 577.5 kHz 或 16 804.5 kHz。

②MF/HF on the frequencies 2,187.5 kHz, 8,414.5 kHz, 4,207.5 kHz, 6,312.5 kHz, 12,577.5 kHz or 16,804.5 kHz.

(13)船舶的 Inmarsat 或其他移动卫星业务提供商的船舶地球站发出的船到岸遇险警报。

(13)A ship-to-shore distress alert transmitted by the ship's Inmarsat or other mobile satellite service provider ship earth station.

(14)由紧急无线电示位标发出的信号。

(14)Signals transmitted by emergency positioning-indicating radio beacons.

(15)无线电通信系统发出的经认可的信号,包括救生艇筏雷达应答器。

(15)Approved signals transmitted by radiocommunication systems, including survival craft radar transponders.

(16)一张橙色帆布上带有一个黑色正方形和圆圈或者其他合适的符号(供空中识别)。

(16)A piece of orange-coloured canvas with either a black-square and circle or other appropriate symbol (for identification from the air).

(17)海水染色标志。

(17)A dye marker.

除为表示遇险需要救助外,禁止使用或显示上述任何信号以及可能与上述任何信号相混淆的其他信号。

The use or exhibition of any of the foregoing signals except for the purpose of indicating distress and need of assistance and the use of other signals which may be confused with any of the above signals is prohibited.

3.2.7　船舶救生信号
3.2.7　Life-saving Signals

船舶救生信号是遇险的船舶、飞机或人员在与救生站、海上救助单位和搜救作业的飞机通信时使用的信号，如表3.2.7至表3.2.12所示。

Life saving signals shall be used by ships, aircraft or persons in distress when communicating with life-saving stations, maritime rescue units and aircraft engaged in search and rescue operations, as shown in Tables 3.2.7 to 3.2.12.

表3.2.7　指引遇险船员或人员的小艇登陆的信号

	手操信号	发光信号	其他信号	意义
白天信号	一面白旗或双臂上下挥动	或发射一颗绿色星光信号	— · — 或用灯光或音响信号发出字母“K”	这是最好的登陆地点
夜间信号	一盏白灯或火焰上下挥动	或发射一颗绿色星光信号	— · — 或用灯光或音响信号发出字母“K”	
	注：可用一盏固定的白灯或火焰放在低处并与瞭望者成一直线作示向标（指示方向）			
白天信号	一面白旗或双臂平举做水平挥动	或发射一颗红色星光信号	· · · 或用灯光或音响信号发出字母“S”	在这里登陆最危险
夜间信号	一盏白灯或火焰上下做水平挥动	或发射一颗红色星光信号	· · · 或用灯光或音响信号发出字母“S”	

续表

	手操信号	发光信号	其他信号	意义
白天信号	1.一面白旗做水平挥动； 2.接着把白旗插在地上； 3.并拿着另一面白旗指示引导的方向	1.或垂直发射一颗红色星光信号； 2.并向较好的登陆地点方向发射一颗白色星光信号	1.如在遇险船艇驶近方向的右边有较好的登陆地点，发出字母“S”（· · ·），接着又发出字母“R”（·—·）； 2.如在遇险船艇驶近方向的左边有较好的登陆地点，发出字母“S”（· · ·），接着又发出字母“L”（·—· ·）	在这里登陆很危险，较好的登陆地点是所指的方向
夜间信号	1.一盏白灯或火焰做水平挥动； 2.接着把白灯或火焰放在地上； 3.并拿着另一盏白灯或火焰指示引导的方向	1.或垂直发射一颗红色星光信号； 2.并向较好的登陆地点方向发射一颗白色星光信号	1.如在遇险船艇驶近方向的右边有较好的登陆地点，发出字母“S”（· · ·），接着又发出字母“R”（·—·）； 2.如在遇险船艇驶近方向的左边有较好的登陆地点，发出字母“S”（· · ·），接着又发出字母“L”（·—· ·）	

Table 3.2.7 Landing signals for the guidance of small boats with crews or persons in distress

	Manual signals	Light signals	Other signals	Signification
Day signals	Vertical motion of a white flag or of the arms	or firing of agreen star signal	— · — or code letter K given by light or sound-signal apparatus	This is the best place to land
Night signals	Vertical motion of a white light or flare	or firing of agreen star signal	— · — or code letter K given by light or sound-signal apparatus	
	Note: a range (indication of direction) may be given by placing a steady white light or flare at a lower level and in line with the observer			

Continued

	Manual signals	Light signals	Other signals	Signification
Day signals	Horizontal motion of a white flag or of the arms extended horizontally	or firing of ared star signal	• • • or code letter S given by light or sound signal apparatus	Landing here highly dangerous
Night signals	Horizontal motion of a light or flare	or firing of ared star signal	• • • or code letter S given by light or sound-signal apparatus	
Day signals	1. Horizontal motion of a white flag, followed by; 2.the placing of the white flag in the ground and by; 3. the carrying of another white flag in the direction to be indicated	1. or firing of a red star signal vertically and; 2.a white star signal in the direction towards the better landing place	1.or signalling the code letter S (• • •) followed by the code letter R (• — •) if a better landing place for the craft in distress is located more to the right in the direction of approach; 2.or signaling the code letter S (• • •) followed by the code letter L (• — • •) if a better landing place for the craft in distress is located more to the left in the direction of approach	Landing here highly dangerous. A more avorable location for landing is in the direction indicated
Night signals	1. Horizontal motion of a white light or flare followed by; 2.the placing of the white light or flare on the ground and by; 3. the carrying of another white light or flare in the direction to be indicated	1. or firing of a red star signal vertically; 2.a white star signal in the direction towards the better landing place	1.or signalling the code letter S (• • •) followed by the code letter R (• — •) if a better landing place for the craft in distress is located more to the right in the direction of approach; 2.or signaling the code letter S (• • •) followed by the code letter L (• — • •) if a better landing place for the craft in distress is located more to the left in the direction of approach	

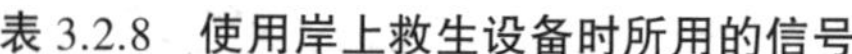

表 3.2.8 使用岸上救生设备时所用的信号

	手操信号	发光信号	其他信号	意义
白天信号	一面白旗或双臂上下挥动	或发射一颗绿色星光信号		一般情况表示：肯定。 特殊情况表示： —火箭绳已握住； —带尾声的滑车已系牢； —缆绳已系牢； —人在裤形救生圈中； —拉走
夜间信号	一盏白灯或火焰上下挥动	或发射一颗绿色星光信号		
白天信号	一面白旗或双臂平举做水平挥动	或发射一颗红色星光信号		一般情况表示：否定 特殊情况表示： —放松； —停拉
夜间信号	一盏白灯或火焰上下做水平挥动	或发射一颗红色星光信号		

Table 3.2.8 Signals to be employed in connection with the use of shore life saving apparatus

	Manual signals	Light signals	Other signals	Signification
Day signals	Vertical motion of a white flag or of the arms	or firing of a green star signal		In general: affirmative. Specifically: —rocket line is held; —tail block is made fast; —hawser is made fast; —man is in the breeches buoy; —haul away
Night signals	Vertical motion of a white light or flare	or firing of a green star signal		
Day signals	Horizontal motion of a white flag or of the arms extended horizontally	or firing of a red star signal		In general: negative Specifically: —slack away; —avast hauling
Night signals	Horizontal motion of a light or flare	or firing of a red star signal		

表 3.2.9 救生站或海上救助单位对船舶或人员发出的遇险信号的回答

	手操信号	发光信号	其他信号	意义
白天信号		 橙色烟雾信号	 或声光混合信号(雷光)三发,每隔 1 min 发射一发	已见到你,将尽快给予援助(重复这种信号时,其意义相同)
夜间信号		 1 min 1 min 白色星光火箭三枚,每隔 1 min 发射一枚		
	注:必要时,白天信号可用于夜间或夜间信号用于白天			

Table 3.2.9 Replies from life saving stations or maritime rescue units to distress signals made by a ship or person

	Manual signals	Light signals	Other signals	Signification
Day signals		 Orange smoke signal	 or combined light and sound signal (thunder-light) consisting of 3 single signals which are fired at intervals of approximately one minute	You are seen, assistance will be given as soon as possible (Repetition of such signal shall have the same meaning)
Night signals		 1 min 1 min White star rocket consisting of 3 single signals which are fired at intervals of approximately one minute		
	Note: if necessary, the day signals may be given at night or the night signals by day			

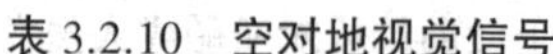

表 3.2.10 空对地视觉信号

飞机在搜寻与救助工作中指导船舶驶向遇险中的飞机、船舶或人员所使用的信号			
飞机先后执行的程序			
1.飞机绕船舶至少转一圈	2.飞机在低空飞行接近船舶船头时,绕船舶的计划航向同时摆动机翼(见注)	3.飞机飞向船舶将被指引的方向	飞机正在指引一艘船舶驶向遇险的飞机或船舶(重复这种信号时,其意义相同)
4.飞机低飞接近船尾,横越船舶的航迹,同时摇摆机翼(见注) 注:开关节流阀(油门)或改变螺旋桨螺距,也可以采用一种如摇摆机翼一样吸引人注意力的方法。然而,由于船舶噪声较高,这种声音信号形式比摇摆机翼的视觉信号效果差			已不需要船舶的援助(重复这种信号时,其意义相同)
船舶回答执行搜救工作的飞机所使用的信号			
悬挂回答旗到顶	改航向到所需方向	或用信号灯发出莫尔斯信号码“T”	告知收到飞机的信号
悬挂国际信号旗“N”(NOVEMBER)		或用信号灯发出莫尔斯信号码“N”	表示不能照办

Table 3.2.10 Air to surface visual signals

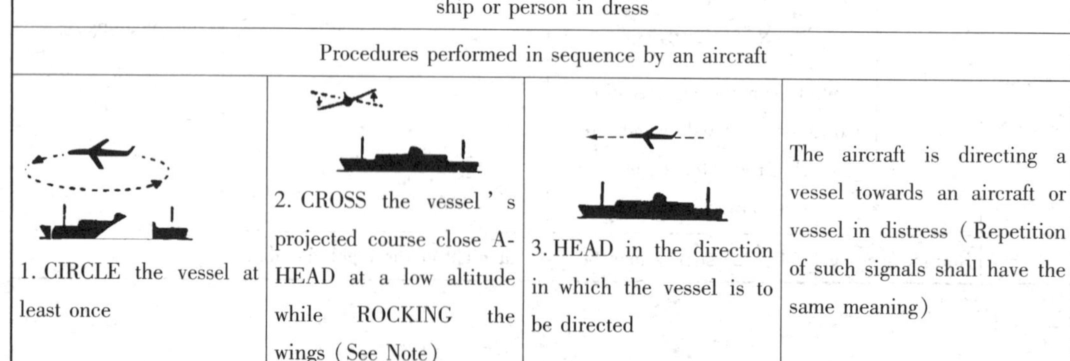

Signals used by aircraft engaged in search and rescue operations to direct ships towards an aircraft, ship or person in dress			
Procedures performed in sequence by an aircraft			
1. CIRCLE the vessel at least once	2. CROSS the vessel's projected course close AHEAD at a low altitude while ROCKING the wings (See Note)	3. HEAD in the direction in which the vessel is to be directed	The aircraft is directing a vessel towards an aircraft or vessel in distress (Repetition of such signals shall have the same meaning)

Continued

 4.CROSS the vessel's wake close ASTERN at low altitude while ROCKING the wings (See Note) Note: Opening and closing the throttle or changing the propeller pitch may also be practiced as an alternative means of attracting attention to that of rocking the wings. However, this form of sound signal may be less effective than the visual signal of rocking the wings owing to high noise level on board the vessel	The assistance of the vessel is no longer required (Repetition of such signals shall have the same meaning)

Signals used by a vessel in response to an aircraft engaged in search and rescue operations			
Hoist "Answering" pendant Close up; or	Change the heading to the required direction; or	— Flash Morse Code signal "T" by signal lamp	Acknowledges receipt of aircraft's signal
Hoist international flag "N" (NOVEMBER); or		— • Flash Morse Code signal "N" by signal lamp	Indicates inability to comply

表 3.2.11 地对空视觉信号

水面船艇或生存者对飞机的通信	
注:在甲板或陆地上显示下列地对空视觉信号中恰当的信号	
信文	国际民航组织/国际海事组织视觉信号
需要援助	V
需要医疗援助	X
不或否定	N
是或肯定	Y
向此方向前进	↑

飞机观察到从水面船艇或生存者发出的上列信号的回答					
投下一封信文(＊能见度高的彩色飘带)	或摆动机翼(白天)	或着陆灯或航行灯开关两次(夜间)	— or • — • 或用灯光发出莫尔斯信号码"T"或"R"	或用其他合适信号	信文收悉
水平直飞不摆动		• — • • — — • — 或用灯光发出莫尔斯信号码"RPT"		或用其他合适信号	信文不明白(请重复)

Table 3.2.11 Surface to air visual signals

<table>
<tr><td colspan="6">Communication from surface craft or survivors to an aircraft</td></tr>
<tr><td colspan="6">Note: Use the following surface-to-air visual signals by displaying the appropriate signal on the deck or on the ground</td></tr>
<tr><td colspan="3">Message</td><td colspan="3">ICAO/IMO visual symbols</td></tr>
<tr><td colspan="3">Require assistance</td><td colspan="3">V</td></tr>
<tr><td colspan="3">Require medical assistance</td><td colspan="3">X</td></tr>
<tr><td colspan="3">No or negative</td><td colspan="3">N</td></tr>
<tr><td colspan="3">Yes or affirmative</td><td colspan="3">Y</td></tr>
<tr><td colspan="3">Proceeding in this direction</td><td colspan="3">↑</td></tr>
<tr><td colspan="6">Reply from an aircraft observing the above signals from surface craft or survivors</td></tr>
<tr><td>Drop a message or (* High visibility colored streamer)</td><td>Rock the wings (during daylight) or</td><td>Flash the landing lights or navigation lights on and off twice (during hours of darkness) or</td><td>— or •—•
Flash Morse Code signal "T" or "R" by light or</td><td>Use any other suitable signal</td><td>Message understood</td></tr>
<tr><td colspan="2">Fly straight and level without rocking wings or</td><td colspan="2">•—• •——• —
Flash Morse Code Signal "RPT" by light or</td><td>Use any other suitable signal</td><td>Message not understood (repeat)</td></tr>
</table>

表 3.2.12 对生存者的信号

<table>
<tr><td colspan="3">飞机完成的程序</td></tr>
<tr><td>投下一封信文
(*能见度高的彩色飘带)</td><td>或投下合适的通信设备来建立直接联络</td><td>飞机希望对生存者发出通知或指示</td></tr>
<tr><td colspan="3">生存者对飞机投下的书信所使用的回答</td></tr>
<tr><td>— or •—•
用灯光发出莫尔斯信号码"T"或"R"</td><td>或使用任何其他合适的信号</td><td>生存者对所投信文收悉</td></tr>
<tr><td>•—• •——• —
用灯光发出莫尔斯信号码"RPT"</td><td></td><td>生存者对所投信文不明白</td></tr>
</table>

Table 3.2.12 Signals to survivors

Procedures performed in sequence by an aircraft		
Drop a message or (* High visibility colored streamer)	Drop communication equipment suitable for establishing direct contact	The aircraft wishes to inform or instruct survivors
Signals used by survivors in response to a message dropped by an aircraft		
— or • — • Flash Morse Code signal "T" or "R" by light or	Use any other suitable signal	Dropped messages is understood by the survivors
• — — • • — — — • — Flash Morse Code signal "RPT" by light		Dropped messages is not understood by the survivors

3.3 船舶操纵性能

3.3 Ship Maneuverability

船舶操纵就是指操船人员对船舶所进行的操作。具体来说,船舶操纵是指操船人员利用船舶操纵设备对船舶运动状态所进行的控制。操船人员更关心的是实施船舶操纵后船舶对操作的反应情况,即船舶的操纵性能状况。

Ship handling refers to the operation of ship handlers on the ship. Specifically, ship handling refers to the control of ship handlers on the state of ship's motion by means of ship handling equipment. Ship handlers are more concerned with the ship's response to the operation after the implementation of ship handling, that is, the state of ship maneuverability.

3.3.1 船舶操纵设备

3.3.1 Ship Handling Equipment

船舶操纵设备也称为船舶运动控制设备,是指船舶本身所装备的有关设备和装置。船舶在不同运动状态下,所使用的操纵设备不尽相同。船舶航行状态下最常用的操纵设备是螺旋桨和舵。进出港和靠离泊操纵时,为了提高船舶在受限水域的操纵性能,有些船舶还配备了侧推器以及特种推进装置等。船舶本身的操纵设备在不能有效控制船舶运动状态的情况下,还需要港作拖船的协助。

Ship handling equipment, also known as ship motion control equipment, refers to the relevant equipment and devices equipped by the ship itself. Various control equipment is used in different states of ship motion. The propeller and rudder are the most commonly used handling equipment when a ship is underway. In order to improve ship maneuverability in restricted waters, some ships are equipped with lateral thrusters, special propulsion devices and so on, when entering and leaving a barbour or berthing and unberthing handling. In the case that the ship handling equipment cannot effectively control the state of ship motion, the harbour tug's assistance is also needed.

3.3.1.1 螺旋桨

3.3.1.1 Propeller

船舶要想以一定的速度航行,必须由主机提供动力来克服船舶阻力,推进船舶航行。该动力即为推进器推力。商船上最常用的推进器是螺旋桨,又称车。螺旋桨是控制船舶速度的重要操纵设备。一般来说,螺旋桨安装于船尾水线以下,由主机获得动力而旋转,推船尾水运动,利用水的反作用力推船移动。操船人员通过操控车钟(如图 3.3.1 所示)控制主机转速,从而控制螺旋桨的转动,以便操纵船舶的速度和方向。

If a ship wants to sail at a certain speed, it must be powered by the main engine to overcome the resistance of the ship and propel the ship to sail. This power is the thrust of the propulsion device. The most commonly used propulsion device in merchant ships are propellers. Propeller is an important equipment to control the ship's speed. Generally speaking, the propeller is installed below the waterline at the stern, which is rotated by the main engine and pushes the water flow at the stern, then causes the ship to move through the water with the reactive force. The ship handler controls the main engine revolution by handling the engine telegraph (see Figure 3.3.1), so as to control the rotation of the propeller and the ship's speed and direction.

图 3.3.1　车钟

Figure 3.3.1　Engine telegraph

螺旋桨主要可分为固定螺距螺旋桨和可调螺距螺旋桨两大类,如图 3.3.2 和图 3.3.3 所示。固定螺距螺旋桨简称固定螺距桨。其螺距是固定不变的(螺距是指螺旋桨旋转一周所前进的距离)。与可调螺距螺旋桨比较,其由于结构简单,维修简便,成本较低,故被广泛使用。可调螺距螺旋桨,又称可变螺距螺旋桨,简称可调螺距桨,可按需要调节螺距,充分发挥主机功率,提高推进效率,船舶前进和后退时可不改变螺旋桨的旋转方向。

Propeller is divided into fixed pitch propeller (FPP) and controllable pitch propeller (CPP), see Figure 3.3.2 and Figure 3.3.3. The pitch of fixed pitch propeller is fixed (pitch refers to the advance distance of propeller rotating one revolution). Compared with controllable pitch propeller, it is widely used because of its simple structure, easy maintenance and low cost. Controllable pitch propeller, also known as variable pitch propeller, which adjusts the pitch as per the requirement to give full play to the power of the main engine and improve the propulsion efficiency, and the rotation direction of the propeller is not changed when the ship goes ahead or astern.

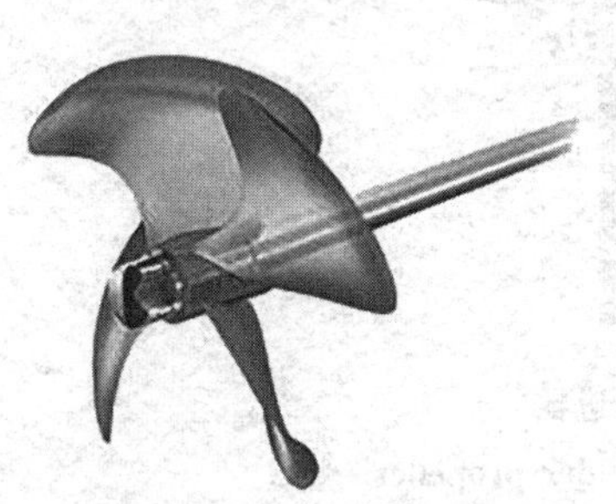

图 3.3.2　固定螺距螺旋桨

Figure 3.3.2　Fixed pitch propeller

图 3.3.3　可调螺距螺旋桨

Figure 3.3.3　Controllable pitch propeller

此外,还有一些特殊螺旋桨的存在,如导管螺旋桨、Z 型推进器、吊舱式推进器、平旋推进器等。导管螺旋桨是在螺旋桨周围加上导流管,增加推力,如图 3.3.4 所示。Z 型推进器可使螺旋桨绕竖轴做 360°转动,任意改变推力的方向,因此又称全回转推进器,如图 3.3.5 所示。吊舱式推进器与 Z 型推进器主要区别是:Z 型推进器的推进电机装在船体内,而吊舱式推进器的推进电机装在吊舱内。因此吊舱式推进器又称全回转吊舱推进器。平旋推进器是在船底旋转圆盘下装有若干可转动的直叶伸入水中,并能产生任何方向推力的螺旋桨,如图 3.3.6 所示。这些特殊螺旋桨具有结构复杂,工艺要求较高等特点,一般用于中小型工程和港作船。

In addition, there are some special propellers, such as ducted propeller, Z-drive, pod propeller, Voith-Schneider Propeller and so on. Ducted propeller is to add a duct around the propeller to increase thrust, see Figure 3.3.4. Z-drive makes the propeller rotate 360° around the vertical axis and change to any direction of thrust, so it is also called azimuth propeller, see Figure 3.3.5. The main difference between pod propeller and Z-drive is that the propulsion motor of the Z-drive is installed in the hull, while that of the pod propeller is installed in the pod. Therefore, pod propeller is also called azipod propeller. Voith-Schneider Propeller is a propeller with perpendicular, rotating blades under a rotating plate on the bottom of a ship that can push in any direction, see Figure 3.3.6. These special propellers have the characteristics of complicated mechanism and higher technology, and are generally used in small and medium-sized engineering ship and harbour craft.

图 3.3.4　导管螺旋桨

Figure 3.3.4　Ducted propeller

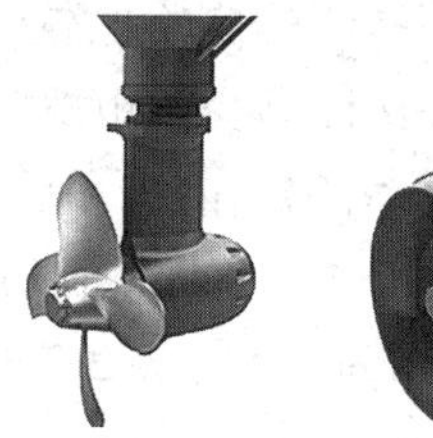

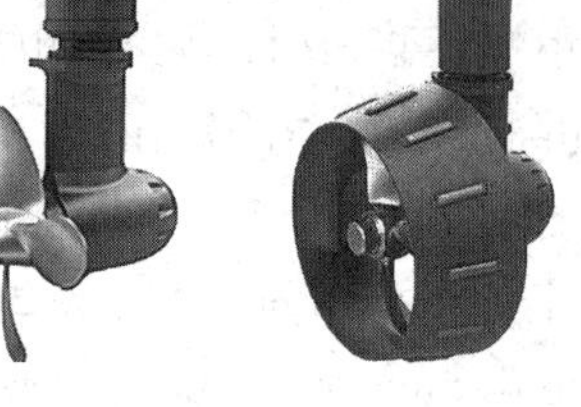

图 3.3.5　Z 型推进器(全回转推进器)

Figure 3.3.5　Z-drive (azimuth propeller)

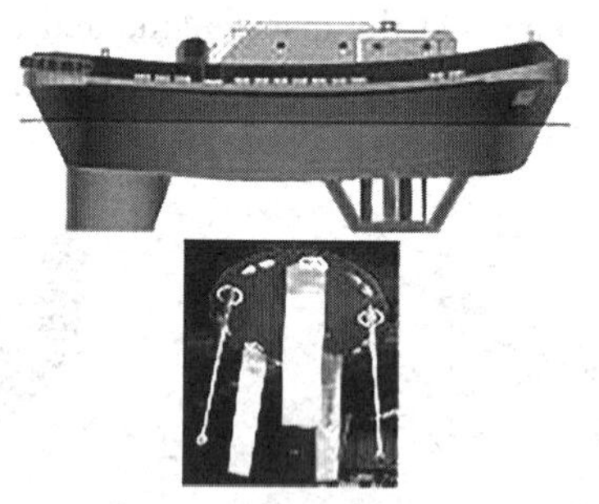

图 3.3.6　平旋推进器

Figure 3.3.6　Voith-Schneider propeller

3.3.1.2　舵

3.3.1.2　Rudder

舵是控制船舶航向的重要操纵设备。舵一般位于螺旋桨的后方,靠近螺旋桨以获取来自螺旋桨的高速水流。该水流经船舶或舵叶在船尾产生一个横向的舵力,从而使船转动。操船人员操控位于驾驶台的舵轮,从而控制舵叶的转动,以便操纵船舶的方向。

Rudder is an important equipment to control the ship's course. The rudder is usually located behind the propeller, close to the propeller to obtain the high speed water flow from propeller. This water flow through the ship or the rudder blade generate a lateral rudder force at the stern, which makes the ship turn. The ship handler handles the steering wheel at the bridge to control the rotation of the rudder blade so as to adjust the ship's direction.

舵的类型较多。按舵杆的轴线位置,舵可分为不平衡舵、平衡舵和半平衡舵。不平衡舵的舵叶面积全部在舵杆轴线的后方,又称普通舵。这种舵有许多支点,舵杆的强度易于保证,舵压力中心至舵轴的距离较大,有利于保持船舶的航向稳定性,但所需的转舵力矩大,所需舵机功率较大。不平衡舵一般用于沿岸航行的小船,如图 3.3.7 所示。平衡舵的舵叶部分面积在舵杆轴线的前方,如图 3.3.8 所示。这种舵的舵压力中心靠近舵轴,不利于保持船舶的航向稳定性,但所需的转舵力矩小,所需舵机功率较小。商船上广泛应用平衡舵。半平衡舵的舵叶部分面积在舵杆轴线的前方,介于普通舵和平衡舵之间,或舵叶的上半部分为不平衡舵,下半部分为平衡舵,如图 3.3.9 所示。这种舵的舵叶的上半部分由挂舵臂支持,使舵坚固可靠,有利于保持航向的稳定性。半平衡舵适合应用于大型船舶。

There are many types of rudder. According to the position of the turning axis of the rudder, rudder divides unbalanced rudder, balanced rudder and semi-balanced rudder. The blade area of the unbalanced rudder is all behind the turning axis, which is also called ordinary rudder. This rudder has many bearing points and is easy to ensure the strength of the rudder stock, and the distance between the center of rudder pressure and the turning axis is large, which is conducive to keep directional stability, but the steering torque is large and the power of the steering engine is high. Unbalanced rudder is usually used for coastal navigation in small boats, see Figure 3.3.7. The parts of blade area of the balance rudder lies in front of the turning axis, see Figure 3.3.8. The center of balance rudder pressure is close to the turning axis, which is not conducive to keep directional stability, but the steering torque is small and the power of the steering engine is low. Balanced rudder is widely used in merchant ships. The blade area of the semi-balanced rudder lies in front of the shaft axis, between the ordinary rudder and the balanced rudder, or the upper part of the rudder is unbalanced and the lower part is balanced, see Figure 3.3.9. The upper part of this rudder is supported by rudder horn, which makes the rudder strong and reliable, and helps to keep directional stability. The semi-balanced rudder is suitable for large ships.

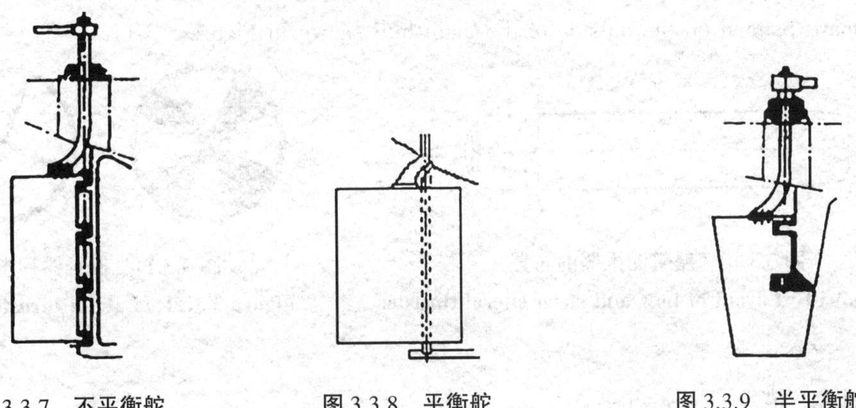

图 3.3.7　不平衡舵　　图 3.3.8　平衡舵　　图 3.3.9　半平衡舵

Figure 3.3.7　Unblanced rudder　Figure 3.3.8　Balanced rudder　Figure 3.3.9　Semi-balanced rudder

3.3.1.3　侧推器

3.3.1.3　Lateral Thruster

侧推器是一种船舶的辅助操纵装置。侧推器一般位于船首或/和船尾横向管道内,由电动机带动侧推器的螺旋桨(一般采用可调螺距桨)旋转,将水推向船侧,利用水的反作用力推船横向运动。操船人员通过操控侧推器控制手柄或旋钮控制侧推器螺旋桨的转速,从而操纵船舶横向运动的速度和方向。船速越高舵控制航向的能力越强。但在船舶进港船速逐渐降低的过程中,操舵控制航向的能力逐渐变差。而侧推器在船舶低速时控制航向的能力强,船速越高侧推器控制航向的能力越弱。

Lateral thruster is a kind of ships' auxiliary control device. Lateral thruster is usually located in the transverse tunnel at the bow or/and stern. The propeller of lateral thruster (usually with controllable pitch propeller) is driven by an electric motor to rotate and pushes the water to any side of the ship, then causes the ship to move laterally through the water with the reactive force. Ship handler controls the propeller revolution of lateral thruster by operating the handle or knob so as to control the ship's lateral speed and direction. The higher the ship's speed is, the better the rudder's ability to control the course is. However, in the process of entering the harbour, the ship's speed gradually decreases, and the ability of steering to control the course gradually becomes worse. While lateral thruster has a strong ability to control the course at low speed, the higher the ship speed is, the weaker lateral thruster's ability to control the course is.

如图 3.3.10 所示,侧推器常安装在靠离泊操纵频率较高的船舶,如滚装船、客船、集装箱船等。一般情况下船首布置艏侧推器,有些船舶在船首、船尾各装上一个至数个侧推器。装有侧推器的船舶在主船体外板上绘有侧推器标志,如图 3.3.11。

As shown in Figure 3.3.10, lateral thruster is usually installed in the ships with high frequency of berthing and unberthing, such as Ro-Ro ship, passenger ship, container ship, etc. Generally, the bow thruster is arranged in the bow, and some ships are equipped with one or more lateral thrusters at the bow and stern respectively. The ship fitted with a lateral thruster has a lateral thruster mark painted on the outside of the main hull shown in Figure 3.3.11.

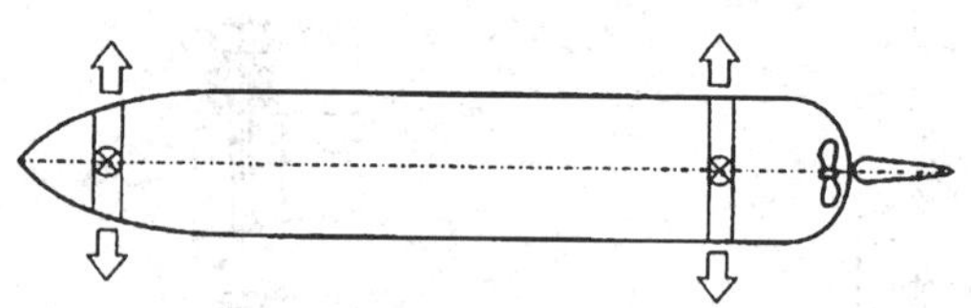

图 3.3.10　艏艉侧推器的布置

Figure 3.3.10　Layout of bow and stern lateral thruster

图 3.3.11　侧推器标志

Figure 3.3.11　Lateral thruster mark

3.3.1.4　锚
3.3.1.4　Anchor

锚是船舶锚泊时所用的设备,也是一种船舶的辅助操纵装置。锚一般位于船首两侧,左舷和右舷各配一只锚,由锚机通过锚链将锚送出或收回。抛锚时,船舶拖着锚使锚爪逐渐抓底。最后当锚抓住海底时,作用在锚上的力达到平衡状态。锚泊时,锚的抓力、锚和锚链的重力、卧底锚链的摩擦力共同抵御风、流等对船的作用力,最终使船舶被系留在指定水域。此外,船舶在航行时,有时抛锚协助掉头或转向;船舶靠离泊时,用拖锚控制船首航向、控制船身或降低船速;在紧急情况下,用拖锚降低船速,避免碰撞;船舶搁浅时,操船人员可沿脱浅方向抛锚,绞收锚链以协助脱浅。霍尔锚和斯贝克锚如图 3.3.12 所示,其中(a)为霍尔锚,(b)为斯贝克锚。

Anchor is used for anchoring and is also a kind of ships' auxiliary control device. Anchors are generally located on both sides of the bow, with an anchor on the port side and an anchor on the starboard side. The anchor is slacked away or heaved in by the windlass with the anchor chain. When anchoring, the anchor is dredged by the ship, so that the anchor claws gradually grasp the bottom. Finally, when the anchor is brought up, the force acting on the anchor achieve a balance. When the ship is at anchor, the anchor's holding power, the weight of anchor and anchor chain, and the friction of ground anchor chain together resist the force of wind, flow and others on the ship, and finally make the ship stay in the designated water area. In addition, when a ship is underway, sometimes the anchor may assist in turning or changing the course; when a ship is berthing and unberthing, the anchor may be used for dragging to control the heading, ship's position or reduce the ship's speed of; in case of emergency, the anchor may be used for reducing the ship's speed and avoid collision; when the ship is stranded, the ship handler may drop the anchor in the direction of refloating, and heave in the anchor chain to assist in refloating. Hall anchor and Spek anchor are shown in Figure 3.3.12, wherein (a) is Hall anchor, (b) is Spek anchor.

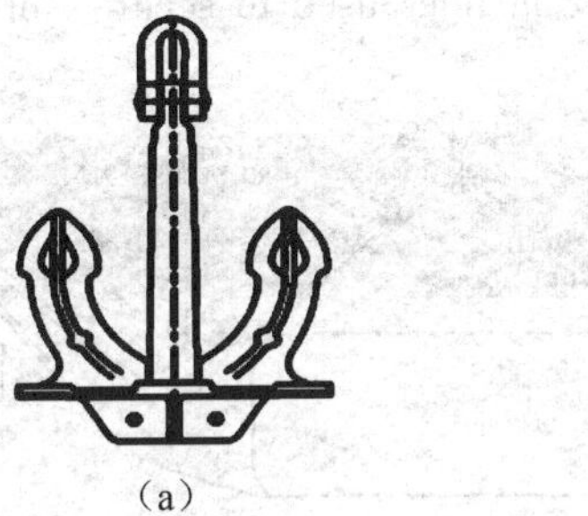
(a)

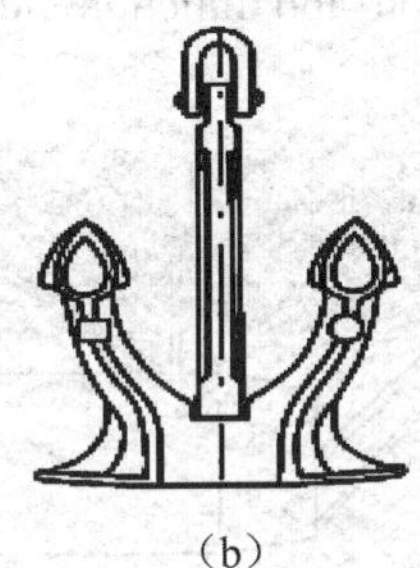
(b)

图 3.3.12　锚

Figure 3.3.12　Anchor

3.3.1.5　系船缆

3.3.1.5　Mooring Line

系船缆是船舶系岸时所用的设备,也是一种船舶的辅助操纵装置。系船缆一般位于船首和船尾,由绞缆机将系船缆送出或收回,使船舶安全地系靠在码头泊位、系船墩或浮筒等固定或活动建筑结构上,以抵御风、流、潮汐等对船舶的作用力。在船舶靠离泊操纵中,系船缆还可用来辅助控制船舶运动。一般船首绞缆机与锚机兼用。

Mooring line is used for making fast to the shore and is also a kind of ships' auxiliary control device. Mooring line is generally located at the fore and aft and end of a ship, which are slack away or heaved in by the mooring winch, so that the ship is safely moored alongside the berth, dolphins, mooring buoys or other fixed or movable structures to resist the force exerted on the ship by wind, currents, tides and so on. Secondly, mooring line is also used to assist to control the ship motion during berthing and unberthing handling. Generally, at the head mooring winch and windlass are combined.

根据缆绳的制作材料不同,系船缆可分为植物纤维缆、化学纤维缆、钢丝缆、钢丝与纤维组成的复合缆四大类。船舶配有多根系船缆，根据各缆绳的位置、出缆方向和作用不同可将其分为六种。靠泊码头时系船缆如图 3.3.13 所示。

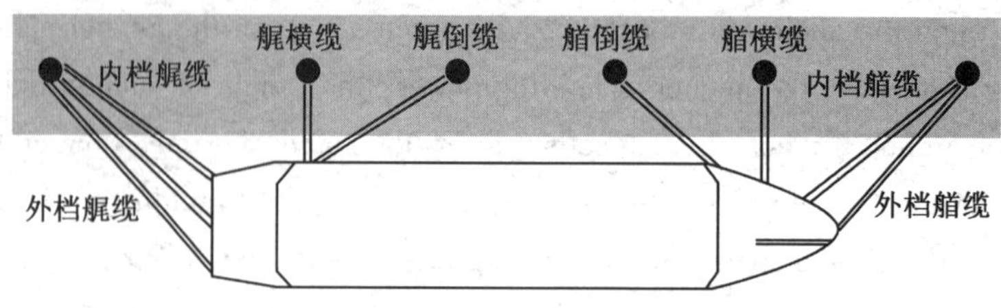

图 3.3.13　靠泊码头时系船缆

According to the types of rope materials, the mooring line is divided into four categories: natural fiber rope, synthetic fiber rope, steel wire rope and compound rope composed of steel wire and fiber. A Ship is equipped with more mooring lines, which are divided into six types according to their position, direction and function. Mooring lines used to secure ship to pier are shown in Figure 3.3.13.

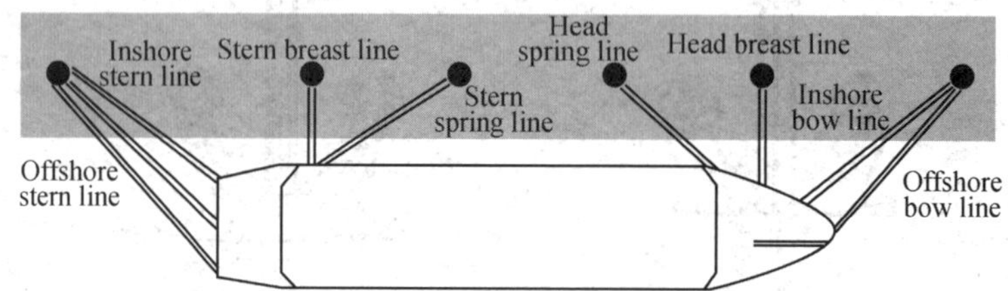

Figure 3.3.13　Mooring lines used to secure ship to pier

(1)艏缆或头缆：位于船首。从外舷出的艏缆称为外档艏缆，从内舷出的艏缆称为内档艏缆，其作用是防止船舶向后移动和船首向外舷偏转。

(1) Head line or bow line: is located at the bow. The head line from the outer side is called offshore bow line, and the head line from the inner side is called inshore bow line, whose function is to prevent the ship from moving backward and the head from moving away from the pier.

(2)艏倒缆或前倒缆：位于船首，其作用是防止船舶向前移动和船首向外舷偏转。

(2) Head spring or forward spring line: is located at the bow, whose function is to prevent the ship from moving forward and the head from moving away from the pier.

(3)艏横缆或前横缆：位于船首，其作用是防止船首向外舷移动。

(3) Head breast or forward breast line: is located at the bow, whose function is to prevent the head from moving away from the pier.

(4)艉缆：位于船尾。从外舷出的艉缆称为外档艉缆，从内舷出的艉缆称为内档艉缆，其作用是防止船舶向前移动和船尾向外舷偏转。

(4) Stern line: is located at the stern. The stern line from the outer side is called offshore stern line, and the stern line from the inner side is called inshore stern line, whose function is to prevent the ship from moving forward and the stern from moving away from the pier.

(5)艉倒缆或后倒缆：位于船尾，其作用是防止船舶向后移动和船尾向外舷偏转。

(5) Stern spring or after spring line: is located the stern, whose function is to prevent the ship from moving backward and the stern from moving away from the pier.

(6)艉横缆或后横缆:位于船尾,其作用是防止船尾向外舷移动。

(6) Stern breast or after breast line: is located the stern, whose function is to prevent the stern from moving away from the pier.

3.3.1.6 拖船

3.3.1.6 Tug

拖船,又名拖轮,是一种船舶,也是一种船舶的辅助操纵手段。拖船结构牢固、设有橡胶护舷、稳定性好、船身小、拖力大、操纵性能良好,没有装卸能力。拖船一般用于协助船舶进出港、协助船舶通过航道或受限水域、协助船舶靠离泊操纵等,如图 3.3.14 所示。

Tug, also known as tugboat, is a kind of ship and also a kind of of ships' auxiliary control device. Tug has strong structure, rubber fender, good stability, small hull, large towing force, good ship maneuverability and no loading and unloading capacity. Tug is generally used to assist ships to enter or leave the harbour, assist ships to pass through the channel or restricted waters, and assist ships to berth and unberth and so on, as shown in Figure 3.3.14.

根据航区不同,拖船可分为外海拖船和港作拖船。外海拖船可分为远洋拖船和沿海拖船。根据用途不同,拖船又可分为运输拖船、港作拖船、救助拖船和海洋开发用拖船。根据推进器的种类不同,港作拖船可分为固定螺距螺旋桨拖船、可调螺距螺旋桨拖船、Z 型推进器拖船和平旋推进器拖船。

According to different navigation areas, tug is divided into offshore tug and harbour tug. Offshore tug can be divided into ocean tug and coastal tug. According to different uses, tug is divided into tug for transportation, harbour tug, salvage tug and tug for marine development. According to the different types of propeller, the harbour tug divided into fixed pitch propeller tug, controllable pitch propeller tug, Z-drive tug and Voith-Schneider propeller tug (VSP tug).

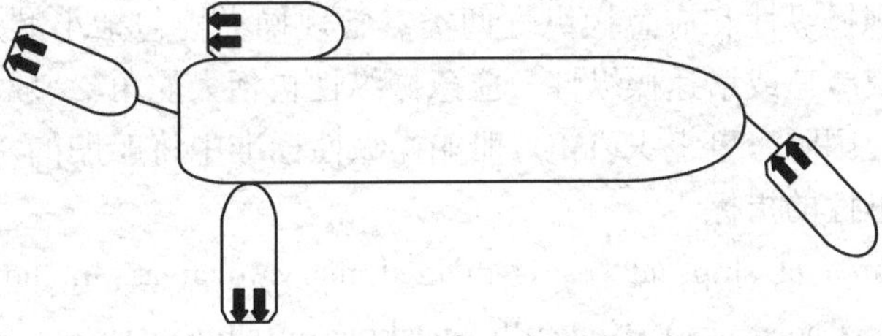

图 3.3.14 拖船协助船舶

Figure 3.3.14 Tugs used to assist a ship

3.3.2 船舶操纵性
3.3.2 Ship Maneuverability

船舶操纵与船舶航行安全直接相关。船舶在海上航行无时不受着风、浪、流等自然环境因素的影响,使船舶运动状态不时发生变化,需要进行船舶操纵以降低其影响。船舶在港内航行时还受到水域宽度和水深等条件的限制,也需要进行船舶操纵使船舶航行在安全水域。因此,船舶操纵也可以理解为保持或改变船速和航向的操作。良好的船舶操纵技术可以减小这些不利因素和条件的影响。因此,船舶操纵的目的就是操船人员利用船舶操纵设备所产生的力和力矩来克服或减小外力和外力矩的影响,使船舶处在安全运动状态或安全水域。

Ship handling is directly related to ship's navigation safety. The ship always suffers the influence of wind, wave, current and other natural environmental factors during sailing at sea, and makes the state of ship motion change from time to time, so that ship handling is required to reduce the influence. When sailing in the harbour, the ship is also restricted by the width and depth of water areas and other conditions, so that ship handling is required to navigate in safe waters. Therefore, ship handling is also known as the operation to keep or change the ship's speed and course. Good ship handling skills reduce the influence of these disadvantageous factors and conditions. Therefore, the purpose of ship handling is that the ship handler overcomes or reduces the influence of external forces and external torques by using ship handling equipment to generate the forces and torques, so that the ship is in a safe state of ship motion or safe waters.

船舶在海上的航区可分为港内和港外(也称为外海)两种区域。一般来说,船舶处于大幅度、频繁使用操纵设备(特别是推进器)的水域或时机时称为"操纵",反之,船舶处于偶尔使用操纵设备的水域或时机时称为"航行"。因此,一般将港内和港外两种航区分别俗称为"港内操纵水域"和"港外航行水域"。在港内,船舶操纵可分为靠离泊操纵、锚泊操纵、进出港操纵、系离浮筒操纵以及系离他船操纵等;在港外,主要有大风浪操纵、避离台风操纵等。船舶操纵性分为常规操纵性和应急操纵性两类。常规操纵性包括小舵角的保向性、中等舵角的初始回转性以及减速或增速操纵性。应急操纵性包括大舵角(一般为满舵)的旋回性和全速倒车的停船性。国际海事组织(IMO)船舶操纵性标准中将船舶的六个显著操纵运动性能作为评价船舶操纵性的指标。

The navigation area of ships at sea is divided into two areas: in the harbour and off the harbour (also known as open sea). Generally speaking, a ship in waters or when ship handling equipment (especially lateral thrusters) is used substantially and frequently is called "maneuvering", whereas a ship in waters or when ship handling equipment is used occasionally called "sailing". Therefore, the two types of navigation areas in the harbour and off the harbour are commonly known as "maneuvering waters in the harbour" and "navigation waters off the harbour" respectively. In the harbour, ship handling is divided into berthing and unberthing handling, anchor handling, entering and leaving handling, mooring and unmooring handling to buoys, mooring and unmooring handling alongside other ships and so on. Off the harbour, ship handling mainly includes ship handling in heavy winds and waves, tropical cyclone avoidance handling and so on. Ship maneuverability consists of conventional maneuverability and emergency maneuverability. Conventional maneuverability includes course-keeping ability with small rudder angle, initial turning ability with medium rudder angle and deceleration or acceleration maneuverability. Emergency maneuverability includes turning ability with large rudder angle (usually hard over) and full astern stopping ability. IMO standards for ship maneuverability identify six significant qualities for the evaluation of ship maneuverability.

3.3.2.1 固有稳定性

3.3.2.1 Inherent Dynamic Stability

固有稳定性又称航向稳定性/直线稳定性,是衡量船舶自动保持直线运动的性能的指标,是船舶固有的操纵性。如图 3.3.15 所示,船舶在直线航行过程中受到某种扰动而改变了原航向,当扰动消失后,不经过操纵就能在新航向上自动恢复直线运动,这样的船舶就具有航向稳定性,反之则不具有航向稳定性。

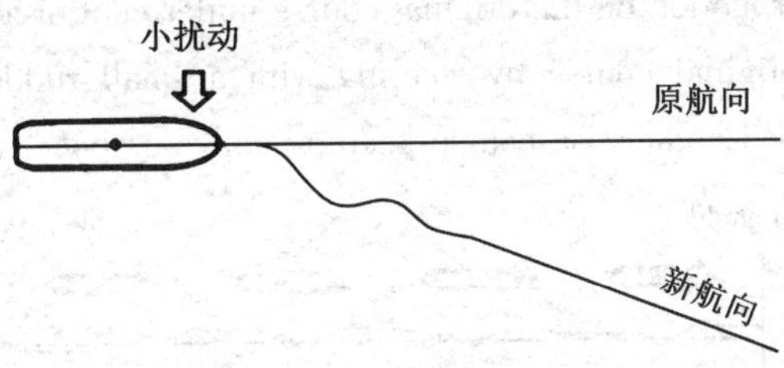

图 3.3.15　固有稳定性

As shown in Figure 3.3.15, inherent dynamic stability is also called directional stability/straight line stability, which is a measure of the ability of the ship to keep the linear motion automatically and is the ship's inherent maneuverability. As shown in Figure 3.3.16, when a ship sails on a straight course, she changes the original course after a small disturbance. After the disturbance disappeared, she recovers the linear motion on a new course without any control actions, so that the ship has inherent dynamic stability, otherwise the ship has no inherent dynamic stability.

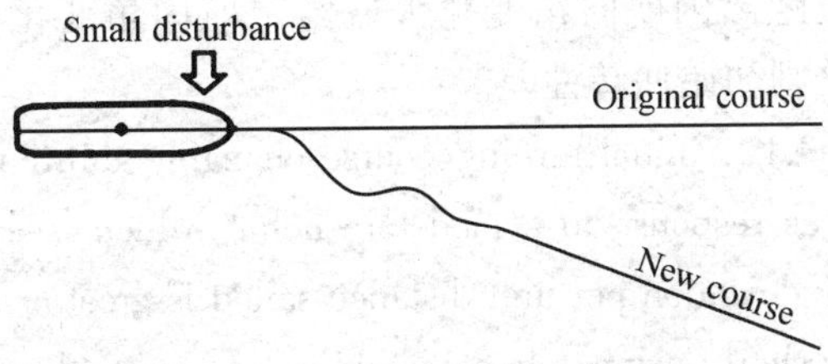

Figure 3.3.15　Inherent dynamic stability

3.3.2.2 保向性
3.3.2.2 Course-keeping Ability

保向性是衡量船舶受控(操舵)时保持直线运动的性能指标。船舶在直线航行过程中受到某种扰动而改变了原航向,通过操纵能使船舶恢复在原航向上做直线运动。如果通过小舵角操纵使船舶在短时间内就能恢复原航向的直线运动,则保向性好,反之则保向性差,如图 3.3.16 所示。

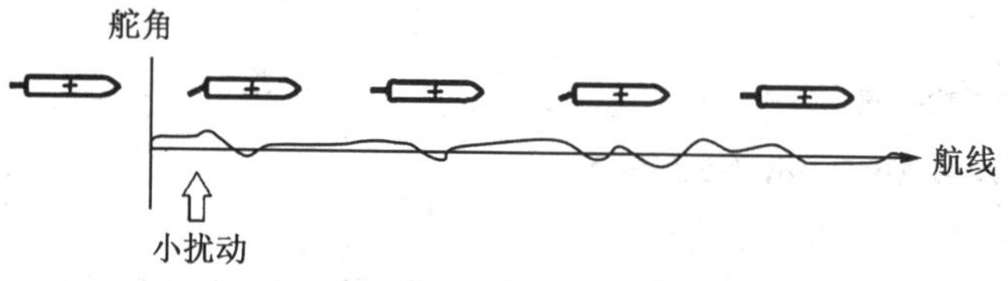

图 3.3.16 船舶保向性

Course-keeping ability is a measure of the ability of the steered ship to keep the linear motion. When a ship sails on a straight course, she changes the original course after a small disturbance, then she recovers the linear motion on the original course under control actions. If the ship recovers the linear motion on the original course by steering with a small rudder angle in a short time, course-keeping ability is good, otherwise course-keeping ability is poor, as shown in Figure 3.3.16.

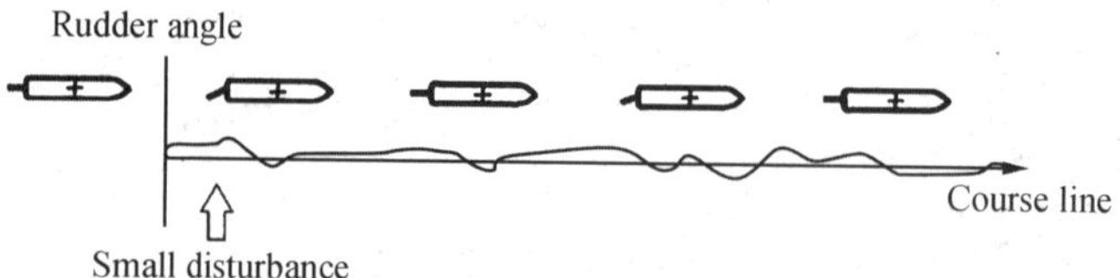

Figure 3.3.16 Course-keeping stability

3.3.2.3 初始回转性/改向性
3.3.2.3 Initial Turning/Course-changing Ability

如图 3.3.17 所示,初始回转性/改向性是船舶对中等舵角的反应能力,衡量船舶改变航向的性能指标。如果单位距离内航向角变化大或给定航向角变化量时船舶所航行的距离短,则初始回转性好,反之则初始回转性差。

As shown in Figure 3.3.17, initial turning/course-changing ability is the ability of the ship to change the original course as response to a moderate helm, which is a measure of the ability of course changing. If heading deviation per unit distance sailed is great or with certain heading deviation unit distance sailed is short, course-changing ability is good, otherwise course-changing ability is poor.

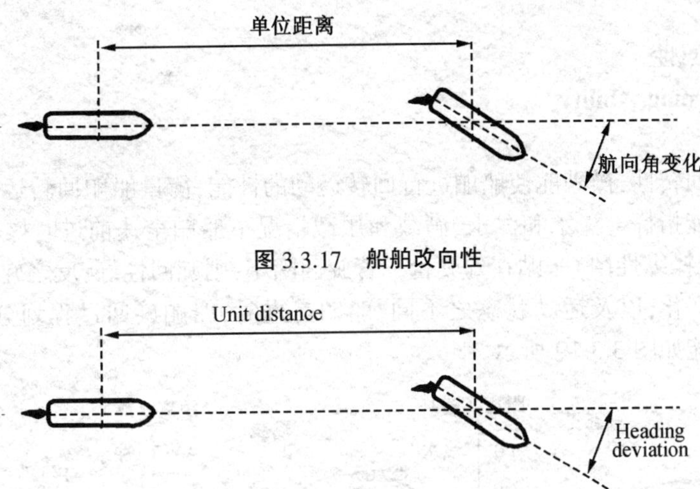

图 3.3.17　船舶改向性

Figure 3.3.17　Course-changing ability

3.3.2.4　艏摇抑制性
3.3.2.4　Yaw Checking Ability

如图 3.3.18 所示，艏摇抑制性是船舶进入一定旋回状态时向旋回相反方向操舵，船舶的反应能力，衡量船舶操舵时抑制船舶转动惯性的性能指标。如果艏向很快就能响应舵的转动，则艏摇抑制性好，反之艏摇抑制性差。

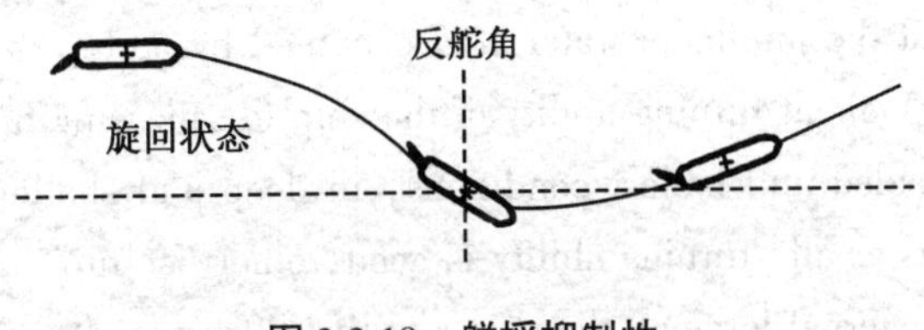

图 3.3.18　艏摇抑制性

Yaw checking ability, the ability of the steered ship to respond to the counter rudder action applied in a certain state of turning, is a measure of the ability of the steered ship to check the ship's rotational inertia. If ship's heading responding to the counter rudder action is quick, yaw checking ability is good, otherwise yaw checking ability is poor.

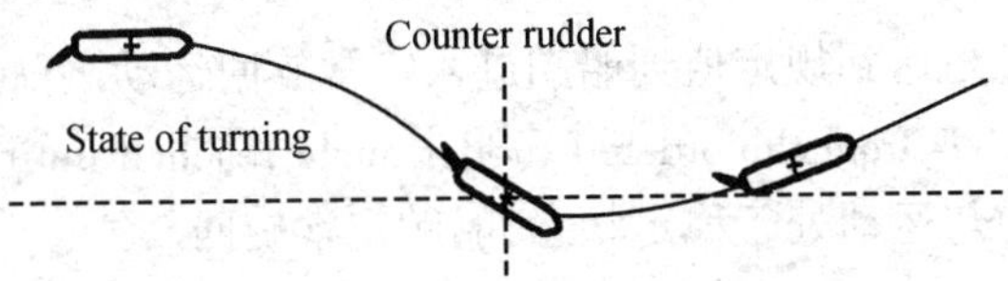

Figure 3.3.18　Yaw checking ability

3.3.2.5 旋回性

3.3.2.5 Turning Ability

旋回性又称回转性，操满舵使船舶进行回转运动的性能，衡量船舶回转运动所占最小水域范围大小的性能指标。深水和浅水、满载和压载情况下船舶全速前进时操满舵旋回性能图表资料（驾驶台操纵性图）张贴在驾驶台。若旋回圈小，则旋回性好；反之旋回性差。根据船舶所受外力的变化，以及运动状态之不同，船舶前进时，船舶旋回过程划分为三个阶段。某船满舵旋回性能如图 3.3.19 所示。

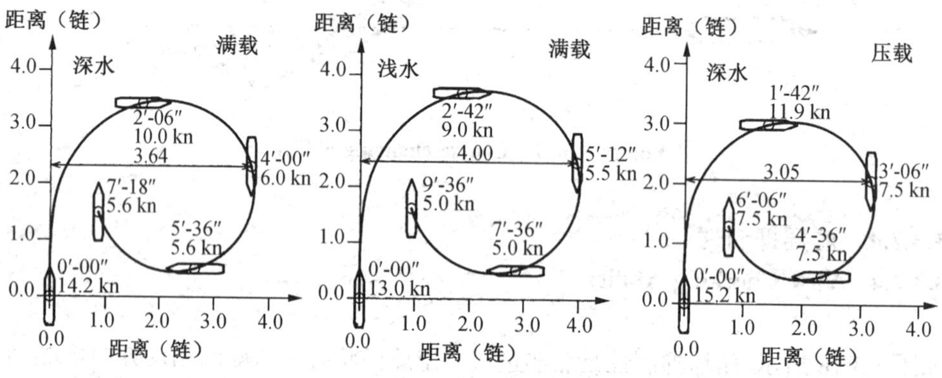

图 3.3.19 某船满舵旋回性能

Turning ability, also called turning performance, is the ability to turn a ship using hard over rudder, and a measure of the minimum water area occupied by a ship's turning motion. Graphic data (wheelhouse poster) about turning ability of the ship to sail using full speed ahead with hard over rudder under full loaded and ballast conditions, in deep and shallow water is posted on the bridge. If turning circle is small, turning ability is good, otherwise turning ability is poor. According to the change of the external force on the ship and the different state of motion, the turning motion is divided into three phases when the ship is going forward. Turning ability of a ship with hard over rudder is shown in Figure 3.3.19.

（1）转舵阶段：从转舵开始到舵角转至规定角度为止。

(1) Rudder turning phase: is from the beginning of steering until the ordered rudder angle reached.

（2）过渡阶段：从舵角达到规定值到船舶进入定常旋回运动之前的动态过程。

(2) Transition phase: is from the ordered rudder angle reached until entering steady turning.

（3）定常阶段：受力与运动处于稳定状态，船舶定常旋回。

(3) Steady turning phase: the force and motion are in a stable state, and the ship is in steady turning.

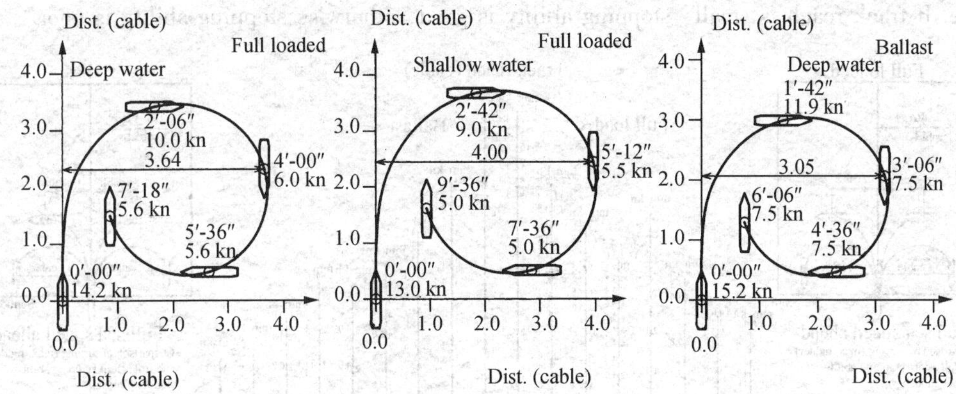

Figure 3.3.19 Turning ability of a ship with hard over rudder

3.3.2.6 停船性

3.3.2.6 Stopping Ability

如图 3.3.20 所示,停船性包括停车性能和紧急停船性能,分别为船舶从任意前进速度使用停车或全速倒车到船舶对水停止移动的性能,衡量船舶纵向运动惯性的性能指标。满载和压载情况下船舶海上全速前进、港内全速前进、港内半速前进和港内慢速前进时全速倒车停船性的图表资料(驾驶台操纵性图)张贴在驾驶台。如果航迹进距短,则停船性好,反之,停船性差。

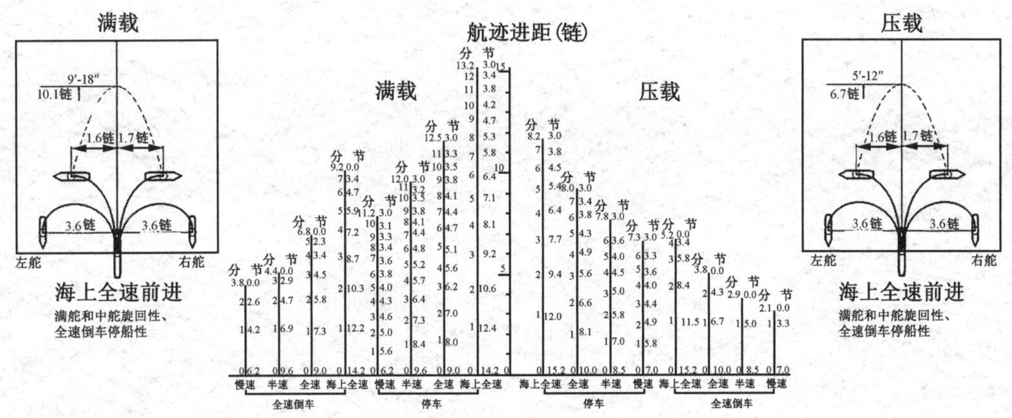

图 3.3.20 某船停船性

As shown in Figure 3.3.20, stopping ability includes inertia stopping ability and crash stopping ability, respectively the ability of ship to stop with engine stopped (inertia stop) or engine full astern (crash stop) from a steady approach at any speed to stopping moving through the water, is a measure of the ability of longitudinal inertia of ship. Graphic data (wheelhouse poster) about stopping the ability of the ship to sail with engine full astern under full loaded and ballast conditions beginning with full sea speed ahead, full ahead, half ahead and slow ahead is posted on the bridge. If track reach is small, stopping ability is good, otherwise stopping ability is poor.

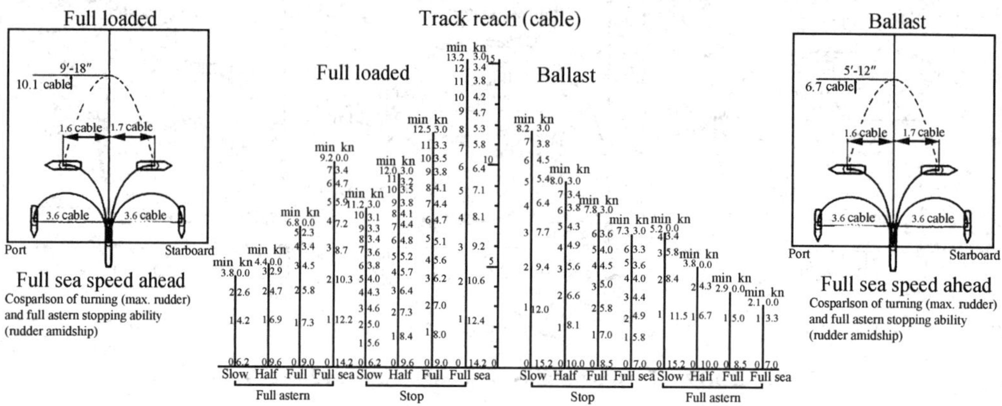

Figure 3.3.20 Stopping ability of a ship

第 4 章　个人安全

Chapter 4 | Personal Safety

4.1　PPE（人员防护设备）要求

4.1　PPE（Personal Protective Equipment）Requirements

4.1.1　个人防护设备综述

4.1.1　PPE（Personal Protective Equipment）Summarize

4.1.1.1　目的

4.1.1.1　Purpose

本指南旨在确定需要使用个人防护设备的地方以及如何对设备进行维护。

This instruction provides guidelines for determining where personal protective equipment is required and how it is to be maintained.

4.1.1.2　适用范围

4.1.1.2　Scope

本指南适用于在需要穿戴个人防护设备的船舶上工作或对船舶进行访问的所有员工、监管人员和访问者。

This instruction applies to all marine employees, regulatory angency personnel, and visitors who work in or visit a vessel where personal protective equipment is required to be worn.

4.1.1.3 责任

4.1.1.3 Responsibilities

HSE(健康、安全、环境保护)经理或DP(指定人员)有责任确保本指南得到遵守。

It is the responsibility of the HSE Manager or DP to ensure these guidelines are complied with.

船长和安全员有责任确保相关人员在船上开展作业时穿戴合适的PPE。

It is the responsibility of the master and safety officer to ensure appropriate Personal Protective Equipment (PPE) is worn during work activities onboard the vessel.

每个人都有责任确保自己根据要求穿戴正确的PPE并且对PPE进行良好的维护。

It is the responsibility of the individual to ensure they wear the correct Personal Protective Equipment (PPE) as required and that it is maintained in a good condition.

4.1.1.4 程序

4.1.1.4 Procedure

(1) 总则

(1) General

本程序旨在为员工和访问者提供关于在船舶上以及作业现场需要穿戴的个人防护设备(PPE)的指导。

The objective of this procedure is to provide guidance on the type of PPE required to be worn by staff and visitors on marine vessels and sites where work activities are being conducted.

物理或化学危险不能通过工程或行政控制措施消除或减少到合适水平时需要穿戴个人防护设备。工程控制是指通过机动方式或通过工艺设计减少或消除危险。行政控制是指将工人暴露在危险中的概率尽可能降至最低的管理程序。

Personal protective equipment is needed for physical or chemical hazards that cannot be eliminated or reduced to acceptable levels through engineering or administrative control measures. Engineering control is the reduction or elimination of hazards by mechanical means or through process design. Administrative controls are management procedures, which reduce worker exposure below permissible exposure limits.

(2) 定义

(2) Definition

个人防护设备(PPE)是指当其他预防措施无法使用或不可行时,需要保护人员免受腐蚀性、有毒、高温、低温或潮湿材料影响而穿戴的设备和衣服。

Personal Protective Equipment (PPE) is equipment and clothing that is worn whenever it is necessary for protection from corrosive, toxic, hot, cold, or wet materials when other preventive measures are not available or practical.

非渗透性衣服和手套可以承受化学物质、碳氢化合物和其他液体的渗透。

Impervious clothing and gloves are capable of withstanding penetration by chemicals, hydrocarbons, and other liquids.

(3)职责和责任

(3) Duties and responsibilities

①监督员责任

①Supervisor Responsibilities

实施了危险评估并且断定危险存在或可能存在后,监督员应当:

After performing a hazard assessment and determining that hazards are present, or likely to be present, the supervisor shall do the following:

- 针对危险评估中识别出来的危险,选择受危险影响的员工需要使用的 PPE 类型。
- Select the types of PPE that the affected employee will use for the hazards identified in the hazard assessment.
- 确保 PPE 数量充足,并且得到合适的保护、维护和卫生消毒。
- Assure the adequacy of the PPE; proper fit protection, maintenance, and sanitation.
- 将选择决定告知每个受危险影响的员工。
- Communicate selection decisions to each affected employee.
- 确保每个受影响员工知晓如何正确使用自己的 PPE。
- Ensure every affected employee knows how to use their PPE correctly.
- 确保每个受影响员工在实施危险评估结果显示需要使用 PPE 的任务时使用所需 PPE。
- Ensure every affected employee uses the required PPE when performing tasks identified in the hazard assessment that require the use of PPE.
- 防止使用有缺陷或已损坏的 PPE。有缺陷或已损坏的 PPE 要进行更换。
- Prevent the use of PPE that is defective or damaged. Defective or damaged PPE must be replaced.
- 千万不要分配需要使用却无法获得 PPE 的任务。
- Never assign a task for which PPE is required but not available.

②员工责任

②Employee Responsibilities

实施风险评估并且确定需要使用 PPE 后,员工应当:

After a hazard assessment has been performed and hazards identified that require PPE, the employee shall do the following:

- 千万不要实施需要使用 PPE 却无法获取 PPE 的任务。
- Never perform a task for which PPE is required but not available.
- 随时正确穿戴和使用所需 PPE。

- Always wear and use required PPE correctly.
- 不使用含缺陷或已损坏的 PPE。
- Never use PPE that is defective or damaged.

(4)一般要求

(4) General requirements

①使用要求

①Required Use

个人防护设备应在任何必要场合或者由于接触、吸收或吸入等危险而容易对身体造成伤害时进行穿戴。

Personal protective equipment shall be worn whenever it is required, or when hazards exist that are capable of causing injury by physical contact, absorption, or inhalation.

②安全设备许可

②Approved Safety Equipment

- 船上使用的个人防护设备和其他安全设备必须由 DP 或 HSE 小组进行选择。使用 PPE 以及其他安全设备的各部门可以提出建议以供 DP 或 HSE 小组考虑。
- Personal protective equipment (PPE) and other safety equipment that is used by marine vessels must be selected by the DP or HSE Group. Various departments which use PPE and other safety equipment may recommend alternative choices for DP or HSE Group's consideration.
- 安全设备应当达到相关标准,要保持高质量、可供获取和存放并且便于使用。
- Safety equipment will be standardized to provide consistent high quality, allow for acquisition and storage, and facilitate issues.
- DP 或 HSE 小组要定期维护、审查和更新标准设备清单。
- A list of standardized equipment will be maintained, reviewed, and updated periodically by the DP or HSE Group.

③获取安全设备

③Obtaining Safety Equipment

- 所有 PPE 和安全设备都要从现场安全员手中获得,并且需要填写带编号的材料收回表,同时要获得相应级别人员的许可。
- All PPE and safety equipment must be obtained from safety officer on site a Materials Withdrawal form with a charge code and the appropriate level of approval.
- 存放、分发和补充 PPE 库存是安全员的责任。他们将维护所需库存并且确保在必要的情况下订购安全设备以保证库存充足。
- Storage, distribution, and replenishment of warehouse stock of PPE is the responsibility of the safety officer. They will maintain the required inventory and will ensure that safety equipment is re-ordered as necessary, so adequate stock is always available.

④针对工作危险

④Specific for the Work Hazard

PPE 必须保护员工免受识别出的危险的伤害,并且要针对具体的工作危险进行穿戴。

PPE must protect employees from the hazards that have been identified and be specific for the work hazard.

⑤照看和存放

⑤Care and Storage

PPE 必须保持干净、可用状态。员工要负责清理和存放发到自己手中的设备。

PPE must be kept in a clean and usable condition. Employees are responsible for cleaning and storing equipment that has been assigned to them.

⑥对访问者的要求

⑥For Visitor Requirements

- 访问者或监管人员处于作业区、在作业现场、在船上或在任何其他工作区时,都必须穿戴适合工作环境的衣服、安全帽、区域内所需任何防护设备以及合适的鞋子。如果访问者和/或监管员提供自己的 PPE,PPE 必须满足船舶的要求并且能够提供足够的保护。
- Whenever visitors or regulatory agency personnel are in an operating area, at a site, on shipboard or in any other working area, they must wear clothing that is appropriate for an industrial environment, a safety helmet, any protective equipment required for the area, and appropriate footwear. If visitors and/or regulatory agency personnel provide their own PPE, it must meet marine vessel requirements and provide adequate protection.
- 访问者走出办公室后不得穿高跟鞋、露趾鞋或凉鞋、夹趾拖鞋、网球鞋或增高鞋或带不平鞋底的鞋子,除非访问者乘坐相关交通工具。
- High-heeled shoes, open-toe shoes or sandals, flip-flops, tennis shoes, or shoes with extra thick or uneven soles are not allowed outside of an office unless the visitor is traveling to or from his/her vehicle.
- 负责访问者的人员必须确保访问者穿上了合适服装。
- The person responsible for the visitor(s) must make sure he/she is wearing the proper attire.
- 本规定只有在得到其指定人员或 HSE 经理的许可之后才能作废。
- This policy can be canceled only with the approval of DP or a HSE Manager.

4.1.2 头部保护
4.1.2 Head Protection

4.1.1.1 总则
4.1.2.1 General

大多数工业头部伤害都是由物体坠落造成的。此类伤害会严重导致丢失工时。尽管物体坠落是造成头部伤害的主要原因,不过头部伤害还有可能由化学物喷溅或熔融物以及与带电设备接触造成。安全帽能够保护人头部免受坠落或飞行物体、高温或危险液体溢到头上以及电击的影响和渗透。安全帽必须达到国际认可的标准。

Most industrial head injuries are caused by falling objects. These injuries can be serious resulting in Lost Time. Although falling objects are the prime cause of head injuries they can also be caused by chemical splash or molten materials, as well as by contact with live electrical equipment. Safety helmets protect the head from impact and penetration by falling or flying objects, overhead spills of hot or hazardous liquids, and electric shock. Safety helmets must meet internationally recognized standards.

4.1.2.2 安全帽政策
4.1.2.2 Safety Helmet Policy

物体坠落可能会对人头部造成潜在伤害,在指定区域内要随时戴安全帽,指定区域包括:

Safety helmets shall be worn at all times where there is potential for injury to the head from falling objects, and in designated areas, including the following:

(1)相关人员可能会因物体坠落导致头部受伤的区域;

(1)There is a possibility that a person may be struck on the head by falling object;

(2)相关人员的头部可能会撞到固定物体的区域;

(2)A person may strike his/her head against a fixed object;

(3)可能会不慎接触到电力危险的区域;

(3)Inadvertent head contact may be made with electrical hazards;

(4)存在头部危险的所有施工区以及其他指定工业区。

(4)All construction sites and other designated industrial areas where overhead hazards exist.

4.1.2.3　安全帽安全守则
4.1.2.3　Safety Helmet Safety Rules

(1)请勿改装悬架,悬架要随时系好。

(1)The suspension shall not be modified and must be properly fastened at all times.

(2)外壳中不要打孔。

(2)Holes shall not be drilled in the shell.

(3)请勿在安全帽上描绘图案。

(3)Safety helmets shall not be painted.

(4)定期检查安全帽,一旦发现破裂、凹痕或其他损坏要立即更换。

(4)Safety helmets should be inspected regularly and replaced at the first sign of cracking, dents, or other damage.

(5)不再使用的(过期的)安全帽必须加以损毁。

(5)Safety helmets that are taken out of service must be destroyed.

(6)船上不允许使用金属安全帽。

(6)Metal safety helmets are not approved for use by marine vessel.

(7)防撞帽不能代替安全帽。

(7)A bump cap shall not be used in place of a safety helmet.

4.1.2.4　清洗和存放安全帽
4.1.2.4　Cleaning and Storing Safety Helmets

(1)安全帽要用温和香皂和温水清洗,切忌使用溶剂、化学物质、汽油或类似物质清洗。

(1)Safety helmets should be cleaned with mild soap and warm water. Solvents, chemicals, gasoline, or similar substances should not be used.

(2)请勿将安全帽长期存放在直接暴露于阳光的地方。

(2)Never store a safety helmet where it is directly exposed to sunlight for long periods of time.

4.1.2.5　防汗带
4.1.2.5　Sweatbands

(1)防汗带可以使额头和眼睛都免受流汗的影响。通过清除水分,防汗带还能帮助减少护目镜和眼睛蒙上水蒸气。

(1)Sweatbands help keep perspiration off the forehead and out of the eyes. By removing moisture, they also help reduce fogging of goggles and glasses.

(2)防汗带可以清洗并且再次使用。

(2) Sweatbands can be washed and reused.

4.1.2.6 冬季衬垫
4.1.2.6 Winter Liners

(1)需要在寒冷天气中工作的员工可以使用均码冬季安全帽衬垫。

(1) Universal-size winter safety helmet liners will be provided to employees who are required to work outside during cold weather.

(2)衬垫变脏后要进行清洗之后才能再次使用。

(2) Liners should be washed when they become soiled and then re-used.

4.1.2.7 再次使用和使用寿命
4.1.2.7 Reissue and Working Life

(1)安全帽只有进行了彻底清洗和检查才能再次使用。

(1) No safety helmets should be reissued unless the safety helmet has been thoroughly cleaned and inspected.

(2)使用时间超过 3 年的安全帽应当进行彻底检查,必要时还应进行更换。

(2) Safety helmets, which have been in service for longer than 3 years, should be thoroughly inspected and replaced as necessary.

(3)束带的塑料部分如果过分使用可能会更快变坏,因此应当每隔不到 2 年的时间更换束带。

(3) Plastic components of harnesses may deteriorate more rapidly under aggressive service conditions and in this case harnesses should be replaced at intervals not longer than 2 years.

4.1.3 眼面防护
4.1.3 Eye and Face Protection

4.1.3.1 总则
4.1.3.1 General

当员工的眼睛或面部暴露于漂浮物质或高温材料或腐蚀性材料中时,需要对眼睛和面部进行保护。当存在眼睛受伤的危险时,要为所有人员提供合适的眼睛保护。典型的危险类型包括:焊接作业、激光、透照器和强热源产生的漂浮微粒喷雾以及尘土、飞溅物质、有害气体、蒸汽以及高强度辐射。工作人员只能戴达到国际认可标准的眼镜、护目镜、护面罩和焊接面罩。

Eye and face protection are required when an employee is exposed to eye or face hazards from flying particles or hot or corrosive materials. Injury to an eye can result in blindness. Appropriate hazard specific eye protection shall be provided for all people where a risk of eye injury exists. Typical hazard might include:flying particles, dust, splashing substances, harmful gases, vapors, aerosols, and high intensity radiation from welding operations, lasers, transilluminators and strong heat sources. Only glasses, goggles, face shields, and welding hoods meeting the requirements of internationally recognized standards may be worn by working personnel.

4.1.3.2 防护镜/安全眼镜

4.1.3.2 Safety Spectacles/Safety Glasses

尽管防护镜/安全眼镜无法提供全部保护,但是它们仍然能够防止一定的危险,尤其是来自眼睛前方的尘土和漂浮微粒。

Although they do not provide complete protection, they do afford useful protection against a number of hazards, particularly dust and flying particles from the front.

此类眼镜要配备结实的框架和抗冲击镜片(聚碳酸酯镜片)以及全塑料侧护板,并且能够提供防紫外线辐射(UV)的保护。

These should have sturdy frames and impact-resistance lenses(Polycarbonate lenses) with full plastic side shields and provide Ultraviolet (UV) protection.

4.1.3.3 化学护目镜

4.1.3.3 Chemical Goggles

(1)需要预防化学物质飞溅、飞屑、尘土时,或可能因暴露于化学物质而对眼睛产生伤害时,请戴化学护目镜。

(1) Chemical goggles shall be worn to protect against splash, flying chips, dust, and whenever there is exposure to chemicals that are capable of causing damage to the eyes.

(2)安全眼镜(即便带有侧护板)不能代替化学护目镜。化学护目镜能够防止眼睛前方、上方、下方和两边带来的危险并且可以替代安全眼镜。

(2) Safety glasses (even those with side shields) cannot be worn in place of goggles. Goggles provide protection from the front, top, bottom, and sides, and are designed to fit over safety glasses.

(3)以下情况应当戴化学护目镜:打磨和有尘作业,使用机床切割电缆,处理矿物棉或纤维玻璃,以及使用便携式手动和电动工具进行钻孔或打磨可能造成化学物质和碳氢化合物喷溅的作业。

(3) Chemical goggles shall be worn for protection during light chipping and dusty work, when cutting wire, using a pedestal grinder, handling mineral wool or fiberglass, doing light grinding or drilling with portable hand and power tools, and pouring chemicals and hydrocarbons where splashing can occur.

(4)化学护目镜不得代替焊工护目镜。

(4)Chemical goggles shall not be used as a replacement for welders' goggles.

4.1.3.4 护面罩

4.1.3.4 Face Shields

(1)必须戴护面罩,防止面部和颈部受到飞溅微粒和腐蚀性液体喷射以及高温的伤害。

(1)Face shields must be worn to protect the face and neck from flying particles and sprays of corrosive liquids and hot solutions.

(2)只戴护面罩不能对眼睛产生完整保护。请务必戴护目镜。

(2)Face shields alone do not provide adequate eye protection. Goggles must also be worn.

除外情况:使用带有护面罩的合格消防帽时可以不再戴护目镜。

Exception:Goggles are not required to be worn with approved fire-fighting helmets that are equipped with a face shield.

4.1.3.5 焊工护目镜

4.1.3.5 Welders' Goggles

(1)带遮面的焊工护目镜能够隔离焊接、切割和燃烧带产生的强光和辐射以及焊渣。使用火炬切割或进行气焊时必须随时戴焊工护目镜。

(1)Shaded welders' goggles protect against glare and radiation from welding, cutting and burning, and welding slag. They must always be worn when cutting with a torch, or when gas welding.

(2)员工要使用带滤光片的护目镜,其明暗度要适宜相关作业,护目镜能防止受到可见光辐射的伤害。镜片的防护明暗度取决于弧电流以及硬钎焊、软钎焊、切割或气焊的类型。

(2)Employees must use goggles with a filtered lens that has a shade number appropriate for the work being performed and that provides protection from injurious light radiation. The protective shade of the lenses is determined by the arc current and the type of brazing, soldering, cutting, or gas welding that will be done.

(3)如果明暗度需要更暗,那么应当使用带滤光片的焊接面罩来保护皮肤和眼睛烧伤。

(3)When a shade darker than necessary, a welding hood with filtered lens is required for protection against skin and eye burns.

(4)焊工护目镜外面请勿再戴护面罩。

(4)A face shield should never be worn over welders' goggles.

(5)焊工护目镜无法防御飞溅事件,因此不能代替化学护目镜。

(5)Welders' goggles do not provide splash protection and should never be worn as a substitute for chemical goggles.

4.1.3.6 焊接面罩
4.1.3.6 Welding Mask

(1)进行电弧焊要戴焊接面罩,从而保护眼睛和面部不受烧伤。滤光片要有能够抵御电弧烧伤的暗面。滤光片的明暗度根据焊接和弧电流的不同类型而不尽相同。

(1) A welding mask is required when arc welding, because it provides both eye and face protection and protects against skin burns. The filtered lens must have a shade darkness that will provide adequate protection from arc burn. The shade of lenses will vary depending upon the type of welding and arc current.

(2)最好能使用配备了翻盖的焊接面罩。

(2) Welding mask that are equipped with a lift-front lens are recommended.

(3)焊工要负责对其焊接面罩进行维护和合理存放。

(3) Welders are responsible for the maintenance and proper storage of their welding mask.

4.1.3.7 照看和存放护目镜、护面罩和焊接面罩
4.1.3.7 Care and Storage of Goggles, Face Shields, Welding Mask

(1)护目镜、护面罩和焊接面罩应当用温肥皂水清洗,然后彻底冲洗最后挂起来晾干,并存放起来。

(1) Goggles, face shields, and welding mask, should be washed with warm soapy water, rinsed thoroughly, and hung to dry before they are stored.

(2)清洗镜片时要使用柔软的纸巾或柔软的抗磨损布料。

(2) A soft tissue or soft nonabrasive cloth should be used to clean the lenses.

(3)护目镜要存放在封闭的容器内,不能用皮带挂起来。

(3) Goggles should be stored in a closed container. They should not be hung by the straps.

(4)焊接面罩里的镜片出现破损或者被刮痕或焊接烧痕遮住视线时要进行更换。

(4) Lenses in welding hoods should be replaced when they become broken, or when vision is obstructed by scratches or weld burns.

4.1.3.8 更换问题设备
4.1.3.8 Replacing Defective Equipment

(1)镜片出现裂缝、凹痕、刮痕或密封处破碎时应当更换护目镜。两边出现损伤或者固定带无法将镜片固定时也要更换护目镜。

(1) Goggles should be replaced when the lenses become cracked, pitted, scratched, or brittle around the sealing area. They should also be replaced when the sides get damaged or the head straps will not hold them in place.

(2)护面罩出现刮痕、裂缝或因长时间使用而破碎时应当更换护面罩。

(2)Face shields should be replaced when they become scratched, cracked, or brittle with age.

(3)焊接面罩出现裂缝或变形,或者镜片支架和/或悬架受损并且/或者无法正常使用时,要更换焊接面罩。

(3)Welding mask should be replaced when they become cracked or distorted, or when the lens holder and/or suspension become damaged and/or do not work properly.

4.1.3.9 烟雾和汗水

4.1.3.9 Fogging and Perspiration

必要时应当在眼睛保护器上使用防雾物质。极端条件下应当使用防汗带。

When necessary, suitable anti-fogging compound should be made available for use with eye protectors. Sweatbands may be necessary for extreme conditions.

4.1.4 听力保护

4.1.4 Hearing Protection

4.1.4.1 总则

4.1.4.1 General

按照法律规定,雇主必须为工作在嘈杂环境中或附近的人员提供必要的个人听力保护。噪声会造成人员身体和心理压力,也会使人无法听到警报信号而导致事故发生。过多的噪声会伤害人耳的听力(噪声导致的听力损伤),并且耳朵一旦受损便很难再修复。身处噪声环境中的员工有时会抱怨自己产生了紧张、失眠和疲劳的问题。过度暴露于噪声环境中也会导致人员工作表现欠佳。

It is a statutory obligation for employers to provide personal hearing protection as necessary for any person working in or near noisy environment. Noise can create physical and psychological stress and contribute to accidents by making it impossible to hear warning signals. Excessive noise can destroy the ear's ability to hear (noise induced hearing loss) and ear damage cannot be repaired. Workers exposed to noise sometimes complain of nervousness, sleeplessness, and fatigue. Excessive noise exposure can also reduce job performance.

身处张贴"需要保护听力"标示的区域并且区域内的设备在运转时,工人和访问者必须戴听力保护设备。

Workers and visitors must wear hearing protection while they are in areas that are posted with "Hearing Protection Required" signs and when equipment in the area is running.

在船上、施工现场、操作设备以及乘坐直升机时可能会听到很大的噪声,此时也需要戴听力保护设备。

Hearing protection is also required when high noise levels are encountered on specific jobs on the ship, on construction sites, while operating equipment, and during travel by helicopter.

4.1.4.2　员工可以戴其中任意一件

4.1.4.2　Employees May Wear Either

(1)由软泡沫或其他合适材料制成并且插入耳孔的一次性可塑性耳塞。

(1) Disposable moldable ear plugs which are made from soft foam or other suitable material and are inserted into the ear hole.

(2)套在耳朵上并且能用头带进行固定的耳罩。头发长、留有鬓角或者因为戴眼镜而在太阳穴上留下痕迹时,耳罩的密封效果会不太好。

(2) Ear muffs which seal around the ear and are held in place with a head band. Muffs do not seal well over long hair, side burns, or the temple bars of glasses.

4.1.4.3　清洁

4.1.4.3　Cleaning

(1)耳罩必须尽可能地经常清洗以保持干净。

(1) Ear muffs must be washed as often as necessary to keep them clean.

(2)一次性耳塞每次使用完后或者变脏后要丢弃。不要水洗并且再次使用一次性耳塞。

(2) Disposable ear plugs should be discarded after each use, or whenever they become dirty. Do not wash and reuse disposable ear plugs.

(3)将耳塞塞入耳内时必须确保手的干净。

(3) Hands must be clean when inserting plugs in the ears.

4.1.5　呼吸道保护

4.1.5　Respiratory Protection

4.1.5.1　总则

4.1.5.1　General

公司应采取一切可行措施确保没有任何员工暴露于可能有害健康的环境。公司还应确保任何人在工作场所都不会暴露于污染浓度超过暴露标准的空气污染或危险大气中。在遵守本要求时,公司应尽可能防止出现此类污染或者通过使用有效吸收污染物的通风或排气系统来控制污染或者适时采用其他防护手段。

The company shall take all practicable measures to ensure that no employee is exposed to an atmosphere that is or may be injurious to health. The company shall also ensure that no person at the workplace is exposed to an atmospheric contaminant at concentration is excess of exposure standards or hazardous atmosphere. In complying with this requirement, the company shall, as far as practicable, avoid the presence of the contaminant concerned or control of the contaminant using ventilation or exhaust system that effectively extract the contaminant or/if impractical use other suitable protection means.

呼吸道保护设备能够抵御尘土、蒸汽、气体和烟雾等空气危险。呼吸器能够减少吸入有害物质的风险,因此可当成预防措施,工程手段或程序文件等其他手段也可用来消除或尽可能降低暴露于此类风险的潜在可能性。

Respiratory equipment provides protection from atmospheric hazards such as dust, vapor, gas and fumes. Respirators reduce the risk of inhaling harmful substances. They should be seen as a precautionary measure and effects taken to eliminate or minimize potential exposure through other means i.e. engineering or procedural.

4.1.5.2 空气净化装置的类型
4.1.5.2 Types of Air Purifying Devices

(1)一次性防尘口罩

(1) Disposable dust mask

此类口罩适用于已知非危险性灰尘,例如木屑/尘土,不能抵御烟雾、蒸汽或石棉的危害。

This type of mask is used for a known non-hazardous dust i.e. wood/soil. They do not provide protection from fumes, vapors or asbestos.

(2)过滤面罩

(2) Cartridges/canisters masks

此类呼吸器能够清除空气中的低浓度危险蒸气和气体。过滤器通常直接附在呼吸器的面罩上。更大容量的过滤器附在面罩的下颚处,或者带有一根安全带并且通过一根呼吸管附在面罩上。此类面罩只能清除空气中的污染物,其用途十分有限。

These respirators are capable of removing low concentrations of hazardous vapors and gases from breathing air. Cartridges usually attach directly to the respirator face piece. The larger volume canisters attach to the chin of the face piece or are carried with a harness and attached to the face piece by a breathing tube. These types of respirators can remove only certain contaminants from air, their use is limited.

此类呼吸器不能用于以下情况:

They should not be used in the following conditions:

①没有足够氧气(体积占20.9%)的空气。

①In atmospheres that do not have a sufficient amount of oxygen (20.9% by volume).

②出现或可能出现未知污染物。

②In the presence or potential presence of unidentified contaminant.

③进入带有未知浓度污染物的不通风或封闭区域。

③For entry into unventilated, or confined areas with unknown concentrations of contaminants.

④带有多于2%的已知污染物的空气。

④In atmospheres containing more than 2% of a known contaminant.

⑤空气湿度太大,可能对过滤器中的溶剂产生不利影响。

⑤In atmospheres containing high humidity with may adversely affect performance of the sorbent inside the cartridges.

⑥污染物对眼睛、鼻子和喉咙等黏膜具有极度刺激性。

⑥For contaminants that are highly irritative to the mucous membrane e.g., eyes, nose and throat.

更换问题设备:

Replacing defective equipment:

①面罩上的橡胶逐渐退化导致密封不好时要更换面罩。

①The face piece should be replaced when the rubber perishes reducing the ability to achieve a good seal.

②安全带破损。

②When the straps are broken.

③达到最长暴露时间或开始新工作之前应更换过滤器。

③The cartridge should be replaced when the recommended exposure time is reached or at the start of the new work.

④空气不容易通过面罩或蒸气很难穿透。

④When the air cannot be easily drawn through the mask or the vapor is difficult to pass through.

4.1.5.3　空气供应装置

4.1.5.3　Air Supplying Devices

此类装置包括航空呼吸器以及自给式呼吸器(SCBA)。使用此设备前要进行仔细培训。此类装置可用于喷砂和消防。

These include airline respirators and self-contained breathing apparatus (SCBA). Use of this equipment requires detailed training. An example of use areas may be spray booth sandblasting and firefighting.

(1) 佩戴

(1) Fitting

达到良好的面部密封十分重要。胡须和鬓角等面部须发会阻碍佩戴效果,眼镜甚至面部不平整也会带来一定的问题。

Achieving a good facial seal is essential. Facial hair as beards and sideburns prevent a close fit and spectacles or even facial irregularity may also present problems.

使用之前要对使用者提供合理的培训。

Appropriate training shall be provided before using.

(2) 维护

(2) Maintenance

所有呼吸防护装置都要根据相关标准和制造商建议定期进行检查,并且存放在合适位置以及进行良好维护、清洁和更换(适时更换面罩和过滤器)。要对设备进行相应监管从而确保遵守相关指南。

All respiratory protective devices shall be regularly checked, properly stored and maintained, cleaned and replaced (both mask and cartridges as appropriate) according to applicable standards and manufacturers' advice. Appropriate supervision shall be exercised to ensure that equipment is used in accordance with instructions.

4.1.6 手部防护

4.1.6 Hand Protection

4.1.6.1 总则

4.1.6.1 General

任何危险地方都要实施手部防护。手套可用来防止物理(割伤和划伤)、化学(皮肤病)、生物(细菌)等潜在危险带来的伤害。

Hand protection shall be provided wherever there is a hazard. Hand gloves are used to protect against injuries resulting from potentially hazardous agents e.g., physical (cuts and scratches), chemical (skin disorders), biological (bacteria).

船上的作业包括对各种材料(如钢丝绳、钢管/固定装置、溶剂、化学物质和废物)进行处理。处理这些材料时通常会接触到人的手部,进而立即或过后带来伤害。

Vessel activities involve the handling of various materials (e.g., wire ropes, steel piping/fixtures, solvents, chemicals and wastes). Handling these materials often brings them into contact with people's hands and can give rise to immediate or delayed injury.

(1)人手接触碳氢化合物、危险物质,或尖锐、粗糙、高温或冰冷物体时要戴手套。

(1)Gloves shall be worn when hands are exposed to hydrocarbons, hazardous substances, or sharp, rough, hot, or very cold objects.

(2)监管员要保证员工配有并使用合适的手套。

(2)Supervisors are responsible for ensuring that their employees have and use the proper gloves.

(3)对于具体工作要求使用的手套类型存在疑问时可咨询HSE小组。

(3)Questions on the type of glove required for specific jobs should be referred to the HSE Group.

4.1.6.2 手套类型

4.1.6.2 Types of Gloves

选择的手套类型必须最适合抵御危险并且能够保证工作的灵活性。使用者首先要确定可能出现的危险,然后从以下几种手套中选择最合适的类型:

The type of glove selected must be the one most suited to protect against the hazard and still provide enough dexterity to do the job. First determine the hazards that are likely to be encountered, and then select the proper type of glove from the following:

(1)皮革手套

(1)Leather-palm gloves

皮革手套能够抵御高温、火花、尖锐和粗糙物体,并且能够缓解撞击带来的影响。维修工和装配工经常使用此类手套进行重型工作。处理货盘、木头、电线、高温设备、高温样品储存器和/或磁鼓时要使用皮革手套。皮革手套只能对碳氢化合物和其他液体带来最低程度的防护,因此处理此类物质时最好不要使用此类手套。

Leather-palm gloves resist heat, sparks, sharp and rough objects, and provide some cushioning against blows. Maintenance workers and riggers often use these gloves for heavy-duty work. Leather-palm gloves should be worn when handling pallets, wood, wire, hot equipment, hot sample containers, and/or drums. Leather-palm gloves provide minimal protection from hydrocarbons and other liquids and are not recommended for this application.

(2)防渗手套(氯丁橡胶、聚氯乙烯、丁腈橡胶)

(2)Impervious gloves (Neoprene, PVC, Nitrile)

①处理碳氢化合物以及酸和腐蚀剂等腐蚀性物质时应当使用防渗手套。选用的手套必须能够抵御所处理的物质的影响。

①Impervious gloves should be used when handling hydrocarbons and corrosive chemicals such as acids and caustics. The gloves selected must be resistant to the material being handled.

②可能出现飞溅事件时应当戴覆盖袖口并且保护手腕和前臂的长手套。

②Gauntlet-type gloves which extend above the cuff and protect the wrist and forearm

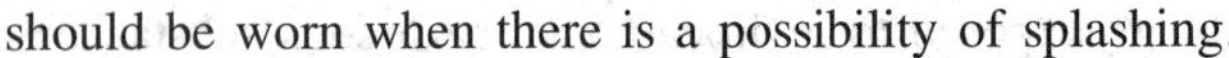

should be worn when there is a possibility of splashing.

③处理油管或受污管以及长时间处理油滑或油性物体时应当戴防渗手套。

③Impervious gloves should be worn when handling oily or contaminated pipe, and during prolonged handling of oily or greasy objects.

(3) 棉手套

(3) Cotton gloves

棉手套能够防尘和抗磨损。但是,此类手套的重量不适合操作粗糙或尖锐材料。手掌位置填入橡胶类材料以及手指位置外面使用橡胶类材料的手套类型能够更利于紧握物体。在不需要皮掌手套时,维修人员会使用这种手套进行较轻的工作。

Cotton cloth-type gloves protect against dirt and abrasion. However, they are not heavy enough for use with rough or sharp materials. The type that has a rubber-like material impregnated in the palm and on the fingers provides an improved grip. Maintenance uses this type of glove for lighter work when leather-palm gloves are not required.

(4) 医用手套

(4) Latex gloves

外科手术型医用手套能够保证最大灵活度,但是保护作用有限。此类手套主要用于非常轻便的作业,从而将皮肤与油料、油脂和液体隔开。医用手套主要用于检验室。

This surgical-type latex glove provides maximum dexterity, but limited protection. It is intended for use in very light service to keep oil, grease, and liquids off the skin. Latex gloves are primarily for laboratory use.

(5) 一次性手套

(5) Disposable gloves

此类轻薄塑料手套主要用于在实验室将手和油料与油脂隔开。诊所和医院的医务人员也会使用一次性手套。他们使用的是自动售货机中有售的单次使用一次性手套。

This is a thin plastic-type glove that is used in the laboratory to keep oil and grease off the hands. Disposable gloves are also used by medical personnel in the clinics and the hospital. The type used is a single-use disposable glove that comes in a dispenser.

(6) 其他手套

(6) Miscellaneous gloves

其他手套包括焊工手套、消防员手套和电工手套。下列手套必须单独进行分配:

These include special-use gloves such as welding gloves, fire fighters' gloves, and electrician gloves. The following gloves must be individually assigned:

①焊工手套是由处理过的皮革制成,能够抵御高温、焊接火花、飞溅和热渣的危害。

①Welders gloves are made from treated leather that provides protection against heat, welding sparks, splatter, and hot slag.

②消防员手套用皮革制成,里面填入了阻燃羊毛材料。它们通常会发给消防部人员。

②Fire-fighting gloves are leather and are lined with a flame-retardant fleece material. They are issued to fire department personnel.

③电工手套用于抵御意外接触通电电力设备产生的电击。电工手套实际上是二合一手套,包括一个内橡胶手套和一个外皮革手套。

③Electrician gloves are used to protect against electrical shock which could result from an accidental contact with energized electrical equipment. Electrician gloves are actually two gloves in one, an inner rubber glove and an outer leather glove.

0 级 1 类手套能抵御 1 000 V 电压。

The Class 0 Type 1 glove provides protection up to 1,000 volts.

4 级 1 类手套能抵御 36 000 V 电压。

The Class 4 Type 1 glove provides protection up to 36,000 volts.

4.1.6.3　检查手套

4.1.6.3　Inspecting Gloves

(1)每次使用手套前都要每天检查手套。

(1)Gloves should be inspected daily before each use.

(2)损坏的手套要进行更换。

(2)Damaged gloves should be replaced.

(3)检查防渗手套是否存在针孔漏气时要向里面吹气。手套破裂或出现小孔时要更换手套。

(3)Impervious gloves should be checked for pinhole leaks by blowing air into them. They should be replaced when they become cracked or develop holes.

(4)检查电工内手套是否出现针孔漏气时要向里面吹气然后把手套放进肥皂水进行检查。外手套要通过肉眼检查是否存在裂缝和针孔。4 级手套必须由外部检查机构每年进行检查。

(4)The inner electrician gloves must be checked for pinhole leaks by blowing air into them and then testing them with soapy water. The outer glove must be visually checked for cracks and holes. Class 4 gloves must be inspected annually by an outside testing agency.

4.1.6.4　维护和清洗

4.1.6.4　Maintenance and Cleaning

受污染或变脏的防渗手套可以使用热肥皂水进行清洗。清洗手套时不能使用溶剂和稀释剂,除非手套能够抵御这些物质的不良影响。

Impervious gloves that are contaminated or dirty can be washed in hot soapy water. Solvents

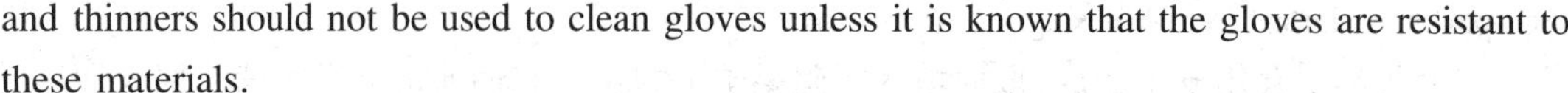

and thinners should not be used to clean gloves unless it is known that the gloves are resistant to these materials.

手套内可以使用滑石粉来减少出汗的影响。

A talcum-type powder can be used inside the glove to reduce the effects of sweating.

手套受到污染或者浸油程度达到能够伤害人的皮肤时，手套应当丢弃。

Gloves that become contaminated, or oil-soaked to the point where the contamination will get on the wearer's skin, should be discarded.

4.1.7 身体防护
4.1.7 Body Protection

4.1.7.1 总则
4.1.7.1 General

必须穿戴合适的身体防护设备将人的身体与酸性、腐蚀性、脏的或易生尘埃材料隔开。所需防护设备类型依据危险性质的不同而有所不同。

Appropriate body protection must be worn to keep acidic, corrosive, oily, dirty, or dusty materials off the body. The type of protection required depends upon the nature of the hazard.

4.1.7.2 工作服
4.1.7.2 Coveralls

工作服由100%轻型棉料制成，包含（阻燃）长袖和一条双向重型拉链，顶部有一个金属拉锁。

Coveralls are to be made from a lightweight 100% cotton material, (flame retardant) have long sleeves and two ways, heavy duty, zipper with a metal snap closer at top.

船上使用的工作服必须使用高能见度材料，上臂和下臂、大腿和小腿以及肩膀周围都要有反光带。

Coveralls for use on vessels must be of high visibility material with reflective tape around the upper and lower arms, upper and lower legs and across the shoulder either side.

4.1.7.3 防渗服装
4.1.7.3 Impervious Clothing

雨衣或防酸衣等防渗服装能够抵御飞溅物的伤害，从事可能接触酸性或腐蚀性材料或碳氢化合物液体的工作时必须穿上防渗服装。

Impervious clothing, such as a rain suit or acid suit, provides protection from splashes and must be worn during jobs where it is possible to come in contact with acidic or corrosive materials or hydrocarbon liquids.

放开绳线、打开设备以及在可能产生腐蚀性或碳氢化合物材料到处飞溅或喷射的环境中工作时要穿上防渗服装。

Impervious clothing is to be worn when opening lines, opening equipment, and working on jobs where corrosive or hydrocarbon materials could splash or spray.

处于潮湿环境、从事暴露于腐蚀性材料的维护作业以及清理水槽中的液体时要穿上防渗服装。

Impervious clothing should be worn under wet conditions, while doing maintenance work where there is exposure to corrosive material, and when cleaning liquid material from a tank.

仓库里要存放防渗外衣、工作服和可拆解头罩。

Impervious jackets, overalls, and detachable hoods are available from the warehouse.

防渗服装一旦破损应当立即处理掉,并且换成新服装。

Torn or damaged impervious clothing should be removed immediately and exchanged for new clothing.

4.1.7.4　一次性工作服

4.1.7.4　Disposable Coveralls and Suits

一次性工作服是为了使工人隔离尘土和干料。此类工作服只能最低限度地抵御液体和油类物质的损害。

Disposable coveralls and suits are designed to keep dust and dry material off the worker. They provide minimal protection against liquids and oily substances.

打扫卫生、清理水槽以及倾倒规定干料时要穿上一次性工作服。

Disposable coveralls are worn during clean-up work, tank cleaning, and while dumping specified dry materials.

清理水槽时可穿上足以抵御非腐蚀性液体伤害的特殊一次性工作服。

Special disposable coveralls that provide adequate protection against non-corrosive liquids are available for tank cleaning.

4.1.7.5　围裙

4.1.7.5　Aprons

在倾倒液体和干料或者使用较脏设备时,应当穿上围裙将尘土和材料与工作服隔开。防渗围裙(PVC 类型)可以抵御油料、溶剂和油脂以及干料飞溅带来的伤害。

Aprons should be worn to keep dirt and material off work clothing when pouring liquids, dumping dry materials, or working with dirty equipment. Impervious aprons (PVC-type) provide splash protection against oils, solvents, and greases, as well as dusty materials.

4.1.7.6 消防战斗服
4.1.7.6 Fireman's Outfit

除了小火之外,所有灭火行动都要求穿上消防战斗服。

Fireman's outfit must be worn when fire-fighting carried out but incipient fires.

消防战斗服由耐火纤维外层、氯丁橡胶防潮层以及耐火纤维制成的热衬垫组成。

Fireman's outfit is made of an outer layer of fire resistant fabric, a neoprene moisture barrier, and a thermal liner made of fire resistant fabric.

4.1.7.7 高能见度防护衣
4.1.7.7 High-Visibility Vests

在出现车辆交通的马路上或在其旁边工作的人员需要穿上高能见度罗网交通防护衣。待命人员和火灾监督员以及地面巡查员都可以穿上此类防护衣从而便于他人辨认。

High-visibility mesh-type traffic vests should be worn by personnel when they are working on or alongside a road where there will be vehicle traffic. These vests can also be used by stand-by and fire watch personnel and building floor wardens so they will be easy to recognize.

4.1.7.8 工作背心/救生衣
4.1.7.8 Work Vest/Life Jacket

(1)工作背心

(1) Work Vest

工作背心主要用于穿上救生衣会导致行动不方便的情况。工作背心由一个马甲组成。得到认可的标准包括美国海岸警卫队及《SOLAS 公约》的相关规定。

Working over water where a full life jacket would make movement difficult. It consists of a waistcoat. Approved standards: the relevent contents of US Coast Guard & SOLAS.

(2)自动膨胀外衣(用于直升机)

(2) Auto Inflate Jacket (Helicopter Use)

得到认可的标准包括 CR 13033、美国海岸警卫队或《SOLAS 公约》的相关规定。

Approved standards: the relevant contents of CR 13033, US Coast Guard or SOLAS.

(3)救生衣

(3) Life Jacket

救生衣必须能够自我调整并且满足《SOLAS 公约》的要求。

Life Jacket must be self-righting and be certified to meet SOLAS requirements.

4.1.8 脚部保护
4.1.8 Foot Protection

4.1.8.1 总则
4.1.8.1 General

员工在可能因物体坠落或滚动而伤及脚部的地方工作时需要穿安全鞋。需要穿安全鞋的区域和工作应由相关设施的监督员或负责人来决定。

Safety footwear shall be worn by employees when they work in an area where there is danger of foot injury due to falling or rolling objects. Areas and jobs which require safety footwear shall be determined by the supervisor or superintendent of the facility.

访问者和监管员只有在参与可能导致脚部受伤的工作时才需要穿安全鞋。但是,他们必须穿上适合相应工作环境的鞋子或靴子。

Visitors and regulatory agency personnel are not required to wear safety footwear unless they engage in work that presents a foot hazard. However, they must wear shoes or boots that are suitable for working environment.

在船舶或设施上不得穿以下鞋子:

The following footwear shall not be worn on marine vessels or facilities:

(1)网球鞋和平底帆布鞋;

(1)Tennis and deck shoes;

(2)超高坡跟靴;

(2)Deep lug boots;

(3)带绉胶、不平整、厚的或不光滑皮革鞋底的靴子和鞋子;

(3)Boots and shoes with crepe, uneven, thick, or rough leather soles;

(4)高跟鞋;

(4)High heeled shoes;

(5)凉鞋和露趾鞋;

(5)Sandals and open-toed shoes;

(6)带有薄的或严重磨损的鞋底的鞋子。

(6)Footwear with thin or badly worn soles.

4.1.8.2 安全鞋标准
4.1.8.2 Safety Footwear Criteria

安全鞋应当达到“个人防护——保护鞋”或者其他国际认可的标准中的相关要求和规格。安全鞋必须具备抗冲击和抗压脚趾保护特性,鞋底要具备防滑和抵抗化学物质影响的特性。

Safety footwear shall meet the requirements and specifications set forth in "Personal Protection—Protective Footwear" or other internationally-recognized standard. Safety footwear must have impact and compression strength toe protection and soles that are slip-resistant and chemical-resistant.

靴子必须至少 250 mm 高(从鞋底底部量起)。

Boots must be a minimum of 250 mm high (measured from the bottom of the sole).

靴子要由皮革制成,并且带有钢质鞋头。

The boot is made of leather with a steel toecap.

必要时还应具备抗油鞋底。

Oil resistant sole where appropriate.

4.1.8.3 使用安全鞋的条件

4.1.8.3 Eligibility for Safety Footwear

公司应向需要安全鞋的员工和劳务合同员工提供所需安全鞋。

Company will furnish safety footwear to employees and personal service contract employees who work in areas requiring them.

接收新安全鞋之前,员工必须向其监督员表明自己之前使用的安全鞋已经不能再用。

Before new safety footwear will be provided, employees must show their supervisor that the pair previously issued is no longer serviceable.

4.1.8.4 领取安全鞋

4.1.8.4 Obtaining Safety Footwear

合格员工可在其监督员的许可下领取安全鞋。领取要求必须包含员工的姓名、员工编号、鞋子尺码,并且得到员工的监督员的许可。

Eligible employees may obtain footwear with their supervisor's approval. The requisition must contain the employee's name, employee number, shoe size, and be approved by the employee's supervisor.

4.1.8.5 橡胶靴

4.1.8.5 Rubber Boots

需要保护脚和鞋子免受过多的水、土、泥、垃圾或腐蚀性材料的影响时应当穿上橡胶靴。此类鞋子应当保护膝盖下半部分的腿免受水和污染物的影响。

Rubber boots should be worn when it is necessary to protect the feet and shoes from excessive water, oil, mud, muck, or corrosive material. They should keep the feet and lower pant legs dry and free from contamination.

4.2 船上安全注意事项

4.2 Safety Regulations on Board

4.2.1 目的

4.2.1 Purpose

确保所有员工以及访问船舶和设施的访问者能够了解工作场所的安全责任。

To ensure all employees, contractors and visitors to marine vessels and facilities are aware of there responsibilities regarding safety while onsite.

4.2.2 适用范围

4.2.2 Scope

本规定适用于所有员工和承包商,以及直接或间接通过承包商受雇在本公司办公楼工作或操作相关设备的员工。

These regulations are applicable to all employees and contractors, also to employees who are employed in/or on buildings or installations of the above mentioned company, either directly or indirectly through contractors.

4.2.3 责任

4.2.3 Responsibilities

经理有责任确保所有新员工都得知本公司的要求。

It is the responsibility of the manager to ensure all new employees are informed of the company requirements.

船舶/设备安全员有责任确保所有员工完全学习并了解其安全责任。

It is the responsibility of the vessel/facility safety officer to ensure all employees are fully inducted and understand their responsibilities regarding safety.

每个人都有责任阅读、理解并遵守上述规定。

It is the responsibility of the individual to read, understand and abide by these regulations.

4.2.4 程序
4.2.4 Procedure

4.2.4.1 总则
4.2.4.1 General

开展作业前风险评定以及根据风险级别进行安全讨论之前,任何工作都不得实施。

Work will not be conducted without a pre-job risk assessment and a safety discussion appropriate for the level of risk.

所有人员都要根据自己从事的工作接受相关培训并提升自己的技能水平。

All persons will be trained and competent in the work they conduct.

根据风险评定结果和最低现场要求需要穿戴 PPE。

PPE will be worn as per risk assessment and minimum site requirement.

开展工作之前要通过审查潜在紧急情况来制定应急方案。

Emergency response plans, developed from a review of potential emergency scenarios will be in place before commencement of work.

每个人都有义务停止不安全的工作。

Everyone has an obligation to stop work that is unsafe.

在所有必要的场合都要遵守安全和卫生规定并且穿戴 PPE。

The regulations with regard to safety and hygiene should be observed and PPE should be worn obligatorily during all activities for which they are considered necessary.

请严格遵守安全长官做出的或他人代表安全员做出的所有安全或卫生指令。

All instructions given by or on behalf of the safety officer regarding safety or hygiene should be followed carefully.

所有员工在工作场所、船舶、办公室和其他公司设施内,都必须保持最高度警惕、有序、整洁和干净。

Every employee must observe the highest possible degree of caution, order, neatness and cleanliness in workshops, on board ships, in offices and other company facilities.

所有员工都应当:

All employees are expected to:

(1)安全、有效地开展工作。

(1) Carry out their jobs in a safe and efficient manner.

(2)使用本公司提供的所有必需的 PPE。

(2) Make use of all required PPE supplied by the company.

(3)就特殊风险与自己的监督者进行协商。

(3) Consult with their supervisor(s) on any job with special risks.

(4)发现材料或设备出现缺陷或损伤之后,每个员工都要告知其监督者或部长和/或安全员。

(4) In the event of detection of defects, damage to material or equipment, every employee is required to inform their Supervisor or Head of Department and/or the safety officer.

(5)所有出口、进入通道、楼梯,尤其是电闸和变电站或消防站的入口要相互隔开,相隔的距离不多于 5 m。

(5) All exits, access ways, stairways and access to switches and transformer substations or fire stations in particular, are always to be kept clear within a range of 5 meters.

(6)请严格遵守所有船上、办公室或公司其他设施上的安全标示。

(6) All safety signs, whether onboard ships, in offices or on other company facilities must be closely observed and followed.

(7)所有员工都要严格遵守口头或书面做出的安全规定和建议或指示。

(7) All employees are required to carefully follow regulations and observe recommendations or instructions, which are given either in writing or verbally with a view to safety.

(8)员工和承包商不得开展可能会对人员或设备造成危险的工作。

(8) Employees and contractors are not permitted to perform jobs in such a way which may cause danger to persons or equipment.

(9)在此及以其他形式为员工做出的通知和规定视作已经传达给每位员工,因此任何人都不得声称自己不了解此通知和规定。

(9) Notices and regulations given here and other forms of media intended for the employees, are considered to have been transmitted to each employee personally, so that nobody can claim to be unfamiliar with such notices and regulations.

(10)任何员工都不得将酒、毒品、有害健康的物质或其他硬质/软质药物带到公司场所,或在公司场所内使用上述物品,亦不得在受上述物品影响期间开展工作。

(10) No employee is permitted to bring to or use on company premises: liquor, intoxicants, substances hazardous to health, or other hard/soft drugs or to carry out their job whilst being under the influence of any of such substances.

(11)任何员工都不得进入与其工作无关的区域。

(11) No employee is permitted access to places where they do not need to be in connection with their job.

(12)请立即将发现的未能完全遵守安全和安保规定的行为汇报给安全与安保部门。

(12) Insufficient safety and security must be reported immediately to the Safety & Security Department.

4.2.4.2 个人防护设备

4.2.4.2 Personal Protective Equipment

进行机器、明火、燃烧、焊接或碾磨作业,处理其他危险物质以及从事可能会有粉尘和其他四处飞溅的物质对眼镜产生伤害的作业时,请务必戴安全眼镜和/或护目镜。

Safety glasses and/or goggles must be worn while working with machinery, fire, burning, welding or grinding and any other hazardous substances and during any activity involving danger to the eyes caused by dust and materials flying about.

在船上、船坞、码头或其他可能会因坠落物体而受伤的地方工作时,请务必戴上安全帽。

Safety helmets must be worn during work on board ships, in the dock, on the wharf or in places where there is a risk of being hit by falling objects.

在船上、船坞以及车间工作时请务必穿上安全鞋。在任何地方都应当穿优质鞋。

Safety shoes must be worn whilst working on board ships, in the dock and in the workshops. Good quality shoes must be worn elsewhere.

喷漆时请务必戴防轻质气体的呼吸器。

A respirator for light gases must be worn while spray painting.

请避免在员工工作的地方释放有毒/有害烟或气或制造尘土。如果无法避免,请务必安装有效装置以吸收此种烟或气,员工也必须戴氧气面罩或防毒面具对自己进行保护。

The emission of toxic/hazardous fumes or gases or creation of dust in spaces where employees are working should be avoided. Where this is not feasible, effective devices must be installed to ensure that such fumes and gases are extracted and employees must wear oxygen masks or gas masks for protection.

在浮动驳船或水上工作时,请务必准备有效的救生装置,比如带有至少 10 m 长的绳索的救生圈。在浮动驳船或水上工作时要在工作场所周边安装栏杆,白天应当在水上准备漂浮旗帜以提醒船舶。晚上则需要配备足够的灯光。

While working on a floating barge or above water, effective life-saving devices, e.g., lifebuoy with a rope of at least ten meters, must be readily available. Railings should be installed around the working area during work on a floating barge or above water and a flag must be flown during daylight hours to alert passing ships of the danger. During the hours of darkness there should be sufficient lighting.

高空作业时要戴安全带。在高空工作时要使用安全系锁而且任何时候都不能解开。该要求适用于在 2 m 甚至更高处且可能会有坠落危险的作业。

Safety harnesses must be worn whilst working at heights. Safety lanyard(s) must be used and should never be disconnected whilst the person is aloft. This requirement is for any work 2 meters or above where the person is at risk of falling.

4.2.4.3 工作服
4.2.4.3 Overall

禁止穿含油或易燃化学物质的工作服或者穿这种不干净衣服进行工作。

It is prohibited to wear overall saturated with oil or inflammable chemicals or to carry out work wearing such contaminated clothing.

禁止穿容易卷入机器的工作服。工人不得在工作场所穿短裤或拖鞋。

Work overall that can easily be trapped in machinery must not be worn. Workers are not permitted on the premises in shorts or slippers.

工作服口袋内不得携带尖锐或凸出物品。

Sharp or pointed objects must not be carried in the pockets of working overall.

工作期间不得戴可能被套住的宽松的腰带、戒指、链子或手镯。

Loose belts or bands on clothing, rings, chains or bracelets must not be worn during work that carries a risk that they may be caught.

焊接工和安装工/切割工不得在工作时在衣服里放置火柴盒和/或打火机。

Welders and fitters/cutters must not work with matchboxes and/or lighters in their working overall.

所有员工在工作场所都要穿工作服。禁止在工作期间穿其他衣服。

All workers must wear overalls when they are working in the production areas. Wearing other clothes during working hours is prohibited.

4.2.4.4 整洁、干净
4.2.4.4 Order and Neatness

禁止在船上到处扔抹布、剩余食物等。这些东西应当放入指定容器内。所有船舶都要遵守“零”舷外排放政策。

It is prohibited to throw overboard: cleaning rags, leftovers of food etc. These shall be disposed of properly in designated containers. A ZERO overboard discharge policy is in force on all vessels.

请立即清理可能导致滑倒的任何溢出液，比如油污。

All spillages which carry a risk of skidding, such as oil spill, should immediately be cleaned.

工作区域必须保持干净。这一规定同样适用于餐厅、休息室、盥洗室、厕所、浴池和衣物储存区。

Places where work is carried out must be kept clean. This also applies to the messroom, lounge room(s), washrooms, toilets, bathing facilities and clothing storage.

部门领导必须确保工作站或工作场所保持干净。

Department heads must ensure that work stations or places where work is done, are clear.

长头发要用帽子遮住。

Long hair must be covered by a bonnet.

4.2.4.5 机器/设备和工具

4.2.4.5 Machinery/Equipment and Tools

未经授权禁止操作机器和其他装置。

It is prohibited to operate machinery and other installations without authorisation.

机器在运转期间并且只要电源未关闭,便不得清理或对机器进行润滑。

It is not permitted to clean or to lubricate machines, while they are running and so long as the power has not been switched off.

安全装置不得从其正常位置上移除或移动。

Safety devices must not be removed or moved from their normal position.

为了在某个机器上工作而移除防护罩的任何员工都必须确保再次使用该机器前恢复该防护罩。

Any employee, who has removed a protective cover for the purpose of performing work on a machine, must ensure that the cover is replaced before the machine is used again.

根据工作需要使用合适的机器、设备和工具。不合适的机器、设备和工具需要立即更换。

Use the proper machinery, equipment and tools for the job for which it is intended. Inadequate machinery, equipment and tools have to be replaced immediately.

所有动力机器、驱动齿轮和设备都必须加以固定和控制,而且必须备有防护罩,以确保实现安全操作。

All power-operated machinery, driving gear and equipment must be secured, controlled and provided with protective covers in such a manner that safe operation is guaranteed.

所有动力机器必须加以固定,操作时要确保达到安全和安保目标,且不得超过安全速度。

All power operated machinery must be secured, handled and operated in such a manner that the safety and security of its operation is guaranteed and a safe speed cannot be exceeded.

在推进器或传动轴上工作时,请务必在机舱里靠近盘车机的旁边贴上"请勿操作"的标示。该机器的操作系统必须完全隔离和锁封,以防止意外启动。

During work on a propeller or propeller shaft, a "DO NOT OPERATE" sign must be posted in the engine room, near the turning engine. The system must be totally isolated and locked out to prevent accidental starting.

对操作中的动力机器进行检测、维护、润滑、清洁、维修和检查时需要十分小心,以避免危险的发生并保证安全。务必使用锁封和签封系统来确保进行作业时设备的安全。

Inspection, maintenance, lubrication, cleaning, overhauling and testing of power operated machinery under operation should be carried out under extreme precautions and in such a manner that danger is avoided and safety is guaranteed. A lock-out and tag-out system must be used to ensure security of the equipment while performing the task.

驱动带、齿轮、链条、绳索和类似传输介质必须得到有效保护和遮盖。

Driving belts, gears, chains, ropes and similar transmission materials must be effectively protected and covered.

操作动力机器的员工不得佩戴项链、手镯、表带和耳环。长袖子必须弄短。

Employees operating power operated machinery must not wear necklaces, bracelets, watchstraps and rings. Overall sleeves should be kept short.

4.2.4.6　压缩气体和焊接设备

4.2.4.6　Compressed gas and welding equipment

压缩后的氧气、乙炔、丙烷、氩气、二氧化碳和空气等如果使用不当会非常危险。只有指定人员和有资质的人员才有权使用和操作压缩气体设备。此类工作应该在通风良好的地方进行,而且必须使用特别为这些气体准备的软管、多支管和调节器。

Oxygen, acetylene, propane, argon, carbon dioxide and air, etc., can be hazardous under pressure if not used properly. Only designated and certified employees are authorised to work with and handle compressed gas equipment. Work should be carried out in a well-ventilated area and hoses, manifolds and regulators specially designed for these gases must be used.

压缩气瓶不能连接在一起,链式气瓶必须靠着墙体、舱壁、气缸、推车、气瓶架或其他架子垂直存放。气瓶应当远离电路和过高温度。

Compressed gas cylinders must not be connected together and chain gas cylinders must always be stored in an upright position against a wall, bulkhead, cylinder, truck, cylinder rack or post. Gas cylinders must be kept away from electrical circuits and excessive heat.

千万不要把气瓶放在人行道、走廊或可能损害气瓶的工作区。气瓶必须进行稳固安装以避免气瓶掉落。

Never place gas cylinders in walkways, passageways or work areas where they could be damaged. Gas cylinders must be installed so that they cannot fall over.

一旦作业中断,请关闭气瓶阀和/或总管阀和放残软管。

In case of interruption of work, close the gas cylinder valve and/or the manifold valve and drain hoses.

空的气瓶必须关闭;先关上气瓶阀,抽掉调节器中的剩余气体,松开调节器然后安装瓶盖。

Empty gas cylinders must be closed; close the gas cylinder valve first, bleed off the remaining gas of the regulator, unscrew the regulator and install the cylinder cap.

除非在以下情况时,否则气瓶(空的或满的)不得移动:

Gas cylinders (empty or full) may only be moved if:

(1)关闭了气瓶阀。

(1)The cylinder valve is closed.

(2)移除了调节器。

(2)The regulator is removed.

(3)安装了瓶盖。

(3)The cylinder cap is installed.

进行切割和焊接作业时,必须在附近地方放置消防设备,尤其是在船上时。

During cutting and welding, there must always be a fire fighting device available in the immediate area, particularly on board vessels.

闪回规避器应当装在乙炔瓶的气焊入口和调节器之间,从而避免乙炔瓶的减速阀发生逆火、闪回和爆炸。

Flashback arrestors should be installed between the torch gas inlets and the regulator of an acetylene cylinder in order to prevent backfires, flashbacks and explosions through the reduction valve in the acetylene cylinder.

禁止在水槽的楼梯间放置氧气或燃气软管。

It is prohibited to place oxygen or gas hoses between the stairs in the tank.

氧气或燃气软管不能在封闭区域内呈加压状态。氧气或燃气软管不得放在吊车轨上。

Oxygen or gas hoses must not be left in a pressurised state in a closed space. Oxygen or gas hoses must not be placed or left on crane rails.

乙炔瓶温度升高时,气瓶不得立即用冷水降温。

In case of rising temperature in an acetylene bottle, the bottle should be cooled immediately with water.

千万不要对气焊工具、调节器、软管、气瓶阀或与氧气接触的任何东西进行润滑。不要把氧气瓶或设备放在可能会有机油滴落到氧气瓶或设备上的地方。不要用带有油渍的手或手套操作氧气设备。

Never oil or grease torches, regulators, hoses, cylinder valves, or anything else that comes into contact with oxygen. Do not place oxygen cylinders or equipment where oil or grease from machinery can drip onto them. Never handle oxygen equipment with greasy or oily hands or gloves.

随时避免油或油类物质与氧气瓶、减速阀、总管阀、软管或切割/气焊工具接触。

Always avoid contact between oil or oil products and oxygen cylinders, reduction valves, manifolds, hoses or cutting/welding torches.

在潮湿或高温区域进行电焊时,请加倍小心,例如要小心进行合理地接。焊接变压器必须配备最大 42 V A/C 的二级电压减压器。

In case of electrical welding in damp or hot spaces, special safety precautions should be taken such as proper grounding. The welding transformer must be provided with a maximum approved secondary voltage reduction relay of 42 V A/C.

停止或中断封闭区域内的作业后,请立即将气焊工具和软管从这些地方移除。

Immediately after termination or interruption of work in closed spaces, torches and hoses have to be removed from these spaces.

务必使燃气软管远离火花、熔金属和熔渣。不要在拖动软管时碰到尖锐物体,使软管远离油脂。避免软管扭折或缠结。软管可能会被附近的设备损害时不得使用软管。

Gas hoses must be protected from sparks, hot metal and slag. Do not drag a hose over sharp objects and keep it away from oil and grease. Prevent kinking or tangling of the hose. Do not run a hose where it can be damaged by nearby equipment.

乙炔设备软管拖动时不能碰到尖锐物体或边缘,从而避免软管破损。

Acetylene equipment hoses must not be dragged over sharp objects or edges in order to avoid the hoses being damaged.

请勿使用没有进行合理外部绝缘的燃气软管以及带有泄漏、烧毁、磨损痕迹或者其他缺陷的燃气软管。

Gas hoses with leaks, burns, worn spots or any other defect and gas hoses without the appropriate outer insulation should not be used.

燃气软管不能用金属丝拴紧。请使用特制夹子以防止软管被割坏或损坏。

Gas hoses must not be fastened by means of iron wire. Special clamps intended for such purpose have to be used in order to prevent the hose from being cut or damaged.

在合适的情况下可大量使用电焊变压器,该变压器可以连接最大 42 V A/C 的常规电压,这种电压由安全变压器的独立的次级绕组所提供。

Electrical welding transformers may be used exclusively if they are suitable for, and connected to, a maximum regular voltage of 42 V A/C, which is supplied by the separate secondary winding of a safety transformer.

在车间或离他人近的地方进行电焊时要使用防护隔板。

Use protective partition screens during electric welding in the workshop or in close proximity to other persons.

开始任何高温作业之前都要先获得作业许可。

A permitto work must be obtained before commencing any hot work.

在危险区域进行高温作业时,至少应当安排一名火灾监督员(随时待命)。

When performing hot work in a hazardous space, at least one fire watchman should be appointed (on standby).

结束工作期限后,须立即:

On termination of the working period:

(1)合理关闭燃气、氧气和水软管、总管阀和/或线路。

(1)Gas, oxygen, air and water hoses, manifolds and/or lines must be properly closed.

(2)储存好燃气、氧气、空气软管和焊接电缆。

(2)Gas, oxygen, air hoses and welding cables must be stored away.

泄漏或损坏的燃气软管必须立即维修或更换。

Leaking or damaged gas hoses must be repaired or replaced immediately.

损坏的焊接电缆必须立即维修或更换。

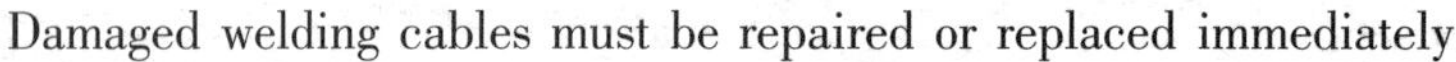

Damaged welding cables must be repaired or replaced immediately.

禁止在距离丙烷储罐很近的地方切割、使用高温或烟。

It is prohibited to cut, apply heat or smoke in the proximity of a propane tank.

4.2.4.7 高空作业

4.2.4.7 Working at Heights

除非达到以下要求,否则不能在距离地面 2 m(6 ft)或更高的地方实施作业:

Working at heights of 2 meters (6 feet) or higher above the ground cannot proceed unless:

(1)使用带有防护装置或扶手,并且由相关人员确认了的固定平台;或者

(1) A fixed platform is used with guard or hand rails, verified by a competent person(s); or

(2)能够承受至少每人 2 275 kg 静载重的重量并且装有以下设备的防坠装置:

(2) Fall arrest equipment is used that is capable of supporting at least a 2,275 kg static load per person and has:

①装有合适的固定物,最好是装在头顶部位;

①A proper anchor mounted, preferably overhead;

②在每个连接头处,均使用双闩锁自锁弹簧钩使身体完全钩住;

②Full body harness using double latch self-locking snap hooks at each connection;

③合成纤维绳;

③Synthetic fibre lanyards;

④减振器;

④Shock absorber;

⑤防坠装置能把自由坠落减少至 2 m(6 ft)或更少;

⑤Fall arrest equipment will limit free fall to 2 meters (6 feet) or less;

⑥完成对防坠装置和系统的目视检查,受损或已经启动的任何设备都不再使用;

⑥A visual inspection of the fall arrest equipment and system is completed and any equipment that is damaged or has been activated is taken out of service;

⑦相关人员有能力进行作业。

⑦Person are competent to perform the work.

4.2.4.7.1 脚手架和梯子

4.2.4.7.1 Scaffolds and Ladders

只有在完全了解脚手架类型的相关负责人的监督下才能建造、拆卸或者大幅度地更换脚手架。

A scaffold must not be built, demolished or substantially changed unless under the supervision of a competent and responsible person, sufficiently familiar with the relevant type of scaffolding.

所有脚手架、梯子和附着设备都必须使用可靠材料,而且必须足以承受可能需要承载的

负荷和压力。

All scaffolds, ladders and associated equipment must be manufactured of reliable material and be strong enough for the load and pressure to which they will be exposed.

在受损部位满足相关要求之前,务必移除并处理受损脚手架,以防有人不慎使用该脚手架。

A damaged scaffold must be removed and disposed of so that accidental use is not possible until the damaged part meets regulations.

离地面 2 m 的任何脚手板:

Any scaffold floor higher than two meters above floor level:

(1)必须有扶手;

(1) Must have rails;

(2)必须带有不到 1.30 m(重载脚手架)和 0.80 m(轻载脚手架)宽的工作面;

(2) Must have a working floor width of less than 1. 30 meters (heavy scaffolds) and 0.80 meters (light scaffolds);

(3)必须进行合理修建,以防木板移动或被风卷起。

(3) Must be adequately constructed so that the boards cannot shift or be lifted by the wind.

4.2.4.7.2 脚手架木板

4.2.4.7.2 Scaffolding Planks

工作面中的木板或用作侧板的木板宽度不得少于 20 cm,并且厚度必须足以确保连接脚手杆(上梁)时的安全。脚手杆(上梁)之间的距离最多 1.80 m,脚手架木板应当在末端安装金属夹以防木板断裂。

Planks forming part of a work floor or that are used as sideboards should not have a width of less than 20 cm and should be thick enough to offer security in connection with the distance between the scaffolding poles (cross-heads). The distance between the scaffolding poles (cross-heads) may be 1.80 meters at the most and planks should be provided with a metal clamp at the ends in order to prevent the plank from splitting.

4.2.4.7.3 扶手

4.2.4.7.3 Railing

2 m 多高的脚手架应当在脚手板上安装 85 cm 高的可靠扶手。

A functional railing of 85 cm height must be installed above the scaffolding floor on scaffolds more than 2 meters high.

4.2.4.7.4 侧板

4.2.4.7.4 Sideboard

脚手架的侧板必须距离工作面足够高,以防材料和设备坠落。侧板最少 20 cm 高,并且要尽可能地紧贴工作面。

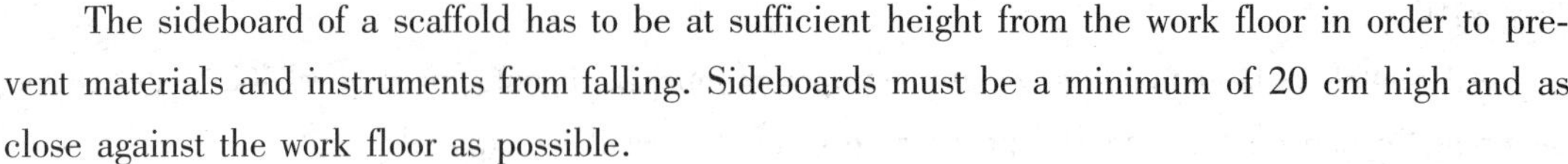

The sideboard of a scaffold has to be at sufficient height from the work floor in order to prevent materials and instruments from falling. Sideboards must be a minimum of 20 cm high and as close against the work floor as possible.

4.2.4.7.5 梯子

4.2.4.7.5 Ladders

梯子应当进行合理维护和清理以防出现滑倒,并且还要加以固定以防坠落或弯曲。

Ladders should be kept well maintained and clean in order to prevent slipping and must be secured to avoid falling or bending.

木梯的横挡应当放在脚手杆的木头里,且无须另外用平头钉或螺丝钉进行固定。

Rungs of wooden ladders should rest in the wood of the poles; they must not be fastened exclusively by hob nails or screws.

请勿给木梯涂漆,但可以上油或者覆盖一层透明清漆。

Wooden ladders must not be painted, but oiled or covered with clear varnish.

4.2.4.8 作业许可

4.2.4.8 Permit to Work

在实施涉及进入封闭区域、吊车作业、跳水、在电动系统上工作、在水中或在 2 m 多高的区域工作、小船作业或在指定高温作业区以外的区域进行高温作业等作业之前,请务必获得满足以下要求的作业许可:

Before conducting work that involves confined space entry, crane operations, diving, work on electrically energized systems, work overboard or at height over 2 meters, small boat operations or hot work outside designated hot work areas, a permit must be obtained that:

(1)划定作业范围;

(1)Defines scope of work;

(2)识别危险和评估风险;

(2)Identifies hazards and assesses risk;

(3)确立控制措施以消除或减少危险;

(3)Establishes control measures to eliminate or mitigate hazards;

(4)将作业与其他相关作业许可或同步作业相联系;

(4)Links the work to other associated work permits or simultaneous operations;

(5)由相关负责人授权;

(5)Is authorised by the responsible person(s);

(6)将上述信息传达给作业相关人员;

(6)Communicates above information to all involved in the work;

(7)确保提供充足的控制措施以返回正常作业。

(7)Ensures adequate control over the return to normal operations.

4.2.4.9 吊车和其他工具

4.2.4.9 Cranes and Other Tools

4.2.4.9.1 一般规定

4.2.4.9.1 General Regulations

吊车司机不得实施任何可能对吊车和/或用吊车移动的负重物产生伤害,或者可能导致自身或他人发生事故的行为。驾驶员必须熟悉安全规定。

A crane driver must not perform any acts that may cause damage to the crane and/or the load to be moved, or that may result in an accident to him or others. He must be familiar with the safety regulations.

只有经过授权的人员才能操作吊车。

Cranes may only be operated by authorised persons.

实习吊车司机只能在有经验的吊车司机(对吊车的操作负责)的直接监督下才能操作吊车。

Trainee crane drivers may only operate a crane under the direct supervision of a competent crane driver who will be responsible for the operation of the crane.

如果吊车司机发现吊车或起重机存在任何问题,该司机需立即放下负重物并且停止吊车。该司机必须立即通知其监督员,监督员将对此采取进一步举措。

If a crane driver detects any defects on a crane or the hoisting gear, he must put down the load immediately and stop the crane. He must notify his supervisor immediately, who will then be responsible for further action.

禁止将工具或材料留在吊机上以防物体发生坠落。任何一次维护后都必须检查吊机。

It is prohibited to leave tools or materials on cranes due to the risk of such objects falling. Cranes must be checked after any maintenance work has been carried out.

吊车司机离开吊车后,所有作业电闸都必须关闭(调到零的位置),总电闸的电源也必须关闭。

When the crane driver leaves the crane, all operational switches must be turned off (in zero position) and the power must be switched off at the main switch.

吊车车厢、步行格栅和吊车上的平台必须没有任何油渍以防出现滑倒。

Access to the crane cabin, walking gratings and platforms on the crane must be kept free of oil and grease in order to prevent slipping.

升起、降下或移动负重物时任何人都不能待在吊车上。

No person is permitted to be on a crane load while the load is hoisted, lowered or moved.

梯子、楼梯、平台等或第三方物品(汽车、船舶等)出现任何损害都必须立即汇报。

Any damage to ladders, stairs, platforms etc. or third party objects (cars, vessels etc.) must be reported without delay.

4.2.4.9.2 操作吊车

4.2.4.9.2 Operating the Crane

进行吊车作业的所有人员都必须根据 PPE 要求至少配备：

All personnel associated with crane operations must wear the following PPE as a minimum:

(1)安全靴；

(1)Safety Boots;

(2)安全帽；

(2)Safety Helmet;

(3)吊装手套；

(3)Rigging Gloves;

(4)工作服。

(4)Overalls.

禁止将负重物移到人员、变电站、建筑、办公室或进行作业的物体上方。

It is prohibited to move a load over persons, transformer stations, buildings, offices or objects where work is being done.

在运送负重物时,要留充足的时间发出清晰的信号(前提是吊车上安装了发出信号的装置)。如果位于吊车下方的人员未能遵守该信号要求,请立即停止作业。

When transporting a load, give clear signals in plenty of time, if the crane is equipped with a device to do so. Stop operations, if persons below the crane fail to act upon the signals.

千万不能将负重物挂在无人看管的吊车上。

Never leave a load hanging from the crane unattended.

如果抓斗不在负重物的垂直上方,千万不要实施升起作业,否则会导致升起期间负重物出现不必要的摇摆。禁止实施移动或升起不在抓斗垂直下方的负重物的作业。

Never hoist when the grab is not vertically over the load, as this may cause unnecessary swinging of the load during hoisting. All actions to move or hoist loads in places that are not vertically under the grab, are prohibited.

除非是在需要特殊许可的特殊场合,否则可使用限位开关以保证最大升吊高度的安全,因为操作开关被禁止使用。请遵守具体的工厂安全规定。

Except in very special cases for which special permission is required, using the limit switch for maximum hoisting-height security as an operating switch is prohibited. The specific factory safety regulations have to be observed.

禁止停用限位开关和刹车等保护装置。请遵守具体的车间安全规定。

It is prohibited to deactivate safeguards such as limit switches and brakes. The specific workshop safety regulations have to be observed.

必要时吊车司机须接收吊车助手(吊物工人)的指令。请严格遵守该指令。

The crane driver receives instructions from the crane assistant (slinger) if that is required for the job. These instructions have to be followed accurately.

如果吊车司机质疑吊车助手所给指令的有效性或者发现正在使用错误的工具或起重

机,吊车司机必须停止吊车操作,从而与吊车助手进行讨论。

If the crane driver doubts the validity of instructions given by the crane assistant, or notices that incorrect tools or hoisting gear are being used, he must stop the crane activities in order to discuss the matter with the crane assistant.

请根据行业标准信号规定的手势信号或通过"无线电话机"进行作业沟通。必须努力确保吊车司机和吊车助手之间不会产生误解。

The working contact is made by means of arm signals in accordance with industry standard signals or by means of a "walkie-talkie". Every effort must be made to ensure that there are no misunderstandings between crane drivers and crane assistants.

所有线缆、吊索、链条、钩环铁以及用于升降或装载的其他类似工具都应由获得授权的人定期检查,其检查结果必须记录在一份证明书或吊车日志簿中。

All cables, slings, chains, shackles and the like that are used for hoisting and lowering or for carrying should be examined regularly by an authorised person, whose findings must be recorded on a certificate or in a crane log book.

维修控制和维护:

Repairs Control and maintenance:

(1)吊车润滑或检查必须由合格人员实施。

(1) Lubricating or examining of the crane must be carried out by a competent person.

(2)维修或维护后的检测必须由吊车司机实施。

(2) Test running after repairs or maintenance has to be carried out by the crane driver.

4.2.4.9.3　升起作业

4.2.4.9.3　Lifting Operations

未达到以下要求时,不得操作电梯式吊车、起重机或其他机械升吊装置:

Lifts utilizing cranes, hoists, or other mechanical lifting devices will not commence unless:

(1)对升吊装置进行评定,相关合格人员要确定升吊方式和设备;

(1) An assessment of the lift has been completed and the lift method and equipment has been determined by a competent person(s);

(2)操作动力起重装置的人必须接受过此种设备作业培训并且得到认可;

(2) Operators of powered lifting devices are trained and certified for that equipment;

(3)装载作业要由相关合格人员实施;

(3) Rigging of the load is carried out by a competent person(s);

(4)在过去(最少)12个月内,升吊装置和设备获得了使用认证;

(4) Lifting devices and equipment have been certified for use within the last 12 months (at a minimum);

(5)负重物不超过升吊装置的动态和/或静态承受能力;

(5) Load does not exceed dynamic and/or static capacities of the lifting equipment;

(6)升吊设备上安装的所有安全装置都是可用的;

(6)Any safety devices installed on lifting equipment are operational;

(7)由相关合格人员实施每次升吊作业之前都要对所有升吊装置和设备进行目视检查。

(7)All lifting devices and equipment have been visually examined before each lift by a competent person(s).

4.2.4.9.4 能源隔离

4.2.4.9.4 Energy Isolation

除非达到以下要求,否则不能实施机械、电力、加工、液压以及其他能源系统的隔离作业:

Any isolation of energy systems:mechanical, electrical, process, hydraulic and others cannot proceed unless:

(1)隔离和释放已存能源的方式要由相关合格人员决定并且由其实施;

(1)The method of isolation and discharge of stored energy are agreed and executed by a competent person(s);

(2)将储存的所有能源释放;

(2)Any stored energy is discharged;

(3)隔离地点要使用锁封和签封系统;

(3)A system of lock-out and tag-out is utilised at isolation points;

(4)实施检测以确保隔离有效;

(4)A test is conducted to ensure the isolation is effective;

(5)定期监控隔离效果。

(5)Isolation effectiveness is periodically monitored.

4.2.4.9.5 电力

4.2.4.9.5 Electricity

除非由具备资质的相关人员进行监督,否则不得实施电力装置、工具、设备或链路维修或此类作业以外的其他活动。

Repairs on electrical instruments, tools, equipment or links, and other activities not part of the operation, may only be conducted under the supervision of staff qualified for such purposes.

如果在带电压的裸线上或附近工作,必须先关掉电源。为了防止电源被意外打开,应当进行锁封/签封,保险丝也要由电工拆掉。

When work is carried out on or near a bare wire under electrical tension, the electricity must be switched off first. In order to prevent the electricity from being switched on unexpectedly, it has to be secured by means of a lock-out/tag-out process, the fuses should also be removed by an electrician.

关闭部分或全部电力装置后,只有在负责人(电工)确认可以安全打开此装置时才能打开此电力装置。

When the electrical installation has been switched off partly or fully, it can only be switched on again after a responsible person (electrician) has personally ascertained that this act can be performed safely.

严厉禁止未经授权的人员操作电力装置、设备或链路。

It is strictly prohibited for unauthorised persons to operate electrical instruments, equipment or links.

4.2.4.9.6　进入封闭区域

4.2.4.9.6　Enclosed Space Entry

除非达到以下要求，否则不能进入封闭区域：

Entry into any enclosed space cannot proceed unless:

(1)没有其他选择；

(1) All other options have been ruled out;

(2)由负责人授权许可；

(2) Permit is issued with authorisation by a responsible person(s);

(3)根据要求将许可传达给所有相关人员并且张贴公布；

(3) Permit is communicated to all affected personnel and posted, as required;

(4)所有相关人员都具备合格的作业资质；

(4) All persons involved are competent to do the work;

(5)影响该区域的所有能源来源都被隔离；

(5) All sources of energy affecting the space have been isolated;

(6)根据评定的结果，尽可能多地对空气进行检测，并且核查和重复该检测；

(6) Testing of atmospheres is conducted, verified and repeated as often as defined by the risk assessment;

(7)备用人待命；

(7) Stand-by person is stationed;

(8)防止人员未经授权时进入。

(8) Unauthorised entry is prevented.

4.2.4.9.7　危险区域/气体检测

4.2.4.9.7　Hazardous Space/Gas Test

请使用获得许可的气体测试方法来检查危险区域是否含有气体。

The investigation to establish whether a hazardous space is gas-free, is made by means of a approved gas test.

安全员完成检查后需要签署一份正式的“气体检测证明”，以证明已经进行检查的相关区域：

When the safety officer has completed his investigation, he will sign an official GAS TEST CERTIFICATE stating that the specified spaces examined:

(1)不存在易燃有毒气体，适合人员进入作业；或

(1) are free from flammable toxic gases, open for persons who are going to work in such spaces; or

(2)存在易燃有毒气体,适合人员进入作业。

(2) are not free from flammable toxic gases, open/accessible for persons who are going to work in such spaces.

本条第(1)和(2)项在表达时应使用以下术语:

Items 1 and 2 of this article are expressed in the following terms:

①“安全且适合工人作业”“不安全,不适合工人作业”;

①“Safe for workers”“Not safe for workers”;

②“安全且适合高温作业”“不安全,不适合高温作业”。

②“Safe for hot work”“Not safe for hot work”.

危险区域包括:

Hazardous spaces are:

①含有、曾经含有或可能有过气体和油的区域;

①Spaces that contain, contained or may have contained gas and oil;

②含有、曾经含有或可能有过化学物质的区域;

②Spaces that contain, contained or may have contained chemicals;

③船舶的油水舱、干隔舱等;

③Ships' tanks, void spaces etc.;

④关闭过一段时间的空置区域。

④Spaces empty and closed for a certain time.

以下人员或部门应收到已签发的每个气体检测证明的副本:

The following persons or departments shall receive a copy of each gas test certificate issued:

①船长;

①the master;

②进入危险区域的人员;

②the person(s) entering the hazardous space;

③部门领班。

③department heads.

气体检测证明的副本应当放在驾驶台或实施作业的区域的附近。

A copy of the gas test certificate shall be placed on the bridge and near the location where work is to be carried out.

只有确认区域内不再存在任何气体、油和/或化学物质后,才能在危险区域实施作业。

Work in hazardous spaces must not be carried out until it has been ascertained that the spaces no longer contain any gas, oil and/or chemicals.

拆下井盖并且进入船舶的危险区域必须先获得船长的许可。

Removing manhole covers and opening hazardous spaces on board ships may only be done with the permission of the master.

需要打开的泵、槽和设备必须不受压力且尽可能无油。获得相关许可后才能开启或解开任何接头。

The pumps, tanks and equipment to be opened, must always be free of pressure and free of oil as far as possible. After the relevant permission has been obtained, all the connections are to be unsealed or uncoupled.

如果对于区域内不再含有气体存在质疑,那么请在实施作业之前开展二次检查以确定气体是否存在。每次存在质疑时都要采取此类方法。

If there is any doubt that a space is no longer free of gas, then another investigation will have to be made to establish the absence of gas, before work may be continued. This must be done each time such suspicion arises.

签发气体检测证明之前禁止在含有、曾经含有或可能有过气体、油和/或化学物质的区域内实施作业。

It is prohibited to carry out work in spaces that contain, contained or may have contained gas, oil and/or chemicals before a gas test certificate has been issued.

在检测出"安全且适合工人作业但不适合高温作业"的区域内不得使用明火或使用其他产生火花的工具,并且要有足够的通风。

In spaces that have been declared "safe for workers, but not safe for hot work", no work with open fire or any other non-spark-free tools must be carried out, and sufficient ventilation must be provided.

在检测出"安全且适合高温作业"的区域内可使用明火作业,前提是接头、阀和法兰都已经松开或打开并且有足够的通风。

In a space that has been declared "safe for hot work", work with an open fire may be carried out, provided the connections, valves and flanges are loosened or opened, and sufficient ventilation is provided.

事故 & 职业病汇报:

Reporting of Accidents & Occupational Illness:

每次发生工伤事故后,船长或队经理都必须填写事故表并在 24 h 内发送给操作经理/公司。

For each industrial accident, the master or party manager must complete an accident form and send it to the operations manager/company within twenty-four hours.

遭遇事故的任何员工都必须尽快(24 h 内)通知安全员,即便此员工认为不需要立即接受医疗救治。如果未在规定的时间内汇报事故,那么事故便不记为工伤事故。

Any employee who has met with an accident must notify the safety officer as soon as possible (within 24 hours), even if he is of the opinion that medical assistance is not required immediately. If the accident has not been reported within the stated time scale, the occurrence is not recorded as an industrial accident.

另外还要尽快将事故和受伤情况告知 HSE 经理,并说明事故发生的时间和地点。

The HSE manager must also be notified of any accident with injuries as soon as possible, stating the time and place of the accident.

根据事故的严重程度,不论是否需要立即提供急救或者受害人是否因为遭遇事故而需要被送往医院,都应将事故告知 HSE 经理。

Depending on the gravity of the accident, whether immediate first aid assistance is required or if the victim has to be transported to a hospital in consequence of the accident, the HSE manager should be informed.

部长必须立即将以下情况通知给安全员:

The head of department must immediately notify the safety officer of:

(1)导致受伤人员需要医疗救治的事故;

(1)accidents of which the injured person or persons require medical assistance;

(2)出现可能导致永久、全部或部分伤残的受伤情况的事故;

(2)accidents that cause such injuries which may result in permanent, full or partial disability;

(3)造成物资损失的事故。

(3)accidents causing material damage.

安全员或队经理必须为所有事故编制事故报告,说明受伤情况和性质,该报告必须提交给本公司。

The safety officer or party manager must create an accident report for all accidents, stating the facts and the nature of the injury, and this report must be sent to the company.

4.3 变更管理

4.3 Management of Change(MOC)

除非完成了变更管理流程,否则由于组织、人员、系统、流程、程序、设备、产品、材料或物质以及法律法规发生变化而产生的作业不得进行。变更管理流程包括:

Work arising from temporary and permanent changes to organization, personnel, systems, process, procedures, equipment, products, materials or substances, and laws and regulations cannot proceed unless a management of change process is completed, where applicable, to include:

(1)受到变更影响的所有人员开展风险评估;

(1)A risk assessment conducted by all impacted by the change;

(2)制订作业计划,以明确变更的时间表以及以下几方面的控制措施;

(2)Development of a work plan that clearly specifies the timescale for the change and any control measures to be implemented regarding;

(3)设备、设施和工艺;

(3)Equipment, facilities and process;

(4)作业、维护、检测程序;

(4) Operations, maintenance, inspection procedures;

(5)培训、人员和沟通;

(5) Training, personnel and communication;

(6)文档编制;

(6) Documentation;

(7)负责人授权的作业计划。

(7) Authorisation of the work plan by the responsible person(s) through completion.

4.4 船上关键设备操作

4.4 Shipboard Key Machine and Equipment

船上关键性机器和设备操作的方案和须知由各轮轮机长和大副负责编制,应指明操作人和责任人。船上关键性机器和设备操作的方案和须知汇总报机务部、海务部审核、批准,分管该轮的机务主管备案。批准后的关键性机器和设备操作的方案和须知送船作为单船操作文件。通常船上关键设备操作包括如下:

The operation plan and instruction of shipboard key machine and equipment shall indicate the operator and the person in liability. C/E and C/O are responsible for compiling them. These procedure and instructions shall be collected to marine department and technical department to audit and approve, tech department should keep all the documents with them. The approved operation plan and instruction of shipboard key machine and equipment shall be distributed on board as the specific ship's operation documentation. Normally including the following items:

(1)主推进系统;

(1) Main propeller system;

(2)船舶电站(发电柴油机、发电机、主配电板、应急发电机及其配电板);

(2) Power station (generator distribution board, emergency switch board, emergency generator);

(3)锅炉;

(3) Boiler;

(4)舵机系统;

(4) Steering gear system;

(5)系离泊设备(锚机、缆机);

(5) Mooring equipments (windlass and winch);

(6)救生艇、救生筏;

(6) Life boat and life raft;

(7)火灾报警系统;
(7) Fire alarm system;
(8)消防泵及应急消防泵;
(8) Fire pump and emergency fire pump;
(9)泡沫灭火系统;
(9) Foam system;
(10)二氧化碳灭火系统;
(10) CO_2 system;
(11)油水分离器及15ppm报警设备;
(11) OWS and 15ppm alarm system;
(12)排油监控系统(ODME);
(12) Oil Discharging Monitoring Equipment (ODME);
(13)生活污水处理装置;
(13) Sewage installations;
(14)焚烧炉;
(14) Incinerator;
(15)全球海上遇险和安全系统;
(15) GMDSS system;
(16)货物系统;
(16) Cargo system;
(17)船长认为必要的其他设备。
(17) Equipments deemed necessary by the master.

第 5 章　船舶保安

Chapter 5 | Ship Security

5.1　船舶保安制度

5.1　Ship Security Regime

5.1.1　保安综述

5.1.1　Ship Security Summarize

2002 年 12 月，国际海事组织（International Maritime Organization, IMO）为了加强船舶和港口设施的保安，在《国际海上人命安全公约》（《SOLAS 公约》）中增加了与保安相关的内容。新增加的内容单独在《SOLAS 公约》第Ⅺ-2 章列明，包括在《国际船舶和港口设施保安规则》（《ISPS 规则》）中"加强海上保安的特别方法"。新增章节自 2004 年 7 月 1 日起正式生效。

In December 2002, the IMO adopted security-related amendments to the SOLAS Convention aimed at enhancing the security of ships and the port facilities. These amendments included a new Chapter Ⅺ-2 in the SOLAS Convention "special measures to enhance maritime security" which enshrined the International Ship and Port Facility Security (ISPS) Code, which took effect by 1 July 2004.

《海员培训、发证和值班标准国际公约》（《STCW 公约》）2010 年马尼拉修正案对于船舶保安相关培训提出了新的要求。这些新要求需要所有受雇到船的或在船上从事相关作业的人员符合《ISPS 规则》的要求。这些要求自 2012 年 1 月 1 日起生效；但是，国际海事组织为了更好地让船舶执行《ISPS 规则》，要求港口国检查官（PSCO）到 2014 年 1 月 1 日才开始强制执行上述规则。

The STCW Convention and Code as amended by the Manila amendments (2010) contains new requirements regarding security training. This training is required by all personnel employed or engaged onboard ships to which the ISPS Code applies. These regulations came into force on 1 January 2012, however, Port State Control Officers (PSCO) have been requested by IMO not to enforce this regulation until 1 January 2014 provided that the vessel otherwise complies with the ISPS Code.

《STCW 公约》2010 年修正案增加了第Ⅵ/5 章"为船舶保安员签发专业证书的强制性最低要求",增加了第 A-Ⅵ/5 节"签发船舶保安员专业证书的强制性最低要求",并规定了签发船舶保安员专业证书的最低适任标准。

The 2010 amendment to STCW Convention added Chapter Ⅵ/5 "Mandatory Minimum Requirements for the Issuance of Professional Certificates for Ship Security Officers", Section A-Ⅵ/5 "Mandatory Minimum Requirements for the Issuance of Professional Certificates for Ship Security Officers", and established minimum competency standards for the issuance of professional certificates for ship security officers.

《STCW 公约》马尼拉修正案对于保安方面提出 3 个新层次的培训内容:

In addition to the existing Ship Security Officer (SSO) training (which is unchanged) the amendments to the STCW Convention brings in three new levels of security training:

(1)保安熟悉培训;

(1) Security-related familiarization training;

(2)保安意识培训;

(2) Security-awareness training;

(3)保安职责培训。

(3) Designated security duties training.

这些变化体现在《STCW 公约》第Ⅵ/6 章节中包括 A-Ⅵ/6 强制部分和 B-Ⅵ/6 指导部分(非强制)。

These changes are embodied in STCW Convention Regulation Ⅵ/6 and Section A-Ⅵ/6 with non-mandatory guidance Section B-Ⅵ/6.

5.1.1.1 保安熟悉培训

5.1.1.1 Security-related Familiarization Training

保安熟悉培训必须由船舶保安员(SSO)或其他有相应资质的人员针对所有受雇上船或在船工作的人员在上船前进行,使其符合《ISPS 规则》中的相关条款。这种培训应将船舶特殊的保安问题着重讲解,使之至少可以令海员做到以下几点:

Security-related familiarization training must be carried out by the SSO, or other equally qualified person, to all persons employed or engaged in any capacity on ships which are required to comply with the provisions of the ISPS Code, prior to them being assigned shipboard duties. This instruction should emphasize ship specific security issues and provide guidance for the seafarer to at least be able to:

(1)报告保安事件,包括海盗、武装劫持威胁和武装袭击;

(1) Report a security incident, including a piracy or armed robbery threat or attack;

(2)懂得当发生保安威胁时应对的程序; 并

(2) Know the procedures to follow when they recognize a security threat ; and

(3)能在发生保安相关紧急情况和意外事故时履行自己的职责。

(3) Take part in security-related emergency and contingency procedures.

5.1.1.2 保安意识培训

5.1.1.2 Security-awareness Training

保安意识培训针对所有受雇上船或在船工作的人员在上船前进行,使其符合《ISPS 规则》中的相关条款。此培训必须符合《STCW 规则》第 A-Ⅵ/6 节第 4 段的要求。此培训结束后经过考试合格将签发《STCW 公约》要求的培训合格证(Z07)。完成此项培训的海员至少可以做到:

Security awareness training must be undertaken by all seafarers employed or engaged in any capacity on ships which are required to comply with the ISPS Code. This training/instruction must meet the requirements of Section A-Ⅵ/6 paragraph 4 of the amended STCW Code. This training leads to the issue of a STCW Certificate of Proficiency. On completion of this training a seafarer will at least be able to:

(1)通过保持高度的保安意识来加强海上保安;

(1) Contribute to the enhancement of maritime security through heightened awareness;

(2)识别保安威胁;并

(2) Recognize security threats; and

(3)懂得采用需要的方式保持保安意识和警惕性。

(3) Understand the need for, and methods of, maintaining security awareness and vigilance.

5.1.1.3 保安职责培训

5.1.1.3 Designated Security Duties Training

符合《ISPS 规则》中的相关条款,根据保安计划要求负有保安职责的船员必须进行保安职责培训。此培训必须符合《STCW 规则》第 A-Ⅵ/6 章第 6~8 段的要求。此培训结束后经过考试合格将签发《STCW 公约》要求的培训合格证(Z08)。完成此项培训的海员至少可以做到:

Training in designated security duties must be undertaken by seafarers, engaged on ships which are required to comply with the provisions of the ISPS Code, who have designated duties under the ships security plan. This training/instruction must meet the requirements of Section A-Ⅵ paragraphs 6 to 8 of the amended STCW Code. This training leads to the issue of an

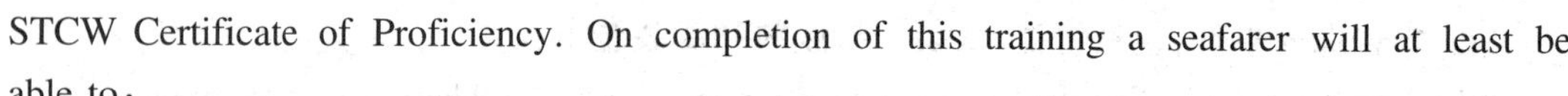

STCW Certificate of Proficiency. On completion of this training a seafarer will at least be able to:

(1)保持船舶保安计划要求的保安状态;

(1) Maintain the conditions set out in a ship security plan;

(2)识别保安风险和威胁;

(2) Recognize security risk and threats;

(3)定期进行保安检查;并

(3) Undertake regular security inspections; and

(4)能正确使用保安设备和系统。

(4) Properly use security equipment and systems.

本课程提供知识给那些被指定履行指定保安职责的海员的责任和职责,如《STCW 规则》中表 A-Ⅵ/6-2 所定义的,特别是协助船舶保安员(SSO)加强船舶保安的职责。

This course provides knowledge to those who may be designated to perform the duties and responsibilities of a seafarers with designated security responsibilities, as defined in Table A-Ⅵ/6-2 of the STCW Code, and in particular the duties and responsibilities with respect to assisting the Ship Security Officer (SSO) in enhancing the security of a vessel.

课程中有 9 个主要的主题,包括:

There are 9 major topics in this course, including:

介绍;海上保安政策;保安责任;船舶保安评估;保安设备;威胁辨认、识别和反应;船保安操作;应急准备、演习和演练;保安管理。

Introduction; Maritime Security Policy; Security Responsibility; Ship Security Assessment; Security Equipment; Threat Identification, Recognition and Response; Ship Security Actions; Emergency Preparedness, Drills and Exercises; Security Administration.

成功完成这门课程的人将有足够的知识和技能:

Those who successfully complete this course will have sufficient knowledge and skills to:

(1)维持船舶保安计划中规定的条件;

(1) maintain the conditions set out in the ship security plan;

(2)提高对保安威胁和义务的认识;

(2) raise awareness of security threats and obligations;

(3)识别和评估保安威胁和风险;

(3) recognize and assess security threats and risks;

(4)使用保安设备和系统;

(4) use the security equipment and system;

(5)定期对船舶进行保安检查。

(5) undertake regular security inspections of the ship.

5.1.2 保安威胁行为
5.1.2 Security Threat Behavior

目前,对船只及船上船员构成威胁的行为不断地出现。这些行为包括恐怖主义、海盗和武装袭击、偷渡、禁运品走私和货物盗窃等。

At the moment, there are continued occurrences of threats to and actions against the ship and her crew from a variety of sources. Such acts include terrorism, piracy and armed attacks, stowaways, contraband smuggling and cargo theft.

5.1.2.1 恐怖主义
5.1.2.1 Terrorism

恐怖主义行为是指以无辜者为目标,用非正常的暴力手段或以暴力相威胁,控制其自由和伤害其生命,造成恐怖效果,以达到某种政治或社会要求的行为。

Terrorist acts refer to actions that target the innocent, use abnormal violent means or threaten violence, control their freedom and harm their lives, causing terronist effects, in order to achieve certain political or social demands.

自"9·11"恐怖袭击以来,恐怖主义已成为世界保安最重要的问题之一。近年来发生的一连串海上袭击表明,恐怖主义确实已经走向了海洋。海上恐怖主义已经成为世界上一个可怕的威胁,其目标是民用和海军舰艇。

Since the attack of "9·11", terrorism has become one of the most important problems to the security of the world. A string of maritime attacks perpetrated in recent years demonstrates that terrorism has indeed gone to sea. Maritime terrorism has emerged as a formidable threat in the world, targeting both civilian and naval vessels.

(1)恐怖主义行为的特点

(1) Characteristics of terrorism act

①恐怖主义行为通常具有政治目的。

①Terrorism act usually have political purposes.

②恐怖主义多采用非正常的暴力手段。

②Terrorism often adopts abnormal violent means.

③袭击对象以无辜者为目标。

③The target of the attack is innocent people.

④新型恐怖主义行为具有国际性、灵活机动、手段先进、高智能化、隐蔽性强及背景复杂等特点。

④New terrorism acts are characterized by international, flexible, advanced means, high in-

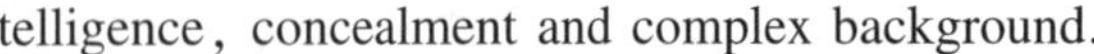

telligence, concealment and complex background.

(2)恐怖主义行为的分类

(2) Classification of terrorism act

恐怖主义行为按性质划分,主要包括政府行为的恐怖主义和非政府行为的恐怖主义。后者的表现形式更为复杂,其又包括以下几种:

According to the nature of terrorism act, mainly including governmental terrorism act and non-governmental terrorism act. The latter has more complex, including the following:

①以民族、种族、宗教为背景的恐怖主义。

①Terrorism against ethnic, racial and religious backgrounds.

②黑社会、黑手党、国际贩毒集团搞的恐怖主义。

②Terrorism by crime groups, Mafia and international drug cartels.

③邪教性质的恐怖主义。

③Cult-like terrorism.

(3)恐怖分子的识别

(3) Terrorist identification

识别恐怖分子没有一个固定而明确的方法。恐怖分子通常都故意隐藏于普通人中,因此看起来可能与普通人没什么两样。下列特点可在识别恐怖分子时作为一定参考:

There is no fixed and clear way to identify terrorists. Terrorists are often deliberately hidden among ordinary people, so they may look like ordinary people. The following characteristics can be used as reference in identifying terrorists:

①单独行动的人或一群同性别的人。

①A person acting alone or a group of persons of the same sex.

②任何时候面部表情都很平静。

②The face is calm at all times.

③激进的年轻男性(也可能有女性)。

③Aggressive young men (and possibly women).

④令人怀疑、飘忽不定的眼神。

④Suspicious, erratic in the eyes.

(4)联合国安理会的行动

(4) UN security council action

联合国安理会第1373号决议(2001)呼吁所有国家,以一切手段打击恐怖主义行为对国际和平与安全造成的威胁,找出办法加紧、加速交流行动情报,尤其是下列情报:

United Nations security council resolution 1373(2001) calls on all states to use all means to combat terrorism act as a threat to international peace and security and to find ways to intensify and accelerate the exchange of operational information, particularly on:

①恐怖主义分子或网络的行动或移动。

①The action or movement of terrorists or networks.

②伪造或变造的旅行证件。

②Forged or altered travel documents.

③贩运军火、爆炸物或敏感材料。

③Trafficking in arms, explosives or sensitive materials.

④恐怖主义集团使用通信技术。

④The use of communications technology by terrorist groups.

⑤恐怖主义集团拥有大规模杀伤性武器所造成的威胁。

⑤The threat posed by the possession of weapons of mass destruction by terrorist groups.

恐怖主义通常包括暴力或暴力威胁,极端组织企图通过恶意手段获取政治目标。恐怖组织可能希望通过使用各种类型的炸弹制造威胁或劫持一艘船来发表声明。越来越多的恐怖分子与极端的宗教教派有联系,教派洗脑政策导致了很多自杀行为以达到恐怖袭击的目的。

Terrorism usually involves violence or threats of violence, and extremist groups attempt to achieve political goals through malicious means. Terrorist groups may wish to make a statement by using various types of bombs, making threats or hijacking a ship. More and more terrorists are linked to extreme religious sects, and sectarian brainwashing has led to a number of suicide attacks.

5.1.2.2　海盗和武装袭击

5.1.2.2　Piracy and Armed Attacks

自古以来,海盗和持械抢劫船只就一直存在于世界各地。在过去的几十年里,在社会和经济问题突出、土地缺乏、海事执法和政治动荡的地区,海盗和武装袭击越来越猖獗。1982年《联合国海洋法公约》第101条,将海盗行为定义为,私人船舶或私人飞机的船员、机组成员或乘客为私人目的,对下列对象所从事的任何非法的暴力或扣留行为,或任何掠夺行为:①在公海上对另一船舶或飞机,或对另一船舶或飞机上的人或财物;②在任何国家管辖范围以外的地方对船舶、飞机、人或财物。另外,国际海事局定义了海盗和武装抢劫:一种登船或企图登船的行为,其明显意图是盗窃或其他犯罪,并明显企图或有能力在该行为的进一步发展中使用武力。

Maritime piracy and armed robbery against ships have been present around the world since ancient time. It has flourished in regions where social and economic problems, lack or weakness of land and maritime law enforcement and political turmoil occur and subsist in the past few decades. The United Nations Convention on the Law of the Sea (UNCLOS 1982), Article 101, defines piracy as any of the following acts:illegal acts of violence or detention of any depredation committed for private ends by crew or passengers of a private ship or private aircraft and directed on the high seas against another ship or aircraft or private aircraft and directed on the high seas

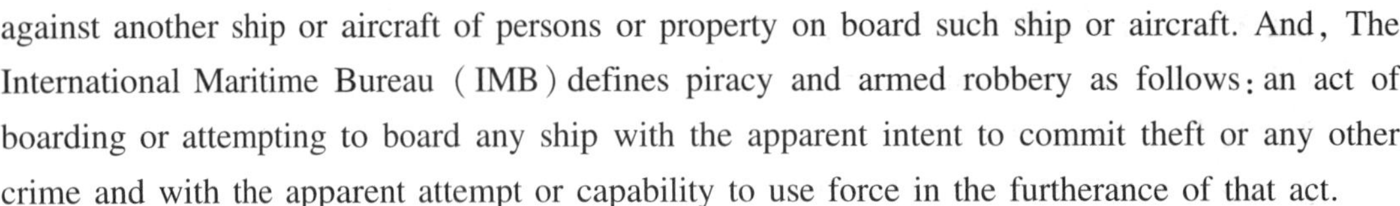

against another ship or aircraft of persons or property on board such ship or aircraft. And, The International Maritime Bureau (IMB) defines piracy and armed robbery as follows: an act of boarding or attempting to board any ship with the apparent intent to commit theft or any other crime and with the apparent attempt or capability to use force in the furtherance of that act.

现代海盗的类型及特点:

Types and characteristics of modern pirates:

海盗是未受任何国家及政府授权,擅自航行海上,以劫掠财物或对人实施暴力行为为目的的人员或组织。其类型主要包括以下三种:

Pirates are the persons or organizations that, without authorization from any state or government, sail the seas without authorization, with the purpose of looting or committing acts of violence against people. It mainly includes the following three types:

5.1.2.2.1 小股海盗

5.1.2.2.1 Small-scale Pirate

小股海盗通常由 4 到 10 人组成,其驾驶快艇对船舶实施攻击。他们惯用的手法是先用钩子钩住船只栏杆或外舷,上船后立即对船员实施抢劫并洗劫船上的货物及金钱。这种海盗是以抢劫财物为目的的,属于游击性质。他们往往先侦察船只是否有利可图且是否容易得手,一般在得手后迅速逃离现场。此类海盗攻击大都发生在内海甚至海岸线附近,并在每年全球海盗攻击案例中占据多数。

Small-scale pirates usually consist of four to ten persons who attack ships in speedboats. Their usual technique is to hook the railings outboard of a ship, and immediately rob the crew of their goods and money. This kind of pirate aims to rob the property and belongs to the guerrilla nature. They often scout out whether a ship is profitable and easy to get, and generally flee the scene quickly. Most of these pirate attacks occur in the inner sea or even near the coastline and account for the majority of global pirate attacks each year.

5.1.2.2.2 属于有组织犯罪团伙的海盗

5.1.2.2.2 A Pirate Belonging to an Organized Criminal Group

这类海盗在实施海上掠夺前通常有详细的计划,并具有牢固的基地和来自可靠渠道的情报,从而可以实施谨慎的有计划攻击。他们有大量的先进武器,并以现代化的通信方式,与世界各地的犯罪集团甚至恐怖分子联系,随时获得商业信息。

Such pirates usually carry out sea raids with detailed planning, strong bases and intelligence from reliable sources, allowing them to carry out carefully planned attacks. They have a large number of advanced weapons and modern means of communication, with criminal groups and even terrorists around the world, access to commercial information.

此类海盗会杀害船员并劫持船舶,属于比较危险的类型。他们在作案时往往会伪装成地方政府执法船只,以例行检查为名强行登船,或者驾驶快艇在货船后高速追赶。有些海盗船联合行动,看起来更像是海上舰队。除了海上远程船只,一些停泊在港口内、近岸的货船也会成为该类海盗洗劫的目标。

Such pirates, who kill crew members and hijack ships, are a more dangerous type. They often commit crimes by disguising themselves as local government law-enforcement vessels, boarding them under the guise of routine inspections, or chasing them at high speed in speed-boats. Some pirate ships operate together, looking more like sea fleets. In addition to the more distant ships at sea, the pirates also target cargo ships that are anchored in ports and close to shore.

他们通常会对所劫持的船舶进行翻新,改变烟囱标志,更改船名、船籍港,修改发动机出厂编号,然后重新配备船员,伪造船舶文件,并航行到其他港口将货物和船舶卖掉。

They often refurbish hijacked ships, changing chimney markings, changing names, port of registry, modifying engine factory numbers, then remanning them, forging ship documents and sailing to other ports to sell the cargo and ship.

5.1.2.2.3 属于分离主义者或恐怖分子的海盗

5.1.2.2.3 Pirates Belonging to Separatists or Terrorists

此类海盗属于一种混合体。他们或实为某分离主义组织与恐怖主义组织的成员,或受这些组织的操纵与控制,其目的是将劫掠的钱财用来资助恐怖行动和分离运动,或者以海盗身份从事恐怖活动。

Such pirates are a mixture. They may be members of a separatist and terrorist organization, or they may be manipulated and controlled by such organizations with the purpose of using the looted money to finance terrorist ACTS and separatist movements, or they may engage in terrorist activities as pirates.

这类海盗主要活跃在阿拉伯海域、斯里兰卡海域、印度尼西亚苏门答腊岛北方靠近亚齐附近海域及靠近南菲律宾海域。他们属于世界上最凶残的海盗,惯用的作案手法是把全体船员杀害后将船只开到隐秘地点,重新油漆,更换船名,再度注册后变成所谓的“幽灵船”,或连同货物一起卖出,或用来作为走私人口和贩卖毒品的工具。此类案例虽然在整个海盗案例中比例很小,每年只有几起左右,但其危害性最大。

The pirates are mainly active in Arabian sea, waters around Sri Lanka, waters around aceh in northern Sumatra, Indonesia, and waters around the southern Philippines. They are among the most ferocious pirates in the world, and their modus vivres are to kill the crew, take the ship to a secret location, repaint it, change its name, re-register it as a “ghost ship”, or sell it with cargo, or use it as a means to smuggle people and drugs. Although such cases make up a small proportion of piracy cases, only a few or so a year, they are the most harmful.

典型的海盗攻击:

Typical pirate attack:

(1)海盗通常使用“母船”(一般是拖网渔船),带两艘或多艘航速在 25 kn、配备机枪和火箭筒等武器的开敞小艇,对过往商船发动袭击。他们经常从船尾两舷靠近目标船,并且似乎更喜欢从左舷船尾登船。

(1) Pirates often use "mother ships" (usually trawlers), two or more open boats with speeds of up to 25 kn, armed with machine guns and rocket-propelled grenades, to attack passing merchant ships. They often approach the target ship from both sides of the stern and seem to prefer to board from the port stern.

(2)海盗"母船"用以运载人员、设备、补给和小的攻击艇,使海盗能在离岸更远的区域发动袭击。

(2) Pirate "mother ships" are used to carry people, equipment, supplies and small attack craft, allowing pirates to launch attacks farther offshore.

(3)海盗将他们的小艇紧贴受袭的船舶,以便让一名或多名武装海盗登船。海盗一般会用绑有挂钩的绳子,或使用轻便长梯从一侧爬上受袭船舶。一旦登船,海盗一般会径直冲向驾驶台,从而控制整个船舶。一旦控制了驾驶台,海盗会要求船舶减速或停船,以便让更多的海盗登船。

(3) Pirates attach their boats to the attacked ship to allow one or more armed pirates to board. Pirates usually use ropes with hooks or long portable ladders to climb up one side of the attacked ship. Once on board, pirates usually run straight to the bridge and take control of the ship. Once in control of the bridge, the pirates ask the ship to slow down or stop to allow more pirates to board.

(4)海盗袭击大部分发生在白天,然而,海盗袭击更可能发生在黎明时分。在夜晚海盗也会发动袭击,但并不常见。

(4) Pirate attacks occur most of the day, however, they are more likely to occur at dawn. Pirates also attack at night, but not often.

(5)海盗通常会使用轻型武器及火箭弹(RPG)来胁迫船长放慢船速或停船以便让更多的海盗登船。无论是在多么困难的情况下,保持船舶全速前进非常重要,或尽可能增加航速,并采用机动操车抵御海盗袭击。

(5) Pirates often use light weapons and rocket-propelled grenades (RPG) to intimidate the captain into slowing down or stopping the ship so that more pirates can board. No matter how difficult the situation is, it is very important to keep the ship at full speed, or increase the speed as much as possible, and to use various speed to resist pirate attacks.

5.1.2.3 偷渡

5.1.2.3 Stowaways

对于航运业来说,偷渡似乎是一个一直存在的问题,尤其是在西非海岸、中美洲、哥伦比亚、委内瑞拉和多米尼加共和国的贸易。除了船舶贸易模式外,这一问题也与船舶和/或货物类型,以及船员的保安培训和保安意识密切相关。2002 年,每个偷渡案件的平均成本约为 7 000 美元。到 2013 年,这一数字大幅增加,达到 2.2 万美元。这些数字不包括会员支付的可扣除的免赔额,因此实际费用要高得多。如果超过一名的偷渡人员偷渡到船上,那么费用就会上升到 10 万美元或更多,因为遣返通常只允许两名保安护送每一名偷渡人员。

Stowaways seem to be an ever-present problem for the shipping industry, in particular to those trading on the coast of West Africa, in Central America, Colombia, Venezuela and the Dominican Republic. In addition to vessels trade patterns, this problem is also closely linked to vessel and/or cargo type, as well as to the security training and awareness of the crew. In 2002, the average cost of each stowaway case was approximately $7,000. By 2013 this figure had increased significantly, to just over $22,000. These numbers do not include the applicable deductibles paid by the member and the actual costs are therefore significantly higher. If more than one stowaway gains access to the vessel, the costs have been known to escalate to $100,000 or more, simply because repatriation is usually only permitted with two security guards escorting each stowaway.

1965 年修订的《国际海上交通便利公约》(《FAL 公约》),将“偷渡”定义为:“一个人未经船东、船长或其他负责人的同意藏在船上,或者藏在船舶装载的货物中,在船舶离开港口后,在船上被发现;或者是在卸货港卸货时被发现,然后由船长将此作为偷渡向有关当局报告。”

The Convention on Facilitation of International Maritime Traffic, 1965, as amended (The FAL Convention), defines stowaway as “a person who is secreted on a ship, or in cargo which is subsequently loaded on the ship, without the consent of the shipowner or the master or any other responsible person and who is detected on board the ship after it has departed from a port, or in the cargo while unloading it in the port of arrival, and is reported as a stowaway by the master to the appropriate authorities”.

船舶上的偷渡人员的存在可能会给船舶带来严重的后果,并延伸到整个航运业。船舶可能在港口延误;将偷渡人员遣返回国可能是一个非常复杂和昂贵的程序,涉及船长、船舶所有人、港口当局和代理人;而偷渡人员的生活可能会受到威胁,因为他们可能要花好几天的时间隐藏起来,有窒息的危险,并且没有任何的水和食物。

The presence of stowaways on board may bring serious consequences for ships and, by extension, for the shipping industry as a whole. The ship could be delayed in port; the repatriation of stowaways can be a very complex and costly procedure involving masters, shipowners, port authorities and agents; and the life of stowaways could be endangered as they may spend several days hidden, with the risk of suffocation and without any water/provisions.

5.1.2.4 禁运品走私

5.1.2.4 Contraband Smuggling

禁运品走私是一种犯罪活动,可能会给船舶所有人带来巨大的经济损失,因为他们的船正被走私犯使用。通常情况下,毒品是走私的商品,它们可能会以许多创造性的方式被带到船上,比如在行李、备品中,或者在一个人的身体内,或者在电子设备上。武器也经常是走私的一个项目。

Contraband smuggling, a criminal activity, may result in large financial loss to the ship owner whose ship is being used by smugglers. Usually, drugs are the commodity being smuggled and they may be brought on board in a number of creative ways such as in luggage, stores, or on a person's body, or in electronic equipment. Weapons are also a frequent item associated with smuggling.

毒品是由世界卫生组织(世卫组织)定义的,它是"任何一种物质,当进入生物体内时,可能会改变生物体的一个或多个功能"。

A drug is defined by the World Health Organization (WHO) as "any substance that, when taken into the living organism, may modify one or more of its functions".

商船是走私和运输非法毒品的首选方式之一,货物和船上的许多空间中有许多隐蔽的机会。毒品运输的高利润吸引了主要的国际犯罪组织和恐怖组织。一些商船海员也被毒贩引诱成为这条运输链的帮凶。

Merchant ships are one of the preferred modes for the smuggling and transport of illegal narcotics, offering many concealment opportunities in the cargo and the many spaces on board. The high profit margins have attracted major international criminal organizations and terrorist groups. Some merchant mariners are also being lured by drug traffickers as accomplices in this transport chain.

某些南美国家一直是毒品生产和出口的焦点。在过去的几年里,委内瑞拉出现了许多严重的毒品案件。海事当局如果在船上发现了毒品,会使船长和船员处于严重的不利情况,他们可能在没有保释或审判、在不确定的情况下被监禁,在一些国家,毒品走私可能导致死刑。这艘船本身可能被暂留,甚至被扣押。

Certain South American countries have been and remain a focal point for production and export by sea of drugs. In the last few years, there has been a number of serious drug cases in Venezuela. The discovery of drugs on board by maritime authorities put the master and the crew in a serious situation and they can be jailed without bail or trial for an indefinite period, while in some countries, drug smuggling can result in the death penalty. The ship itself can be suspended or even detained.

众所周知,潜水员可能会在水下将容器焊接到船体上,并在船舵杆中隐藏药物。船舶周围的气泡可能是任何此类活动的迹象。

Divers are known to weld receptacles to the vessel's hull underwater and to conceal drugs in rudder trunks. Air bubbles in the water around the vessel may be an indication of any such activities.

非法药物和精神药物可以通过许多巧妙的方式走私到船上,包括:

Illicit drugs and psychotropic substances can be smuggled on board in many ingenious ways, including:

(1)在船的结构和住宿生活区;

(1) inside the vessel's structure and accommodation;

(2)在船的货舱和货物之间;

(2) inside the vessel's holds and amongst the cargo;

(3)在船体开口,如冷却水通海阀箱。

(3) inside vessel openings in the hull, such as cooling water sea chest.

5.1.2.5 货物盗窃和附带损害

5.1.2.5 Cargo Theft and Collateral Damage

货物盗窃是一个由来已久的问题,它一直困扰着海事行业,并给海事行业造成了巨额的经济损失。预防通常是应对这种安全威胁的最有效方法。虽然在大多数货物盗窃案件中可能没有涉及暴力或政治问题,但这一问题仍然在保安威胁清单上居高不下,需要在本课程中讨论其解决方案。货物盗窃只是对货物安全的各种威胁之一。

Cargo theft, an age-old problem, continues to plague the maritime industry and causes financial losses in staggering amounts. Prevention is normally the most effective method of dealing with this security threat. Although there may not be violence or political issues involved in most cargo theft cases, this matter remains high in the list of security threats. Cargo theft is only one of various threats to the security of cargo.

5.2 船上保安设备及措施

5.2 Security Equipment and Security Measures

5.2.1 船舶保安报警系统(SSAS)

5.2.1 Ship Security Alert System (SSAS)

如图5.2.1所示,船舶保安报警系统安装到船,目的是将保安警报发送到岸上,向主管当局表明该船的保安受到威胁或已被破坏。它至少包含两个激活点,这两个激活点应该在驾驶台和一个其他位置。它们应该受到保护,以免被误操作。安装该系统的目的是允许对岸上的主管当局发出警报,并不会在船上发出警报,也不会向其他船只发出警报。

As shown in Figure 5.2.1, the ship security alert system is provided to a ship for the purpose of transmitting a security alert to the shore to indicate to a competent authority that the security of the ship is under threat or has been compromised. It comprises a minimum of two activation points, which should be capable of being used on the navigation bridge and in other locations. They should be protected against inadvertent operations. These initiate the transmission of a ship security alert. The system is intended to allow a covert activation to be made which alerts the competent authority ashore and does not raise an alarm on board nor alert other ships.

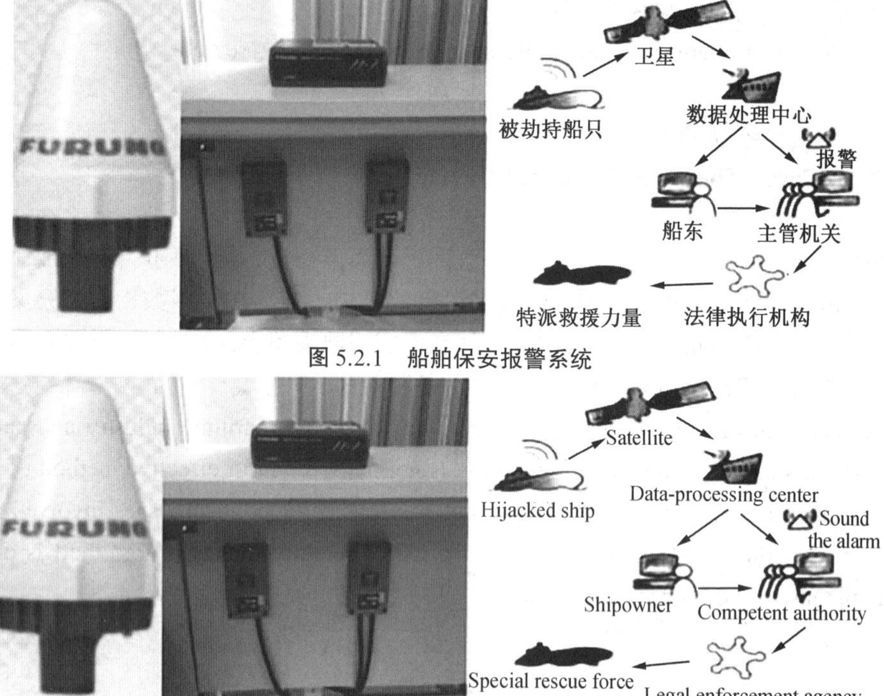

图 5.2.1 船舶保安报警系统

Figure 5.2.1 Ship Security alarm system

当被激活时,船舶保安报警系统应继续保持船舶保安警报,直到被关闭或重新设置。此外,它还应该能够进行测试。

The ship security alert system, when activated, should continue the ship security alert until deactivated and/or reset. In addition, it should be capable of being tested.

船舶保安报警系统的动力来自船舶的主要电力来源,除此之外,它还应该可以从另一个适当的电源系统中运行该系统。

Where the ship security alert system is powered from the ship's main source of electrical power, it should, in addition, be possible to operate the system from another appropriate source of power.

根据政府的要求,收到警报的主管当局通知其政府内的海洋保安主管部门,即其附近的沿海国家或其他缔约国政府。

As required by its Administration, the competent authority receiving the alert notifies the authority responsible for maritime security within its Administration, the coastal state(s) in whose vicinity the ship is presently operating, or other contracting governments.

在所有情况下,由船舶保安报警系统激活点启动的传输应该包含一个唯一的代码/标识符,表明警报没有根据 GMDSS 的遇险过程生成。该传输应包括船舶身份和当前位置。这种传输应该被传送到一个海岸站,不应该被发送到船舶站。

In all cases, transmission initiated by security alert system activation points should include a unique code/identifier indicating that the alert has not been generated in accordance with GMDSS distress procedures. The transmission should include the ship identity and current position. The transmission should be addressed to a shore station and should not be addressed to ship stations.

5.2.2 自动识别系统(AIS)
5.2.2 Automatic Information System (AIS)

如图 5.2.2 所示,自动识别系统被设计成能够自动向其他船只和海岸当局提供信息。当AIS 数据与现有的雷达系统融合时,当局能够更容易地区分船只。AIS 数据可以自动处理,即自动为单个船只创建规范化的活动模式,当被破坏时,创建一个警报,从而突出潜在的威胁,以便更有效地使用保安资产。AIS 改善了海事领域的意识,并允许加强保安和控制。

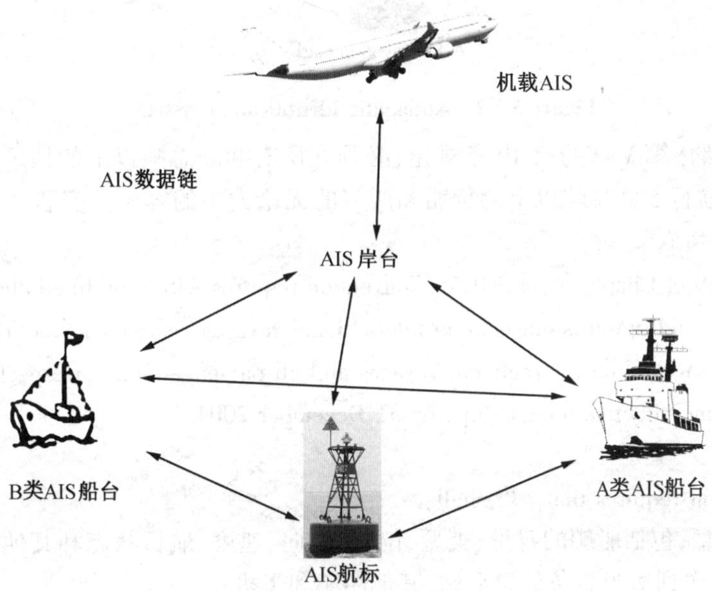

图 5.2.2 自动识别系统

As shown in Figure 5.2.2, automatic identification systems are designed to be capable of providing information about the ship to other ships and to coastal authorities automatically. When AIS data is fused with existing radar systems, authorities are able to differentiate between vessels more easily. AIS data can be automatically processed to create normalized activity patterns for individual vessels, which when breached, create an alert, thus highlighting potential threats for more efficient use of security assets. AIS improves maritime domain awareness and allows for heightened security and control.

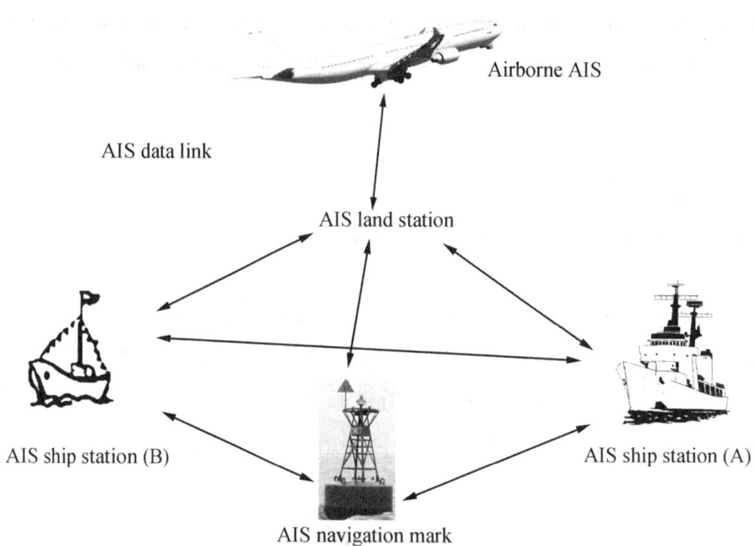

Figure 5.2.2 Automatic Identification system

《SOLAS 公约》第Ⅴ章的第 19 条规定,必须在所有 300 总吨以上的从事国际航行的船舶、不从事国际航行 500 总吨以上的货船和所有的无论大小的客船上安装。该要求于 2004 年 12 月 31 日起生效。

Regulation 19 of Chapte Ⅴ of SOLAS Convention requires AIS to be fitted aboard all ships of 300 gross tonnage and upwards engaged on international voyages, cargo ships of 500 gross tonnage and upwards not engaged on international voyages and all passenger ships irrespective of size. The requirement became effective for all ships by 31 December 2004.

规定要求:

The regulation requires that AIS shall:

(1)提供信息,包括船舶的身份、类型、位置、航向、速度、航行状态和其他与保安有关的信息——自动发送到适当装备的岸上站、其他船舶和飞机;

(1)provide information, including the ship's identity, type, position, course, speed, navigational status and other safety-related information—automatically to appropriately equipped shore stations, other ships and aircraft;

(2)安装在船舶上类似的设备会自动接收这些信息,监视和跟踪船舶;

(2) receive automatically such information from similarly fitted ships, monitor and track ships;

(3)与岸上设施交换数据。

(3)exchange data with shore-based facilities.

除国际协议、规则或标准为保护航行信息外,配备在船舶上的 AIS 任何时候都应保持正在运行中。

Ships fitted with AIS shall maintain AIS in operation at all times except where international agreements, rules or standards provide for the protection of navigational information.

如果船长认为 AIS 持续的运行可能会危及船舶的保安,或者在保安事故即将发生时,可能会关闭 AIS,船长就应该这样做:

If the master believes that continual operation of AIS might compromise the safety of the ship, or where security incidents are imminent, the AIS may be switched off. In doing so, masters should:

- 请记住,攻击者可能监视船只到岸的通信,并使用拦截的信息来选择他们的目标;
- bear in mind the possibility that attackers are monitoring ship-to-shore communications and using intercepted information to select their targets;
- 要知道,在高危地区关闭 AIS 会降低支持海军舰艇跟踪和追踪可能需要援助的船只的能力;
- be aware that switching off AIS in high-risk areas reduces the ability of the supporting naval vessels to track and trace vessels which may require assistance;
- 在发生攻击的地区,通过无线电将货物或贵重物品的信息传送到船上时,要小心谨慎;
- exercise caution when transmitting information on cargo or valuables on board by radio in areas where attacks occur;
- 使用专业判断来决定是否应该关闭 AIS 来避免受到攻击;
- use professional judgement to decide whether the AIS should be switched off to avoid being attacked;
- 能够察觉海盗活动猖獗的地区;
- detection when entering areas where piracy is an imminent threat;
- 平衡攻击的风险和维护航行安全的需要;
- balance the risk of attack against the need to maintain the safety of navigation;
- 根据国际海事组织的指导材料采取行动;
- act in accordance with IMO guidance material;
- 要知道在高危地区运营的其他船舶可能已经决定关闭他们的 AIS 系统;并且
- be aware that other ships operating in high-risk areas may have taken a decision to switch off their AIS system; and
- 在发生攻击时,确保在一定程度上能够再次打开并传送信息,以使保安部队能够定位船只。
- in the event of an attack, ensure to the extent feasible that AIS is turned on again and transmitting information to enable security forces to locate the ship.

5.2.3 远程识别和跟踪(LRIT)系统

5.2.3 Long-range Identification and Tracking (LRIT) System

如图 5.2.3 所示,远程识别和跟踪系统是在国际海事组织的领导下,作为一种加强海事保安的手段,通过提供船舶身份和当前位置信息,使缔约国政府能够评估一艘船在其海岸附近的保安风险,并在必要时做出反应。一个强有力的国际海上远程识别和跟踪系统是海上保安的重要和不可分割的组成部分。

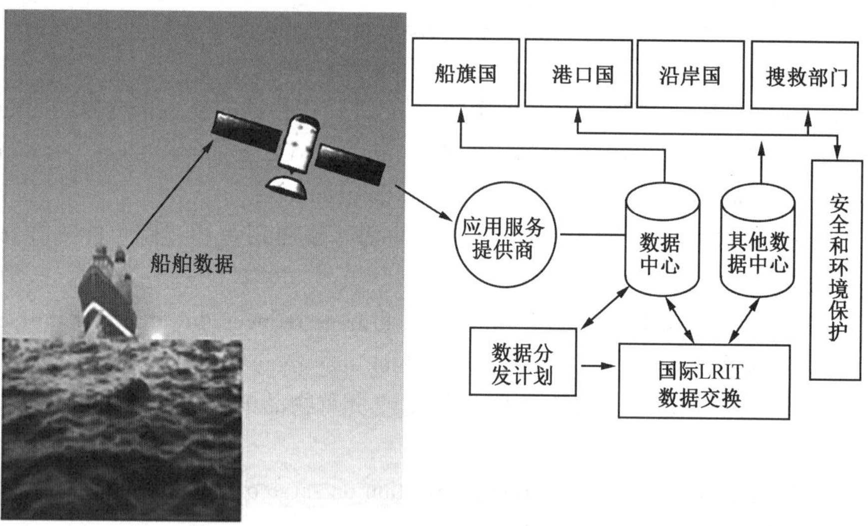

图 5.2.3　远程识别和跟踪系统轮廓图

As shown in Figure 5.2.3, Long-range Information and Tracking system was spearheaded at the IMO as a means of enhancing maritime security by providing ship identity and current location information in sufficient time for a Contracting Government to evaluate the security risk posed by a ship near its coast and to respond, if necessary. A robust international scheme for long-range identification and tracking system of ships is an important and integral element of maritime security.

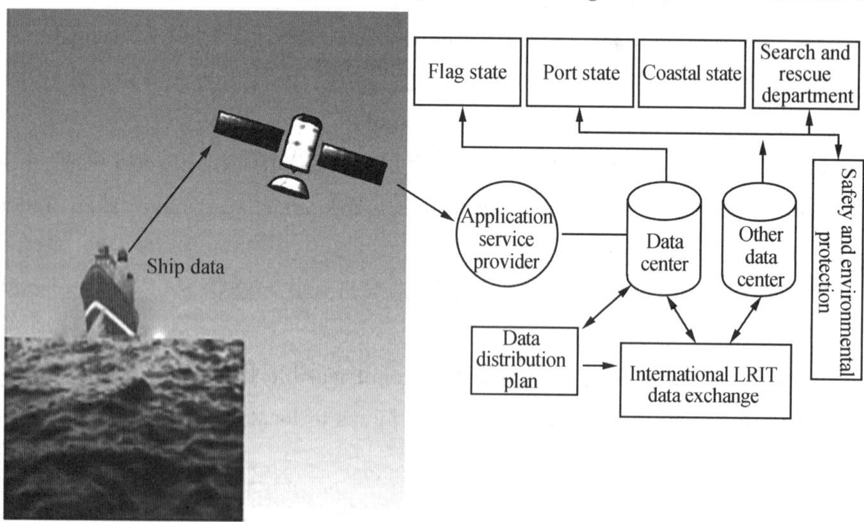

Figure 5.2.3　Outline of long-range identification and tracking system

LRIT 系统包括船载 LRIT 信息传输设备、通信服务提供商、应用服务提供商、LRIT 数据中心, 包括任何相关的船舶监控系统、LRIT 数据分发计划和国际 LRIT 数据交换。LRIT 系统的性能的某些方面是由 LRIT 的协调员代表所有的《SOLAS 公约》缔约国查看或审核。

The LRIT system consists of the shipborne LRIT information transmitting equipment, the Communication Service Provider(s), the Application Service Provider(s), the LRIT Data Center(s), including any related Vessel Monitoring System(s), the LRIT Data Distribution Plan and the International LRIT Data Exchange. Certain aspects of the performance of the LRIT system are reviewed or audited by the LRIT Coordinator acting on behalf of all SOLAS contracting governments.

与 AIS 不同,LRIT 通信是被编址的(也就是说,它是信息的安全点对点传输),而不是广播。LRIT 信息会提供给各《SOLAS 公约》缔约国政府和搜救服务中心,当提出申请时,信息将通过使用国际 LRIT 数据交换系统的国家、区域和 LRIT 数据协调中心的系统获得。为了满足安全或其他方面的需要,政府随时可能决定不向另一个缔约国政府提供船舶的 LRIT 信息。

Unlike AIS, LRIT communication is addressed (i.e. it is a secure point-to-point transmission of information) rather than a broadcast. LRIT information is provided to contracting governments to the SOLAS Convention and search and rescue services entitled to receive the information, upon request, through a system of national, regional and cooperative LRIT Data Centers using the International LRIT Data Exchange. An administration may at any time, in order to meet security or other concerns, decide not to provide LRIT information about its ships to another contracting government. Ships should only transmit the LRIT information to the LRIT Data Center selected by their administration.

每个政府都应向其所选择的 LRIT 数据中心提供一份有权悬挂其旗帜的船舶名单,以及其他重要的细节,并应在发生变化时及时更新这些名单。船舶只应将 LRIT 信息传输到其管理所选定的 LRIT 数据中心。

Each administration should provide to the LRIT Data Center which has selected a list of the ships entitled to fly its flag, which are required to transmit LRIT information, together with other salient details and should update, without undue delay, such lists as and when changes occur. Ships should only transmit the LRIT information to the selected LRIT Data Center by their Administration.

在特殊情况下,在最短的时间内,如果 LRIT 在使用时被船长认为危及船舶的安全或保安,就可以关闭 LRIT 系统。在这样的情况下,要求船长在不延误的情况下通知管理部门,并将发生的原因和关闭持续时间记录下来。

In exceptional circumstances and for the shortest duration possible, the LRIT system can be switched off if its operation is considered by the master to compromise the safety or security of the ship. In such instances, the master is required to inform the administration without undue delay and record the occurrence with the reason for the decision and duration of non-transmittal.

5.2.4 探测系统
5.2.4 Detection System

探测系统的目的是跟踪、观察和暴露在任何给定的地方可能发生的不能预想的情况。系统被划分为几个主要的组,随后将被处理。

The purpose of a detection system is to trace, observe and expose unwanted situations that can occur at any given place. The systems are subdivided into several main groups that will be treated subsequently.

5.2.4.1 照明
5.2.4.1 Lighting

在必要时进行船舶/港口接口活动,或在港口设施或锚地,船舶的甲板和通道应在数小时的黑暗和低能见度的时间内给予照明。在航行时在必要的时候,船舶应根据《国际海上避碰规则》的规定,使用不影响安全航行的最大照明。

The ship's deck and access points to the ship should be illuminated during hours of darkness and periods of low visibility while conducting ship/port interface activities or at a port facility or anchorage when necessary. While underway, when necessary, ships should use the maximum lighting available consistent with safe navigation, having regard to the provisions of the International Regulations for the Prevention of Collisions at Sea in force.

在确定适当的照明强度和位置时,应考虑以下几点:

The following should be considered when establishing the appropriate level and location of lighting:

- 船舶的人员应当能够探测到船舶以外的活动,无论是在岸上还是在水面上;
- the ship's personnel should be able to detect activities beyond the ship, on both the shore side and the waterside;
- 覆盖范围应包括船舶周围和周围的区域;
- coverage should include the area on and around the ship;
- 覆盖范围应便于在通道控制人员识别;并
- coverage should facilitate personnel identification at access points; and
- 可以通过与港口设施协调来提供相应覆盖范围的照明。
- coverage may be provided through coordination with the port facility.

5.2.4.2　X 射线扫描仪
5.2.4.2　X-ray Scanner

最常用的检查大量行李和个人物品的方法是用 X 射线扫描仪扫描。现代设备能够根据穿透的图像做出很好的判断,但是 X 射线检查在识别药物方面比物理搜索的效果差,尽管货物、包装或容器中的假隔间或空心部分可以被发现。

The most usual method of screening high volumes of baggage and personal belongings is to use X-ray scanner. Modern equipment is capable of producing images of good definition and penetration, but X-ray examination can be less effective than physical search in identifying drugs, although false compartments or hollow sections in goods, packaging or containers can be revealed.

X 射线设备提供了一种快速方便的方法,可以在不需要打开或损坏物品的情况下查看内部物品。通道尺寸多种多样,如典型的宽 600 mm、高 400 mm 通道设备,用于筛查乘客行李;通过宽 1 650 mm、高 1 500 mm 的设备用于扫描货物;专业系统具备筛查整个集装箱和车辆的能力。这种灵活性将允许大多数物品可以方便地移动到设备上并产生 X 射线图像的物体。保安检测 X 射线包裹扫描仪如图 5.2.4 所示。

X-ray equipment provides a fast and convenient way of seeing inside objects without the need to unpack or damage them. It can be bought with various tunnel sizes, such as the typical 600 mm wide and 400 mm high tunnel equipment that is used for screening passengers' bags; through the 1,650 mm wide and 1,500 mm high equipment which is used to screen cargo; to specialized systems capable of screening whole containers and vehicles. This flexibility will allow most objects that can conveniently be moved to be passed through the equipment and produce an X-ray image. Security detection X-ray package scanner is shown in Figure 5.2.4.

图 5.2.4　保安检测 X 射线包裹扫描仪

Figure 5.2.4　Security detection X-ray package scanner

5.2.4.3 金属探测器
5.2.4.3 Metal Detectors

金属探测器是一种能探测附近金属的电子仪器。金属探测器可以用来寻找隐藏在物体内部的金属夹杂物,其分为两类,包括手持金属探测器和固定金属探测器。

A metal detector is an electronic instrument which detects the presence of metal nearby. Metal detectors are useful for finding metal inclusions hidden within objects and divided into two kinds including the hand-held metal detectors and walk-through metal detectors.

手持金属探测器是一种优良的便携式保安设备,它能探测到各种金属,并探索潜在危险,帮助海员以非侵入性的方式对游客进行检查。另一种常见的类型是固定金属探测器,用于在监狱、法院和机场的接入点进行安全检查,以探测人的身上隐藏的金属武器。金属探测器在探测到金属时,将会利用声音或振动发出警报。两种金属探测器如图 5.2.5 所示。

The hand-held metal detector is an excellent portable security equipment, which can find out explore kinds of metals and explore the potential danger, helping the seafarers to inspect the visitors in non-intrusive way. Another common type are stationary walk-through metal detectors used for security screening at access points in prisons, courthouses, and airports to detect concealed metal weapons on a person's body. The metal detector will transmit an acoustic sound or a vibration if metal is detected. Two kinds of metal detector are shown in Figure 5.2.5.

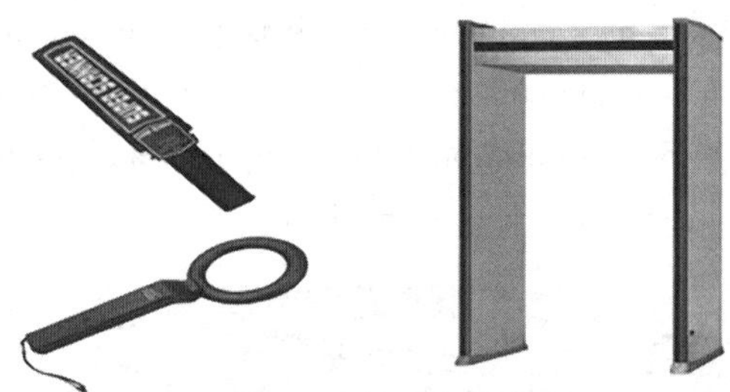

图 5.2.5 两种金属探测器

Figure 5.2.5 Two kinds of metal detector

5.2.4.4 爆炸物探测器
5.2.4.4 Explosive Detector

爆炸检测是一种非破坏性的检测过程,以确定一个容器是否含有爆炸物质。爆炸物探测器通常用于机场、港口和边境控制。手持爆炸物探测器如图 5.2.6 所示。

Explosive detection is a non-destructive inspection process to determine whether a container contains explosive material. Explosive detector is commonly used at airports, ports and for border control. Handheld explosive detector is shown in Figure 5.2.6.

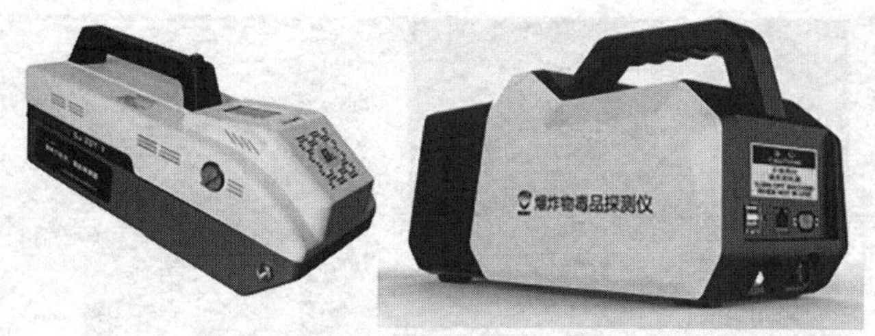

图 5.2.6 手持爆炸物探测器

Figure 5.2.6 Handheld explosive detector

用于爆炸物探测的比色测试套件是最古老、最简单、使用最广泛的探测爆炸物的方法之一。对爆炸物的比色检测包括将一种化学试剂应用到未知的材料或样品中,并观察一种颜色的反应。常见的颜色反应是已知的,如果有爆炸性的物质存在,在许多情况下会表明该物质来源于哪种类型的炸药。主要的炸药是硝基芳香炸药、硝酸酯炸药和硝胺炸药。一些类型的炸药不含硝基,其中包括无机硝基炸药、氯酸盐炸药和过氧化氢炸药。

The use of Colorimetric test kits for explosive detection is one of the oldest, simplest, and most widely used methods for the detection of explosives. Colorimetric detection of explosives involves applying a chemical reagent to an unknown material or sample and observing a color reaction. Common color reactions are known and indicate to the user if there is an explosive material present and in many cases the group of explosives from which the material is derived. The major groups of explosives are nitroaromatic explosives, nitrate ester and nitramine explosives. Improvised explosives not containing nitro groups include inorganic nitrate-based explosives, chlorate-based explosives, and hydrogen peroxide-based explosives.

5.2.4.5 闭路电视(CCTV)系统
5.2.4.5 Closed Circuit Television (CCTV) System

如图 5.2.7 所示,闭路电视系统是一个有(旋转/倾斜)摄像机和监视器的系统,它能监视一定距离内的进出的通道、房屋、栅栏、棚屋、起重机、水侧和船只。

As shown in Figure 5.2.7, CCTV is a system with (rotating /tilting) cameras and a monitor to enable a security guard to observe the access roads, the premises, the fencing, sheds, cranes, the waterside and ships from a distance.

该系统可以在机舱和其他位置安装摄像头,以方便保安监测、预防危险和保护船上人员的安全。它有以下优点:

This system onboard can facilitate safety, prevention of danger, and security of the crew with the cameras installed in the engine room and other locations. It has the following advantages:

- 通过监测指定人员或地点加强安全;
- To enhance safety via monitoring designated persons or locations;
- 在必要的时候确保保安安全;
- To ensure security for certain purposes when necessary;

图 5.2.7　闭路电视系统

Figure 5.2.7　Closed circuit television system

- 促进对人类控制范围之外的地点的安全和持续管理；
- To facilitate safe and constant management of the locations beyond the reach of human control;
- 克服了用肉眼辨别物体的局限性；
- To overcome the limitation in distinguishing objects with the naked eye;
- 用于记录存档的可视数据；
- To record visual data for archive;
- 通过减少人力来提高效率。
- To improve efficiency by reducing manpower.

数据的记录通常是由计算机执行的。此信息的备份应定期执行。

Recording of data is usually performed by a computer. A back-up of this information should be performed at regular intervals.

5.2.4.6　入侵探测系统

5.2.4.6　Intrusion Detection System

入侵检测系统是一种设备或软件应用程序，用于监视网络或系统的恶意活动或违反策略。最基本的系统由一个或多个传感器组成，用来检测入侵者，以及用警报装置来指示入侵。

An intrusion detection system is a device or software application that monitors a network or systems for malicious activity or policy violations. The most basic system consists of one or more sensors to detect intruders, and an alerting device to indicate the intrusion.

传感器可以通过各种各样的方法检测入侵者，例如监测打开的门和打开的窗户，或者通过监测未被占用的内部运动、声音、振动或其他干扰。传感器包括但不限于被动红外探测器、微波探测器、超声波探测器、运动传感器等。最常见的警报装置包括钟、警报器和/或闪烁灯，这两种功能都具有双重目的：一是警告使用者有入侵者，二是有可能吓走入侵者。

Sensors can detect intruders by a variety of methods, such as monitoring doors and windows for opening, or by monitoring unoccupied interiors for motions, sound, vibration, or other disturbances. The sensors including and are not limited to, passive infrared detectors, microwave detectors, ultrasonic detectors, motion sensors, etc. Most commonly, the alerting device includes bells, sirens, and/or flashing lights, which serves the dual purposes of warning occupants of intrusion, and potentially scaring off occupants of intrusion.

入侵检测系统还可以与闭路电视(CCTV)监视系统相结合,以自动记录入侵者的活动,并可通过电子门锁进入控制系统。

Intrusion detection systems may also be combined with closed-circuit television (CCTV) surveillance systems to automatically record the activities of intruders, and may interface to access control systems for electrically locked doors.

5.2.4.7 狗或其他动物
5.2.4.7 Dogs and Other Animals

经过特殊训练的狗或其他动物在搜索汽车、行李和货物方面非常有效。狗也可以用来在船上进行搜索,但需要熟悉海洋环境才能达到效果。

Specially trained dogs and other animals can be very effective in searching for cars, baggage and freight. Dogs can also be used for searching in ships but need to be familiar with the sea-going environment to achieve results.

5.2.5 通信手段
5.2.5 Means of Communication

5.2.5.1 全球海上遇险和安全系统
5.2.5.1 Global Maritime Distress and Safety System

全球海上遇险和安全系统,如图5.2.8所示,是一个国际公认的安全规程、设备的类型和通信协议,用于提高安全性和便于救援陷入困境的船只和飞机。

The Global Maritime Distress and Safety System, see Figure 5.2.8, is an internationally agreed-upon set of safety procedures, types of equipment, and communication protocols used to increase safety and make it easier to rescue distressed ships, boats and aircraft.

系统旨在执行以下功能:报警(包括单位遇险的定位)、搜救协调、定位(导航)、海上安全信息广播、一般通信和船间的通信。特定的广播运输需求取决于船舶的操作,而不是它的吨位。系统还提供了冗余的遇险报警和应急电源。

The system is intended to perform the following functions: alerting (including position determination of the unit in distress), search and rescue coordination, locating (navigation), maritime safety information broadcasts, general communications, and ship-to-ship communications. Specific radio carriage requirements depend upon the ship's area of operation, rather than its tonnage. The system also provides redundant means of distress alerting, and emergency sources of power.

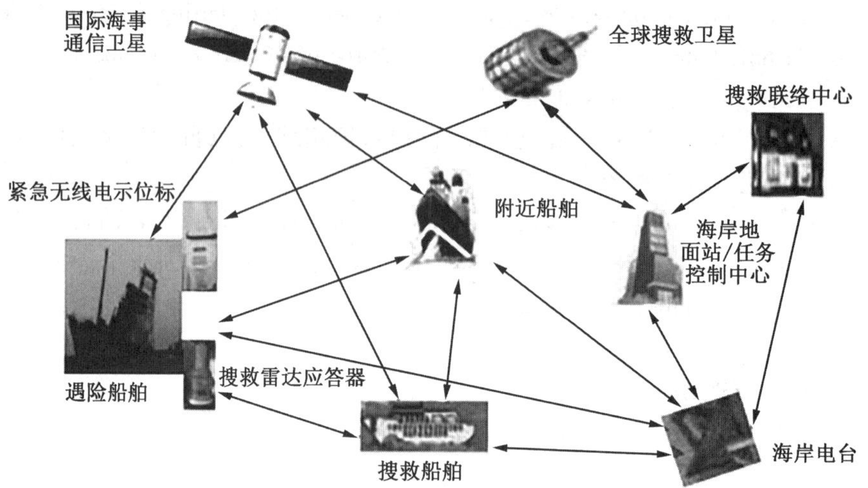

图 5.2.8 全球海上遇险和安全系统

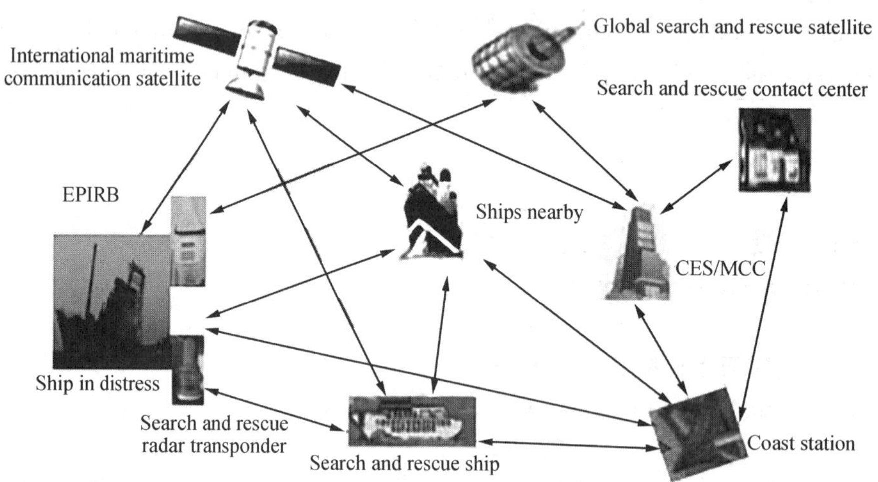

Figure 5.2.8 Global Maritime Distress and Safety System

5.2.5.2 甚高频(VHF)无线电

5.2.5.2 Very High Frequency (VHF) Radio

甚高频无线电是无线电频率介于 156.0 MHz 和 162.025 MHz 之间,具有一定的包容性。"甚高频"区间的频率非常高。它有广泛用途,包括召唤救援服务和与港口、船闸、驾驶台和码头沟通。

VHF radio refers to the radio frequency range between 156.0 and 162.025 MHz, inclusive. The "VHF" signifies the very high frequency of the range. It is used for a wide variety of purposes, including summoning rescue services and communicating with harbours, locks, bridges and terminal.

一套海洋甚高频设备包括发射机和接收机,并且仅仅在标准下操作,国际频率称为信道。信道 16(156.8 MHz)是国际电话和遇险通道。海洋甚高频大多使用“单工”传播,交流只能发生在一个方向。然而,一些信道是“双工”通信的传输通道,可以同时在两个方向交流,两端设备允许的时候为全双工,否则为半双工。

A marine VHF set is a combined transmitter and receiver and only operates on standard, international frequencies known as channels. Channel 16 (156.8 MHz) is the international calling and distress channel. Marine VHF mostly uses “simplex” transmission, where communication can only take place in one direction at a time. Some channels, however, are “duplex” transmission channels where communication can take place in both directions simultaneously when the equipment on both ends allow it (full duplex), otherwise “semi-duplex” is used.

如图 5.2.9 所示,甚高频设备可以固定或移动。固定设备通常具有更可靠的电源,更高的传输能量,具有一个更大的和更有效的天线及一个更大的显示和按钮。便携式设备(通常是防水的甚高频对讲机设计)在紧急情况下可以带到一个小艇或救生艇上,其有自己的电源,如果经 GMDSS 组织认可则需要防水。

As shown in Figure 5.2.9, VHF sets can be fixed or portable. A fixed set generally has the advantages of a more reliable power source, higher transmit power, a larger and more effective aerial and a bigger display and buttons. A portable set (often essentially a waterproof, VHF walkie-talkie in design) can be carried on a kayak, or to a lifeboat in an emergency, has its own power source and is waterproof if GMDSS organization approved.

图 5.2.9　固定和手持甚高频 VHF

Figure 5.2.9　Fixed and handheld VHF

5.2.5.3　公共广播系统

5.2.5.3　Public Address (PA) System

公共广播系统是一种带有麦克风、扩音器和扬声器的电子扩音和分发系统,用于在公开场合、机构、商业建筑等位置发布公告,如学校、体育场馆、大型客运船舶和飞机。

A public address system (PA system) is an electronic sound amplification and distribution system with a microphone, amplifier and loudspeakers, used to make announcements in public, institutional and commercial buildings and locations, such as schools, stadiums and large passenger vessels and aircraft.

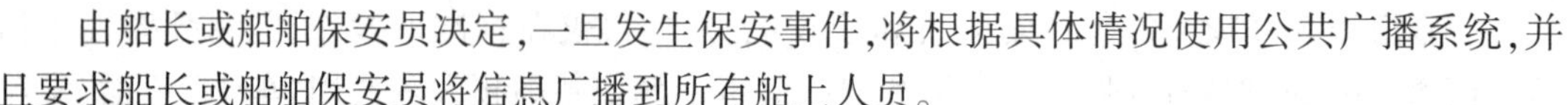

由船长或船舶保安员决定，一旦发生保安事件，将根据具体情况使用公共广播系统，并且要求船长或船舶保安员将信息广播到所有船上人员。

The master or the ship security officer decides, in case of the occurrence of the security incident and in accordance with the specific situations, the use of the public address system, and the master or the ship security officer performs the broadcasting to the whole personnel on board.

5.2.5.4 内部电话系统

5.2.5.4 Internal Telephone System

内部电话系统是设计在船上一些固定和关键位置的通信系统，如房间、驾驶台、集控室、舵机间等。内部电话系统可能包括：共电式电话系统、声力电话系统和本质安全电话系统。内部电话系统都是用于驾驶室、集控室和舵机间之间的正常状态或紧急和必要时的沟通，或需要的房间之间的通信。

Internal telephone system is a system designed to communicate at some fixed and critical locations in the vessel, such as cabins, bridge, engine control room, steering gear room and so on. The internal telephone system may include: common battery telephone system, sound-powered telephone system and intrinsically safe telephone system. All of them are used for communicating with bridge, engine control room, and steering gear room in case of normal condition or emergency and for communicating between the areas or rooms when necessary.

5.2.6 阻止和减轻海盗攻击及持械抢劫船只的设备和系统

5.2.6 Equipment and Systems of Deter and Mitigate Attacks by Pirates and Armed Robbers Against Ships

5.2.6.1 行业最佳管理实践(BMP)

5.2.6.1 Industry Best Management Practices (BMP)

在高风险地区，为了帮助船只避免、阻止或延缓海盗袭击，由石油公司国际海洋论坛(OCIMF)发布的行业最佳管理实践(BMP)，给出了很多建议性保护措施和设备。

For the purpose of assisting ships to avoid, deter or delay piracy attacks in the high risk area, the Industry Best Management Practices (BMP), which was published by Oil Companies International Marine Forum (OCIMF), gives a lot of recommended protection measures and equipment.

5.2.6.1.1 当前的海盗现状

5.2.6.1.1 Current Pirate Status

目前，海盗、恐怖分子仍以远洋船舶为主要攻击对象。根据相关国际法和港口所在地的法律，民用船只一般是不允许携带武器装备的，因此很容易受到海盗、恐怖组织或武装分子的劫持。一旦遭遇劫持,船只不但会损失大量的财物,影响船期和运输进度,船员还可能面临生命危险,这一情况在索马里海域和其他海域时常发生。

At present, pirates and terrorists are still taking ocean-going ships as the main target of attack. Civilian ships are generally not allowed to carry weapons under international law and the laws of the ports, so making them vulnerable to piracy, terrorist groups or militants. In the event of hijacking, not only can a ship lose a lot of money and belongings, affect the shipment schedule and transportation schedule, but also the crew members may be at risk of their lives, as is often the case off Somalia and elsewhere.

现在在亚丁湾的海军或其他军事力量,集中在国际推荐的航道(IRTC)附近,这大大降低了海盗袭击这个地区的概率。由于海军或其他军事力量集中在这个领域,索马里海盗活动被迫进入阿拉伯海及其他地区。然而,我们仍应高度重视,海盗活动还严重和持续威胁着亚丁湾。

The presence of naval/military forces in the Gulf of Aden, concentrated on the Internationally Recommended Transit Corridor (IRTC), has significantly reduced the incidence of piracy attack in this area. With naval/military forces concentrated in this area, Somali pirate activity has been forced out into the Arabian Sea and beyond. However, it is important to note that there remains a serious and continuing threat from piracy in the Gulf of Aden.

由于索马里海盗袭击发生在亚丁湾、阿拉伯海和印度洋北部,已严重影响该地区所有航运。最近劫持商船活动有所增加,使用渔船和帆船作为"母船"携带快艇(小艇)和武器进行攻击,使海盗活动从索马里扩展到极端的范围。

Based that Somali pirate attacks have taken place throughout the Gulf of Aden, Arabian Sea and Northern Indian Ocean, seriously affecting all shipping in the region. The recent increasing of hijacked merchant ships, using fishing vessels and dhows as "motherships" carrying attack craft (skiffs) and weapons that enable pirates to operate at extreme range from Somalia.

海盗活动:

Pirate activity:

(1)在高风险地区海盗活动频率的变化是由气候条件的改变和海军/军事力量行动决定的。

(1) The level of pirate activity varies within the high risk area due to changing weather conditions and activity by naval/military forces.

(2)受西南季风的影响,此地区海盗活动通常会减少,并在季风后增加。

(2) Pirate activity generally reduces in areas affected by the southwest monsoon, and increases in the period following the monsoon.

(3)通常东北季风比西南季风对海盗活动影响要小。

(3) The onset of the northeast monsoon generally has a lesser effect on piracy activity than the southwest monsoon.

(4)海盗活动在一个高风险区域减少,可能会在另一个区域增加(如在肯尼亚和坦桑尼亚、亚丁湾和曼德海峡海域,根据一般经验,在西南季风盛行期间海盗活动有所增加)。

(4) When piracy activity is reduced in one area of the high risk area, it is likely to increase in another area (e.g., the area off Kenya and Tanzania, the Gulf of Aden and Bab-el-Mandeb area. generally experience, an increase in pirate activity during the southwest monsoon).

高风险区域常有海盗活动和/或攻击发生。出于最佳管理实践的目的,高风险区域是从苏伊士到霍尔木兹海峡以北作为边界,南到10°S,东到78°E。[注意:英国海上贸易组织(UKMTO)自愿报告面积略大,因为它包括阿拉伯海湾。]袭击大都发生在高危区域的周边。袭击向南部延伸至莫桑比克海峡。即使在高风险地区的南部界限以南,也应保持高度戒备和警戒状态。

The high risk area defines itself by where pirate activity and/or attacks have taken place. For the purpose of BMP, the high risk area is an area bounded by Suez and the Strait of Hormuz to the north, 10°S and 78°E. (Note that the UKMTO Voluntary Reporting Area is slightly larger as it includes the Arabian Gulf). Attacks have taken place at most extremities of the high risk area. Attacks to the south have extended into the Mozambique Channel. A high state of readiness and vigilance should be maintained even to the south of the southerly limit of the high risk area.

重要的是,使用规划路线通过高风险区域应获得海盗活动最新的信息。同样重要的是,根据由航行警告和/或海军军事力量提供的信息,船舶在短时间内可以改变航向来避开海盗活动。在规划路线通过高风险区域时,天气也可以构成被海盗认可的一个障碍因素。建议从非洲之角航运中心、北约航运中心和英国海上贸易组织获取关于海盗的活动范围和位置的最新建议/更新。强烈建议在高危地区应用最佳管理实践。

It is important that the latest information on the location of where pirates are operating is used when planning routes through the high risk area. It is also important that vessels are prepared to alter course at short notice to avoid pirate activity when information is provided by NAV WARNINGS and/or naval/military forces. Weather can also constitute an obstacle to pirates and can be considered a factor when planning a route through the high risk area. It is recommended that the latest advice/updates be obtained from MSCHOA, NATO Shipping Center, and the UKMTO on the extent and latest location of pirate activity. It is strongly recommended that BMP is applied throughout the high risk area.

目前,索马里部分海域有中国等国家的海军担负护航,相对比较安全,但远洋船舶在其他大部分没有护航的海域航行时,危险依然存在。例如,在西非、几内亚湾、南菲律宾、马六甲海峡及其外锚地,海盗活动和恐怖袭击依然猖獗。面对广袤的海洋及星罗棋布的全球航线,海军护航不可能做到时间上和海域上的全覆盖。当远洋船舶航行在危险水域时,船上人员会长期处于提心吊胆、惶恐不安的状态。为避开海盗袭击,有些船舶在运输重要货物时不得不绕道航行,而绕道航行将大幅增加航行时间与营运成本。

At present, some waters near Somalia are protected by the navies of China and other countries and more scure. However, dangers still exist when ocean-going ships sail in other waters that are mostly unescorted. For example, piracy and terrorist attacks are still rampant in West Africa, the Gulf of Guinea, the Southern Philippines, the Malacca Strait and its outer anchorage. In the face of vast oceans and interconnected global shipping routes, it is impossible for naval escorts to achieve complete coverage in time and sea area. When ocean-going ships are sailing in dangerous waters, the people on board will be in a state of fear and anxiety for a long time. To avoid pirate attacks, some ships have to take detours when transporting vital cargo, which greatly increases voyage time and operating costs.

近年来,在几内亚湾海域的海盗越来越猖獗,频繁抢劫来往商船,甚至绑架船员,使该地逐渐成为海盗事故高发区。该海域位于尼日利亚、贝宁、多哥等众多较为落后国家的交界地带,每个国家的政府军事能力有限,当前并没有足够的能力彻底剿除该海域的海盗。虽然其中一些国家派出海军力量进行巡航,但还是不足以给海盗带来致命的打击。2019 年几内亚湾地区发生的 77 起海盗和海上武装抢劫事件,数量上虽然比 2018 年略有下降,但绑架案却达到了近 11 年来的最高水平。2020 年前两个月发生了 3 起船员被绑架事件和 6 起海盗成功登船事件。2020 年 11 月,西非东海岸就发生了 8 起海盗劫持事件。这足以表明几内亚湾海域在短时间内依旧会处于海盗事故高发区。

In recent years, pirates have become more and more rampant in the Gulf of Guinea, frequently robbing merchant ships and even kidnapping crew, which has gradually become a high incidence area of piracy accidents. The sea lies at the border of Nigeria, Benin, Togo and a number of other less developed countries, each of which has limited military capabilities and currently lacks the capacity to completely eradicate piracy in the area. Some of these countries have sent naval forces to patrol, but not enough to deal a fatal blow to the pirates. The 77 incidents of piracy and armed robbery at sea in the Gulf of Guinea region in 2019 were slightly lower than in 2018, but the number of kidnappings reached the highest level in nearly 11 years. In the first two months of 2020, there were three kidnappings of crew and six successful boarding by pirates. In November 2020, there were eight hijackings by pirates near the east coast of West Africa. This suggests that the Gulf of Guinea will remain a piracy hotspot for a while yet.

5.2.6.1.2 船舶保护措施
5.2.6.1.2 Ship Protection Measures

(1)加强值班

(1) Strengthen watchkeeping

进入高风险区域之前,建议按照要求做好准备,提高警惕:

Prior to entering the high risk area, it is recommended that preparations are made to support the requirement for increased vigilance by:

①每班提供额外的观察瞭望。额外的观察瞭望应充分了解险情。

①Providing additional lookouts for each watch. Additional lookouts should be fully briefed.

②为了最大化瞭望的警觉性,可考虑短的轮值周期。

②Considering a shorter rotation of the watch period in order to maximize alertness of the lookouts.

③确保增强的驾驶台团队有足够的双筒望远镜,最好是防眩光的。

③Ensuring that there are sufficient binoculars for the enhanced bridge team, preferably anti-glare.

④考虑使用夜视光学仪。

④Considering use of night vision optics.

⑤保持谨慎雷达瞭望。

⑤Maintaining a careful radar watch.

⑥逼真的假人放在船舶战略位置可以给人有很多人值班的印象。

⑥Well constructed dummies placed at strategic locations around the vessel can give an impression of greater numbers of people on watch.

(2)增强驾驶台保护

(2) Enhanced bridge protection

驾驶台通常是所有海盗攻击的焦点。在最初的部分攻击中,海盗一般用武器直接对驾驶台开火试图迫使船停下来。海盗如果能够登上船,通常想控制驾驶台。

The bridge is usually the focus for any pirate attack. In the initial part of the attack, pirates direct weapons fire at the bridge to try to coerce the ship to stop. If they are able to board the vessel, the pirates usually try to make for the bridge to enable them to take control.

下面的进一步增强保护措施可能会被考虑:

The following further protection enhancements might be considered:

①在攻击中,凯芙拉材料的防弹衣和头盔可以为驾驶台团队提供一定程度的保护。(如果可能,防弹衣和头盔应该用非军事的颜色)。

①Kevlar jackets and helmets available for the bridge team to provide a level of protection for those on the bridge during an attack. (If possible, jackets and helmets should be in a nonmilitary colour).

②虽然大多数驾驶台窗口是薄板状的,为进一步防止玻璃飞溅可以应用安全玻璃膜,通常称为防爆膜。前后驾驶台的窗口和驾驶台翼门的窗户可以使用金属板材(钢/铝),在海盗攻击时以便可以迅速获得保护。

②While most bridge windows are laminated, further protection against flying glass can be provided by the application of security glass film, often called blast resistant film. Fabricated metal (steel/aluminium), plates for the side and rear bridge windows and the bridge wing door windows, which may be rapidly secured in place in the event of an attack.

③驾驶台两翼甲板后部(常开),可以用沙袋墙保护。

③The after part of both bridge wings (open always), can be protected by a wall of sandbags.

④驾驶台的两侧和后方,以及驾驶台两翼,可以用两层带刺铁丝网围栏保护。

④The sides and rear of the bridge, and the bridge wings, may be protected with a double layer of barbed wire fence.

(3) 控制进入驾驶台、生活区和机械空间通道

(3) Control of access to bridge, accommodation and machinery spaces

为阻止或延迟海盗成功登上船舶并且试图进入生活区或机械空间,控制进入通道是非常重要的。应该认识到如果海盗顺利通过上层甲板通道,他们会很容易进入生活区,特别是很容易进入驾驶台。因此,强烈建议进入高风险区域之前要尽最大努力对上层甲板通道加以控制,以阻止海盗进入生活区和驾驶台。

It is very important to control access routes to deter or delay pirates who have managed to board a vessel and are trying to enter accommodation or machinery spaces. It is very important to recognize that if pirates do gain access to the upper deck of a vessel, they will be tenacious in their efforts to gain access to the accommodation section and in particular the bridge. It is strongly recommended that significant effort is expended prior to entry to the high risk area to deny the pirates access to the accommodation and the bridge.

这些控制措施包括但不限于:

These controls include, but are not limited to:

①所有通向驾驶台、生活区和机械空间的舱门和舱口应妥善锁闭,防止他们被海盗打开。

①All doors and hatches providing access to the bridge, accommodation and machinery spaces should be properly secured to prevent them being opened by pirates.

②为了给予船舶最大的保护,应仔细考虑舱门和舱口锁闭的手段。

②Careful consideration should be given to the means of securing doors and hatches in order to afford the ship the maximum protection possible.

③当舱门或舱口位于生活区的逃生路线上时,有必要使试图从该路线逃生的船员能够打开舱门或舱口。当舱门或舱口被锁上时,钥匙必须放在舱门或舱口附近的位置(仅供船员使用)。

③Where the door or hatch is located on an escape route from a manned compartment, it is essential that it can be opened by a seafarer trying to exit by that route. Where the door or hatch is locked, it is essential that a key is available, in a clearly visible position by the door or hatch.

④建议一旦锁闭门和舱口,指定用于常规通道的数量应该限制,通道的使用由值班驾驶员严格控制。

④It is recommended that once doors and hatches are secured, a designated and limited number are used for routine access when required, their use being strictly controlled by the officer of the watch.

⑤应该考虑对生活区外部的梯子进行阻挡或吊升,以防止其被使用,并且应限制外部通向驾驶台的通道。

⑤Consideration should be given to blocking or lifting external ladders on the accommodation block to prevent their use, and to restrict external access to the bridge.

⑥如果为了水密完整性,舱门和舱口需要关闭,确保除了锁以外所有闭门器也要完全锁

住。在可能的情况下,使用额外的锁闭加强措施,如用铁丝锁紧可增强舱口的安全。

⑥Where doors and hatches are required to be closed for watertight integrity, ensure all clips are fully dogged down in addition to any locks. Where possible, additional securing such as with wire strops may enhance hatch security.

⑦海盗知道可以通过舷窗和窗户作为通道进入船舶,在舷窗和窗户上安装钢筋将可以防止这种情况发生,即使他们会设法打破窗户。

⑦Pirates have been known to gain access through portholes and windows. The fitting of steel bars to windows will prevent this even if they manage to shatter the window.

⑧进入高风险区域之前制定并实施控制通过生活区、机械空间和存储房间通道的程序。

⑧Prior to entering the high risk area procedures for controlling access to accommodation, machinery spaces and store rooms should be set out and practiced.

(4)物理障碍(见图 5.2.10)

(4)Physical barriers (see Figure 5.2.10)

海盗通常使用长的、重量较轻的钩梯、带抓钩的绳子和长杆连钩并带爬绳的装置连接到船舶,进而攀爬到船上。应该利用物理障碍增加海盗攀登的高度和攀爬的难度,使他们的攀爬尽可能困难而无法上船。

Pirates typically use long lightweight hooked ladders, grappling hooks with rope attached and long hooked poles with a climbing rope attached to board the vessels. Physical barriers should be used to make it as difficult as possible to gain access to vessels by increasing the height and difficulty of any climb for an attacking pirate.

图 5.2.10　船上的铁丝网

Figure 5.2.10　Barbed wire on a ship

这些设备包括:

These equipment including:

①刀片刺网

①Razor Wire

刀片刺网(也称为刺带)可以创建一个有效的障碍,但只有精心部署才可以。钢丝上的倒钩设计用于产生穿刺和刮人的作用。刀片刺网的质量(钢丝规格和倒刺的频率)和类型会相差很大,应该注意选择合适的刀片刺网。质量差的刀片刺网达不到预期的防御效果。

Razor wire (also known as barbed tape) creates an effective barrier but only when carefully deployed. The barbs on the wire are designed to have a piercing and gripping action. Care should be taken when selecting appropriate razor wire as the quality (wire gauge and frequency of barbs) and type will vary considerably. Lower quality razor wire is unlikely to be effective.

通常有三种主要类型的刀片刺网可用:

Three main types of razor wire are commonly available:

- 未弯曲型(直接链);
- Unclipped (straight strand);
- 螺旋形(如电话绳);和
- Spiral (like a telephone cord); and
- 笼形(串联螺旋)。
- Concertina (linked spirals).

推荐使用笼形刀片刺网作为最有效的屏障。这样的刀片刺网要求由高强度的钢丝制成,这样难以用手工工具切断。推荐使用的刀片刺网线圈直径为 730 mm 到 980 mm。在部署刀片刺网时,需要使用个人防护设备来保护手、手臂和脸。移动铁丝网应使用钢丝钩(如挂肉钩),而不是通过戴手套的方式直接接触,这样可以降低手受伤的风险。建议提供短段的铁丝网(例如 10 m 一节),因为它使用起来明显比沉重而笨拙的大段更容易和更安全。

Concertina razor wire is recommended as the linked spirals make it the most effective barrier. Concertina razor wire should be constructed of high tensile wire, which is difficult to cut with hand tools. Concertina razor wire coil diameters of approximately 730 mm or 980 mm are recommended. When deploying razor wire personal protective equipment to protect hands, arms and faces must be used. Moving razor wire using wire hooks (like meat hooks) rather that by gloved hand reduces the risk of injury. It is recommended that razor wire is provided in shorter sections (e.g., 10-meter section) as it is significantly easier and safer to use than larger sections which can be very heavy and unwieldy.

结实的刀片刺网障碍对于防止海盗登船是特别有效的,如:

A robust razor wire barrier is particularly effective if it is:

- 构造舷外的船舶结构(即悬臂)加上刀片刺网,使海盗在登船梯/抓钩钩船的结构时更困难。
- Constructed outboard of the ship's structure (i.e. overhanging) to make it more difficult for pirates to hook on their boarding ladder/grappling hooks to the ship's structure.
- 安装双层笼形的刀片刺网,一些船只使用三层笼形的刀片刺网更加有效。
- Constructed of a double roll of concertina razor wire, some vessels use a treble roll of concertina razor wire which is even more effective.
- 妥善固定刀片刺网,防止海盗拉掉刀片刺网,例如海盗利用登船梯的钩拉掉刀片刺网。还应该考虑利用钢丝穿过铁丝网进一步固定铁丝网,防止脱落。
- Properly secured to the vessel to prevent pirates pulling off the razor wire, with for exam-

ple the hook of a boarding ladder. Consideration should also be given to further securing the razor wire with a wire strop through the razor wire to prevent it being dislodged.

也有一些船舶利用顶部有锋利尖端的固定金属架作为一个有效的屏障。

Some vessels utilize fixed metal grills topped with metal spikes as an effective barrier.

电网是不建议用于运送烃类易燃物品的船舶上,但有一个完整的风险评估后,可以适当地和有效地利用到一些其他类型的船舶上。

Electrified barriers are not recommended for hydrocarbon carrying vessels, but, following a full risk assessment, can be appropriate and effective for some other types of vessel.

使用带电栅栏或屏障时,建议在船内一侧使用英语/船员的语言进行危险警示,对船外面一侧使用英语及当地语言进行危险警示。

It is recommended that warning signs of the electrified fence or barrier are displayed inward facing in English/language of the crew, outward facing in English/language of the local.

这种向外的使用警告标语也可能被视为一种威慑,即使障碍的部分实际上是没有带电的。

The use of such outward facing warning signs might also be considered as a deterrent even if no part of the barrier is actually electrified.

②水喷淋和泡沫发生器

②Water Spray and Foam generators

用水喷雾和/或泡沫发生器可有效阻止或延迟企图登船的海盗。水的使用可以使海盗小艇很难保持与船舶贴合,使海盗更难以试图爬上船舶,如图 5.2.11 所示。

The use of water spray and/or foam generator has been found to be effective in deterring or delaying pirates attempting to board a vessel. The use of water can make it difficult for a pirate skiff to remain alongside and makes it significantly more difficult for a pirate to try to climb onboard, see Figure 5.2.11.

图 5.2.11 用喷水延迟海盗登船

Figure 5.2.11 Using water spray to delay pirate boarding

这些方法包括:

These methods include:

· 消防水龙和泡沫发生器——手工操作的消防水龙和泡沫发生器不推荐,因为这可能会把操作人员置于一个特别暴露的位置而产生危险，因此建议消防水龙和泡沫发生器应该固定在海盗可能登船的位置。

- Fire hoses and foam generator—Manual operation of fire hoses and foam generator is not recommended as this is likely to place the operator in a particularly exposed position and therefore it is recommended that fire hoses and foam generator (delivering water) should be fixed in position to cover likely pirate access routes.
- 高压水枪——这种设计旨在提供高压水垂直扫弧，从而保护更大的船体部分。
- Water cannons—These are designed to deliver water in a vertical sweeping arc thus protecting a greater part of the hull.
- 压载泵——在可能的情况下，船舶可以利用它们的压载泵供水溢流到甲板，从而在船边形成一个高效的水幕。
- Ballast pumps—Where possible to do so ships may utilize their ballast pumps to flood the deck with water, thus providing a highly effective water curtain over the ship's side.
- 蒸汽——利用热水或通过一个扩散器喷嘴产生蒸汽来阻止海盗也是非常有效的阻止海盗攻击的方法。
- Steam—Hot water, or using a diffuser nozzle to produce steam to deter pirates has also been found to be very effective in deterring attacks.
- 固定喷水管路——有些船舶安装了固定喷水管路，使用玻璃钢水管，用喷雾喷嘴产生水幕覆盖更大的保护领域。
- Water spray rails—Some ships have installed spray rails using Glass Reinforced Plastic (GRP) water main, with spray nozzles to produce a water curtain to cover larger areas.

③操船实践

③Maneuvering Practice

进入高风险区域前练习操纵船舶防止海盗登船是非常有益的，这样能确保熟悉船舶的操纵特点和如何操作，可以有效抗击海盗登船，与此同时保持最好的速度。

It is highly beneficial to practice maneuvering the ship before entering high risk areas to prevent pirates from boarding. This ensures familiarity with the ship's maneuvering characteristics and operational procedures, enabling effective resistance to pirate boarding while maintaining optimal speed.

④安全集合点/安全舱

④Safe Muster Points/Citadels

船舶在可能遭受海盗威胁的水域航行时的任何决定，都需要仔细考虑和详细规划，以确保船员和船只的安全。应该考虑建立一个安全集合点或安全舱，通常要求如下：

Any decision to navigate in waters where the vessel's security may be threatened requires careful consideration and detailed planning to ensure the safety of the crew and vessel. Consideration should be given to establishing a safe muster point or secure citadel, an explanation of each follows:

安全集合点：

Safe Muster Point:

· 安全集合点是选择一个指定区域对船员提供最大实物保护，最好是在船舶的低处。
· A safe muster point is a designated area chosen to provide maximum physical protection to the crew, preferably low down within the vessel.
· 在发生可疑的事件时，船员不需要在驾驶台或机舱控制室召集。
· In the event of a suspicious approach, members of the crew not required on the bridge or the engine control room will muster.
· 一个安全集合点是一个短期的避风港，当海盗开始小型武器或便携式火箭炮射击时将提供保护。
· A safe muster point is a short-term safe palace, which will provide ballistic protection when the pirates commence firing with small arms weaponry or RPGs.

安全舱：

Citadel：

安全舱是预先在船上指定的计划好的区域构建的一个舱室，在海盗即将登船时，所有船员将进入其中寻求保护。设计和建造安全舱可以对海盗试图进入抵制一段时间以赢得救援（关于安全舱，在非洲之角和北约航运中心网站上有详细的文档，其中包含指导和建议）。对于安全舱的使用有一点需要注意，即如果在关闭前有任何船员被留在外面，安全舱就失去意义了。

A citadel is a designated pre-planned area where is purposed built into the ship, in the event of imminent boarding by pirates, all crew will seek protection. A citadel is designed and constructed to resist a determined pirate trying to gain entry for a fixed period of time (A detailed document about citadel containing guidance and advice is included on the MSCHOA and NATO Shipping Center website). The whole concept of the citadel approach is lost if any crew member is left outside before it is secured.

安全舱的设置应满足隐秘性、安全性、一致性的原则。

The setting of citadel should meet the principles of privacy, safety and consistency.

安全舱应至少满足：

The citadel shall be fitted for at least：

· 能够便于有效防止海盗进入，能够满足船员的基本生存需求，能够保障与外界通信畅通，能够维持必要的卫生健康条件等基本功能需求。
· It can facilitate and effectively prevent the entry of pirates, meet the basic survival needs of the crew, ensure smooth communication with the outside world, and maintain necessary health conditions and other basic functional requirements.
· 安全舱的布置应综合考虑船舶结构、船员数量及安全舱的功能需求等因素，进行合理布置。应尽可能考虑方便船员对船舶关键设备进行适当控制，以避免或削弱外来人员对船舶进行控制或操纵的可能性。可以由船上的其他舱室兼作安全舱。安全舱的布置应在船舶保安计划中进行详细描述。
· The layout of the citadel shall be reasonably arranged by taking into account such factors as the structure of the ship, the number of crew and the functional requirements of the

citadel. As far as possible, consideration should be given to facilitating appropriate control of critical equipment of the ship by the crew so as to avoid or weaken the possibility of control or manipulation of the ship by other personnel. Other cabins may dual-purpose as citadel. The arrangement of the citadel shall be described in detail in the relevant documents.

- 安全舱应配备应急照明系统、个人防护设施、食品、饮用水、储存各类废弃物或排泄物的容器、必要的药品、适当的通信设备。对安全舱内的设备、设施、出入口、通风等,船员应能在安全舱内对其进行有效控制。
- The citadel shall be equipped with emergency lighting system, personal protective facilities, food, drinking water, containers for storing all kinds of waste or excreta, necessary medicines, and appropriate communication equipment. The crew shall effectively control the equipment, facilities, exit and ventilation in the citadel.
- 对船舶操纵设备、主推进装置或发电机等关键设备,船员应能在安全舱内对其进行适当监控、控制或能削弱、延缓外部的控制。
- The crew shall be able to properly monitor, control or weaken or delay external control of key equipment such as ship control equipment, main propulsion equipment or generator in the citadel.

安全舱配备的设备、设施、食品、药品等应保持适当的维护保养,以保证其维持必要的功能。船员进入安全舱后,食品及饮用水应由专人负责管理,分配时应考虑个人需求及在安全舱内可能停留的时间。船舶应制定安全舱撤离程序,并进行适当的演练。

The equipment, facilities, food, medicines, etc. provided in the citadel shall be maintained properly to ensure the maintenance of necessary functions. After the crew enters the citadel, the food and drinking water shall be managed by a special person, and the personal needs and the possible stay time in the citadel shall be taken into account in the distribution. The ship shall formulate procedures for citadel evacuation and conduct appropriate drills.

⑤海上私人武装保安组织

⑤Armed Private Maritime Security Contactors

船舶操作者根据自己的船舶航行风险评估来决定使用或不使用海上私人武装保安组织,如果使用,则需要得到船旗国的批准。

The use, or not, of armed private maritime security contractors onboard merchant vessels is a matter for individual ship operators to decide following their own voyage risk assessment and approval of respective flag States.

根据风险分析,船舶操作者在考虑使用海上私人武装保安组织时,应慎重规划以保护容易被海盗袭击的船舶。海上私人武装保安组织应作为比较实用的额外的保护,而不是代替最佳管理实践中要求的保护措施。

According to the risk analysis, when considering the use of private armed security contactors at sea, ship operators should carefully plan to protect ships that are vulnerable to piracy. Private armed security contactors at sea should serve as a more practical additional protection, not as a

substitute for protection measures required by best management practices.

国际海事组织利用国际海事组织通告的形式指导船舶运营商、船长和船旗国在高风险地区使用海上私人武装保安组织。

IMO uses the form of IMO circulars to guide ship operators, captains and flag States on the use of private armed maritime security contactors in high-risk areas.

5.2.6.2 海军护航

5.2.6.2 Naval Escort

军事方面对海盗袭击的反应,让一些国家罕见地展现了团结。曾经有3个国际海军特遣部队在索马里海域执行任务,护送众多国家的船只进入和离开该地区,并且参与打击海盗行动的时间长短不一。它们分别是联合特遣部队150(其使命是持久自由行动)、联合特遣部队151(成立于2009年,专门打击海盗)和欧盟海军亚特兰大特遣部队。

The military response to the pirate attacks has produced a rare show of unity among some countries. There were three international naval task forces in the region, with numerous national vessels and task forces entering and leaving the region, engaging in anti-piracy operations for various lengths of time. The three international task forces which compose the bulk of anti-piracy operations are Combined Task Force 150 (whose overarching mission is operation enduring freedom), Combined Task Force 151 (which was set up in 2009 specifically to run anti-piracy operations) and the EU Naval Task Force operating under Operation Atalanta.

所有反海盗行动都通过名为"共享意识和消除冲突"的每月会议进行协调。最初只有北约、欧盟和驻巴林的多国海军部队(CMF)参与,后来吸引来自20多个国家的武装力量参与。

All anti-piracy operations are coordinated through a monthly planning conference called Shared Awareness and Deconfliction (SHADE). Originally having representatives only from NATO, the EU, and the Combined Maritime Forces (CMF) HQ in Bahrain, it now regularly attracts representatives from over 20 countries.

这些武装力量包括:

These forces include:

(1)多国海军部队

(1) Combined Maritime Forces (CMF)

多国海军部队由25个国家联盟致力于确保相关地区安全。多国海军部队行动符合相关国际法并得到联合国安理会支持,通常执行3个不同的任务。联合特遣部队150在红海、亚丁湾、印度洋、阿拉伯海和阿曼湾进行海上保安相关操作;联合特遣部队151在亚丁湾、索马里海盆和印度洋进行威慑、打击和抑制海盗行为,保护海上任何国籍的船只安全通过;联合特遣部队152在阿拉伯海湾开展海上保安行动,作为海湾合作委员会的合作伙伴来防止一些海上的破坏活动。

Combined Maritime Forces is a 25 nations coalition committed to ensuring regional security.

CMF operates in accordance with international law and relevant United Nations Security Council Resolutions and is supported by three distinct missions. Combined Task Force (CTF) 150 operates in the Red Sea, Gulf of Aden, Indian Ocean, Arabian Sea and the Gulf of Oman conducting. Maritime Security Operations. CTF 151 operates in the Gulf of Aden and Somali Basin and the Indian Ocean to deter, disrupt and suppress piracy, protecting the safe passage of maritime vessels of any nationality. CTF 152 operates in the Arabian Gulf conducting maritime security operations in conjunction with Gulf Cooperation Council (GCC) partners in order to prevent destabilizing activities.

(2)欧盟海军部队(EU NAVFOR)

(2) The European Union Naval Force

欧盟海军部队作为国际海军力量的一部分,在打击非洲之角的海盗中扮演着重要的角色。在公共保安与防务政策下的欧盟推出欧盟索马里海军——亚特兰大特遣部队。这个特遣部队致力于保护人道主义援助、减少运输路线的中断和保护该地区海洋环境不受破坏。

The European Union Naval Force, as part of the international effort, EU NAVFOR plays a significant role in combating piracy off the coast of the Horn of Africa. The European Union under the Common Security and Defence Policy (CSDP) launched EU NAVFOR Somalia—Operation Atalanta. This operation is working to protect humanitarian aid and reduce the disruption to the shipping routes and the de-stabilising of the maritime environment in the region.

到目前为止,有26个国家参与了特遣部队。亚特兰大特遣部队的部署随季风季节波动而变化,因为季风决定了海盗出没的频率。该部队通常由5~10艘水面舰艇、1~2艘辅助船和2~4架海上巡逻和侦察飞机组成;包括地面人员,亚特兰大特遣部队共有约2 000名军事人员。欧盟海军部队保护区域包括红海南部、亚丁湾和印度洋的西部,涵盖塞舌尔,面积达2 000 000平方海里。

To date, 26 countries have brought some kind of contribution to the operation. At any one time, the European force size fluctuates according to the monsoon seasons, which determine the level of piracy. It typically consists of 5 to 10 surface combatants (naval ships), 1 to 2 auxiliary ships and 2 to 4 maritime patrol and reconnaissance aircraft. Including land-based personnel, Operation Atalanta consists of a total of around 2,000 military personnel. EU NAVFOR operates in a zone comprising the south of the Red Sea, the Gulf of Aden and the western part of the Indian Ocean including the Seychelles, which represents an area of 2,000,000 square nautical miles.

(3)海洋盾特遣行动

(3) Operation Ocean Shield

海洋盾特遣行动是北约对国际社会打击非洲之角海盗行动的贡献。海洋盾特遣行动具有独特的北约的特色,集中力量采取更全面的方法打击海盗。北约专注于在海上打击海盗行动,支持海运组织采取行动来减少海盗袭击的发生率,以及区域国家的反海盗能力建设。海洋盾特遣行动的目的是补充该地区现有的国际组织和增强部队反海盗行动的能力。

Operation Ocean Shield is NATO's contribution to international efforts to combat piracy off

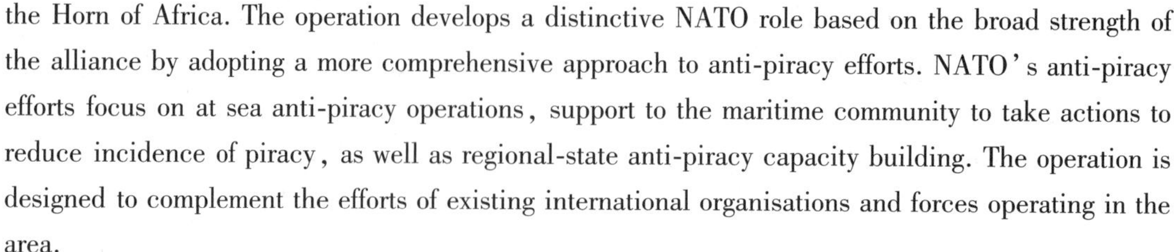

the Horn of Africa. The operation develops a distinctive NATO role based on the broad strength of the alliance by adopting a more comprehensive approach to anti-piracy efforts. NATO's anti-piracy efforts focus on at sea anti-piracy operations, support to the maritime community to take actions to reduce incidence of piracy, as well as regional-state anti-piracy capacity building. The operation is designed to complement the efforts of existing international organisations and forces operating in the area.

(4) 中国海军编队

(4) Chinese Naval Convoy Forces

2008 年 12 月 26 日,中国派遣 2 艘驱逐舰“海口号(171)”、“武汉号(169)”和 1 艘补给舰到亚丁湾地区,同时配备了海军陆战队武装,包括一组 16 名中国特种部队成员与武装直升机。根据最初的部署,中国由指定的三舰编队(包括 2 艘驱逐舰和 1 艘补给舰)在亚丁湾地区开始护航任务。

On 26 December 2008, China dispatched two destroyers, Haikou (171), Wuhan (169) and the supply ship, to the Gulf of Aden. It is also armed with marines, including a group of 16 Chinese special forces members and helicopter gunships. According to the initial deployment, China began the escort mission in the Gulf of Aden area with a designated three-ship formation, including two destroyers and a supply ship.

此外,其他非北约和欧盟国家也会采取一些行动打击海盗行动。中国、澳大利亚、巴基斯坦、伊朗、日本、韩国、马来西亚、俄罗斯、泰国和沙特阿拉伯都派出了军舰、侦察机和武装人员到相关区域,有时加入现有的特遣队,有时独立操作。

Additionally, other non-NATO and non-EU countries have, at one time or another, contributed to counter-piracy operations. China, Australia, Pakistan, Iran, Japan, Republic of Korea, Malaysia, Pakistan, Russia, Thailand, and Saudi Arabia have all sent ships, surveillance aircraft or personnel to the region, sometimes joining with the existing CTFs, sometimes operating independently.

如图 5.2.12 所示,2016 年 4 月 7 日,第 23 批护航编队由导弹护卫舰“湘潭号(531)”、“舟山号(529)”以及综合补给舰“巢湖号(890)”组成,携带舰载直升机 2 架、特战队员数十名,共 700 余名官兵。

As shown in Figure 5.2.12, on April 7, 2016, the 23rd Naval Convoy Forces consisted of the guided missile frigate Xiangtan (531), Zhoushan (529), and the comprehensive supply ship Chaohu (890), carried 2 shipboard helicopters and dozens of special operations personnel, totaling 700 other officers and soldiers.

图 5.2.12　第 23 批护航编队

Figure 5.2.12　The 23rd Naval Convoy Forces

2008 年 12 月 31 日以来，中国船东协会正式接受了亚丁湾和索马里海域护送船只过境申请，西行报告线在 057°E 和东行报告线在 15°N（红海附近）。船只悬挂中华人民共和国国旗的及悬挂方便旗但属于中国船东和运营商可以申请护航。悬挂中国香港特别行政区旗帜的船只护航应该通过我国香港相关海事部门申请。中国台湾地区旗帜的船只应在中国船东协会申请护航。

Since December 31st, 2008, China Shipowners' Association formally accepted the escort application for ships transiting the Gulf of Aden and waters off Somalia, with westbound reporting line at 057°E and eastbound reporting line at 15°N (off the Red Sea). Ships flying the flag of People's Republic of China. Chinese shipowners and operators flying the flag of convenience may apply for the escort. Ships flying the flag of Hong Kong Special Administrative Region of China should apply for the escort in Hong Kong Maritime Department. Ships flying the flag of Taiwan of China should apply for the escort in China Shipowners' Association.

申请程序：

Procedures for application:

（1）申请护航的人税务应该注册在中国船东协会秘书处，包括名字、电话号码、税号码、联系人的电子邮件和地址。子公司应通过其总部注册公司。中国船东协会只接受已经通过注册的公司的护航申请。

(1) Those who apply for the escort should be registered in the secretariat of China Shipowners' Association by tax in which name, telephone number, tax number, e-mail and address of contact person should be entered. Subsidiary companies should be registered through its headquarter company. China Shipowners' Association only accepted the escort application filed by those companies which have gone through registry.

（2）请登录 http://www.csoa.cn 下载报告列表船舶申请护航服务电子格式（访问格式）。

(2) Please log in http://www.csoa.cn to download the reporting list for Ships Applying for Escort Service in electronic format (in access format).

（3）参照指导在船舶申请护航服务名单上填好信息。申请在船只抵达报告线七/五/三/一天前请发送电子邮件到 escort@ csoa.cn。

(3) Fill in the blanks on the List for Ships Applying for Escort Service, with reference to the instruction. Please send an e-mail to escort@ csoa. cn for the application, seven/five/three/one day before ships arriving at the reporting line.

(4)所有的申请文件都应该于每天上午10点之前发送,中国船东协会将向交通运输部(MOT)递交收集到的申请文件。

(4) All the application documents should be due before 10 am every day and China Shipowners' Association will report to the Ministry of Transport (MOT) with the collected documents.

(5)通过交通运输部批准,中国船东协会将及时联系申请人。

(5) With the approval by MOT, China Shipowners' Association will promptly contact the applicant.

(6)申请人应及时选择供选择的护航编队并报告中国船东协会秘书处。接受护航服务后,所有人包括船长应该服从海军的命令,并保持所有可用的联系。

(6) Applicants should in time choose the escorting alternative and report to the secretariat of China Shipowners' Association. Those who are in the escort service, including the masters on board, should obey the navy orders, and keep all means available to be contacted.

(7)中国船东协会的联系信息:

(7) Contact information of China Shipowners' Association:

电话:+86-10-85110162,85110160。

Telephone: +86-10-85110162, 85110160.

传真:+86-10-65122718。

Fax: +86-10-65122718.

第6章 工作用语

Chapter 6 | Working Expressions

6.1 值班用语

6.1 Watch-keeping Expressions

6.1.1 课前准备

6.1.1 Warming Up

海上事故的发生多由沟通不畅造成,主要的问题是:来自不同国家的船员第一语言并不是英语。国际海事组织致力于敦促航运公司遵守标准海事通信用语的规定,并就认证船舶人员的不同方式提供建议。国际海事组织强调雇用没有持国际海事组织标准海事通信用语培训证书的值班驾驶员是非法的,因为他们在船工作期间由于语言沟通不畅,容易造成误解和过失。

Many of the accidents at sea occur due to poor communication, identifying a major problem: seamen on board, coming from many different nationalities, do not use English as first language. IMO urges shipping companies to comply with the SMCP (Standard Marine Communication Phrases) law and advises on the different ways to certify ship's personnel. IMO highlights that it is illegal to use watch officers who are not certified in the IMO SMCP, as they are prone to misunderstandings and mistakes during operations on board.

6.1.1.1 港内值班

6.1.1.1 Watch-keeping at Port

船舶在港货物作业和值班程序包括很多复杂的方面,尤其是货物装卸的各方面要予以

充分考虑。值班驾驶员和值班水手要遵循下列程序要求：

Ships cargo handling at port and watch-keeping procedures involve many complexities and careful consideration will need to be made for all aspects of loading and unloading. The duty deck officer (OOW) and the crew of the watch shall carry out their duties in compliance with the below procedures:

(1)时刻遵守所有相关规则、规定和法律。

(1) All relevant rules, regulations and laws must be observed at all times.

(2)值班驾驶员要观测天气，当天气发生剧烈变化时向船长或副报告。

(2) The OOW shall observe the weather and report any drastic changes to the master or the Chief Officer.

(3)根据船舶保安计划进行梯口值班和巡逻。所有限制区域保持关闭或派人值守。

(3) Gangway watch and patrols shall be carried out in accordance with the vessels Ship Security Plan. All restricted areas must remain secured or manned.

(4)值班驾驶员和值班水手要定期查看船舶周围水域以防止污染，尤其是在排压载水和油类转运期间。

(4) The OOW and the crew of the watch shall periodically monitor the water surrounding the vessel, for marine pollution, especially during de-ballasting and oil transfer operations.

(5)在系岸期间，值班驾驶员要定期检查照管好舷梯和系泊缆绳，充分考虑当地潮汐及天气变化以及由货物作业、压载水和燃油调整造成的船舶吃水变化，采取必要措施以确保船舶系泊安全。

(5) While moored at a shore facility, the OOW shall periodically check and tend the gangway and moorings, and take any action necessary to ensure the safe mooring of the vessel, considering local changes in weather and tide, as well as changes in draft due to cargo transfer operations, ballast operations or bunker fuel transfer operations.

(6)靠泊期间确保防鼠挡安放就位。

(6) Rat guards are to be always in place on mooring ropes while at berth.

(7)甲板排水口除下雨排水期间可暂时开启，其余时间要保持封堵状态。

(7) Deck scuppers are to remain plugged at all times except briefly opened to drain rain water.

(8)不得排放污水。

(8) Bilges are not to be pumped out.

(9)值班驾驶员要按照《国际海上避碰规则》正确显示号灯、号型和旗帜，鸣放声响信号（锚泊时、雾中）。

(9) The OOW shall ensure that all lights, shapes and flags are displayed and sound signals (at anchor, in fog) used in accordance with the International Regulations for Preventing Collisions at Sea (COLREGs).

(10)值班驾驶员要根据在港值班检查表定期开展检查。

(10) The OOW shall make a periodical inspection according to the Check List for Watch in Port.

6.1.1.2 锚泊值班

6.1.1.2 Anchor Watch

为了确保船舶安全,锚泊期间值班驾驶员及值班人员要根据船长命令保持锚泊值班。充分理解船长常规命令中关于锚泊值班的要求。值班驾驶员要理解夜航命令,有任何疑问须向船长确认。船长随时可以提供帮助。

For the safety of ship, anchor watches shall be maintained by the OOW and the crew of the watch in accordance with master's orders. The master's standing orders must be fully understood regarding anchor watches. OOW must be sure that he understands the night orders, if in any doubt ask the master to clarify. The master is always available to help.

锚泊值班期间,值班驾驶员要考虑下列基本检查项目:

Following are the basic check items that should be taken into account by deck officer while performing anchor watch:

(1)尽快确定船位,并将其标记在合适的海图上。

(1) Determine and plot the ship's position on the appropriate chart as soon as practicable.

(2)若当时环境允许,值班驾驶员需通过测固定助航标志或可用显著陆标的方位来定期核对船舶是否保持稳定锚泊状态。

(2) When circumstances permit, check at sufficiently frequent intervals whether the ship is remaining securely at anchor by taking bearings of fixed navigation marks or readily identifiable shore objects.

(3)保持正规瞭望。

(3) Ensure that a proper lookout is maintained.

(4)确保定期进行绕船巡逻检查。

(4) Ensure that inspection rounds of the ship are made periodically.

(5)观察气象和潮汐状况及海况。

(5) Observe meteorological and tidal conditions and the state of the sea.

(6)船舶一旦走锚,通知船长并采取必要措施。

(6) Notify the master and undertake all necessary measures if the ship drags anchor.

(7)确保主机和其他机械按照船长指令处于随时可用的状态。

(7) Ensure that the state of readiness of the main engines and other machinery is in accordance with the master's instructions.

(8)若能见度变差,通知船长。

(8) If visibility deteriorates, notify the master.

(9)确保船舶根据相关规则显示相应的号灯、号型,鸣放相应声响信号。

(9) Ensure that the ship exhibits the appropriate lights and shapes and that appropriate sound signals are made in accordance with all applicable regulations.

(10)遵守防污染规则,采取措施防止船舶造成环境污染。

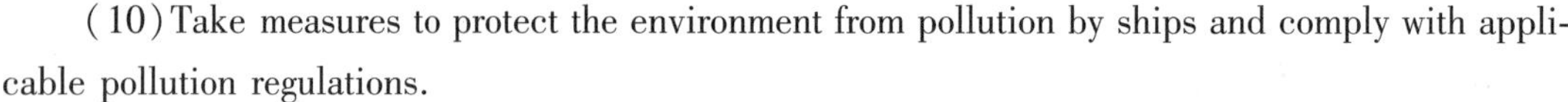

(10)Take measures to protect the environment from pollution by ships and comply with applicable pollution regulations.

6.1.2 对话练习
6.1.2 Dialogue Practice

对话 1

Dialogue 1

A:早上好,大副。我来自国家商检局,被委任前来进行货舱检验。

A:Good morning, Mr. Chief. I'm from State Commodity Inspection Bureau and appointed for your ship's cargo hold survey.

B:欢迎您,检验员先生。我船已经按照租船人指示准备好了。我们希望您会对我船的状况感到满意。

B:Welcome, Mr. Surveyor. Our ship has already been prepared according to the Charterer's instructions. We hope you will be satisfied with her condition.

A:希望如此。首先,请给我一份你船的船舶参数和暂定计划。

A:I hope so. Firstly, please give me one copy of your ship's particulars and of the tentative plan.

B:给您。

B:Here you are.

A:谢谢。你船上最后拉载过的三种货物是什么?

A:Thank you. What are the kinds of the last three cargoes carried on board?

B:煤炭、玉米和铁矿石。

B:Coal, corn, and iron ore.

A:好的。我们去看一看货舱吧。

A:Well. Let's go for a glimpse of cargo hold.

B:好的,这边请。

B:OK, this way please.

A:现在我们在 1 号货舱。

A:Now we are at No.1 cargo hold.

B:我来看看。橡胶垫圈状态良好,排水管道系统运转正常。我认为货舱的水密性也不错。

B:Let me have a look. The rubber gaskets are good and draining canals work well. I think the cargo hold's watertightness is also in good condition.

A:我完全同意您的看法。

A:I totally agree with you.

B:大副,舱口梁上有些松散的钢铁氧化皮和一些成片剥落的漆。

B:Mr. Chief, there are some loose scales and flaking paint in the hatch beam.

A:哦,抱歉。我会让人马上进行清理的。

A:Oh, sorry. I will ask my hand to clean them right away.

B:好的。检查结束了。一切都满足《国际散装谷物安全运输规则》的要求,将为你船颁发允许运输散装谷物的证书。

B:That's fine. The inspection is over. And everything satisfies the requirements of the International Code for the Safe Carriage of Grain in Bulk. The Document of Authorization for the Carriage of Grain will be issued to you.

对话 2

Dialogue 2

A:大副,我是您的理货员。

A:Chief, I'm your tally man.

B:欢迎您,先生。

B:Welcome, sir.

A:您有单证给我吗?

A:Do you have some papers for me?

B:给您,一份积载图和一份货物清单。

B:Here you are, one copy of stowage plan and one copy of cargo list.

A:谢谢。让我看看。

A:Thank you. Let me have a look.

B:我们将在贵港卸载 120 个集装箱,同时装载 150 个集装箱。

B:We will discharge 120 containers in your port and load 150 containers at the same time.

A:好的。顺便说一下,有一些特种集装箱。

A:Fine. By the way, there are some special containers.

B:是的。它们是 5 个冷藏集装箱和 10 个危险品集装箱。请格外关注它们。

B:Right. They are 5 reefer containers and 10 dangerous containers. Please pay extra attention.

A:我会的。

A:I will.

B:您知道我船开始作业时间及开航时间吗?

B:Do you have any idea about what time will start working and our sailing time?

A:是的,装卸工人上午 9 点开始工作,6 小时后,你船可以开航。

A:Yes, the stevedores will start working at 9 o'clock in the morning, and 6 hours later, your vessel will be sailing.

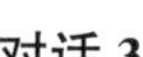

对话 3

Dialogue 3

A:船长,我们打算进入货舱检查货物。您能发一张工作许可证吗?

A:Captain, we plan to enter the hold for cargo inspection. Would you please issue a permit-to-work?

B:好的。您认为进行货物检查要花多长时间?

B:All right. How long do you think it will take for the job?

A:有很多机械货物要再次检查绑扎情况。也许要整个上午。

A:There are a lot of machinery cargoes to be double checked for the lashing. Maybe it will take all the morning.

B:您做了哪些准备?

B:What preparations have you made?

A:我打开了通风口,启动了风扇。

A:I have opened ventilators and started fans.

B:哦,您进行环境测试了吗?

B:Oh, have you carried out atmospheric testing?

A:还没有。我们将在进入货舱前进行测试。

A:Not yet. This will be conducted before we enter the hold.

B:我恐怕货舱会缺氧,特别是装有谷物的货舱。

B:I' m afraid there exists oxygen deficiency, especially in the hold for corn.

A:这也正是我所担心的。

A:That' s also my concern.

B:还有其他的问题吗?

B:Anything else?

A:我会在货舱内安装一些货舱灯。每个下到货舱的船员会随身带一个手电筒。

A:We will fix some cargo lights inside. Each crew down to the hold will bring a torch with himself.

B:嗯。

B:Hmm.

A:每个船员应该配备安全装备。

A:Every crew should wear safety equipment.

B:您安排与驾驶台沟通的人员了吗?

B:Have you arranged some guy to communicate with bridge?

A:是的,他还负责救助任务。

A:Yes, he is also responsible for rescue task.

B:最好在附近准备一些急救设备。

B:Better get some first-aid equipment nearby.

A:没问题。我会在工作开始前做一个简要说明,并指定水手长负责操作过程。

A:No problem. And I will give a briefing before the job and appoint Bosun to be in charge of the operation in progress.

B:很好！这是工作许可证。按您刚才说的去做,要格外小心。

B:Good! Here is permit-to-work. Just do as what you have said and keep extra caution.

6.1.3 句型操练
6.1.3 Sentence Pattern Drills

6.1.3.1 舷梯值班
6.1.3.1 Gangway Watch

(1)对不起,先生,有什么可以帮助您的吗?

(1)Excuse me, sir. What can I do for you?

(2)我能看看您的身份证吗?

(2)Could I have your ID, please?

(3)我们船长正在办公室等您。

(3)Our captain is expecting you in the office.

(4)船上的所有空间应当保持关闭。

(4)Every space on board the ship should be kept locked.

(5)对不起,您不能在船舶周围徘徊。

(5)Sorry, you are not allowed to wander around the ship.

(6)您能填写访客记录并在这个位置签字吗?

(6)Could you fill out the visitor's log and sign here, please?

(7)在您登船前我需要看看您的身份证。

(7)I need to see your ID before your boarding.

(8)多谢配合。

(8)Thanks for your cooperation.

6.1.3.2 接班
6.1.3.2 Taking over Watch

(1)救生艇里的饮用水上次更换是哪一天?

(1)When was the drinking water of the lifeboat last changed?

(2)救生筏释放指南已按要求张贴。

(2)Life raft launching instructions are exhibited as prescribed.

(3)消防设备上次检查是什么时候?

(3)When the fire-fighting appliances were last checked?

(4)二氧化碳灭火器上次称重是什么时候?

(4)When the CO_2 fire extinguishers were last weighed?

(5)你能给我演示一下舱盖作业程序及注意事项吗?

(5)Could you show me the hatch cover operation procedures and cautions?

(6)驾驶台上的航行设备都是可用的。

(6)The navigational equipment on the bridge are all operational.

(7)备车程序是什么?

(7)What's the standing-by engine procedure?

(8)有什么特殊规定或特殊要求吗?

(8)Are there any specific rules or special requirements?

(9)我已了解关于三副职责的众多要求。

(9)I've understood the various procedure pertaining to 3rd officer's duties.

(10)已经进行了简要介绍,告知了众多文件位置并已理解。

(10)Briefing has been carried out and various files location shown and understood.

(11)交接班工作已经平稳进行。

(11)The handing and taking over of duties has been carried out smoothly.

(12)我需要检查一下救生艇的位置。

(12)I need to check lifeboats station location.

(13)我来检查一下应急队和弃船职责。

(13)Let me check emergency party and abandon ship duties.

(14)检查应急集合地点的位置。

(14)Check the location of emergency muster station.

(15)检查从我的房间和工作场所至救生艇位置和应急集合站位置的逃生通道。

(15)Check escape routes from my cabin and workplace to lifeboat station and emergency muster station.

(16)我了解船舶安全及应急程序的要求。

(16)I understand ship specific safety and emergency procedure and arrangements.

(17)我已检查过急救和医疗设备的位置。

(17)I've checked where the first aid and medical equipment is situated.

(18)我已阅读过位于公共区域的安全管理手册的第三卷。

(18)I've read the Volume Three of the SMM (Safety Management Manual) situated in public areas.

6.2 航行值班用语

6.2 Navigation Watch-keeping Expressions

6.2.1 课前准备
6.2.1 Warming Up

海上航行期间,值班驾驶员作为船长的代表,要确保有效航行值班并保证值班期间船舶的安全。他的主要职责是无论是否有其他人协助,时刻保持正规瞭望。他的主要航行职责还包括定期核对船舶航向、比对陀螺罗经和磁罗经航向。瞭望人员的主要职责是对所有影响船舶航行安全的危险物体保持瞭望。他必须对此项工作保持全神贯注并向值班驾驶员进行报告。

When navigating at sea, the OOW, on behalf of the master, must supervise the efficient running of the watch and ensure the safe navigation of the vessel throughout the watch period. His main duty is to maintain a proper lookout whenever the vessel is at sea, regardless of other personnel engaged on a similar duty. His navigational duties also include the regular checking of the ship's course and the comparison of the gyrocompass with the magnetic compass. The principal duty of the lookout is to maintain a continuous watch for all hazards that may impair the safe navigation of the vessel. He is obliged to give his full uninterrupted attention to this duty, reporting to the officer of the watch.

舵工的职责是在船舶未使用自动舵驾驶的时候操纵船舶。在大型客船上,执行操舵任务的人经常被称作"quartermaster",商船上"quartermaster"和"helmsman"都很常用。因为船舶的安全航行由舵工来控制,所以操舵任务是十分紧张和劳累的,并需要经常换班以保证有效操舵。

The function of the "helmsman" is to steer the vessel when it is not engaged on automatic pilot. On large passenger vessels the steering duty is normally carried out by the "quartermaster" and the terms "helmsman" and "quartermaster" are both in common use in all merchant vessels. The duty can be tedious and tiring and regular reliefs are employed to maintain efficiency, since the responsibility for the safe passage of the vessel lies in the hands of the man steering.

当船舶沿岸航行时,通常雇用引航员并使用手动操舵。舵工从引航员处得到舵令后需向引航员逐字逐句重复其下达的每一命令之后再去执行。舵工需牢记引航员是船长及其代表(值班驾驶员)的建议者,船长或值班驾驶员可能会更改引航员的命令。

When a vessel is navigating in coastal waters, a pilot is generally employed and manual steering is used. The helmsman should take orders for the wheel movements from the pilot and repeat each order, word for word, back to the pilot before executing the movement. The man at the wheel should bear in mind that the pilot is an adviser to the master and his representative (OOW), and at any time the master or the officer of the watch may countermand the orders of the pilot.

上述提到的人员和组织之间要相互配合和保持良好的沟通以保证船舶的在航安全。

All these people and organizations mentioned above should cooperate with each other and keep close communication so as to keep the vessel's safety at sea.

6.2.2 对话练习
6.2.2 Dialogue Practice

对话 1

Dialogue 1

A:Avonport 港调,我是机动船蓝鲸号。我的雷达失灵了。岸基雷达协助可使用吗?完毕。

A:Avonport port control, this is MV Blue Whale. My radar is not working. Is shore-based radar assistance available? Over.

B:机动船蓝鲸号,我是 Avonport 港调。可以,岸基雷达协助可以使用。你需要航行协助吗? 完毕。

B:MV Blue Whale, this is Avonport port control. Yes, shore-based radar assistance is available. Do you require navigational assistance? Over.

A:Avonport 港调,我是机动船蓝鲸号。是的,我需要航行协助。完毕。

A:Avonport port control, this is MV Blue Whale. Yes, I require navigational assistance. Over.

B:机动船蓝鲸号,我是 Avonport 港调。你的位置在哪? 完毕。

B:MV Blue Whale, this is Avonport port control. What is your position? Over.

A:Avonport 港调,我是机动船蓝鲸号。我的位置在入口浮筒 115°方位,距离 3 海里处。完毕。

A:Avonport port control, this is MV Blue Whale. My position is bearing 115 degrees, distance three miles from entrance buoy. Over.

B:机动船蓝鲸号,我是 Avonport 港调。你的位置是如何获得的? 完毕。

B:Blue Whale, this is Avonport port control. How was your position obtained? Over.

A:Avonport 港调,我是机动船蓝鲸号。我的位置是通过交叉方位获得的。完毕。

A:Avonport port control, this is Blue Whale. My position was obtained by cross-bearing. Over.

B:机动船蓝鲸号,我是 Avonport 港调。我在我的雷达屏幕上找不到你。你当前的航向和航速是多少? 完毕。

B:Blue Whale, this is Avonport port control. I cannot locate you on my radar screen. What is your present course and speed? Over.

A:Avonport 港调,我是机动船蓝鲸号。我当前的航向和航速是 060°、18 节。完毕。

A:Avonport port control, this is Blue Whale. My present course and speed are 060 degrees, 18 knots. Over.

B:机动船蓝鲸号,我是 Avonport 港调。我已经在我的雷达屏幕上找到你了。结束。

B:Blue Whale, this is Avonport port control. I have located you on my radar screen. Out.

对话 2

Dialogue 2

A:机动船蓝鲸号,我是 Avonport 港调。这个区域有带有浮标的渔网。请小心驾驶。完毕。

A:MV Blue Whale, this is Avonport Port Control. Nets with buoys in this area. Please navigate with caution. Over.

B:Avonport 港调,我是机动船蓝鲸号。我将小心驾驶。完毕。

B:Avonport Port Control, this is Blue Whale. I will navigate with caution. Over.

A:机动船蓝鲸号,我是 Avonport 港调。让清航道。搜救作业正在进行中。完毕。

A:MV Blue Whale, this is Avonport Port Control. Keep clear of the fairway. Search and rescue in progress. Over.

B:Avonport 港调,我是机动船蓝鲸号。我将让清航道。完毕。

B:Avonport Port Control, this is Blue Whale. I will keep clear. Over.

A:机动船蓝鲸号,我是 Avonport 港调。你的航向正在偏离雷达参照线。完毕。

A:MV Blue Whale, this is Avonport Port Control. Your course is deviating from the radar reference line. Over.

B:Avonport 港调,我是机动船蓝鲸号。你建议我以什么航向行驶?完毕。

B:Avonport Port Control, this is Blue Whale. What course do you advise? Over.

A:机动船蓝鲸号,我是 Avonport 港调。建议走航向 120°。完毕。

A:MV Blue Whale, this is Avonport Port Control. Advise make course 120 degrees. Over.

B:Avonport 港调,我是机动船蓝鲸号。正在改向至 120°。完毕。

B:Avonport Port Control, this is Blue Whale. Making course 120 degrees. Over.

A:机动船蓝鲸号,我是 Avonport 港调。你船北面有一艘大型油船正在离开航道。你必须等候她从你船船首方向横穿。完毕。

A:MV Blue Whale. This is Avonport Port Control. There is a large tanker to the north of you is leaving the fairway. You must wait for her to cross ahead of you. Over.

B:Avonport 港调,我是机动船蓝鲸号。我将等候那艘大型油船清爽。结束。

B:Avonport Port Control, this is Blue Whale. I will wait for the large tanker to clear. Out.

对话 3

Dialogue 3

A:我们前面的船看起来好像减速了。三副,我们距离那艘船多远?

A:The ship ahead of us seems to have reduced its speed. Third mate, what is our distance from the ship?

B:3 海里,船长。它的速度是 11 节。她已经稍微减速。我们越来越靠近她了。

B:Three miles, Captain. Her speed is 11 knots. She has slowed down a bit. We are getting closer to her.

A:明白。我们的速度是 12 节。我们也减速。把主机转速降到每分钟 75 转。

A:Roger. Our speed is 12 knots. Let's reduce our speed, too. Bring down the engine revolution to 75 r/min.

B:好的。主机转速正降到每分钟 75 转。航速将降低。

B:Roger. Engine revolution bringing down to 75 r/min. Speed will be reduced.

A:收到。

A:Roger.

对话 4

Dialogue 4

A:你好,大副。现在是你的幸福时光了。

A:Hi, Chief mate. It's your good time now.

B:你终于来了。你已经调整好夜视了吗?

B:Really miss you. Have you completed your adjustment to night vision?

A:我能毫不费力地看到你。

A:I can catch you without any difficulty.

B:好的,现在船舶正在靠近直布罗陀海峡,并且马上将进入分道通航制区域。

B:OK. Now the ship is approaching Gibraltar Strait, and will enter traffic separation scheme soon.

A:船首向和船速是多少?

A:What is the heading and speed?

B:船首向设定在 080°,对地航速是 18 节,核对陀螺罗经和标准罗经,+2°的差值。

B:Heading sets 080 (zero eight zero) degrees, speed over aground 18 knots, check up gyro and standard compass, +2 degrees in difference.

A:好的,这艘船已经正常航行了。

A:Good, the ship is in her own way.

B:微风,能见度不怎么好,有时有薄雾。

B:The wind is soft and visibility is not so good. Sometimes mist appears.

A:明白。

A:Understood.

B:左侧雷达的量程为12海里。附近有很多船只。

B:Port radar is working at 12 nautical miles scale. There is a lot of traffic nearby.

A:我看一下。左舷船首那艘距离为7海里的船是什么情况?

A:Let me have a look. How about the port bow vessel, 7 nautical miles away?

B:她是一艘对遇船,到目前为止与我们没有冲突。

B:She is a head-on vessel, no conflict with us till now.

A:明白了。

A:I see.

B:航行灯工作正常,所有的航行和安全设备状况良好。

B:Navigational lights work well and all navigational and safety equipment are in good condition.

A:好的,还有什么特殊指示吗?

A:Alright. Have any special instructions?

B:就这么多。如果有任何问题,请立刻呼叫船长。

B:That's all. If there is any question, please call the captain immediately.

6.2.3 句型操练
6.2.3 Sentence Pattern Drills

6.2.3.1 航行值班
6.2.3.1 Navigational Watch-keeping

(1)下一转向点距目前位置还有2.5海里。

(1)The next way point is 2.5 nautical miles from the present position.

(2)对地航速15节。/对水航速17节。

(2)Speed over ground is 15 knots./Speed through water is 17 knots.

(3)磁罗经误差是2°东。

(3)Magnetic compass error is 2 degrees east.

(4)当前最大吃水是7米。

(4)Present maximum draft is 7 meters.

(5)艏吃水是8米。

(5)Draft forward is 8 meters.

(6)船舶将让路。

(6)The vessel will give way.

(7)船舶正直航。

(7)The vessel is standing on.

(8)一船正从右舷穿越。

(8) A vessel is crossing from starboard side.
(9)我们将向右转向以让路。
(9) We will alter course to give way.
(10)我们北方的船舶和我航向相同。
(10) A vessel north of us is on the same course.
(11)该处交通繁忙。
(11) There is heavy traffic in the area.
(12)雷达上没有危险目标。
(12) There are no dangerous targets on the radar.
(13) GPS 没有工作。
(13) GPS is not in operation.
(14)航行灯已打开。
(14) Navigational lights are switched on.
(15)南风蒲福 7 级。
(15) The wind is southerly force Beaufort 7.
(16)海况预计会在 40 分钟内改变。
(16) The sea state is expected to change within 40 minutes.
(17)能见度预计会在半小时内降低到 2 海里。
(17) Visibility is expected to decrease to 2 nautical miles within half an hour.
(18)气压正在快速下降。
(18) Barometer is dropping rapidly.
(19)最近的一次保安巡逻是协调世界时 1800。
(19) The latest security patrol was at 1800 hours UTC.
(20)班交给你了。
(20) You have the watch now.
(21)班交给我吧。
(21) I have the watch now.
(22)浓雾。保持警觉瞭望。谨慎驾驶。
(22) Dense fog. Keep a sharp lookout. Navigate with caution.
(23)到成山角的时候叫醒我。
(23) Wake me up while arriving at Cheng Shanjiao.
(24)发现任何异常立即叫我。
(24) Call me at any time if you find something abnormal.
(25)密切关注前方渔船。
(25) Pay much attention to fishing boat ahead.
(26)第二台雷达没有扫描线。
(26) The second radar has no sweeping line.
(27)注意,车钟的全速倒车更慢了。

(27) The full astern of the telegraph is much later, pay attention.
(28)在当前位置抛锚比较危险。
(28) It is dangerous to anchor in your present position.
(29)不要穿越航路。
(29) Do not cross fairway.
(30)建议你从失控船的西侧通过。
(30) Advise you pass west of disabled vessel.
(31)你目前的航向比较危险。
(31) You are steering dangerous course.
(32)你正驶入危险之中,前方有浅滩。
(32) You are running into danger. Shallow water ahead of you.
(33)雷达有盲区吗?
(33) Has radar any blind sectors?
(34)是的,雷达盲区从001°到004°。
(34) Yes, radar has blind sectors from 001 to 004 degrees.
(35)雷达量程调成3海里。
(35) Change radar to 3 nautical miles range scale.
(36)挂起2个黑球,表明船舶失控。
(36) Let's hoist two black balls to signal that the vessel is not under command.
(37)船长,我看见了一盏灯。好像是手电筒发出的灯光。
(37) Captain, I saw a light. It seems that the light was made by an electric torch.

6.2.3.2 甚高频通信
6.2.3.2 VHF Communications

(1)你船船名、呼号是什么?你的识别码是多少?
(1) What is your name, call sign? What is your identification?
(2)你船是哪国船旗?你的登记港是哪?
(2) What is your flag state? What is your port of registry?
(3)你船最大吃水是多少?
(3) What is your maximum draft?
(4)我船最大淡水吃水是13米。
(4) My maximum draft in fresh water is 13 meters.
(5)你船船宽多少?
(5) What's your width?
(6)我的信号强度如何?我收听到你的信号强度为1/5。
(6) How do you read me? I read you with signal strength one/five.
(7)航向为210的船舶,这里是机动船Utopia,意图:我将以25节的速度从你船右舷追

越。完毕。

(7) Vessel on course 210 degrees, this is MV Utopia. Intention: I wish to overtake you on your starboard side with 25 knots. Over.

(8)根据 ARPA 读数,CPA 是 2.5 海里。我可以过你船头吗？完毕。

(8) According to the ARPA reading, the CPA is 2.5 n mile. May I pass you at your bow? Over.

(9)我将过你船船尾。我会向右转向。完毕。

(9) I will pass at your stern. I will change my course to starboard. Over.

(10)我将向右转向,我们左对左通过。完毕。

(10) I will change my course to starboard. Let's pass each other port-to-port. Over.

(11)多谢合作。祝您航安。转换至 16 频道,结束。

(11) Thank you for your cooperation. Bon voyage. Swtich to channel 16. Out.

6.3 日常甲板维护用语及升旗用语

6.3 Daily Deck Maintenance Expressions and Flag Hoisting Expressions

6.3.1 课前准备

6.3.1 Warming Up

船舶保养包括检查、清洗、养护、加油润滑和调整(根据需要)。船舶常规保养工作包括很多方面,例如除锈、刷漆、冲洗甲板和货舱,保养船舶索具和甲板机械等。除此之外可能需要在船员能力范围内做一些小型部件的更换。作为船舶的操作者,你必须要采取积极行动以保障你的船舶处于最好的营运状况。这其实并不简单,因为你需要对抗盐水和含盐空气的腐蚀作用。风浪作用同样使船舶及其主机遭受很强的应力和应变。所以保养工作绝不可停歇。本部分主要包括船舶在预防性保养过程中的沟通及要求。

Vessel maintenance includes inspecting, cleaning, servicing, preserving, lubricating, and adjusting (as required). These routine maintenance works include many aspects, for example de-rusting and painting, washing the decks and holds, maintenance of ship's rigging and deck machinery, and so on. It can also require minor parts replacement within the capability of the crew. As a watercraft operator, you must take an active part in keeping your vessel at its peak operating condition. This is not an easy or simple task because you are constantly battling against the corrosive effects of salt water and salt air. The wind and sea also subject a vessel and its engines to strong stresses and strains. It takes day-by-day work and watchfulness to cope with all of these conditions. Maintenance never ceases. This part covers the communication about procedures for preventive maintenance and the required maintenance aboard ship.

这些常规的、每天的保养任务必须进行以预防或者至少可以延缓船舶设备锈斑的形成或状况的恶化。进行船舶保养的第一步也是最重要的一步是保持船舶清洁。这对于船舶健康和有效营运也很有必要。

These are the routine daily tasks that must be done aboard ship to prevent, or at least to hold back, the formation of rust or deterioration of the ship's equipment. The first and most important step in proper maintenance is to keep a vessel clean. This is necessary for good health and efficient operation.

油漆通常用作保持船体表面清洁。它可以密封钢铁部分并防止铁锈的形成。油漆还可以用作很多其他目的。由于其防腐特性,油漆可以帮助保持清洁和卫生。另外,还可以用以反射、吸收或分散亮光。例如,浅色漆可以用在船舶内部以发散自然光和人造光以达到最好的效果。这些反射和吸收特性顺带也使它们可能被用作装饰。

Paint is used primarily for preserving surfaces. It seals the pores of steel and helps to keep rust from forming. Paint also serves a variety of other purposes. It is valuable as an aid to cleanliness and sanitation because of its antiseptic properties and smooth, washable surface. Paint is also used to reflect, absorb, or redistribute light. For example, light-colored paint is used for the interior of the ship to distribute natural and artificial light to the best advantage. These same properties of reflection and absorption, incidentally, make camouflage painting possible.

6.3.2　对话练习
6.3.2　Dialogue Practice

对话 1

Dialogue 1

A:今天我们将对 3 号货舱的甲板板进行日常保养。

A:Today we'll carry out routine maintenance from deck plating in way of No.3 cargo hold.

B:好的。

B:All right.

A:记住,我们只做修补作业。就是说,首先确认船壳、结构或者相关设备的损坏和恶化情况。

A:Remember, just do patch work. That is to say, firstly identify any damage or deterioration of the vessel's hull, structure or related equipment.

B:没问题。

B:No problem.

A:我发现有些菌形通风筒已经严重磨损,有些灭火器生锈了,所以我觉得有必要进行动火作业,一会儿我会申请许可。

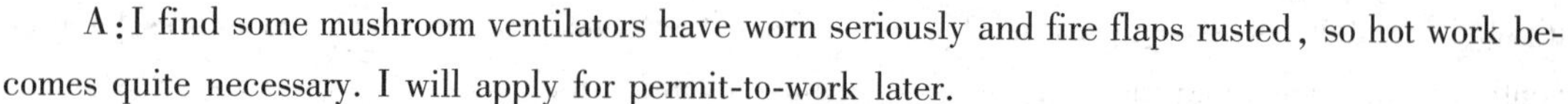

A:I find some mushroom ventilators have worn seriously and fire flaps rusted, so hot work becomes quite necessary. I will apply for permit-to-work later.

B:我会准备好乙炔和氧气,包括灭火设备。

B:And I will keep the acetylene and oxygen ready, including firefighting equipment.

A:对于测深和通风的管道,你最好关注一下底部,看看是否出现了严重的腐蚀。

A:As for the pipes for sounding and venting, you'd better keep a sharp eye on the bottom and check if heavy corrosion occurs.

B:好的。我还会确认一下盖子是否就位。

B:Certainly. I will also confirm whether the cap is in place.

A:你有没有发现什么情况会影响船壳强度和水密完整性?

A:Have you found anything that can affect ship's hull strength and watertight integrity?

B:是的。有很多垃圾挡着通往消防总管的路。恐怕压力大一点的话管道会破裂。最好移除这些垃圾。

B:Yes. There are heavy wastes in way of fire mains. I'm afraid the pipes could break while the pressure is a bit higher. Better crop those wastes.

A:好的。我们会照办。

A:OK. We will do what you say.

B:顺便说一下,舱口围板的一些肘板出现了裂缝,怎么处理?

B:By the way, some brackets in the hatch coaming have cracked. How to deal with this problem?

A:重焊一下就好。以后我会继续留意的。

A:Just re-weld them. I will pay further attention in the future.

B:明白。

B:I see.

A:你想用电锤和气动锤吗?

A:Do you intend to use electric hammer and pneumatic hammer?

B:是的,需要进行大面积的除锈。

B:Yes, because there is a large area to be chipped.

A:但是你要小心,因为它们总是引起危险。

A:But you have to take care since they always cause some dangers.

B:我已经检查了它们,并且我让所有的工人在作业过程中都戴了护目镜和手套。

B:I have already inspected them and asked all hands to properly wear goggles and gloves during operation.

A:很好!记着,表面一定要彻底地打磨干净。

A:Great! Please remember that surface preparation should be polished and clean thoroughly.

B:明白。

B:I see.

对话 2

Dialogue 2

A:大副,物料间里应该放什么?

A:What should be kept in the store on board the ship, Chief?

B:能够满足日常需求的物料,比如说食物、淡水、清洁材料、医疗用品、安全用品、备用品等。

B:Certainly, the inventory that can meet its daily requirements, such as food, water, cleaning supplies, medical supplies, safety supplies, spare parts, etc.

A:这么多东西呀! 你怎么管理它们?

A:So many things! How do you manage them?

B:这个工作不简单的。你看,从计划、申请、库存、维修保养到申报,每一步都需要大量的工作。

B:It is not an easy job. You see, from plan, application, inventory, upkeep to declaration, every link involves a lot of work.

A:天呀,你能告诉我保管物料间的基本原则吗?

A:Oh, gosh! Would you please tell me the basic rule to keep ship's store?

B:好的。我们准备物料的目的是保证整个航次期间船舶的正常运行。每条船都不一样的。

B:OK. We should prepare our store to guarantee the ship's normal operation during the whole voyage. It varies from one ship to another.

A:你想,每一项都可能有不同的名字和规格,你如何才能拿到正确的呢?

A:You know, one item may have different names and specification, so how could you make sure that you can get the correct one?

B:这要感谢由 IMPA 制作的船用物料指南,它整合了全世界知名厂家的材料的特征。

B:Thanks to the marine store guide produced by IMPA, it integrates the materials' feature from the various world-famous manufacturers.

A:你能举例说明吗?

A:Can you give an example?

B:如果你想要抗咬合剂喷雾,你只要写六个数字 45 08 46 就可以了。

B:If you want to get anti-seize spray, just write down the six-digit number 45 08 46.

A:很好,但是你如何确保所有的必需品都能填写到申请表里呢?

A:Great! But how can you make sure that all necessities have been entered into the application form?

B:那很简单。我会按照它们的功能来写下要求,然后认真编写。

B:Aha, that is easy. I will collect all requirements under the scope of their responsibilities, and compile them carefully.

A:顺便问一下,材料到了船边以后,我们应该做什么?

A:By the way, upon the materials coming alongside the ship, what measures shall we take?

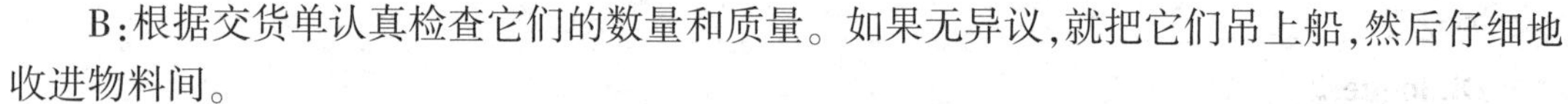

B:根据交货单认真检查它们的数量和质量。如果无异议,就把它们吊上船,然后仔细地收进物料间。

B:Carefully check their quantity and quality in the light of the delivery note. If no discrepancy, lift them on deck, keep them in the store properly.

A:明白。在航行中如何保管它们呢?

A:I see. Then how to upkeep them during the voyage?

B:水手长会把物料整理并绑扎好,尤其是特殊物料,比如油漆和化学品。

B:Bosun would tidy and secure the store, keep them in good condition, especially for some special materials such as paints, chemicals, etc.

A:懂了。还有一件事,我知道船舶物料在每一个挂靠港都要申报。那个文件是什么?

A:I get it. One more thing, I have ever learned that ship stores should be declared at every port of call. What is the document?

B:是船舶物料申报单。

B:It is Ship's Stores Declaration.

A:在这个文件中需要清晰地说明什么?

A:What should be stated clearly in this document?

B:它需要说明物料的名字、数量、储藏位置,并且要说明船上的所有物料都要有合法的用途。

B:It should state article's name, quantity, and place of storage and demonstrate that all materials on board are of legal use.

6.3.3 句型操练

6.3.3 Sentence Pattern Drills

(1)发现左舷吊艇钢丝部分磨损,下次进坞时掉头。

(1)Found the port boat fall partly abrasion, to be end to end when vessel dry dock.

(2)任何人在进入全封闭救生艇内从事保养工作之前应该事先得到值班驾驶员的许可。

(2)Anybody who wishes to enter the enclosed lifeboat for maintenance work shall get duty office's approve in advance.

(3)检查发现,用于救生艇的艇首索在靠港期间丢失,通知水头立即放一个新的。

(3)Check and find the paints for lifeboat lost during call at this port, ask Bosun to put a new one in position immediately.

(4)检查救生艇的船名、船籍港标志清晰,反光带状态良好。

(4)The marker of ship's name and register port which the lifeboat belong to is in clear condition, retro-reflective tape in good condition.

(5)艇内船员座位的标志模糊,安排水手重新用白油漆标志。

(5)The seat position marker inside port lifeboat is indistinct, arrange AB remark it with white paint.

(6)艇内的压缩饼干将在下月到期,要求船舶供应商在本港按需要供给56包饼干。

(6)The ship's bread in the lifeboat is due next month. Ask the local ship chandler to supply 56 packages as required.

(7)检查救生艇的结构包括固定部件和活动部件,未见异常。

(7)Check the condition of lifeboat structure including fixed and loose equipment, no abnormal found.

(8)启动艇机之前的一个必要步骤就是要检查艇机是否有足够的燃油。

(8)One necessary step before starting the engine is to check whether the engine has sufficient oil in side.

(9)更换救生艇吊艇钢丝并将更换日期标注在救生艇下面的艇甲板上。

(9)Renew boat fall and label the renew date on the boat deck under the lifeboat.

(10)脱钩装置释放手柄上的安全插销生锈了,拔出加油后再放回去。

(10)The release handle safety pin seized by rust, pull it out with force, grace it, refit it again.

(11)打开电源启动艇机,以前进和后退的方式运转共3分钟,正常。

(11)Switch on power and start the engine, running engine in ahead and astern mode for 3 minutes, satisfactory.

(12)拧开救生艇的艇底塞放出艇内的积水,再拧上艇底塞。

(12)Screw off the boat plug to drain out all free water, then screw up again.

(13)定期保养救生艇艇架系统,确保其处于随时可用的状态。

(13)Regular maintain the boat davit system to ensure the system ready for immediately use.

(14)移走其他杂物,确保登乘区域清爽。

(14)Remove any other unnecessary objects and ensure embarkation area is free of obstructions.

(15)拆检右舷救生艇齿轮箱进行清洁,并重新装回。

(15)Overhaul the gearbox on starboard lifeboat, refit in position after cleaning.

(16)定期检查救生艇内的蓄电池的状态,需要时进行充电。

(16)Check the status of store battery inside lifeboat periodically, recharge it if necessary.

(17)对照防火控制图检查每一便携式灭火器,确保每一灭火器都正确放置。

(17)Check each portable fire extinguisher against the fire control plan to ensure that each extinguisher is proper placed.

(18)船舶离港前所有救生设备都应处于良好且立即可用的状态。

(18)Before vessel leaving a port, each of her life-saving appliances shall be in good order and ready for immediate use.

(19)每周检查所有救生艇筏、救助艇及降落设备,以确保其随时可用。

(19)All survival craft, rescue boats and launching appliances shall be inspected weekly to ensure they are ready for use.

(20)应该为救生装置提供备件和修理设备。

(20) Spares and repair equipment shall be provided for life-saving appliances.

(21)一些容易磨损的部件应定期更换。

(21) Some components which are easily worn need to be replaced regularly.

(22)检查应包括,但不限于吊钩状态、吊钩与救生艇的连接以及适当和完全复位的承载释放装置的状况。

(22) The inspection shall include, but is not limited to, the condition of hooks, their attachment to the lifeboat and the on-load release gear being properly and completely reset.

(23)如果可行的话,救生艇和救助艇的发动机每周应运转 3 分钟以上。

(23) Engines in lifeboats and rescue boats shall be run for a total period of not less than 3 minutes every week if possible.

(24)在艇筏演习的过程中检查其释放系统未见异常。

(24) Check the on-load release system for any trouble during boat drill, satisfactory.

(25)使用手摇柄启动艇机,测试发现一切正常。

(25) Start engine with hand crank, test and found in normal condition.

(26)在救生艇下降前确认所有水密门窗是关闭的,艇员已经就位。

(26) Before lowering lifeboat, make sure that all watertight doors of the lifeboat are closed and each boatman has stationed.

(27)检查救生艇内的安全带是否处于良好状态。

(27) Check seat belts in the lifeboat whether in good condition.

(28)维持艇内食物、水和设备处于良好的状态,按需随时更新。

(28) Maintain food, water and equipment in lifeboat in sound condition, replacement in due time as necessary.

(29)将释放手柄一次拉到完全打开位置。

(29) Pull the release handle to the fully open position by one action.

(30)确认救生艇处于接近水面的位置,但未进入水中,静水压力内锁装置没有触发。

(30) Confirm that the lifeboat is as close as possible to the water surface, but that the hydrostatic interlock is not triggered.

(31)将右舷的救生艇放至水面并操纵数分钟,收上并放回原位。

(31) Launch starboard lifeboat to water surface and maneuver in the water for minutes, retrieve and restored in position.

(32)在救生艇和艇架之间安装悬挂索,检查救生艇脱钩装置。

(32) Rig hanging-off pennants between the lifeboat and davit and check lifeboat releasing gear.

(33)救生艇操作说明因风化而变得模糊,重新张贴一张新的。

(33) The lifeboat operate instruction became indistinct due to weather, re-placard a new one.

(34)清除艇底塞孔内的杂物,检查其放置情况。

(34) Removed any dirt of drain valve and checked correct operation.

(35)当地的船舶供应商将三个救生筏拉到岸上去进行检验,并于开航前送回,附带检验证书。

(35)Local ship chandler take 3 life rafts ashore for annual inspection and send back prior to vessel sailing, together with annual inspection certificate.

(36)三副召集所有新上船的船员做消防的培训,并现场演示如何释放便携式二氧化碳灭火器。

(36)3/O call all new joining crew together for firefighting training and demonstrate how to release portable CO_2 extinguisher to them.

(37)检查消火栓、皮龙带和水枪状态是否良好。

(37)Check fire hydrants, hoses and nozzles whether in good condition.

(38)船舶航次修理时,用压缩空气吹通二氧化碳管系。

(38)Blew out CO_2 pipe system with pressure air when vessel in voyage repair.

(39)检查所有消防站的消防员装备,状况良好。

(39)Check the fireman outfitting at all fire stations and find in order.

(40)测试厨房区域烟雾报警系统,符合要求。

(40)Test smoke alarming system at the galley area, satisfactory.

(41)在演习中发现两个消防皮龙渗漏,立即更新。

(41)2 fire hoses were found leakage during firefighting drill, renew them immediately.

(42)把皮龙带从皮龙箱中拿出,重新正确卷起后再放回。

(42)Take fire hose out from the hydrant and re-roll them up correctly then put it back.

(43)两个皮龙箱在本航次的大风浪中严重变形,通知船长。

(43)2 fire hydrants were serious deformed by rough sea during voyage, report to captain at once.

(44)在左舷舷梯旁的救生圈上的救生绳有些乱,三副整理并重新盘放好。

(44)Lifeline attached to lifebuoy at port side gangway in confusion, 3/O sort and re-coil it up in order.

(45)收到5件新的救生衣,按需要用油漆刷上船名和船籍港。

(45)Received 5 new life jacket, paint them with ship's name and register port as necessary.

(46)日常保养中意外地释放了驾驶台左翼的烟雾信号,用VHF通知附近所有的船舶。

(46)Accidentally activate smoke signal at port bridge wing during daily maintenance, inform all nearby vessel via VHF.

(47)测试紧急无线电示位标和搜救雷达应答器未见异常,更换搜救雷达应答器下月即将到期的电池。

(47)Test EPIRB and ASRT found they are in good condition, replaced the battery for SART as it to be expired next month.

(48)吊艇架上所有活动部件加油润滑。

(48)Lubricate all moving parts on the lifeboat davit.

(49)检查救生艇的吊艇架,未见腐蚀和变形,所有的标志都很清楚。

(49) Visually check the lifeboat davit, no corrosion and deformation, all marks in clear.

(50)用沙袋对两个救生艇的释放装置按规定进行试验,未见变形。

(50) Operationally test release gear with sand in bag as per requirement for the both lifeboats, no deform were found.

6.4 船舶靠离码头和抛锚的英语口令

6.4 Ship Mooring and Unmooring Orders and Anchoring Orders

6.4.1 课前准备

6.4.1 Warming Up

船舶锚泊、靠离泊作业期间,船头和船尾以及驾驶台应有足够数量的人员以确保作业安全。

During anchoring, mooring and unmooring operations, a sufficient number of personnel should always be available at each end of the vessel to ensure a safe operation.

各队应有一名驾驶员负责,各负责驾驶员应和驾驶台团队建立有效沟通。若沟通工具用到便携式无线电,沟通时应清晰说明船名以防误解。所有参与锚泊和靠离泊作业的人员应正确穿着防护服装。

A responsible officer should be in charge of each of parties and a suitable means of communication between the responsible officers and the bridge team should be established. If this involves use of portable radios, the ship should be clearly identified by name to prevent misinterpretation. All personnel involved in anchoring and mooring operations should wear suitable protective clothing.

船长应当确保锚泊及靠离泊作业(包括和拖船互动)安全并着重强调以下事项:

The master shall ensure that anchoring and mooring operations (including interaction with tugs) are carried out in a safe manner and the following items are properly addressed:

(1)合理计划和监督。

(1) Suitable planning and supervision.

(2)正确沟通。

(2) Proper communication.

(3)人员适任。

(3) Competency of personnel.

(4)靠离泊和锚泊作业团队人员充足。

(4) Sufficient members in the mooring and anchoring teams.

(5)熟悉靠泊、锚泊、过往交通和潮汐/天气状况的特殊要求。

(5) Familiarity with any specific requirements relating to anchoring, shore moorings, passing traffic and tidal/weather conditions.

在开安全会议时,要发现、评估并记录所有任何不安全的情况。若有必要,应当采取相应的改正措施。

Any unsafe situations shall be identified, evaluated and recorded in the Safety & Health Committee Meeting. Corrective actions shall be implemented as necessary.

6.4.2 对话练习

6.4.2 Dialogue Practice

对话 1

Dialogue 1

A:大副,我是船长。我们要带 3 条拖船。两条拖拽,一条顶推。准备好系拖船。

A: Chief mate, this is Captain. We will take three tugs. Two tugs will pull, and one tug will push. Stand by for making fast the tugs.

B:船长,我是大副。已准备好。

B: Captain, this is Chief mate. Standing by.

A:大副,使用左舷船首导缆孔。送撇缆上拖船。

A: Chief mate, use the fairlead on port bow. Send heaving lines to the tug.

B:撇缆送到拖船,船长。

B: Heaving lines being sent to the tugs now, Captain.

A:送两根拖缆上拖船。

A: Send two towing lines to the tugs.

B:两根拖缆送至拖船,船长。

B: Two towing lines being sent to the tugs, Captain.

A:船头拖船系左舷船首,船尾拖船系右舷船尾。

A: Make fast the forward tugs on port bow, and the aft tug on the starboard quarter.

B:前后拖船系好,船长。

B: Tugs fore and aft are made fast now, Captain.

A:大副,把拖缆眼环上桩。

A: Chief mate, put the eyes of the towing lines on bitts.

B:船长,拖缆上桩。我们准备好解拖船。

B: Captain, towing lines are on bitts now. We are standing by for letting go to the tugs.

对话 2

Dialogue 2

A：大副，抛左锚。

A：Chief mate, let go port anchor.

B：明白，抛左锚。

B：Roger, port anchor let go.

A：锚链方向如何？

A：Where is cable leading now?

B：两节甲板，锚链向前。

B：Two shackles on deck, cable leading forward.

A：继续松出锚链。

A：Keep paying out the cable.

B：明白，松出锚链。目前 3 节入水。

B：Roger, pay out cable. Three shackles in water now.

A：明白，刹住。

A：Roger, hold on.

B：刹住。锚链不吃力。

B：Hold on. Now chain is slack away.

A：好的，继续松出锚链，6 节入水。

A：OK, continue paying out the chain to 6 shackles in water.

B：明白，现在 6 节入水。锚链 10 点钟方向。

B：Roger, 6 shackles in water now, cable leading at ten o'clock.

A：锚是否抓底？

A：Is anchor brought up?

B：是的，已经抓底。

B：Yes, already brought up.

A：可以了，升起锚球。

A：OK, hoist the anchor ball.

对话 3

Dialogue 3

A：Avonport 引航站，这是机动船蓝鲸号。引航艇就位了吗？完毕。

A：Avonport Pilot Station, this is MV Blue Whale. Is the pilot boat on station? Over.

B：机动船蓝鲸号，这是 Avonport 引航站。引航艇已经驶向你船。完毕。

B：MV Blue Whale, this is Avonport Pilot Station. The pilot boat is coming to you. Over.

A：Avonport 引航站，这是机动船蓝鲸号。我在什么位置接引航员？完毕。

A：Avonport Pilot Station, this is MV Blue Whale. In what position can I take the pilot? Over.

B：机动船蓝鲸号，这是 Avonport 引航站。停在目前的位置等待引航员。完毕。

B:MV Blue Whale, this is Avonport Pilot Station. Stop in the present position and wait for the pilot. Over.

A:Avonport 引航站,这是机动船蓝鲸号。我会停在目前的位置。引航员何时登船?完毕。

A:Avonport Pilot Station, this is MV Blue Whale. I will stay in the present position. When will the pilot embark? Over.

B:机动船蓝鲸号,这是 Avonport 引航站。引航员将在当地时间 1130 登船。完毕。

B:MV Blue Whale, this is Avonport Pilot Station. The pilot will embark at 1130 hours local time. Over.

A:机动船蓝鲸号,这是 Avonport 引航站。将引航艇置于你船东南向。完毕。

A:MV Blue Whale, this is Avonport Pilot Station. Keep the pilot boat southeast of you. Over.

B:Avonport 引航站,这是机动船蓝鲸号。好的。我会将引航艇置于我船东南向。完毕。

B:Avonport Pilot Station, this is MV Blue Whale. Yes, I will keep the pilot boat southeast of me. Over.

A:机动船蓝鲸号,这是 Avonport 引航站。守听 12 频道直至引航员登船结束。完毕。

A:MV Blue Whale, this is Avonport Pilot Station. Stand by on VHF Channel 12 until pilot transfer is completed. Over.

B:Avonport 引航站,这是机动船蓝鲸号。守听 12 频道。结束。

B:Avonport Pilot Station, this is MV Blue Whale. Standing by on VHF Channel 12. Out.

对话 4

Dialogue 4

A:三副,安放舷梯,与引航员软梯组合安放。

A:Third mate, rig the accommodation ladder in combination with the pilot ladder.

B:引航员先生,舷梯和引航员软梯安放在右舷。是否需要扶手绳?

B:Mr. Pilot, accommodation ladder and pilot ladder are rigged on the starboard side. Are manropes required?

A:是的,需要扶手绳。在引航员软梯处准备一根撇缆。

A:Yes, manropes are required. Have a heaving line ready at the pilot ladder.

B:撇缆准备好了,先生。

B:Heaving line is ready, Sir.

A:三副,在你船右舷做下风。

A:Third mate, make a lee on your starboard side.

B:是,先生。我将为你做下风。

B:Yes, sir. I will make a lee for you.

A:登船速度 6 节。

A:Make a boarding speed of 6 knots.

B:是,先生。登船速度会是 6 节。

B:Yes, sir. I will make a boarding speed of 6 knots.

B:引航员先生,可以登船了吗?

B:Mr. Pilot, is embarkation possible now?

A:是的,现在可以登船了。

A:Yes, embarkation is possible now.

6.4.3 句型操练

6.4.3 Sentence Pattern Drills

6.4.3.1 靠离泊

6.4.3.1 Berthing & Unberthing

(1)我们将左舷靠泊。

(1)We will berth port side alongside.

(2)我们将系浮筒。

(2)We will moor to dolphins.

(3)泊位上有碰垫吗?/是的,泊位上有碰垫。

(3)Are fenders on the berth? /Yes, fenders are on the berth.

(4)送出头缆。

(4)Send out the head lines.

(5)送出艏倒缆。

(5)Send out the springs forward.

(6)你们有自动调节缆车吗?/是的,我们船头有自动调节缆车。

(6)Do you have tension winches? Yes, we have tension winches forward.

(7)艏艉准备好撇缆。

(7)Have the heaving lines ready forward and aft.

(8)向岸上打出撇缆。

(8)Send the heaving line(s) ashore.

(9)用中间导缆孔/巴拿马导缆孔。

(9)Use the center lead/panama lead.

(10)停止绞缆。

(10)Stop heaving.

(11)松艏倒缆。

(11)Slack away the forward spring.

(12)溜艉倒缆。

(12)Check the aft springs.

(13)报告船头/船尾到码头的距离。

(13) Report the forward/aft distance to the pier.
(14)艉部距离1号浮筒1.5米。
(14) The aft distance to No.1 Buoy is 1.5 meters.
(15)船舶就位。
(15) We are in position.
(16)船头船尾系牢。
(16) Make fast forward and aft.
(17)备车。
(17) Stand by engines.
(18)我们将在20分钟内做好开航准备。
(18) We will be ready to get underway in 20 minutes.
(19)准备解缆。
(19) Stand by for letting go.
(20)单绑头缆和艏倒缆。
(20) Single up to the head line and forward spring.
(21)解开船头所有缆绳。
(21) Let go all forward.
(22)解开拖缆。
(22) Let go the towing line(s).

6.4.3.2 锚泊命令

6.4.3.2 Anchoring Orders

(1)备好左锚,准备抛锚。/备好双锚,准备抛锚。
(1) Stand by port anchor for letting go./Stand by both anchors for letting go.
(2)我们将抛左/右锚。
(2) We will let go port/starboard anchor.
(3)3节锚链入水。
(3) Put 3 shackles in the water.
(4)抛右锚。
(4) Let go starboard anchor.
(5)锚链什么方向?
(5) How is the cable leading?
(6)锚链向左/右。
(6) The cable is leading to port/starboard.
(7)锚链包绕船头。
(7) The cable is round the bow.
(8)锚链垂直。

(8)The cable is up and down.
(9)锚抓牢了吗？/是的,已经抓牢。
(9)Is she brought up? /Yes, she is brought up.
(10)打开锚灯。
(10)Switch on the anchor light(s).
(11)升锚球。
(11)Hoist the anchor ball.
(12)测方位检查锚位。
(12)Check the anchor position by bearings.
(13)驾驶台,通知机舱送锚链水。
(13)Bridge, ask the engine room for water.
(14)准备绞锚。
(14)Stand by for heaving up.
(15)合上锚机离合。/锚机离合已合上。
(15)Put the windlass in gear./The windlass is in gear.
(16)绞双锚链。
(16)Heave up both cable(s).
(17)停止绞锚。/已停止。
(17)Stop heaving./Heaving stopped.
(18)锚离底。
(18)The anchor is aweigh.
(19)锚链清爽。
(19)The cables are clear.
(20)锚清爽海底/水面。
(20)The anchor is clear of bottom/water.
(21)锚缠绞。
(21)The anchor is foul.
(22)锚已固定。
(22)The anchor is secured.

6.4.3.3 拖船协助

6.4.3.3 Tug Assistance

(1)向拖船送撇缆。
(1)Send heaving lines to the tugs.
(2)把拖船系在左舷船头。
(2)Make fast the tugs on port bow.
(3)拖船系在了右舷船头。

(3)The tug is fast on starboard bow.

(4)远离拖带缆绳。

(4)Keep clear of towing line(s).

(5)准备解拖船。

(5)Stand by for letting go the tug(s).

(6)解开拖船。

(6)Let go the tug(s).

6.4.4　标准船舶口令

6.4.4　Standard Orders on Board Vessel

6.4.4.1　标准舵令

6.4.4.1　Standard Wheel Orders

(1)舵工应当复诵所有下达的舵令,值班驾驶员应当保证舵令被立即正确执行。所有舵令在撤销前应当执行。如果船舶对舵没有反应,舵工应当立即报告。

(1)All wheel orders given should be repeated by the helmsman and the officer of the watch should ensure that they are carried out correctly and immediately. All wheel orders should be held until countermanded. The helmsman should report immediately if the vessel does not answer the wheel.

(2)如果注意到舵工精力不集中,应当向他提问:"什么航向?"他应当回答:"航向……度。"

这是提醒舵工注意操舵。

(2)When there is concern that the helmsman is inattentive he should be questioned:"What is your course?" And he should respond:"My course ...... degrees."

This is a reminder to the helmsman to mind your helm.

(3)舵令和含义

(3)Orders and Meanings

①正舵:将舵转到船首尾位置。

①Midships:Rudder to be held in the fore and aft position.

②左舵 5/10/15/20/25:将舵转到左舵 5°/10°/15°/20°/25°。

②Port five/ten/fifteen/twenty/twenty-five:5°/10°/15°/20°/25°of port rudder to be held.

③左满舵:将舵向左转到头。

③Hard-a-port:Rudder to be held fully over to port.

④右舵 5/10/15/20/25:将舵转到右舵 5°/10°/15°/20°/25°。

④Starboard five/ten/fifteen/twenty/twentyfive:5°/10°/15°/20°/25° of starboard rudder to be held.

⑤右满舵:将舵向右转到头。

⑤Hard-a-starboard:Rudder to be held fully over to starboard.

⑥回舵到 5/10/15/20:减小舵角到 5°/10°/15°/20°并把定。

⑥Ease to five/ten/fifteen/twenty:Reduce amount of rudder to 5°/10°/15°/20°and hold.

⑦把定:尽快减小摆动。

⑦Steady:Reduce swing as rapidly as possible.

⑧照直走:操舵使船舶稳定在下舵令时罗经指示的船首向。舵工必须复诵舵令并当接收到该舵令时报出罗经船首向。当船稳定在该航向时,舵工必须大声报告“把定在……度”。

⑧Steady as she goes:Steer a steady course on the compass heading indicated at the time of the order. The helmsman is to repeat the order and call out the compass heading on receiving the order. When the ship is steady on that heading, the helmsman is to call out “Steady on ……”.

⑨把浮标/标志/立标放在……左/右舷。

⑨Keep buoy/mark/beacon……on port side/starboard side.

⑩如果舵无反应,立即报告。

⑩Report if she does not answer wheel.

⑪完舵。

⑪Finished with wheel.

(4)当值班驾驶员要求操某一罗经航向时,他应当先说舵轮转动的方向接着逐个说出每个数字,包括零数字,例如“左舵,航向 182°”“右舵,航向 082°”。

(4)When the officer of the watch requires a course to be steered by compass, the direction in which she/he wants the wheel turned should be stated followed by each numeral being said separately, including zero, for example:“Port, steer one eight two”“Starboard, steer zero eight two”.

如果要对着某一选定的物标航向,应给舵工下舵令:

“对着……浮标/……标志/……立标走。”

下舵令的人对舵工的回答应当予以确认。

If it is desired to steer on a selected mark the helmsman should be ordered to:

“Steer on……buoy/……mark/……beacon.”

The person giving the order should acknowledge the helmsman's reply.

6.4.4.2 标准车钟令

6.4.4.2 Standard Engine Orders

(1)车钟令应当由操纵车钟的人复诵,值班驾驶员应当保证命令被立即正确地执行。

(1)Any engine order given should be repeated by the person operating the bridge telegraph(s) and the officer of the watch should ensure the order is carried out correctly and immediately.

(2)命令和含义。

(2)Orders and meanings.

①前进三(全速前进):向前推进的最大主机转数。

①Full ahead: Maximum maneuvering engine revolutions for ahead propulsion.

②前进二(半速前进):按命令指示的转数。

②Half ahead: Revolutions as indicated in ship's orders.

③前进一(慢速前进):按命令指示的转数。

③Slow ahead: Revolutions as indicated in ship's orders.

④微速前进:按命令指示的转数。

④Dead slow ahead: Revolutions as indicated in ship's orders.

⑤停车:主机停转。

⑤Stop engine(s): No engine revolutions.

⑥微速后退:按命令指示的转数。

⑥Dead slow astern: Revolutions as indicated in ship's orders.

⑦后退一(慢速后退):按命令指示的转数。

⑦Slow astern: Revolutions as indicated in ship's orders.

⑧后退二(半速后退):按命令指示的转数。

⑧Half astern: Revolutions as indicated in ship's orders.

⑨后退三(全速后退):按命令指示的转数。

⑨Full astern: Revolutions as indicated in ship's orders.

⑩紧急全速前进/后退。

⑩Emergency full ahead/astern.

⑪备车:机舱人员完全做好操纵准备,驾驶台要下达车钟令。

⑪Stand by engine: Engine-room personnel fully ready to maneuver and bridge manned to relay engine orders.

⑫完车:不再需要主机运转。

⑫Finished with engine(s): Movement of engine(s) no longer required.

(3)如果船舶配备有双推进器,影响双车的车钟令前应当加上"双"字,例如"双车前进三""双车后退一",例外的情况是使用"双车停"。当要独立操纵两个推进器时,应当指明,例如"右车前进三""左车后退二"等。

(3) In vessels fitted with twin propellers, the word "both" should be added to all orders affecting both shafts, e.g., "Full ahead both" "Slow astern both", except that the words "Stop all engines" should be used, when appropriate. When required to maneuver twin propellers independently, this should be indicated, i.e. "full ahead starboard" "half astern port", etc.

(4)当使用船首侧推器时,使用以下命令:

(4) Where bow thrusters are used, the following orders are used:

①艏推全速/半速向左/右:船首在侧推作用下向左/右转动。

①Bow thrust full/half to port/starboard side: Ship's head to move to port/starboard with power as specified.

②艉推全速/半速向左/右:船尾在侧推作用下向左/右转动。

②Stern thrust full/half to port/starboard side: Ship's stern to move to port/starboard with

power as specified.

③艏(艉)侧推停车。

③Bow (stern) thrust stop.

(5)对配备有可调螺距推进器的船舶,车钟令的含义包括命令中螺距和转数的组合。

(5) For vessels with variable pitch propellers, the meaning of the order would include the combination of pitch and revolutions as indicated in ship's orders.

6.4.4.3 系/解缆令

6.4.4.3 Mooring/Unmooring Orders

(1)单绑;

(1)Single up;

(2)船尾缆全部解掉;

(2)All let go aft;

(3)……缆解掉;

(3)Let go……line;

(4)船尾全部清爽;

(4)All clear aft;

(5)带……缆;

(5)Send out……line;

(6)……缆上车(绞缆机滚筒);

(6)Put……line on winch (or capstan windlass);

(7)……缆上桩;

(7)Put……line on bitts;

(8)停绞;

(8)Stop heaving (or avast heaving);

(9)……缆放松;

(9)Slack away……line;

(10)准备绞……缆;

(10)Stand by to heave……line;

(11)……缆收紧;

(11)Take in the slack on……line;

(12)绞……缆;

(12)Heave away……line;

(13)挽牢;

(13)Make fast;

(14)放松一点;

(14)Slack a little;

(15)向前(后)移……米;
(15)Shift (or move)ahead (or astern)……meter(s);
(16)刹住(或拉住);
(16)Hold on;
(17)就位;
(17)In position;
(18)溜一溜……缆。
(18)Check……line.

6.4.4.4 标准锚泊令
6.4.4.4 Standard Anchor Order

(1)准备绞(起)锚。
(1)Stand by (to) heave away anchor.
(2)准备左(右或双)锚。
(2)Stand by port (starboard or both) anchor(s).
(3)抛(左或右)锚。
(3)Let go (port or starboard) anchor.
(4)刹住。
(4)Hold on.
(5)停止绞锚。
(5)Stop heaving or avast heaving.
(6)锚链方向如何?
(6)How is chain leading?
(7)放松锚链。
(7)Slack away chain.
(8)*X* 节锚链下水(甲板或锚链筒)。
(8)*X* shackles in water (on deck or hawse pipe).

6.5 应急状况的工作表达和命令

6.5 Working Expressions and Orders in Emergency

6.5.1 课前准备

6.5.1 Warming Up

随着国际安全管理体系的建立,船上所有应急状况都已能够实现调查并形成后续的文件备案。这也为船长在发生海上紧急事故时做出决定提供了指南。国际安全管理体系也整合了在这个理想和法律均想建立绿色环境的时代所必须具备的岸基支持。

With the establishment of the International Safety Management (ISM) system all shipboard emergencies have been investigated and subsequently documented. This action has provided ship's masters with guidelines to support his/her decision-making in the event of a real-time emergency at sea. The system has also incorporated the shore side back-up support, deemed necessary in the age of the desired and legally required green environment.

《SOLAS 公约》修正案及其决议希望船舶能配备合适的、和谐的"应急计划"以为众多船舶应急状况下的行动提供指导。这些应急状况的例子如下,包括但不限于:

Amendments and Resolutions to the SOLAS Convention now expect vessels to carry appropriate harmonized "Emergency Plans" to provide guidelines for shipboard contingency planning for various types of emergency. Typical examples of such emergencies are as follows, but should not be limited to:

(1)火灾;

(1) Fire;

(2)船舶损坏;

(2) Damage to the ship;

(3)污染;

(3) Pollution;

(4)威胁到船舶及其旅客和船员的违法行为;

(4) Unlawful acts threatening the safety of the ship and the security of its passengers and crew;

(5)货物相关的事故;

(5) Cargo related accidents;

(6)个人事故;

(6) Personnel accidents;

(7) 对他船的紧急救助。

(7) Emergency assistance to other vessels.

6.5.2 对话练习

6.5.2 Dialogue Practice

对话 1

Dialogue 1

A:机动船蓝鲸号,驾驶台呼叫驾驶员。旋出 1 号救生艇并报告。完毕。

A:MV Blue Whale, Bridge to Mate. Swing out Lifeboat No.1 and report. Over.

B:机动船蓝鲸号,驾驶员呼叫驾驶台。1 号救生艇旋出,船长。

B:MV Blue Whale, Mate to Bridge. Lifeboat No.1 swung out, sir.

A:机动船蓝鲸号,驾驶台呼叫驾驶员。降下 1 号救生艇靠在登艇甲板并报告。完毕。

A:MV Blue Whale, Bridge to Mate. Lower Lifeboat No.1 alongside the embarkation deck and report. Over.

B:机动船蓝鲸号,驾驶员呼叫驾驶台。1 号救生艇靠在登艇甲板,船长。

B:MV Blue Whale, Mate to Bridge. Lifeboat No.1 is alongside the embarkation deck, Sir.

A:机动船蓝鲸号,驾驶台呼叫驾驶员。经由登乘梯进入救生艇。完毕。

A:MV Blue Whale, Bridge to Mate. Enter the lifeboat via ladders. Over.

B:机动船蓝鲸号,驾驶员呼叫驾驶台。已进入 1 号救生艇。完毕。

B:MV Blue Whale, Mate to Bridge. Lifeboat No.1 entered. Over.

A:机动船蓝鲸号,驾驶台呼叫驾驶员。通知海岸无线电台每一救生艇的船员数量并报告。完毕。

A:MV Blue Whale, Bridge to Mate. Inform coast radio stations of the number of crewmembers in each lifeboat and report. Over.

B:机动船蓝鲸号,驾驶员呼叫驾驶台。已通知海岸无线电台。完毕。

B:MV Blue Whale, Mate to Bridge. Coast radio stations informed. Over.

A:机动船蓝鲸号,驾驶台呼叫驾驶员。让清大船并报告。完毕。

A:MV Blue Whale, Bridge to Mate. Stand clear of the vessel and report. Over.

B:机动船蓝鲸号,驾驶员呼叫驾驶台。1 号救生艇让清大船。完毕。

B:MV Blue Whale, Mate to Bridge. Lifeboat No.1 standing clear of the vessel now. Over.

A:机动船蓝鲸号,驾驶员呼叫船长。应急艇船员已集合。完毕。

A:MV Blue Whale, Mate to Captain. Emergency boat crew mustered. Over.

B:机动船蓝鲸号,驾驶台呼叫驾驶员。有人从右舷落水,准备降下救助艇。完毕。

B:MV Blue Whale, Bridge to Mate. We' ve got a man overboard on the starboard side. Prepare to lower the rescue boat. Over.

A:机动船蓝鲸号,驾驶员呼叫船长。救助艇准备降下,先生。

A:MV Blue Whale, Mate to Captain. Rescue boat ready for lowering, Sir.

B:机动船蓝鲸号,驾驶台呼叫驾驶员。明白。降下救助艇。完毕。

B:MV Blue Whale, Bridge to Mate. Understood. Lower the rescue boat. Over.

A:机动船蓝鲸号,驾驶员呼叫船长。降下救助艇,先生。救助艇让清吊索并驶离。完毕。

A:MV Blue Whale, Mate to Captain. Lower the rescue boat, Sir. Rescue boat clear of falls and away, Sir. Over.

B:机动船蓝鲸号,驾驶台呼叫驾驶员。明白。救助艇让清吊索并驶离。请持续通知我。完毕。

B:MV Blue Whale, Bridge to Mate. Understood. Rescue boat clear of falls and away. Keep me advised. Over.

A:机动船蓝鲸号,驾驶员呼叫船长。我持续通知你。完毕。

A:MV Blue Whale, Mate to Captain. I will keep you advised. Over.

对话 2

Dialogue 2

A:你能告诉我救生筏是什么吗?

A:Would you please tell me what liferaft is?

B:救生筏是一种提供紧急运输,使人员远离下沉或危险船舶的安全设备。

B:It is one of safety equipment used to provide emergency transportation to get people away from a sinking or endangered vessel.

A:但我们的船舶已配备了救生艇。

A:But our vessel has already been equipped with lifeboats.

B:救生筏很轻并且便于操作。

B:The raft is very light and can be handled very easily and conveniently.

A:哦,我认为它容易在海上正浮。

A:Oh, but I' m afraid it' s liable to turn upside down at sea.

B:正确。这就是平衡水袋和海锚连接于救生筏的原因。海锚也用来使救生筏偏离袭来的海浪。

B:Exactly. That' s why water pockets and sea anchor are attached to it. The sea anchor also serves to turn the raft away from oncoming waves.

A:那么救生筏是如何操作的?看起来绑定得很紧。

A:Then how does liferaft work? It looks likely to be bound tightly.

B:静水压力释放器将辅助救生筏自动释放而不需要人为干预。

B:Hydraulic Release Unit will help to release the liferaft automatically without any human interference.

A:我明白啦。

A:I see.

B:你同样也可以手动释放。

B:You can also manually release it.

A:那该如何操作?

A:Then how?

B:找到并释放手动脱钩,然后将救生筏扔向水中,拖住系艇索直到其胀开。

B:Locate and release manual slip hook, then throw liferaft into water, tug on the painter until it inflates.

A:听起来不是很困难。

A:It sounds not so difficult.

对话 3

Dialogue 3

A:有人知道在海上如何求生吗?

A:Is there anyone know how for survival at sea?

B:当然。这取决于你使用救生设备的知识和能力,你处理所面临危险的专业技能和求生欲望。

B:Of course. It depends upon your knowledge and ability to use the survival equipment available, your special skill to be applied to cope with the hazards you face and your will to live on.

A:但是如何获得所有这些知识呢?

A:But how to get all this knowledge?

B:当上船时,试着弄清楚救生设备和装置是什么,在哪里存放,以及包括什么。

B:When boarding a ship, try to find out what survival equipment and appliances are, where they are stowed, and what they include.

A:我明白了。那么求生技能是什么?

A:I see. Then what are the survival skills?

B:这些技能可能包括救生衣的正确穿着,防止晕船和体温过低,合理的水与粮食的配给等。

B:Those skills may include correct donning of jacket, protection against seasickness and hypothermia, good ration of water and food, etc.

A:如何形成求生心态?

A:How to develop the survival mindset?

B:有特定的策略和精神工具能够帮助人员更好地应对求生环境。

B:There are certain strategies and mental tools that can help people cope better in a survival situation.

A:你能告诉我一些细节吗?

A:Can you tell me some details?

B:首先,保持其简单化,意思是识别最需要做什么,然后每次进行简单的一步。

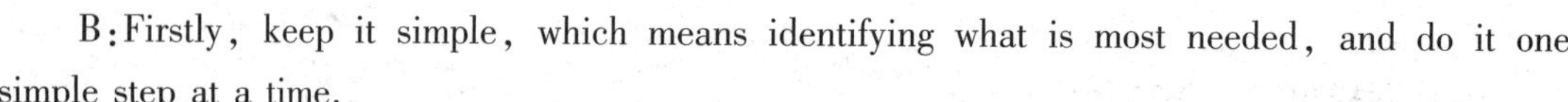

B:Firstly, keep it simple, which means identifying what is most needed, and do it one simple step at a time.

A:这样能帮助保持注意力并且不用担心将来。

A:This helps to keep focused and not to worry about the future.

B:是的。第二点,有 B 计划可用。

B:Yes. Secondly, have a plan B available.

A:这意味着多种选择可能是安全出路。

A:It means the alternative that may be our way to safety.

B:十分正确。下一步就是指挥你的船舶。你对自己的生命以及发生的状况负责。

B:You are quite right. The next is to captain your own ship. You are responsible for taking control of your life and what happens to it.

A:还有吗?

A:And what's more?

B:注意节制。最好屈尊忍耐并承认已经发生的事情。

B:Beware of denial. It's best to put our pride in our pocket and admit what has happened.

6.5.3 句型操练
6.5.3 Sentence Pattern Drills

6.5.3.1 堵漏
6.5.3.1 Damage Control

(1)水密门将在 2 分钟内可用。

(1)Watertight door control will be operational in 2 minutes.

(2)应急发电机可用。

(2)Emergency generator is operational.

(3)所有堵漏设备完整可用。

(3)All damage control equipment is complete and available.

(4)堵漏队已经人员齐整集合待命。

(4)Damage control team stand complete and mustered.

(5)堵漏材料可用。

(5)Damage control material available.

(6)机舱内水密门手动关闭。

(6)Watertight doors in the engine room closed by hand.

(7)污水泵已开启。

(7)Bilge pumps are switched on.

(8)在步话机上保持无线电联系。

(8) Maintain radio contact on walkie-talkie.
(9)堵漏队必须穿着防护服。
(9) Damage control team must have protective clothing.
(10)从内部堵漏不能实现。
(10) Stopping flooding from inside not possible.

6.5.3.2　火灾、爆炸
6.5.3.2　Fire, Explosion

(1)机动船 Seagull 轮机舱/货舱/上层建筑/生活区着火。
(1) MV Seagull is on fire in engine-room/holds/superstructure/accommodation.
(2)危险品着火了吗?/是的,危险品着火了。
(2) Are dangerous goods on fire?/Yes, dangerous goods on fire.
(3)有爆炸危险吗?/是的,有爆炸危险。/不,没有爆炸危险。
(3) Is danger of explosion?/Yes, danger of explosion./No, no danger of explosion.
(4)所有便携式灭火器可用。
(4) All portable extinguishers are operational.
(5)二氧化碳已经完全释放。
(5) The carbon dioxide has been fully released.
(6)准备好应急消防泵并报告。/应急消防泵已准备就绪。
(6) Stand by emergency fire pumps and report./Emergency fire pumps standing by.
(7)检查消防员装备并报告。/消防员装备完整且可用。
(7) Check the firemen's outfits and report./Firemen's outfit operational and complete.
(8)探测火灾的确切位置。/火灾位于厨房/生活区/物料间。
(8) Detect the exact location of the fire./Fire is in the galley/accommodation/stores.

6.5.3.3　进水
6.5.3.3　Flooding

(1)机动船 Blue Pearl 轮水线以下渗水。
(1) MV Blue Pearl has leak below water line.
(2)进水已经被控制了吗?/进水已经被控制。
(2) Is flooding under control?/Flooding under control.
(3)堵漏队正在堵漏。
(3) Damage control teams are fighting the flooding.
(4)布置堵漏值班并报告。
(4) Post damage control watch and report.
(5)水面上升很快。

(5) The water level rises fast.

(6)我们已经启动1号海水泵进行排水。

(6) We have started No.1 seawater pump to drain water.

(7)污水泵保持准备状态。

(7) Bilge pumps remain on standby.

(8)5号货舱有一个大洞。

(8) There is a big hole in No.5 hold.

(9)3号货舱有一条裂纹。

(9) There is a crack in No.3 hold.

(10)我们将检查机舱水位。

(10) We will check the water levels in engine room.

6.5.3.4 碰撞

6.5.3.4 Collision

(1)机动船 Glory 轮和机动船 Breeze 轮/不明船舶/物标/一条灯船/冰山……发生了碰撞。

(1) MV Glory has collided with MV Breeze/unknown vessel/object/a light vessel/iceberg……

(2)机动船 Glory 轮仅能慢速前进。

(2) MV Glory can only proceed at slow speed.

(3)机动船 Glory 轮需要两艘拖船。

(3) MV Glory requires 2 tugs.

(4)检查受损程度。

(4) Check the extent of the damage.

(5)对所有压载舱和燃油舱进行测深。

(5) Sound all ballast and fuel oil tanks.

6.5.3.5 搁浅

6.5.3.5 Grounding

(1)机动船 Flying Fish 轮在 01°00′N,132°00′E 位置搁浅。

(1) MV Flying Fish is aground in position 01°00′N, 132°00′E.

(2)机动船 Flying Fish 轮船头/船尾/船中搁浅。

(2) MV Flying Fish is aground forward/aft/in the middle.

(3)机动船 Flying Fish 轮将抛货以脱浅。

(3) MV Flying Fish will jettison cargo to refloat.

(4)机动船 Flying Fish 轮将在 03°00′N,134°00′E 位置处抢滩。

(4)MV Flying Fish will beach in position 03°00′N,134°00′E.

6.5.3.6 倾覆危险
6.5.3.6 List-danger of Capsizing

(1)机动船 Sky 轮向左舷/右舷横倾严重。
(1)MV Sky has heavy list to port side/starboard side.
(2)机动船 Sky 轮有倾覆危险。
(2)MV Sky is in danger of capsizing.
(3)机动船 Sky 轮抛货以控制横倾。
(3)MV Sky jettisoned cargo to stop listing.

6.5.3.7 沉没
6.5.3.7 Sinking

(1)机动船 Courage 轮碰撞之后在 18°00′S, 109°15′E 位置处沉没。
(1)MV Courage is sinking in position 18°00′S, 109°15′E after collision.
(2)机动船 Courage 轮在搁浅进水爆炸后沉没。
(2)MV Courage sinking after grounding flooding explosion.
(3)机动船 Hope 轮正驶往你处援助。
(3)MV Hope proceeds to your assistance.
(4)机动船 Hope 轮预计在 2 小时内/协调世界时 1430 抵达你处。
(4)MV Hope expects to reach you within 2 hours/at 1430 UTC.

6.5.3.8 失控和漂航
6.5.3.8 Disabled and Adrift

(1)机动船 Utopia 轮在 18°00′S, 109°15′E 位置处失控。
(1)MV Utopia is not under command in position 18°00′S, 109°15′E.
(2)机动船 Utopia 轮正以 5 节速度向 135°方向漂航。
(2)MV Utopia drifting at 5 knots to 135 degrees.
(3)机动船 Utopia 轮需要拖船援助。
(3)MV Utopia requires tug assistance.

6.5.3.9 弃船
6.5.3.9 Abandoning Vessel

(1)我们必须要弃船了。

(1) We have to abandon our ship.

(2) 在落放的过程中要抓紧你座位上的绳索。

(2) Hold on to ropes on your seat when launching.

(3) 跟随救生艇员到登乘甲板的救生艇站去。

(3) Follow lifeboat men to lifeboat stations on embarkation deck.

(4) 操作救生艇主机并报告。

(4) Operate lifeboat engines and report.

(5) 穿好救生衣。

(5) Don your lifejacket.

第 7 章　日常生活用语

Chapter 7 | Daily Common Expressions

◇◆ 7.1　交通用语

7.1　Traffic Expressions

7.1.1　课前准备

7.1.1　Warming Up

船舶挂靠外国港口时,移民局官员会登船进行检查。船长应该准备好海员护照,海员证和两份船员名单。移民局官员通常会要求船长在大厅集合所有船员进行检查。检查后,移民局官员会给你一份登陆证申请表格,填好表格并签名后,移民局官员会给船员签发登陆证。另外,如果船上有乘客,移民局官员会要求乘客名单,一式两份,其中一份盖章后,返回给船长。

When the ship calls at a foreign port, the immigration officers will come on board for inspection. The master should get seafarers' passports, seaman's books and two copies of crew list ready. The immigration officer usually require master to muster all crew in the saloon for the inspection. After inspection, the immigration officers will give you the application form for shore pass. When you fill in the form and sign it, the immigration officers will issue shore passes for the crew. Moreover, the immigration officers require a passenger list in duplicate if any on board, one of these shall be returned to the master after stamping.

请注意,没有携带登陆证和护照的人员不允许上岸。任何人必须遵守登陆证背面印刷的当地法规,外国海员不允许携带相机上岸。在离港前,应将登陆证返回给移民局。在登陆证背面有张地图,你可以很容易找到购物中心、超市、海员俱乐部、银行、博物馆、戏剧院、电影院、书店、饭店和酒吧。

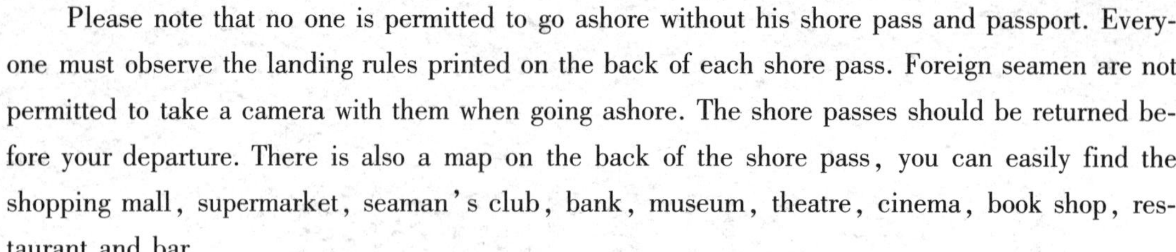

Please note that no one is permitted to go ashore without his shore pass and passport. Everyone must observe the landing rules printed on the back of each shore pass. Foreign seamen are not permitted to take a camera with them when going ashore. The shore passes should be returned before your departure. There is also a map on the back of the shore pass, you can easily find the shopping mall, supermarket, seaman's club, bank, museum, theatre, cinema, book shop, restaurant and bar.

7.1.2 对话练习

7.1.2 Dialogue Practice

对话 1

Dialogue 1

A：打扰一下，请问你能告诉我怎么去伦敦吗？

A：Excuse me. Could you please tell me the way to London?

B：当然。你应该在"National Station"这一站乘地铁去。

B：OK. You should take metro at National Station.

A：但是地铁站在哪？

A：But how can we find the station.

B：直走在第二个交叉口左转，再沿着街道直走，地铁站就在你的正前方，你不会错过的。

B：Go ahead and turn left at the second crossing. Go along the street and station is right in front of you. You won't miss it.

A：谢谢。顺便问一下，在乘坐地铁的时候需要换乘吗？

A：Thank you. By the way, do we have to change anywhere by metro?

B：不需要。记得在"Longchamp Avenues"这一站下车就行。

B：Not necessary. Just remember to get off when you arrive at Longchamp Avenues.

A：还有其他方式去哪吗？

A：Is there any other way to get there?

B：当然最简单的方式是乘坐出租车，但是更贵。

B：the simplest way is by taxi, of course. But it's much more expensive.

A：我还是乘坐地铁吧，非常感谢。

A：I will take the metro. Thank you very much.

B：不用谢。

B：You are welcome.

对话 2

Dialogue 2

A：打扰一下，我想上"蓝鲸"号船舶。服务艇什么时候离开？

A:Excuse me, we want to board Motor Vessel Blue Whale. When dose the service boat leave?

B:海事1号艇下午1点离开,它在那边。

B:Maine No.1 leaves at 1 PM. She is over there.

A:谢谢。顺便问一下,我想买些点心,附近有商店吗?

A:Thank you. By the way, I'd like to buy some snack. Is there a shop around here?

B:沿着这条街往下走有个便利店。

B:There is a convenience store further down the street.

A:怎么走呢?

A:How can I get there?

B:从那儿出去,拐角处左拐,然后直走大约200米,便利店就在你的右边。

B:Well, go out there, turn left at the corner, and then go straight for about 200 meters. You'll find it on your right.

A:非常感谢。

A:Thank you very much.

B:不用谢,记得不要错过服务艇。

B:That's all right. Be sure not to miss the service boat.

对话3

Dialogue 3

A:打扰一下,请问邮局在哪?

A:Excuse me, where is the post office, please?

B:邮局?离这里很远啊。

B:Post office? It's very far from here.

A:我怎么到那儿呢?

A:How can I get there?

B:你可以乘坐公交车。

B:You can take the bus.

A:乘坐哪路公交车呢?

A:What bus can I take?

B:3路公交。

B:No.3 bus.

A:非常感谢。顺便问一下,公交车站在哪儿?

A:Thank you. By the way, where is the bus stop?

B:你沿着这条路一直走到第一个交通灯,然后右拐,再沿着公路直走大约500米,车站在你右边。

B:You can walk this way till the first traffic light, then turn right and go along the road for about 500 meters. You will find it on your right.

A：非常感谢。

A：Thank you very much.

B：不用谢。

B：You are welcome.

7.1.3 句型操练
7.1.3 Sentence Pattern Drills

(1)打扰一下，附近有酒吧吗？

(1)Excuse me, is there any pub around?

(2)当然，穿过这条街道就是。

(2)Yes, just across the street.

(3)打扰一下，请问邮局在哪？

(3)Excuse me, where is the post office, please?

(4)离这儿不远。

(4)It's not far from here.

(5)从这儿到这个地址有多远？

(5)How far is this address from here?

(6)很近。沿着这条街道往下走然后左拐。

(6)Oh, it's quite near here. Go down the street and turn left.

(7)请问花园酒店在哪？

(7)Where is Garden Hotel, please?

(8)走路太远了，你最好乘公交车。

(8)It's too far to walk. You'd better take a bus.

(9)打扰一下，到中国领事馆怎么走？

(9)Excuse me, how can I get to Chinese Consulate?

(10)恐怕你走错方向了。

(10)I'm afraid you are going the wrong direction.

(11)到港口在哪换乘？

(11)Where should I change for the harbour?

(12)在第四站下车。

(12)Get off at the fourth stop.

(13)请问，你能告诉我到"Blossom Peach"怎么走吗？

(13)Can you tell me the way to Blossom Peach, please?

(14)当然。向北走，出了这个区，然后通过酒店、医院和"Santy"村庄，一直到穿过那座小桥。

(14)Sure. Go north out of town. Continue past the hotel, the hospital and the village of Santy, until crossing the small bridge.

(15)现在看一下地图,从铁路站开始,沿着"Orange"街道向下,在第三个路口右转,然后再走两个街区。

(15) Now look at the map. Start at the railway station. Go down Orange Street. Take the third turning on the right then go two blocks.

(16)打扰一下,怎么去最近的纪念品商店?

(16) Excuse me, how can I get to the nearest souvenir shop?

(17)一直向前走,在第二个路口向右转。商店就在你前面。

(17) Go straight ahead and turn right at the second crossing. The shop is just in front of you.

(18)你要去哪,先生?

(18) Where will you go, sir?

(19)第126号"Smithdown"路。

(19) No.126 Smithdown Road, please.

(20)我要在10点之前到达机场,你能做到吗?

(20) I need to get to the airport before 10 clock. Can you make it?

(21)我不能保证,但是我会尽力的。

(21) I can't promise, but I'll do my best.

7.1.4 词汇
7.1.4 Words and Expressions

harbour	[ˈhɑːbə]	*n.*	海港
port	[pɔːt]	*n.*	港口
bank	[bæŋk]	*n.*	银行
post office			邮局
shopping center			购物中心
pub	[pʌb]	*n.*	酒吧
bar	[bɑː(r)]	*n.*	酒吧
airport	[ˈeəpɔːt]	*n.*	机场
hotel	[həʊˈtel]	*n.*	酒店,旅馆
embassy	[ˈembəsi]	*n.*	大使馆
consulate	[ˈkɒnsjələt]	*n.*	领事,领事馆
address	[əˈdres]	*n.*	地址
anchorage	[ˈæŋkərɪdʒ]	*n.*	锚地
avenue	[ˈævənjuː]	*n.*	林荫道,大街,路
bakery	[ˈbeɪkəri]	*n.*	面包店
berth	[bɜːθ]	*n.*	泊位

cinema	[ˈsɪnəmə]	*n.*	电影院
church	[tʃɜːtʃ]	*n.*	教堂
gallery	[ˈgæləri]	*n.*	画廊
museum	[mjuˈziːəm]	*n.*	博物馆
railway station			火车站
supermarket	[ˈsuːpəmɑːkɪt]	*n.*	超级市场
traffic light			交通信号灯
underground	[ˌʌndəˈgraʊnd]	*adj.*	地下的
tube	[tjuːb]	*n.*	地铁
subway	[ˈsʌbweɪ]	*n.*	地铁,地下通道
wharf	[wɔːf]	*n.*	码头
pier	[pɪə(r)]	*n.*	码头

7.2 海关用语

7.2 Custom Expressions

7.2.1 课前准备

7.2.1 Warming Up

海关官员的主要职责是检查船上的文件,例如海关申报表格、船员名单、船员个人物品清单、库存和伙食清单、进口货物舱单、上一港口清关单等。为避免海员走私,海关官员通常会将烟酒库封起来。没有海关官员在场,海员绝不能解封烟酒库,直到开航前海关官员解封。

The main duties of the custom officers are to check the documents on board, such as the Customs Declaration Form, Crew Lists, Crew Personal Articles Lists, Stores and Provisions List, the Import Cargo Manifest, Last Port Clearance and so on. To avoid seafarers smuggling, the custom officers usually seal the ship's bonded store. The seafarers can never unseal the store without custom officers on the spot until the custom officers unseal it before sailing.

海关官员登船前,船长应该准备好所有必要的文件和表格,并告知船员海关检查规则。贵重物品必须申报,否则将被视为走私物品。

Before customs officers come on board, the captain should get all necessary documents and forms ready and inform the crew about the customs regulations. Valuable possessions must be declared, otherwise, they will be regarded as smuggled goods.

7.2.2　对话练习

7.2.2　Dialogue Practice

对话 1

Dialogue 1

A：你已经办好海关手续吗？

A：Have you gone through the customs formalities?

B：还没有，我们正在办理。

B：Not yet. We are just going to do it.

A：你把进口舱单准备好了吗？

A：Do you have the import manifest ready?

B：当然，给你。

B：Yes, of course. Here you are.

A：所有的货物都在这个港口卸吗？

A：Are all the cargo to be discharged in this port?

B：不，这里卸大约三分之二，剩下的在宁波港卸。

B：No. About two-thirds are to be landed here, and the rest at Ningbo Port.

A：请填写一下这些海关申报单，好吗？

A：Could you please fill out this customs declaration?

B：当然，我会让管事现在就填。

B：Sure. I'll ask my purser to do that right now.

A：船上有麻醉药吗？

A：Do you have any narcotic on board?

B：有，船上有 50 克吗啡。我已经把麻醉药清单插入到这个表格中了，可以吗？

B：Yes, we have 50 grams of morphine. I have inserted a list of narcotics on this form. Is that OK?

A：可以，这样就行。

A：Yes. That's fine.

对话 2

Dialogue 2

A：船长，我们开始海关检查吧。

A：Captain, let's begin the customs inspection.

B：好的！

B：OK!

A：请出示一下进口货物舱单？

A:Please show me the Import Cargo Manifest.

B:好的,给你。

B:Yes, here you are.

A:在这个港口,你准备如何处理你船上的货物呢?

A:How are you going to deal with your cargo in this port?

B:我们准备在这一港卸大约三分之一的货物,剩下的将在后面的挂靠港上海和鹿特丹卸。

B:We're going to discharge about one-third of the cargo here, and the rest will be discharged in our next ports of call, Shanghai and Rotterdam.

A:你能填写一下海关申报单吗?

A:Could you please fill out the Custom Declaration?

B:我告诉二副立刻去做。

B:I'll tell my 2nd officer to do that right now.

A:你们船上有麻醉药吗?

A:Do you have any narcotic on board?

B:有,船上有 60 克吗啡。我已经把麻醉药清单插入到这个表格中了,可以吗?

B:Yes, we have 60 grams of morphine. I have inserted a list of narcotics on this form. Is that OK?

A:可以,这样就行。

A:Yes. That's fine.

对话 3

Dialogue 3

A:你从哪来?

A:Where are you from?

B:我来自中国。

B:I am from China.

A:你来这儿是做生意还是观光?

A:Are you here on business or for sightseeing?

B:做生意。

B:On business.

A:你身上有多少外币?

A:How much foreign currency have you got?

B:400 美元。

B:400 dollars.

A:请出示一下你的护照?

A:Your passport, please?

B:在这儿。

B:Here it is.

A:请把你的行李箱放在柜台上并打开。

A:Please put your trunk on the counter and open it.

B:好的,你看,所有东西都是我的私人物品。

B:OK. You see, all of them are my personal belongings.

A:你有什么东西要申报吗?

A:Have you anything to declare?

B:有,我有一小瓶香水要申报。

B:Yes, I've got a small bottle of perfume.

A:还有其他要申报的吗?

A:Anything else?

B:有,我用100美元买了一块手表,90美元买了一件新T恤。它们免税吗?

B:Yes, I've bought a watch at 100 dollars and a new shirt at 90 dollars. Are they duty-free?

A:你有100美元的免税额,T恤需要征税。

A:You are allowed 100 dollars duty-free, so the shirt is dutiable article.

B:税费是多少啊?

B:How much is the duty?

A:10美元。

A:It is 10 dollars.

7.2.3 句型操练

7.2.3 Sentence Pattern Drills

(1)你有要申报的物品吗?

(1)Do you have anything to declare?

(2)你有应交税的物品吗?

(2)Have you got anything dutiable?

(3)你有酒精或烟草类的物品吗?

(3)Have you got any alcohol or tobacco products?

(4)你带有被禁止的物品吗?

(4)Have you got anything prohibited?

(5)你有多少外币?

(5)How much foreign currency have you got?

(6)你来这儿是做生意还是观光啊?

(6)Are you here on business or for sightseeing?

(7)请出示一下你的护照?

(7)Show me your passport, please.

(8)请把它放在柜台上并打开?

(8)Please put it on the counter and open it.

(9)清关,请通过。

(9)Cleared.Pass on, please.

(10)这是应缴税的物品。

(10)This is dutiable article.

(11)税费是10美元。

(11)The duty is 10 dollars.

(12)税费是多少?

(12)How much is the duty?

(13)它是免税的吗?

(13)Is it duty-free?

(14)我可以带走我的东西吗?

(14)May I take my things away?

(15)我必须打开它吗?

(15)Must I open it?

(16)我没有携带被禁止的物品。

(16)I have nothing prohibited.

(17)我有一小瓶香水威士忌。

(17)I have a small bottle of perfume whiskey.

(18)它们都是要用的。

(18)All of them are for use.

(19)对不起,我们还没办好海关手续。可以推迟到今天下午吗?

(19)I am sorry we are not quite ready for the customs formalities. Is it possible to have them postponed to this afternoon?

(20)没有我们的人在现场的话,你不能打开任何封好的仓库。

(20)You can never unseal any sealed store without our people present on the spot.

(21)请填一下这个海关申报单。

(21)Please fill out this customs declaration.

(22)外国海员要在港门口左边的海关室申报自己的外币。

(22)Foreign seamen required to declare their foreign currency at the customs house on the left of the harbor gate.

(23)请告诉我每一件设备的尺寸和重量。

(23)Please inform me of the dimensions and weight of each piece of equipment.

(24)海关允许的香烟和酒精的额度是多少?

(24)What's the customs allowance of cigarettes and spirits?

(25)每人每天的允许额度是50支香烟和一瓶烈性酒。

(25)Its allowance is 50 cigarettes and a bottle of spirits for each person a day.

(26)有多少乘客在上一挂靠港上船?

(26) How many passengers did you take on at your last port of call?

(27)这是乘客名单的复印件,我们总共只有3名乘客,1名乘客入境,2名乘客过境。

(27) Here is a copy of passengers list for you. We have got only three passengers, one inward and two through.

7.2.4 词汇

7.2.4 Words and Expressions

custom	[ˈkʌstəm]	*n.*	海关
passport	[ˈpɑːspɔːt]	*n.*	护照
perfume	[ˈpɜːfjuːm]	*n.*	香水
foreign currency			外币
declare	[dɪˈkleə(r)]	*v.*	申报
business	[ˈbɪznəs]	*n.*	商业,生意
sightseeing	[ˈsaɪtsiːɪŋ]	*n.*	观光,游览
duty	[ˈdjuːti]	*n.*	税收,关税
dutiable	[ˈdjuːtɪəbl]	*adj.*	应纳税的
clear	[klɪə(r)]	*v.*	允许(入境、处境)
alcohol	[ˈælkəhɒl]	*n.*	酒精
tobacco	[təˈbækəʊ]	*n.*	烟草
counter	[ˈkaʊntə(r)]	*n.*	柜台
article	[ˈɑːtɪkl]	*n.*	物品,文章
duty-free	[ˈdjuːtɪˈfriː]	*adj.*	免税的
whisky	[ˈwɪski]	*n.*	威士忌酒
personal belongings			个人用品
customs formalities			海关手续
import	[ˈɪmpɔːt]	*n.*	进口商品
manifest	[ˈmænɪfest]	*n.*	舱单
narcotic	[nɑːˈkɒtɪk]	*n.*	麻醉剂,镇定药
purser	[ˈpɜːsə(r)]	*n.*	管事,事务长
gram	[græm]	*n.*	克
morphine	[ˈmɔːfiːn]	*n.*	吗啡
insert	[ɪnˈsɜːt]	*v.*	插入,嵌入
postpone	[pəˈspəʊn]	*v.*	推迟,延缓
unseal	[ˈʌnˈsiːl]	*v.*	开封
spot	[spɒt]	*n.*	地点,现场

dimension	[daɪˈmenʃn]	*n.*	尺寸,大小
weight	[weɪt]	*n.*	重量
equipment	[ɪˈkwɪpmənt]	*n.*	设备,器材
allowance	[əˈlaʊəns]	*n.*	限额
cigarette	[ˌsɪgəˈret]	*n.*	香烟
spirit	[ˈspɪrɪt]	*n.*	烈性酒
passenger	[ˈpæsɪndʒə(r)]	*n.*	乘客
wine	[waɪn]	*n.*	白酒

7.3 购物用语

7.3 Shopping Expressions

7.3.1 课前准备

7.3.1 Warming Up

当你乘船去国外时,你可能会买一些感兴趣的东西作为纪念品。你也会买一些新鲜的蔬菜和水果进行营养补充。因为在长航次后,船员几乎吃完了船上的蔬菜和水果。另外,一些船员会为自己买一些衣服,为朋友买一些礼物,当然,有一些特定的物品会有折扣。请记住,在一些小商店,你不能使用自己的信用卡,只能现金支付。

When you go abroad by ship, you may prefer to buy something interested as a souvenir. Also, you can buy some fresh vegetables and fruits for nutrition supplements. Because after a long voyage, the crew almost eat up the vegetables and fruits on board. Moreover, some crew prefer to buy some clothes for themselves and some gifts for their friends. Of course, you can get a discount for particular articles. Please note that you can't use your credit card in small shops and you can only pay cash.

7.3.2 对话练习

7.3.2 Dialogue Practice

对话 1

Dialogue 1

A:早上好,先生,需要帮助吗?

A:Good morning, sir. Can I help you?

B:是的,我想看看 T 恤衫。

B:Yes, I'd like to see a T-shirt.

A:什么尺寸?

A:What size?

B:L 号。

B:Size L.

A:你喜欢什么颜色?

A:What color do you prefer?

B:我喜欢深色。

B:I prefer the dark color.

A:这个怎么样?

A:How about this one?

B:看起来不错,我可以试一下吗?

B:It looks nice. May I try it on?

A:当然。

A:Certainly.

B:它很适合我,多少钱?

B:It fits me well. How much is it?

A:99 美元。

A:99 dollars.

B:太贵了,可以便宜点吗?

B:It's too dear. Can't you make it cheaper?

A:当然,但是我只能给你打 10%的折扣。

A:OK, but I can only give you 10% off.

B:我买了。

B:I'll take it.

对话 2

Dialogue 2

A:早上好,先生,需要帮助吗?

A:Morning, sir. Can I help you?

B:我想买条领带配我的西装,你可以给我一些建议吗?

B:I want to buy a tie to match my suit. Could you give me some suggestion?

A:当然,先生。这条黑色的怎么样?它是纯丝绸的,在年轻人中非常流行。

A:Of course, sir. How about this black one? It is 100% silk and very popular among young people.

B:我看看。看起来很好,多少钱?

B:Let me see. Oh, it looks nice. How much is it?

A:85 美元。

A:85 dollars.

B:好的,我买了。

B:OK, I'll take it.

A:我可以使用信用卡吗?

A:Can I use my credit card?

B:对不起,你不能使用信用卡,只能付现金。

B:Sorry, you can't use the credit card, you can pay cash only.

A:好的,这是 100 美金。

A:OK. Here is 100 dollars.

B:谢谢。这是找给你的零钱,再见。

B:Thank you. Here is the changes. Bye.

A:再见。

A:Bye.

对话 3

Dialogue 3

A:早上好,先生,需要帮助吗?

A:Morning, sir. Can I help you?

B:这块手表多少钱?

B:How much is the watch?

A:400 美金。

A:It's 400 dollars.

B:太贵了,这是促销价吗?

B:That's too expensive. Is it the sale price?

A:不是,可以给你打 10%的折扣。你想要几块?

A:No, you can have a 10% discount. How many do you want?

B:一块。

B:Just one.

A:这是最便宜的价格了,如果你买两块以上,我还可以给你每块再打 10%的折扣。

A:That's the lowest price. If you take two or more, I will give you another 10% discount for each one.

B:我看一下,它的质量好吗?

B:Let me see. Is the quality good?

A:当然,它质量非常好。

A:Yes, it's very good quality.

B:好的。我将买两块,一共多少钱?

B:OK. I will take two. How much for those?

A:总共 640 美元。

A:It's 640 dollars totally.

B:这是 700 美元。

B:Here is 700 dollars.

A:谢谢,这是找给你的零钱。再见。

A:Thank you. Here is the changes. Bye.

B:再见。

B:Bye.

7.3.3　句型操练
7.3.3　Sentence Pattern Drills

(1)我能为你做什么?

(1)What can I do for you?

(2)我能为你做些什么呢?

(2)Is there anything I can do for you?

(3)早上好,先生,需要帮助吗?

(3)Good morning, Sir. Can I help you?

(4)我想买一件 T 恤衫。

(4)I want to buy a T-shirt.

(5)我想买一块手表。

(5)I'd like to see a piece of watch.

(6)我想买一条领带。

(6)I'm looking for a tie.

(7)你穿多大号的?

(7)What size do your wear?

(8)大号(小号、中号)

(8)Size Large (Small, Medium).

(9)这种颜色(类型、材质)怎么样?

(9)How about this color (style, material)?

(10)请给我拿件小号(大号、中号)。

(10)Give me a smaller (larger, medium) size, please.

(11)我喜欢浅色(深色)。

(11)I prefer a light (dark) color.

(12)你能给我一些建议(主意、意见)吗?

(12)Could you give me some advice (idea, suggestion)?

(13)它是纯(真正的)丝绸(棉花、皮革)的吗?

(13) Is it pure (real, genuine) silk (cotton, leather)?
(14)我可以试一下吗?
(14) May I try it on?
(15)这个多少钱?
(15) How much is it?
(16)这个需要多少钱?
(16) How much does it cost?
(17)它的价格是多少钱?
(17) What's the price of it?
(18)它在促销。
(18) It's on sale.
(19)它打20%的折扣。
(19) It's 20% off.
(20)它太贵了,有便宜一些的吗?
(20) It's too dear (expensive). Have you anything cheaper?
(21)你不能卖得便宜点吗?
(21) Can't you make it cheaper?
(22)你能给我打一些折扣吗?
(22) Can you give me a discount?
(23)它很适合我。
(23) It fits (suits) me well.
(24)他们看起来非常好。
(24) They look very nice.
(25)我不认为它配我的鞋子。
(25) I don't think it matches my shoes.
(26)我买它了。
(26) I'll take it.
(27)我买下它们了。
(27) I'll buy them.
(28)我能使用信用卡吗?
(28) Can I use my credit card?
(29)给你钱。
(29) Here the money.
(30)这是找你的零钱。
(30) Here is the change.

7.3.4 词汇

7.3.4 Words and Expressions

popular	[ˈpɒpjələ(r)]	*adj.*	流行的,受欢迎的
prefer	[prɪˈfɜː(r)]	*v.*	更喜欢
certainly	[ˈsɜːtnli]	*adv.*	当然,确定
suggestion	[səˈdʒestʃən]	*n.*	建议,意见
change	[tʃeɪndʒ]	*v.*	改变,变化
		n.	零钱
size	[saɪz]	*n.*	尺寸,大小
pure	[pjʊə(r)]	*adj.*	纯的,纯正的
color	[ˈkʌlə(r)]	*n.*	颜色,色彩
style	[staɪl]	*n.*	款式,类型
material	[məˈtɪəriəl]	*n.*	材料,材质
medium	[ˈmiːdiəm]	*adj.*	中等的
light color			浅颜色
genuine	[ˈdʒenjuɪn]	*adj.*	真正的,纯种的
silk	[sɪlk]	*n.*	丝绸,丝织物
cotton	[ˈkɒtn]	*n.*	棉,棉织品
leather	[ˈleðə(r)]	*n.*	皮,皮革
dear	[dɪə(r)]	*adj.*	昂贵的
expensive	[ɪkˈspensɪv]	*adj.*	昂贵的,豪华的
cheaper	[ˈtʃiːpər]	*adj.*	廉价的,低廉的
discount	[ˈdɪskaʊnt]	*n.*	折扣
credit card			信用卡
match	[mætʃ]	*n.*	手表,火柴
		v.	相称,相配
dark color			深颜色

7.4 就医用语

7.4 Hospitalizing Expressions

7.4.1 课前准备
7.4.1 Warming Up

海员如果没有穿安全鞋或甲板上有水和油迹时,有时会摔伤胳膊和腿,当梯子没有固定好时,海员也会摔倒。为防止摔断胳膊和腿,海员一定要穿上安全鞋。当发生火灾或化学品泄漏时,海员可能会烧伤自己。为防止烧伤,一定要遵守"禁止吸烟"和安全程序。海员在使用锋利机器时不小心,可能会切伤自己的手指。为防止切伤,一定要戴上安全手套。海员在使用机器时,可能会弄伤自己的眼睛。如果灰尘、火星或化学品进入眼睛会非常危险。为防止眼睛受伤,一定要戴上护目镜。

Seafarers sometimes break their arms and legs. It happens when they don't wear safety boots or when decks are wet and oily. Seafarers also fall when ladders are not secure. To prevent broken arms and legs, it is important to wear safety boots. Seafarers can burn themselves when there is a fire or chemical spill. To prevent burns, it is important to obey "No Smoking" signs and safety procedures. Seafarers may cut their fingers when they are careless with sharp machinery. To prevent cuts, it is important to wear safety gloves. Seafarers sometimes injure their eyes when they work with machinery. Dust, sparks and chemicals are very dangerous when they enter the eye. To prevent eye injuries, it is important to wear safety goggles.

7.4.2 对话练习
7.4.2 Dialogue Practice

对话 1

Dialogue 1

A:出什么问题了?

A:Now, what's the problem?

B:医生,我想我昨天扭伤了背! 非常疼,事实上,我几乎不能动了!

B:Oh, doctor, I think I strained my back yesterday! It's very painful. In fact, I can hardly move!

A：好的。我看一下，怎么弄伤的？

A：Right. Let me see. How did it happen?

B：我在工作间抬一块钢板时，扭伤了背。钢板太重了。

B：I strained my back because I lifted a steel plate in workshop. It was very heavy.

A：你是一个人还是有别人在你旁边呢？

A：Were you alone or was there anyone else there?

B：就我自己。

B：I was alone.

A：你没看到起重机吗？

A：Did you see a hoist?

B：没，我没看见。起重机坏了，我没修理它。

B：No, I didn't. The hoist broke but I didn't repair it.

A：你太粗心了。你看多么容易受伤啊，把这些止疼药吃了，告诉大副你必须休息24小时。

A：Well, that was careless. You see how easy it was to injure yourself. Take these painkillers and tell the Chief you must rest for 24 hours.

对话2

Dialogue 2

A：早上好，医生。

A：Good morning. Doctor.

B：早上好，今天你的脚踝怎么样了？

B：Good morning. How is your ankle today?

A：非常糟糕。我根本不能走路了！我确定脚踝骨折了！

A：Terrible. I can't walk at all! I'm sure my ankle is broken!

B：不，不，不。你的脚踝没有骨折！我昨天告诉过你，你只是扭伤了，仅此而已。

B：No, no, no. You don't have a broken ankle! I told you yesterday. You bruise it, that's all.

A：你怎么知道我没有骨折？真的非常疼！

A：How do you know it's not broken? It hurts!

B：因为在X光照片上你没有骨折。你在甲板上滑倒的时候，你扭伤了它，不是很严重。

B：Because there are no broken bones on the X-ray. When you slipped on the deck, you bruised it, it's not serious.

A：到处都是油，所以我才滑倒了。

A：Well, there was oil everywhere, that's why I slipped.

B：是啊，那你穿的是什么鞋呢？

B：Yes, but what shoes did you have on?

A：我的训练鞋。

A: My training shoes.

B:你看,这是你自己的错。当你工作的时候,你一定要穿上工作鞋,工作鞋能保护你的脚和脚踝。现在休息一天,不要抱怨了。

B: You see, it was your own fault. When you're working, you must wear your boots. They protect your feet and ankles. Now rest for a day and don't complain.

对话 3

Dialogue 3

A:你好,感觉怎么样?

A: Hello there, how are you feeling?

B:不太好,医生,我头疼。

B: Not so good, Doctor. My head hurts.

A:是啊,你摔倒的时候,撞到了头,非常严重。很幸运你没有割伤。有大约 5 分钟的时间你是没有意识的。

A: Yes, you hit your head very hard when you fell. It's lucky that you didn't cut it. You were unconscious for about 5 minutes.

B:是啊,他们打了我之后,我就记不清发生什么了?医生,我应该怎么办?我一直感到眩晕。

B: Yeah. I can't remember what happened after they hit me. What should I do, Doctor? I still feel dizzy.

A:你必须休息,我建议你不要工作,至少休息两天。

A: You must rest. I advise you not to work for at least two days.

B:好的,我知道了,我的鼻子怎么样啊?你觉得骨折了吗?真的很疼,那个海盗打我太用力了。

B: Oh, I see. What about my nose? Do you think it's broken? It really hurts, that pirate hit me very hard.

A:很不幸,你的鼻子骨折了。你应该做一下 X 光检查。

A: Well, I'm sorry to say that you have nose broken. You should have an X-ray to check.

B:你认为我应该去医院吗?

B: Oh. Do you think I should go to hospital then?

A:是的,我建议你上岸去医院两天。我会跟船长说你今天晚上必须上岸。

A: Yes. I recommend you go on shore to hospital for two days. I'm going to tell the Captain that you must go ashore this evening.

B:不,我不喜欢医院。我真的不喜欢手术。

B: Oh, no. I don't like hospitals. And I really don't like operations.

A:但是,你不需要做手术,你只需要进行 X 光检查和一个全面检查。不用担心,只需要两天。

A: But you don't need to have an operation! You only need to have an X-ray and a complete check-up. Don't worry. It's only for two days.

B:我待在船上,吃点药,可以吗?

B:Maybe I can take some medicine and stay on board?

A:不,你不用吃药,现在在船上休息就行。我会安排把你转移到岸上,你应该睡一会儿。

A:No, you don't need medicine. Just rest in bed now. I'm going to organize your transfer on shore. You should try to sleep for a while.

B:好的,谢谢!

B:OK, then. Thanks!

7.4.3 句型操练
7.4.3 Sentence Pattern Drills

描述不适状况及用药和治疗

Describing uncomfortable conditions and the need of medicine and treatment

(1)我觉得不舒服/恶心/发冷/头晕。

(1)I feel so ill/sick/rather chilly/dizzy.

(2)我的胃部/后背疼。

(2)I've a pain in my stomach/back.

(3)我耳鸣。

(3)I have running noise in my ears.

(4)我腹泻/食欲不佳/发烧。

(4)I've a diarrhea/a poor appetite/a fever.

(5)我的手腕扭了,伤势很严重。

(5)I sprained my wrist badly.

(6)我把手指割破了。

(6)I've cut my finger.

(7)我胸部痛。

(7)My chest hurts.

(8)我的胳膊抬不起来。

(8)I can't lift my arms.

(9)我全身痛。

(9)I seem to have pain all over.

(10)我昨晚吐血了。

(10)I vomited blood last night.

(11)出血了/麻木了。

(11)It's bleeding/numb.

(12)我嘴里有苦味。

(12) There is a bitter taste in my mouth.

(13)所有骨节都痛。

(13) Every bone is aching.

(14)这里痛。

(14) The pain is here.

(15)我咳嗽得很厉害。

(15) I coughed a lot.

(16)一会儿痛,一会儿不痛。

(16) The pain is off and on.

(17)我一直失眠。

(17) I' ve been loosing sleep.

(18)她伤了胳膊,但是她没有伤到腿。

(18) She injured her arm but she didn' t injure her leg.

(19)跌倒的时候,我摔坏了腿。

(19) I broke my leg when I fell.

(20)当我抬一些设备的时候扭伤了背。

(20) I strained my back when I was lifting some equipment.

(21)当我撞到桌子的时候擦伤了膝盖。

(21) I bruised my knee when I bumped into the table.

(22)当凿子滑落的时候,切伤了我的手指。

(22) I cut my finger when the chisel slipped.

(23)在歧管处,消防软管没有固定,船员拆开管路的时候受伤了。

(23) The fire-fighting hose was not secured at the manifold but the crewman was injured when he disconnected the hose.

(24)由于没有穿安全鞋,很多船员在甲板上滑倒。

(24) Many seafarers slip on deck because they don' t wear safety boots.

(25)钢板落下来的时候,砸伤了一个船员的胳膊。

(25) A seafarer broke his arm because a steel pipe fell on him.

(26)在 3 号货仓,一个海员摔断了腿,立即送到了岸上。

(26) A sailor fractured his leg at Hold No.3 and was sent ashore at once.

(27)把它包扎一下。

(27) Get it bandaged.

(28)给我扎一针吧。

(28) I' d like an injection.

(29)我要做个胸部透视。

(29) I want to have a chest X-ray.

(30)这个药如何服用?

(30) How should I take the medicine?

(31)您觉得我得了什么病?
(31)What do you think is wrong?
(32)这种药有副作用吗?
(32)Dose the medicine have any side-effect?
(33)我对青霉素过敏。
(33)I' m allergic to penicillin.
(34)每次一片,每日三次。
(34)Take one tablet one time, three times a day.
(35)每4小时服用一丸。
(35)Take one capsule every four hours.
(36)是病毒感染吗?
(36)Is it virus infection?
(37)给我开点止痛药吧。
(37)Give me some pain-killers, please.
(38)我需要一瓶止咳糖浆。
(38)I need a bottle of cough syrup.
(39)给我开个药膏。
(39)Send me some ointment.
(40)我更喜欢中药。
(40)I prefer Chinese traditional medicine.
(41)每天在伤处涂一次药膏。
(41)Put the ointment on the sore once a day.
(42)清洗一下伤口。
(42)Wash the wound.
(43)每4小时滴五滴。
(43)Five drops every four hours.
(44)使用前请摇晃一下。
(44)Shake well before using it.
(45)这是退烧药。
(45)The medicine can keep your fever down.
(46)这是口服药。
(46)This is for oral.
(47)这个护肤液只能外用。
(47)This lotion is for external use only.

7.4.4 词汇

7.4.4 Words and Expressions

pain	[peɪn]	*n.*	疼,痛
fever	[ˈfiːvə(r)]	*n.*	发烧
bleeding	[ˈbliːdɪŋ]	*n.*	出血,流血
injection	[ɪnˈdʒekʃn]	*n.*	注射
ointment	[ˈɔɪntmənt]	*n.*	药膏
capsule	[ˈkæpsjuːl]	*n.*	胶囊
allergic	[əˈlɜːdʒɪk]	*adj.*	过敏的
appetite	[ˈæpɪtaɪt]	*n.*	食欲
bandage	[ˈbændɪdʒ]	*n.*	绷带
catch/take a cold			感冒,受凉,伤风
chest	[tʃest]	*n.*	胸部,胸腔
chilly	[ˈtʃɪli]	*adj.*	冷的
diarrhea	[ˌdaɪəˈrɪə]	*n.*	痢疾,腹泻
dizzy	[ˈdɪzi]	*adj.*	眩晕的
external	[ɪk'stɜːnl]	*adj.*	外用的
headache	[ˈhedeɪk]	*n.*	头痛,令人头痛之事
hurt	[hɜːt]	*v.*	刺痛,受伤
infection	[ɪnˈfekʃn]	*n.*	感染
lotion	[ˈləʊʃn]	*n.*	洗液,洗剂
numb	[nʌm]	*adj.*	麻木的
penicillin	[ˌpenɪˈsɪlɪn]	*adj.*	青霉素,盘尼西林
sprain	[spreɪn]	*v.*	扭伤
stomach	[ˈstʌmək]	*n.*	胃口,胃部
virus	[ˈvaɪrəs]	*n.*	病毒
vomit	[ˈvɒmɪt]	*v.*	呕吐
side-effect	[ˈsaɪdɪfˈekt]	*n.*	副作用
syrup	[ˈsɪrəp]	*n.*	糖浆,糖汁
pain-killer	[ˈpeɪnkˈɪlər]	*n.*	止痛药
sore	[sɔː(r)]	*n.*	伤处,痛处
shake	[ʃeɪk]	*v.*	摇动,震动
oral	[ˈɔːrəl]	*n.*	口服

7.5 日常交流用语

7.5 Daily Communication Expressions

7.5.1 课前准备

7.5.1 Warming Up

机动船“蓝鲸”号共有五层甲板,机舱在第一层甲板之下。在一层甲板上有三个房间:厨房、洗衣间和库房。在洗衣间的上方是医疗室,医疗室在二层甲板,紧挨着普通船员餐厅。普通船员餐厅的右边是办公室。二层甲板没有船员房间,但在三层甲板有船员房间,一个房间是引航员房间,一个房间是大副房间,在两者之间是高级船员餐厅。船长房间在四层甲板,两边分别为无线电间和轮机长房间,无线电间在船长房间的左边。驾驶台在五层甲板。

On the MV Blue Whale there are five decks. The engine room is below the first deck. There are three rooms on the first deck: the galley, the laundry and the storeroom. Above the laundry there is a hospital. It is on the second deck next to the ratings' mess-room. To the right of the ratings' mess-room is an office. There are no cabins on this deck, but there are cabins on the third deck. There is one cabin for the pilot and one for the Chief Officer. Between them is the officer's mess-room. There is a cabin for the master on the fourth deck between the radio room and the Chief Engineer's cabin. The radio room is to the left of the master's cabin. The bridge is on the fifth deck.

7.5.2 对话练习

7.5.2 Dialogue Practice

对话 1

Dialogue 1

A:你好,杰克,今天下午你什么时候结束值班?

A:Hi, Jack. When will you finish your watch this afternoon?

B:你好,皮特,我 1600 下班。

B:Hi, Peter. At 1600.

A:好的。你有特别的事情要忙吗?我们一起看个电影吧?

A:OK. Do you have anything particular in mind? Shall we watch a movie together?

B:好的。你想看什么?

B:Yeah, OK. What do you want to watch?

A:船长 Harworth 希望每个人都看看关于船舶安全的录像。

A:Well. Captain Harworth wants everyone to watch a safety video.

B:好吧,安全问题比较重要。但是我更愿意看个喜剧放松一下。

B:Well, it's important to know more about safety. But I'd prefer comedy for relaxation.

A:嗯,有些喜剧不错,但是我喜欢动作片。

A:Uh, some comedies are OK, but I really like action movies.

B:我讨厌动作片,看着吓人!

B:But I hate action movies, they are awful!

A:好吧,我们先看安全视频吧,然后再挑个好片子看。

A:OK, let's watch the safety film first, then choose a good video.

B:好的,我知道有个新恐怖片很棒。

B:Yeah, I'm sure there's a new horror film, that's very good.

A:没问题,只要不是音乐剧就好,那个太糟糕了。那就 4 点见。

A:Well, anything but musicals, they are terrible! OK, see you at four o'clock.

B:好的,再见。

B:OK, see you.

对话 2

Dialogue 2

A:你洗完了吗?

A:Is your washing finished?

B:快了。现在正在甩干。

B:It will be soon. It's now in the spin cycle.

A:我看到有人用自来水冲洗东西,那不是浪费吗?

A:I saw someone rinsing something under running water. Isn't that wasteful?

B:是的。虽然我们可以从机舱造水机处获得足够多的淡水,但我们依然要养成节约用水的习惯。

B:Yes. Even though we can get as much water as we need from the engine room evaporator, we still need to make a habit of saving water.

A:对的,我尽量少用点清洁剂。这样漂洗衣服的时候可以少用点水。

A:Right. I also try not to use too much detergent. That way takes less fresh water to rinse my laundry.

B:清洁剂效果很好,只需要一勺就够了。另外,它极易分解,减少了对海洋的污染。

B:The detergent we have is really strong, so just one little scoop does the job. Besides, it helps reduce marine pollution as it breaks down easily.

B:我洗好了。我得去晾衣服了。哇,你有这么多衣服要洗啊!

B:OK, I'm done. I will hang up my clothes now. Wow, you have a lot of clothes to wash!

A:我一直很忙,再不洗就没有干净衣服穿了。

A:I've been very busy and hardly have anything clean to wear.

B:你得保持卫生,不然你会生病。

B:You have to stay clean or you'll get sick.

对话3

Dialogue 3

A:你不该吃这么快!

A:You shouldn't eat so quickly!

B:我饿了。食物很美味,我就忍不住了。

B:I'm starving. And the food is so good that I can't help it.

A:多咀嚼食物有益于你的身体健康。

A:Chewing your food well helps you in good health.

B:我知道。

B:I see.

A:你不喜欢蔬菜吗?

A:Don't you like vegetables?

B:是的,我不喜欢。蔬菜没什么味道,肉和鱼是我的最爱。

B:Yes, I do. Vegetables are tasteless. The meat and fish is my favorite.

A:在船上保存鱼和肉很简单,而保存蔬菜很困难。这些剩下的蔬菜太浪费了。

A:It's easier for us to serve meat and fish on board. It is harder to preserve vegetables. And it's wasteful to have all these leftover vegetables.

B:我听说肉更有营养,吃肉比吃蔬菜能获得更多的能量。

B:I heard that meat is more nutritious and that eating meat gives you more energy than eating vegetables.

A:但是最重要的是饮食平衡。

A:But a good balanced meal is the most important thing.

B:我懂了。

B:I see.

7.5.3　句型操练

7.5.3　Sentence Pattern Drills

(1)我来自中国浙江。

(1)I'm from Zhejiang, China.

(2)我们船上有另外一个中国人,他是水手长,名字叫丹峰。

(2)We have another Chinese on board:the Bosun. His name is Danfeng.

(3)早上好,船长。我是新来的大副。

(3)Good morning, Captain. I am the new Chief Officer.

(4)船长想让每个人都看看安全视频。

(4)Captain wants everyone to watch a safety video.

(5)我们需要了解更多关于 ISPS 的知识。

(5)We need more knowledge on ISPS.

(6)有些喜剧不错,但我却喜欢动作片。

(6)Some comedies are OK, but I really like action movies.

(7)不行! 太可怕了! 那些兰博电影太不好看了!

(7)No way! They are awful! Those Rambo movies are really bad!

(8)从 Caracas 到 Lima 以 15 节的速度大约需要 20 个小时。

(8)It's approximately 20 hours with a speed of 15 knots from Caracas to Lima.

(9)我看到很多的塑料瓶漂在周围。

(9)I saw a lot of plastic bottles floating around.

(10)在港期间,禁止向水中倾倒任何东西。

(10)It's forbidden to dispose of anything in the water when in a harbor.

(11)你在空闲时间干些什么?

(11)What do you do in your spare time?

(12)我通常听音乐,读书和看电视。

(12)I often listen to music, read books and watch TV.

(13)二副房间在三层甲板,在医疗室的上面。

(13)The Second Officer's cabin is on the third deck. It's above the hospital.

(14)船长房间在引航员房间和二副房间之间。二副房间在右边。

(14)The Captain's cabin is between the Pilot's and the Second Officer's. The second Officer's cabin is on the right.

(15)泵间在一层甲板,正好在普通船员餐厅的下面。

(15)The pump room is on the first deck, just below the rating's mess-room.

(16)每天早上,我 0700 起床,0730 吃早饭,0750 上驾驶台从大副处接班。

(16)Every morning I get up at 0700. I have breakfast at 0730, then at 0750 I go to the bridge and take over the watch from the Chief Officer.

(17)服务生会教你如何使用洗衣机。

(17)The steward will show you how to use the washing machine.

(18)请记住这些细节并且熟悉船舶的安全特点。

(18)Please note these particulars and get familiar with the ship's safety features.

(19)用那种方式冲洗洗衣间用水量不多。

(19)That way takes less fresh water to rinse my laundry.

(20)我的集合站在我房间的外面,紧挨着医疗室。

(20) My muster station is outside my cabin next to the hospital.

(21)首先,我们能看到驾驶台。请向右转,然后走上这些台阶,向上一层。它就在你的前面。

(21) First, we can see the bridge. Please turn right and go up these stairs one level. It's in front of you there.

(22)船上在很多地方都有消防警报,比如走廊,甲板,厨房,靠近机舱的墙上等。

(22) The fire alarms are in many places on board, such as in the corridor, on deck, in the galley, on the wall next to the engine room, etc.

(23)这些肉足够船上20个人吃30天了。这是50千克的冻鸡和100千克的鱼。

(23) The meat is enough for 30 days of 20 men's consumption onboard. So that's 50 kilos of frozen chicken and 100 kilos of fish.

(24)我想要500升果汁,5千克茶叶和10千克咖啡。

(24) I'd like 500 liters of juice, 5 kilos of tea, and 10 kilos of coffee.

(25)我可以有更多的免税额度吗?

(25) Do I have more duty-free allowances?

(26)我想把这个包裹发往中国。

(26) I'd like to send this parcel to China.

(27)我想去外币兑换处。

(27) I want the foreign exchange department.

(28)目前,有两个空房间,但是,它们只是今天晚上是空着的。

(28) There are two rooms free at the moment, but they are only available tonight.

(29)每天早上,大副给我一份要做的工作清单。

(29) Every morning the Chief Officer gives me a list of jobs to do.

(30)工作后,我有一些空闲时间,我经常和我的朋友下棋。

(30) I have some free time after work so I often play chess with my friend.

(31)在睡觉之前,我有时会读一些书。

(31) I sometimes read a book before going to sleep.

(32)我和另外一名实习生共住一个房间。

(32) I share my cabin with another cadet.

(33)我很喜欢这艘船上的新工作。

(33) I really like my new job on this vessel.

7.5.4 词汇

7.5.4 Words and Expressions

rank	[ræŋk]	*n.*	等级,职务
captain	[ˈkæptɪn]	*n.*	船长

master	[ˈmɑːstə(r)]	*n.*	船长
officer	[ˈɒfɪsə(r)]	*n.*	高级船员
chief officer, C/O or chief mate			大副
second officer, 2/O, 2nd/O or second mate			二副
third officer, 3/O, 3rd/O or third mate			三副
bosun/boatswain	[ˈbəʊsn]	*n.*	水手长
engineer	[ˌendʒɪˈnɪə(r)]	*n.*	轮机员
chief engineer, C/E			轮机长/老轨/大车
second engineer, 2/E			大管轮/二轨/二车
third engineer, 3/E			二管轮/三轨/三车
fourth engineer, 4/E			三管轮/四轨/四车
chief motorman or No.1 oiler			机工长
rating	[ˈreɪtɪŋ]	*n.*	普通船员
steward	[ˈstjuːəd]	*n.*	服务员
cadet	[kəˈdet]	*n.*	见习生
cook	[kuk]	*n.*	厨师
pilot	[ˈpaɪlət]	*n.*	引航员
agent	[ˈeidʒənt]	*n.*	代理
chandler	[ˈtʃɑːndlə]	*n.*	杂货供应商
board	[bɔːd]	*n.*	甲板
		v.	登船
introduce	[ˌɪntrəˈdjuːs]	*v.*	介绍
allow	[əˈlaʊ]	*v.*	允许
born	[bɔːn]	*v.*	出生
certificate	[səˈtɪfɪkət]	*n.*	证书,证明书
Medical Certificate			体检证书
Health Certificate			健康证明书(我国船员用)
particular	[pəˈtɪkjələ(r)]	*n.*	特点,细节
safety video			安全录像
comedy	[ˈkɒmədi]	*n.*	喜剧
relaxation	[ˌriːlækˈseɪʃn]	*n.*	放松,消遣
action movie			动作影片
awful	[ˈɔːfl]	*adj.*	糟糕的,可怕的
choose	[tʃuːz]	*v.*	选择
horror film			恐怖影片
musical	[ˈmjuːzɪkl]	*n.*	音乐片
terrible	[ˈterəbl]	*adj.*	可怕的,极度的
spin cycle			甩干筒

rinsing	[ˈrɪnsɪŋ]	*v.*	漂洗
wasteful	[ˈweɪstfl]	*adj.*	浪费的
evaporator	[ɪˈvæpəˌreɪtə]	*n.*	蒸发器
detergent	[dɪˈtɜːdʒənt]	*n.*	洗涤剂
laundry	[ˈlɔːndri]	*n.*	洗衣间
scoop	[skuːp]	*n.*	勺,铲
marine pollution			海洋污染
starve	[stɑːv]	*v.*	挨饿
vegetable	[ˈvedʒtəbl]	*n.*	蔬菜
tasteless	[ˈteɪstləs]	*adj.*	无味的,乏味的
favorite	[ˈfeɪvərɪt]	*adj.*	喜爱的,喜欢的
preserve	[prɪˈzɜːv]	*v.*	保存,保鲜
leftover	[ˈleftəʊvə(r)]	*adj.*	剩余的,吃剩的
nutritious	[njuˈtrɪʃəs]	*adj.*	有营养的
energy	[ˈenədʒi]	*n.*	能量,精力
approximately	[əˈprɒksɪmətli]	*adv.*	大约地,近似地
plastic	[ˈplæstɪk]	*n.*	塑料
forbidden	[fəˈbɪdn]	*adj.*	禁止的
dispose	[dɪˈspəʊz]	*v.*	处理,处置
mess-room	[mes ruːm]	*n.*	餐厅
feature	[ˈfiːtʃə(r)]	*n.*	特征,特点
corridor	[ˈkɒrɪdɔː(r)]	*n.*	走廊,通道
consumption	[kənˈsʌmpʃn]	*n.*	消费,消耗
duty-free allowance			免税额度
parcel	[ˈpɑːsl]	*n.*	包袱,包裹
exchange	[ɪksˈtʃeɪndʒ]	*n.*	交换,交易
		v.	互换,兑换

7.6 公文用语

7.6 Correspondence Expressions

7.6.1 公文用语格式

7.6.1 Format of Correspondence Expression

公文有各种各样的格式。我们必须遵从国际惯例,选择某一种国际上认可的格式。一般,应注意按美观、大方、正式化等几方面要求来选用格式。在船上,利用计算机撰写这方面的信函很方便,而且可利用计算机中商务信函模板制得相当规范的文件。这里我们推荐下述格式供我国船员在航海生产中参考。

Correspondence has various forms. We have to follow international practice and choose a format that is approved internationally. In general, attention should be paid to the selection of format according to the requirements of beauty, generosity, formalization and so on. On board, it is convenient to use the computer to write this type of letter, and you can use the business letter template in the computer to produce fairly standard documents. Here we recommend the following format for the reference of Chinese sailors in navigation practice.

①公文纸的文头

①At the top of the stamped paper

一般应包括公司标志、公司名称、地址,电话、电报、电传、传真等号码,电子邮件地址和因特网主页地址等。

Generally, it should include the company logo, company name, address, telephone, telegraph, telex, fax and other numbers, e-mail address and Internet homepage address.

该部分内容一般为固定内容,以彩色印刷文本为佳。

This part of the content is generally fixed content, color printed text is preferred.

②本船船名及地址

②Name and address of the ship

与①隔一或两个行位,打印本船船名;本船所在地,一般是船舶所在的港口名称。

One or two rows apart from ①, print the name of the ship. The place of the ship is generally the name of the port where the ship is located.

有时港口很小,后要接国家名称甚至洲名;有时港口很大,前要加泊位、码头名称。地名、国家名、泊位和码头等专有名称的首字母要大写。各行右对齐。

Sometimes the port is small, followed by the name of the country or even the continent name;

Sometimes the port is very large, preceded by the name of the berth, wharf. Proper names such as place names, country names, berths and wharves should be capitalized. Align the rows to the right.

③日期

③Date

与②隔一或两个行位打印日期,一般应是信函拟发出之日期,而不是撰稿之日期。同本船船名及地址一样,采用右对齐格式。

The date of printing, one or two lines apart from ②, should generally be the date when the letter is intended to be sent, not the date when it was written. As with the name and address of the ship, use the right alignment format.

④对方地址

④Address of the other party

与③隔一或两个行位,打印对方所在部门,先写小部门,后写大部门,中间用“,”分隔;对方所在公司名称;对方公司所在地址,小地址在前,大地址在后,中间用“,”分隔。字母大小写的原则同前。各行左对齐。

One or two lines apart from ③, print the department of the other party, small department first, then large department, separated by a “,”; The company name of the other party; Address of the other company, the small address is first, the large address is last, and the middle address is separated by a “,”. The principle of capital or lower-case letter is the same as before. Align the lines to the left.

⑤称呼

⑤Salutation

· 不知对方姓名时

· The other's name unknown

—男士:Sir,Sirs,Dear Sir,Dear Sirs,Gentleman,Gentlemen。

—Man:Sir, Sirs, Dear Sir, Dear Sirs, Gentleman, Gentlemen.

—女士:Madam,Mesdames,Dear Madam,Ladies。

—Woman:Madam, Mesdames, Dear Madam, Ladies.

· 已知对方姓名时

· The other's name known

—男士:Mr.…,Dear Mr.…,Messrs.…,Dear Messrs.…

—Man:Mr.…, Dear Mr.…, Messrs.…, Dear Messrs.…

—女士未婚:Miss …,Misses.…,Dear Miss.…,Dear Misses.…

—Woman unmarried:Miss.…,Misses.…,Dear Miss.…,Dear Misses.…

—女士已婚:Mrs.…,Mmes.…,Dear Mrs.…,Dear Mmes.…

—Woman married:Mrs.…, Mmes.…,Dear Mrs.…,Dear Mmes.…

—女士不论婚否:Ms.…,Dear Ms.…

—Ladies whether married or not:Ms.…,Dear Ms.…

· 不知发向何人时

· Send to whom unknown

不知发向何人时可用这一短语:To whom it may concern.

You can use this expression:To whom it may concern.

· 称呼后人名的接法

· Name connected followed by salutation

称呼后可接姓或全名。名前不能加称呼。外国人有时将名写在前面,姓写在后面,但也有将名写在前姓写在后的情况。我们应弄清楚并适应这种习惯。华人的名字一定要姓在前,名在后。我们要坚持自己的文化尊严,而不能用颠倒自己姓名的方法来给外国人提供方便;而且许多外国人知道中国人的姓名顺序,我们自己颠倒了反而会造成误会。

A salutation may be followed by a surname or full name. There is no salutation before a given name. Foreigners sometimes put their first name before the family name, but sometimes they put their family name before the first name. We should understand and adapt to this habit. Chinese names must be the family name first, the first name last. We should insist on our own cultural dignity and not make things easier for foreigners by reversing our own names. Moreover, many foreigners know the order of Chinese names, which will cause misunderstanding if we reverse it ourselves.

· 一些职务前可加 Mr.

· Add Mr. before post

在船长、轮机长、引航员等比较有身份的职务前可加 Mr.,如 Mr. Captain、Mr. Chief Officer、Mr. Cook、Mr. President、Mr. Agent、Mr. Pilot。

Mr. May be added before more prestigious post such as captain, captain, pilot, etc. For example, Mr. Captain, Mr. Chief Officer, Mr. Cook, Mr. President, Mr. Agent, Mr. Pilot.

· 一些职务可用作称呼

· Some post can be used salutation

一些比较有身份的职务,如船长、轮机长、引航员等,可用作称呼,如 Captain Wang, Dr.Lin。

Some post with more status, such as Captain, chief engineer, pilot, etc., can be used as salutations, such as Captain Wang, Dr. Lin.

· 人名后接“,”

· Name followed by“,”

早些年在人名后接“:”,现在一般用“,”。称呼后空一或两行位。

In earlier years, a person's name was followed by a “:”, but now a “,” is commonly used. Leave one or two lines after the salutation.

⑥正文

⑥Text

第一行可以缩进若干个字母,如 4~10 个或更多,也可以顶格。建议在中文中采用如下原则:

The first line can be indented by a number of letters, such as 4 to 10 or more, or it can be delimited. It is recommended to adopt the following principles in Chinese:

- 不用"-"号换行,必要时将整个单词移到下一行,最好利用计算机自动换行;
- Line feed without "-", if necessary, the whole word will be moved to the next line, had better use computer word wrap;
- 不要使用"、",而要使用",";
- Don't use "、", but to use ",";
- 句号用实心点,不用空心圆;
- Full stop with a solid point, not hollow circular;
- 不用书名号,而用大写首字母来代表书名、规则、公约等的名称,或者将这类名称用斜体书写;
- Don't use quotation marks, and use capital letters to represent the name of the book title, rules and conventions, or such names are written in italics.
- 段落间用空行的方式来区别;
- Separated by the empty line between paragraphs;
- 每一句首字母必须大写。
- The first letter in each sentence must be capitalized.

船上干部船员的职务、姓名,港口官员职务与姓名及其他有关官员的职务与姓名的首字母要大写。正文后空一或两行位。

The first letter is capitalized for the rank of the crew, name, port officials, name and other relevant officials, name. Leave one or two lines after the text.

⑦致谢或盼望

⑦Acknowledgement and hope

提前感谢你对此事的关心。

Thank you in advance for your kind attention to this matter.

谢谢您的合作。

Thank you for your cooperation.

我期待着尽快收到你的来信。

I am looking forward to hearing from you as soon as possible.

如能及时关注此事,我们将不胜感激。

Your prompt attention to this matter will be much appreciated.

近些年,人们常用现在分词短语来表示致谢或盼望,其意义更加明确和生动,如:

In recent years, people often use the present participle to express gratitude or hope, which has a more explicit and vivid meaning, such as:

提前感谢您对此事的关心。

Thanking you in advance for your kind attention to this matter.

感谢您的合作。

Thanking you for your cooperation.

期待尽快收到您的来信。

Looking forward to hearing from you as soon as possible.

其后空一或两行位。

It is followed by one or two lines blank.

⑧客套话

⑧Pleasantries

常与发信人地址及日期对齐,常有如下几种用法:

Often aligned with the sender's address and date, it is often used in the following ways:

Yours truly, Truly Yours,

Yours very truly, Very truly yours,

Yours faithfully, Very faithfully yours,

Yours sincerely, Sincerely yours,

Yours respectfully, Respectfully yours,

此外,偶尔还可用下列几种形式:

In addition, it may occasionally be used in the following forms:

Gratefully yours,

Expectantly yours,

Hopefully yours,

Patiently yours,

Urgently yours,

Regretfully yours,

Cooperatively yours,

注意,这一短语后一定加“,”而不用“.”,其后空一或两行位。

Note that this phrase must be followed by " , ", instead of " . ", followed by one or two lines.

⑨职务与签名

⑨Post and signature

签名和职务前后应空若干行位,取决于纸张的大小。

There should be a number of blank lines before and after the signature and post, depending on the size of the paper.

⑩附件

⑩Attachment

常用的短语为:

Common phrases are:

Enclosed herewith

Enclosures

附件名称应准确列出,并且应与所附文件名称一致。附件多于一份时常应编号。

The name of the attachment should be listed accurately and should correspond to the name of the attached document. More than one copy of attachments should always be numbered.

①	
空 1~2 行 Leave one or two lines	
②	
空 1~2 行 Leave one or two lines	
③	
空 1~2 行 Leave one or two lines	
④	
空 1~2 行 Leave one or two lines	
⑤	
空 1~2 行 Leave one or two lines	
⑥	
空 1~2 行 Leave one or two lines	
⑦	
空 1~2 行 Leave one or two lines	

⑧	______________
空 1~2 行 Leave one or two lines	
视纸张大小空若干行 Empty several lines based on paper size	
⑨	______________ ______________
视纸张大小空若干行 Empty several lines based on paper size	
⑩	______________ ______________ ______________

7.6.2 范例
7.6.2 Example

范例 1:船舶载重量声明

Puerto Limon, Costa Rica
2015 年 10 月 14 日

泛美海运船队公司
Puerto Limon

先生,

请知悉在我控制下的机动船"Gluckaulf"夏季载重线的载重量为 12 431 t,包装容积为 18 439 m^3,散装容积为 19 941 m^3。

此致敬礼,
"Gluckaulf"船船长______________
C.Clifford

递交日期:2015 年 10 月 14 日地方时 1000
接受日期:2015 年 10 月 14 日地方时 1000

代理______________
Montague Moody

Example 1: Declaration of DWC

Puerto Limon, Costa Rica
14th October, 2015

Pan America Marine Fleet Co.
Puerto Limon

Dear Sirs,

Be it known that MV Gluckaulf under my command has a DWC of 12,431 M/T on summer loadline, and a bale capacity of 18,439 Cu. M. and a grain capacity of 19,941 Cu. M.

Truly yours,
Master of MV Gluckaulf ________________.
C. Clifford

Delivered at: 1000 h LT, Oct. 14th, 2015
Accepted at: 1000 h LT, Oct. 14th, 2015

Agent ________________
Montague Moody

范例 2:海事声明

"自由"号船舶,黄埔港
2016 年 3 月 11 日

公证处
黄埔

先生,

2016 年 3 月 11 日, Yugoslav"自由"号机动船船长 A. J. Nicholas 在公证处声明:他船装载 5 934 t 杂货在 2 月 5 日从 Yugoslavia 的 Rijekac 出发, 2 月 10 日到达黄埔港,由于航行过程中遇到大风浪,担心船体,机器和货物损坏或灭失,针对所有的灭失和损坏,他在此发表海事声明,并且在必要的时间和地点保留延伸海事声明的权利。

此致敬礼,
机动船"自由"号船船长________________
L. Keller

Example 2: Marine Note of Protest

MV Freedom, Port Huangpu
11th March, 2016

Notary Public Office
Huangpu

Dear Sirs,

On this Eleventh day of March 2016, Captain A. J. Nicholas, Master of Yugoslav MS Freedom declares at this Notary Public Office that his vessel sailed from Rijeka, Yugoslavia, on the Fifth day of February with 5,934 M/T of general cargo, and arrived at Huangpu on the Tenth day of this month, and that fearing loss or damage that might have been sustained by the vessel's hull, machinery and cargo through rough and boisterous weather during the passage, he hereby notes his protest against all losses and damages caused thereby, reserving the right to extend the same whenever and wherever necessary.

Yours truly,
Master of MV Freedom ________________
L. Keller

范例 3：许可请求

横滨，日本
2017 年 9 月 4 日

港长
横滨

先生，

请求在本月 5 日 0900 到 6 日 1700 进行主机定期检查。本次检查不会影响货物操作，但在检查完成后，必要时主机启动需要 4 h 的准备时间。

如果你能尽快许可本次检查，不胜感激。

此致敬礼，
机动船“西岛”号船长________________
N. More

Example 3: Request for permission

Yokohama, Japan
4th September. 2017

Harbour Master

Yokohama

Dear Sirs,

Permission is kindly requested to carry out the periodical survey for the main engine from 0900 hrs on 5th to 1700 hrs on 6th this month. The survey will in no way affect cargo operation, but the main engine will require four hours' notice to be ready if necessary after completion of the survey.

Your prompt approval of this matter will be highly appreciated.

Yours truly,

Master of MV West Island ________________

N. More

7.6.3 词汇

7.6.3 Words and Expressions

declaration	[ˌdekləˈreɪʃn]	*n.*	宣布,宣告
command	[kəˈmɑːnd]	*n.*	命令,控制
load-line	[ləʊdlaɪn]	*n.*	载重线
capacity	[kəˈpæsəti]	*n.*	容量,能力
deliver	[dɪˈlɪvə(r)]	*v.*	投递,递送
Notary Public Officer			公证处
sustain	[səˈsteɪn]	*v.*	遭受
machinery	[məˈʃiːnəri]	*n.*	机器,机械装置
boisterous	[ˈbɔɪstərəs]	*adj.*	狂暴的,喧闹的
protest	[ˈprəʊtest]	*n.*	声明,抗议
reserve	[rɪˈzɜːv]	*v.*	保存,保留
permission	[pəˈmɪʃn]	*n.*	允许,批准,认可
periodical	[ˌpɪəriˈɒdɪkl]	*adj.*	周期的,定期的
affect	[əˈfekt]	*v.*	影响
completion	[kəmˈpliːʃn]	*n.*	完成,实现
approval	[əˈpruːvl]	*n.*	同意,批准
appreciate	[əˈpriːʃieɪt]	*v.*	感激,欣赏

参考文献

References

[1] 郭禹，张吉平，戴冉. 航海学. 大连：大连海事大学出版社，2014.

[2] KHALIQUE A. Nav basics：the earth，coastal navigation，tides & passage planning. 2nd ed. Edinburgh，UK：WITHERBY Publishing Group Ltd，2011.

[3] BOWDITCH N. The american practical navigator. Bethesda，Maryland：National Imagery and Mapping agency，2019.

[4] CUTLER J T. Dutton 's nautical navigation. 15th ed. Annapolis Maryland：Naval Institute Press，2004.

[5] HOBBS R R. Marine navigation；piloting and celestial and electronic navigation. 4th ed. Annapolis Maryland：Naval Institute Press，1997.

[6] THE UNITED KINGDOM HYDROGRAPHIC OFFICE. Admiralty tide tables vol. 1-8. Taunton：UKHO，2023.

[7] THE UNITED KINGDOM HYDROGRAPHIC OFFICE. Symbols and abbreviations used on admiralty paper charts-int1. 8th ed. Taunton：UKHO，2020.

[8] THE UNITED KINGDOM HYDROGRAPHIC OFFICE. The mariner's handbook（np100）. 13th ed. Taunton：UKHO，2023.

[9] THE UNITED KINGDOM HYDROGRAPHIC OFFICE. Iala maritime buoyage. 8th ed. Taunton：UKHO，2018.

[10] DOKKUM V K. Ship knowledge：a modern encyclopedia. 12th ed. Enkhuizen：Dokmar，2020.

[11] 李伟. 船舶结构与设备. 大连：大连海事大学出版社，2008.

[12] 魏云雨. 船舶信号与 VHF 通信. 大连：大连海事大学出版社，2008.

[13] 吴兆麟，赵月林. 船舶值班与避碰. 5 版. 大连：大连海事大学出版社，2021.

[14] 史国友. 船舶操纵. 大连：大连海事大学出版社，2024.

[15] 国际海事组织. 国际信号规则. 中国人民解放军海军司令部航海保证部，译. 天津：中

国航海图书出版社, 2011.
[16] 田佰军, 王文新. 船舶货运. 大连:大连海事大学出版社, 2024.
[17] 田佰军, 王洪贵. Marine cargo operation. 大连: 大连海事大学出版社, 2017.
[18] 田佰军. 船舶结构与货运(大副). 大连: 大连海事大学出版社, 2022.
[19] 田佰军. 船舶结构与货运(二/三副). 大连: 大连海事大学出版社, 2022.
[20] 中华人民共和国海事局. 1978 年海员培训、发证和值班标准国际公约马尼拉修正案 大连: 大连海事大学出版社,2010.
[21] 陈秋妹. 船舶保安意识与职责. 大连: 大连海事大学出版社,2012.
[22] 盛清波. 船舶保安员. 大连: 大连海事大学出版社,2012.
[23] 戚发勇, 王岩. 基本安全——个人安全与社会责任. 大连: 大连海事学院出版社,2013.
[24] 郝勇. 熟悉与基本安全——个人安全与社会责任. 武汉: 武汉理工大学出版社,2013.
[25] 国际海事组织. 国际海上人命安全公约. 北京: 人民交通出版社,2014.
[26] 中华人民共和国海事局. 船舶保安员(中英对照). 大连: 大连海事大学出版社,2016.
[27] 戚发勇, 陈秋妹. 海船船员专业培训合格证书知识更新. 大连: 大连海事大学出版社,2017.
[28] 徐敏, 张浩. 劳动防护用品知识学习手册. 北京:中国劳动社会保障出版社,2018.
[29] 范中洲, 刘新卓. 船舶保安意识与职责. 大连: 大连海事大学出版社,2021.
[30] 船舶检修检测劳动防护及职业道德. 北京: 人民交通出版社,2021.
[31] 中国海事服务中心. 船舶保安. 大连: 大连海事大学出版社,2022.
[32] 中国海事服务中心. 船舶保安意识与职责. 大连: 大连海事大学出版社,2022.
[33] 中国海事服务中心. 船舶保安员. 大连: 大连海事大学出版社,2023.
[34] 戚发勇, 曹铮, 代俊林. 基本安全——个人安全与社会责任(2023 版). 大连: 大连海事大学出版社,2023.
[35] 中华人民共和国海事局. 国际海事组织标准航海通信用语. 北京:人民交通出版社, 2008.
[36] 黄岗, 惠小锁, 刘俊. 中级航海英语. 大连: 大连海事大学出版社, 2022.
[37] 沈江, 黄岗, 惠小锁. 航海英语写作. 大连: 大连海事大学出版社, 2016.
[38] 姜朝妍. 航海英语(二三副). 大连: 大连海事大学出版社, 2020.
[39] 姜朝妍, 仇旭燕. 航海英语听力与会话. 大连: 大连海事大学出版社, 2022.